P...iculum

This reader is one part of an Open University integrated teaching system and the selection is therefore related to other material available to students. It is designed to evoke the critical understanding of students. Opinions expressed in it are not necessarily those of the course team or of the University.

Policies for the Curriculum

edited by
**Bob Moon, Patricia Murphy
and John Raynor**
at the Open University

Hodder & Stoughton
LONDON SYDNEY AUCKLAND TORONTO
in association with the Open University

ISBN 0 340 51436 1

First published 1989

Typeset by Wearside Tradespools, Fulwell, Sunderland.
Printed in Great Britain for the educational publishing division of
Hodder and Stoughton Limited, Mill Road,
Dunton Green, Sevenoaks, Kent
by Richard Clay Ltd, Bungay, Suffolk.

Contents

Background Note

This reader has been prepared as part of a course Curriculum Learning and Assessment from the Open University MA in Education. An accompanying volume, *Developments in Learning and Assessment*, provides a further source of readings. The two volumes together, along with other set texts, provide the background for a study guide focusing on the specific aspect of curriculum examined by the course. Further details are available from the Open University, Walton Hall, Milton Keynes, MK7 6AA.

Acknowledgment

The articles in this reader were selected and commissioned over a six-month period. In the week that the manuscript was completed John Raynor died while on a visit to East Africa. We would therefore wish to make a special acknowledgment to the experience, perception and good humour John brought to this task.

Bob Moon
Patricia Murphy

Introduction

Curriculum controversies now occupy the central ground of educational policy making. An increased public and bureaucratic involvement in curriculum decision making can be observed in most countries of the world. This reader, perhaps more appropriately seen as a source book, looks at a number of aspects of these developments. The focus is on those countries entering a third or fourth decade of curriculum renewal. All the articles, papers and speeches, with the exception of Appendix 3, have been taken from the last decade. Particular attention is given to events in Britain through the late 1970s and 1980s. The change from a devolved apparently *laissez faire* style of curriculum control to a centralised, highly prescriptive legislative framework has attracted widespread interest. In many ways the formula is more binding than many countries with a long tradition of government statutory controls. By design, and to some extent as the outcome of political expediency, England and Wales, with Scotland and Northern Ireland reluctantly following, have combined the North American traditions in testing and assessment with the Continental practice of a statutory programme or syllabus.

There are many reasons why curriculum policies have attracted increasing attention. The controversial linking of school performance and curriculum relevance to prevailing economic conditions is one example. This is a debate with long historical antecedents. The knock to economic confidence, for example, that followed the oil crisis of 1973 is seen to have left a lasting imprint on social and educational consciousness. Alongside this a number of critics had become increasingly disenchanted with the way the social and political ambitions for schooling seemed constrained by curriculum practice. Decades of institutional reorganisation to promote democratisation, particularly at the secondary level, seemed to founder on divisive styles of curriculum implementation. Inevitably the rather isolated attempts to change this attracted widespread educational and political interest. Out of a progressive rhetoric of reform came an equally polemical plea and nostalgia for traditional modes of curriculum. The unfortunately titled Black Paper in Britain and the *Why Johnny Can't Read* series in the USA had their counterparts in many countries.

Neither the left nor the right could establish coherent policies against the fluctuations of public mood and attitude. In the early 1980s, therefore, in France a socialist government with a socialist President managed to espouse progressive curriculum policies under one Minister, Alain Savary, and highly traditionalist approaches under his successor, Jean Pierre Chevènement. In Britain during the same period one Secretary of State, Keith Joseph, accepted the principle of devolved curriculum control while his successor, Kenneth Baker, took precisely the opposite view. The word 'quality', a touchstone for education reform in the 1980s, has received advocacy across the political spectrum. Definitions have become problematic.

Curriculum, an interdisciplinary study, inevitably reflects the prevailing intellectual interests of the time. Psychological orthodoxies of the late 1950s heavily influenced the planning models that dominated the first phase of national and project based curriculum development. The late 1960s and early 1970s saw the demise of psychology and a surge of interest in what came to be called the new sociology of education. Optimism about the potentialities and possibilities of curriculum reform were buffeted by fierce debates both within the field of sociology and outside. A more eclectic and pragmatic approach to theory may be evolving in part as a defensive response to, for many, a hostile political climate but also as a way of conceptualising some of the pressing issues that have become established on the curriculum agenda.

This reader, therefore, provides a range of material to stimulate an interest in both the historical background of curriculum policies and the contemporary concerns of decision makers. An emphasis has been given to curriculum change. Successful implementation depends on the astute development of strategies sensitive to local social and political contexts. Awareness of the evidence available about such processes is significant for curriculum policies.

Selection has been made from a variety of sources. Significant political statements, such as the much quoted but not easily available Ruskin College Speech, are set alongside more analytical reviews of policies and events. Chronologies have been provided, as a response to a high level of interest in curriculum history and as an incentive to delve more deeply.

SECTION 1

Contexts for the Curriculum

Introduction

This section presents two different perspectives on the context within which curriculum is developed. Anyone who has come remotely near a curriculum decision knows how fraught the process is. Most involve jettisoning some aspects of the status quo in favour of some, as yet unproven, alternative. It is rare, if it exists at all, to find any evidence from curriculum research or practice which points unavowedly to one direction for future reform. Malcolm Skilbeck analyses the changes that have affected curriculum development in a wide range of countries over the last four decades. This study arose from a review of policies in OECD countries that has acted as the prelude to a number of specific international investigations carried out by the Centre for Educational Research and Innovation of the OECD. He illustrates the breadth and depth of public involvement in curriculum. The Japanese National Council for Educational Reform met 668 times and heard the views of 483 experts! In Saskatchewan 40,000 written responses were received to a consultation exercise. To this can be added the 17,000 responses received to a similar exercise but carried out over a period of a few weeks when the British government published a consultative paper. Curriculum policy as set out here is rarely a concerted drive, more often a form of power struggle, and the issue and participants in that impinge directly on decisions about the curriculum.

Mike Golby, while considering social and economic forces, is concerned to examine the way curriculum enquiry has been conceptualised in the twentieth century. He outlines the work of a number of significant curriculum specialists and summarises the critiques that have developed around each. Recent developments in national curriculum policies are examined against the different traditions of curriculum thinking.

1.1

A Changing Social and Educational Context

Malcolm Skilbeck

The curriculum and its attendant pedagogy are the principal means whereby the school pursues its educational purposes and organises and structures learning. The curriculum is everywhere changing, however imperceptibly. But by what means can we characterise change? How can we relate it to the broader social and educational context?

Language and experience of change

Metaphors for educational and other dimensions of social reform abound. In 1971, while Western European countries were still experiencing the frisson of politically radicalised youth and workers, new social and educational visions were in the air. Queen Elizabeth of England communicated her belief to the then Prime Minister, the late Harold Macmillan, that social order was about to collapse. Macmillan, famous for unflappability, shrewdly replied that in his view all was well since the pendulum, having moved so far, was about to swing back towards stability. Not much later, the oil crisis gave rise to a further swing or perhaps, for a time, a spin. But the fires of '68 were already cooling and the crisis of oil helped to turn education back on itself.

The swinging pendulum is an image of social and indeed educational change. A related image, more akin to a gyration, is that of the roundabout: the reforms in education today might be likened to those of 20 or 30 years ago in as much as education as a means of nation building or rebuilding is once again high on the agenda. Yet again, there is the metaphor of the linear accelerator: the reform gathers momentum and when maximum acceleration is reached fundamental changes occur.

While pendulums, swings and roundabouts are much in favour in studies of change, the accelerator is, or so it appears in the eyes of the typical researcher concerned with change processes in education, rather less apposite. It is affirmed in the literature that educational reforms in fact often stop short of the point where fundamental changes occur: situations are partially transformed and reforms are described as patchy, partial or incomplete.[1] Thus, in the United States in the 1960s the transformation of high school mathematics and science was a ragged affair; in Britain the Plowden Committee's recommended reform of primary education proved to be more a commentary on what had been partially achieved in individual local education authorities and schools than a firm direction for future development. In Ireland, there has been disappointment over the limited take up in schools of the far-sighted reform proposals for primary schooling dating from 1971.[2]

In more recent days, the introduction of microcomputers illustrates another issue: the revolutionary potential for transforming pedagogy is mediated through teacher values, skills and attitudes, resource constraints, and the technical imbalance between hardware and software. Seldom are countries able to work comprehensively and consistently on all of these fronts, thus progress is uneven.

It must also be conceded that some reforms in schooling can be retrogressive or at least have unwelcome unintended consequences, such as the lowering of standards of student attainment or excessive costs for minimum gains. Educational technology has provided examples of the latter, including the early experiments with language laboratories and computer assisted learning. In addition to the metaphors signifying movement, energy, dynamism, there is also the educational dead end. 'Reform' and 'progress' are not always the same. This lesson has been well learnt by educators during the past three decades.

But perhaps the most universal of these change metaphors is suggested by the shunting locomotive. At least to people in schools the change process is often experienced as a series of sharp shocks as one determined locomotive after another moves them across endless tracks. The rationality of the yard supervisor and locomotive driver (who in any case keep changing) is not always apparent to the impacted wagons.[3]

A backward glance

What is clear is that since the 1950s many member (OECD) countries have experienced a succession of significant impulses in educational reform, which have varied widely in range and intensity. They have occurred in school reorganisation and development, new approaches to curriculum scope and content, innovatory practices in teaching and learning and the expansion and enlargement of teacher education. It is useful in attempting to assess the significance of current movements to set them against this backcloth of a generation or more of continuing changes in curriculum and pedagogy in many member countries.

The early postwar initiatives, for example in the United States in the 1950s, either took the overall curriculum and school organisation very largely for granted or sought adaptations and adjustments to meet perceived student characteristics. There was a strong emphasis on pedagogy: ways of improving learning and organising classrooms for instruction. 'Life adjustment' education is a case in point, reflecting a changing highschool population and a felt need to modify teaching content and methods.[4] The educators were for a short while in the saddle in a period of rapid expansion of the school system. Their critics were not, however, content to leave them there. The heated debates of the 1950s were followed by an era of very largely subject specific projects which, again, took the overall shape of the curriculum for granted and aimed to update content and introduce new, psychologically oriented learning strategies.

These subject-specific projects of the 1960s, starting with mathematics and physical sciences, are often treated as the beginning of the modern movement of curriculum reform. This is certainly to oversimplify, yet it is the case that the changes in teaching content in such subjects as mathematics and sciences gave impetus to subject centred curriculum and a new vigour in pedagogy around the world. Fresh life was also given to the essential philosophy of education: universal core subjects, enduring and rigorous standards, authoritative knowledge and resurgence of interest in cognitive or process skills across the curriculum. Such was the aspiration. The school practice did not, however, change on the scale or in quite the ways that had been hoped.

It is significant that the drive for reform in the USA in the Sputnik era was as much political-economic-administrative as educational: the nation was perceived to be at risk then, as in the 1980s. Apart from the limitations of the projects as change strategies they did not capture the national imagination or command the political agenda in the way that the reforms of the 1980s have done.

In some countries, such as Australia, Japan, Sweden, Scotland, England and Wales, reform programmes and experiments from the 1950s onwards related to the reorganisation of secondary education along comprehensive lines, centred on the structure of schooling and expansion of provision. In the 1960s and 1970s we observe similar trends in France, Finland, Turkey and Italy (but not Germany where the tripartite system of Hauptschule, Realschule and Gymnasium seem firmly rooted in the enduring Humboltian tradition). Much of the impetus was provided by concerns other than international trends in politics and economics. These include social justice, equality of opportunity and national efficiency. Thus we have the spectacle of the national state bent on reforming itself but, quite willing, as was the case of Sweden for example, to learn from the American experiment in democratic schooling.[5]

Education for all in a comprehensive setting was clearly related to the advancement of the nation as well as meeting the needs of the individual. School reform was seen as a concomitant if not a cause of social progress. These changes, however, were not usually accompanied by significant widespread changes in the nature and the delivery of the processes of teaching and learning except insofar as subject content was updated and small-scale pedagogical reforms occurred. A commentary by the Inspectorate in England and Wales makes the point that all to often what occurred was that the old curricula for selective schools were somewhat modified and inserted into the new institutions.[6] Similarly, the Finnish report notes that changes in school practice did not, in the 1970s, match the reorganisation of 1972. Content and methods are the focus of reform there in the 1980s. At the elementary stage there was in several countries a release from the restrictions of selection for particular types of secondary schools with a consequent freeing of the curriculum and pedagogy. This, in turn, provoked a 'back to basics' reaction which has persisted to the present.

Policy concerns

It is not possible here, nor is it necessary, to outline the succession of reform endeavours in school development and learning or to go further into the forms and processes of change from the 1950s to the 1970s, in order to address the first of our major concerns in this paper: the current debate and the context in which it is occurring. Crucial to understanding that debate, however, is awareness that practically all of the major public education policy issues now under review are part of broad and complex socio-cultural movements which are being increasingly related to economic, political and strategic concerns in member countries. These concerns are of a diverse, indeed amorphous nature. Matters commonly raised in OECD and other reports cover birth rate decline (except in Ireland), changing family structures, high divorce rates, ageing societies; unemployment; the participation of women in the workforce; migration and multiculturalism; structural change in the economy; the impact of technological change; environmental degradation; law and order; information processing and the media-directed society.

The trends and concerns identified in the previous paragraph might seem to set the agenda. To many politicians and commentators they do. Yet there is more to it than that. From even a brief listing of such a wide range of concerns and trends, it is evident that the challenges to education require considerable analysis and refinement. There is not an obvious transfer from 'social issue' to 'educational action' and this itself constitutes a problem for the commentators and the politicians who are calling for action as much as it does for the educators.

More than any other factors it is the sense of a vast array of issues to be addressed through a huge number of institutions – schools – that is resulting in a two-way power shift: concentration of policy and dispersion of responsibility for action. The trend towards concentration of educational control is a striking development, alongside devolution of responsibility. Accountability is the connecting mechanism which is increasingly seen as the means of linking these two ships that might otherwise pass in the night. But that, too, is an oversimplified view.

The concentration of control is not necessarily into single national ministries or centres but into functional agencies which, enlisting modern communications technology, are able to aspire to if not always maintain close, system-wide control or surveillance of the field of action. Such concentration should not be seen in terms of the conventional distinction between centralised and decentralised patterns of educational organisation. It is in effect a redistribution of functions and authority in which both central agencies and the field play new roles. There is, moreover, a distinction to be drawn between central control of broad policy, resources and curricula on the one hand and autonomy in pedagogical practice on the other.

Noteworthy in this context is the increased trend towards community political-bureaucratic control of major educational decisions and consequent uncertainty and ambiguity in the role of the specialist professional educator. The trend, by the way, does not preclude occasional coalitions on specific issues. It follows that the renewed interest in the learning process, teaching methods, the selection of content, school environment and their interrelationships can only be partially understood if we focus on the internal dynamics of the educational sector. What must be recognised, above every other consideration, is the public profile of education: its prominence in the public consciousness; hence its political salience. Public education is public business; educational decisions and the uses of educational resources are a matter of public concern. This manifests itself, of course, in the very considerable media attention and in the widely publicised debates and controversies in several – but not all – countries.

What is the source of these concerns? Is it some objective demonstration of the shortcomings of schooling or of the ways in which particular pedagogical practices (such as highly directed instruction, or frequent testing of learning outcomes) can foster substantial improvements or changes? The answer to these questions is that an impartial appraisal of educational practices and the research literature does not justify either the extreme criticism in some countries or the excessively optimistic expectation of an earlier generation of reformers that widely dispersed curriculum and pedagogical changes hold the key to dramatic short-term gains in learning and in life chances.

While attending directly to the need to attain high standards, relevant learnings and other desiderata in mass educational systems, we must keep in mind changes in the wider social, economical, political and cultural arena. These changes, as much as what has or has not been done in schools, help to explain what has become, especially within English-speaking countries, a chronic disquiet about the public education system. This disquiet manifests itself in concern about basic skills, academic standards, the ability or willingness of schools to prepare for employment, the expectation that the school will educate for improved public morality and standards of behaviour and the belief that it is to schooling – or education more broadly – that we must look for economic/social development. Generally speaking, the Anglo-Saxon countries are moving towards the kinds of national frameworks for curriculum (and other) decisions commonly found in Continental Europe and Japan. There is in some countries, and particularly in this context the United States, Great Britain and Australia, a trend to deflect upon the school the economic and social problems of the day. While this manifests itself in criticisms that are often wide of the mark where they are not quite superficial, the obverse of those criticisms is the expectation that improved education is vital for national well-being.

There has been, especially since the late 1970s, a considerably heightened expectation of the social and economic benefits to be derived from qualitative improvements in schooling: in curriculum and in learning outcomes. While the 1960s' and 1970s' themes of democratisation, access and equity have not disappeared they are now milder, more sporadic. They have been overtaken by the economic and technological imperatives. The note of 'efficiency' sounds more frequently than 'equity'.

In the case of one country, Australia, in a 1987 OECD review the role of the school in economic recovery was highlighted. Subsequently, the Australian Minister for Employment, Education and Training in chairing the 1988 OECD Intergovernmental Conference on Education and the Economy in a Changing Society and presenting the Australian position made it perfectly clear that schooling must perform an instrumental role of adjustment to economic and other kinds of macro-social changes. The OECD programme of conferences and report on *Quality in Education* amply demonstrate that there is a broad spectrum of political and administrative opinion in member countries supporting such approaches. It is, therefore, necessary to remind ourselves, in the words of George Papadopoulos, speaking at the 1987 Kyoto Conference, that 'education must not be assumed merely to respond to change ... education itself is a factor of change. Education has its own life, has its own objectives very often, and is an instrument in societies for bringing about change.'[7]

In the light of this observation and essentially pedagogical concerns it expresses, what is needed is a new balance. The view that education is a public good which represents an enduring part of our values structure is as relevant to the debate as is the perception of education as an instrument – and servant – of public policy aimed at achieving specified economic and social outcomes in given circumstances. The OECD seems an appropriate forum for the necessary debate that must precede any new concord between the education purists, the economic rationalists, and the political realists – provided, that is, discussion can take place across as well as within these several domains.

Demographic, economic and political factors

We turn now to three of the changes which in the member country reports preparatory to this study were identified as highly significant for curriculum policies and pedagogical practice. These can be broadly described as demographic, economic and political trends. Demography is identified as a major consideration affecting thought and action on the curriculum, for example in Australia, England and Wales, the United States, New Zealand and the Netherlands where rolls are more or less stable or are declining. Not uniform either by level of schooling or by region, these declines in some countries constitute a major challenge whether in resourcing schools, training and employing teachers, or determining priorities for curriculum development. Such demographic trends underline the value of flexible structures, staffing policies and resource allocation procedures. Most countries, however, are struggling to achieve such flexibility.

Overall stability or decline of school population can mask significant sectoral growth, as in the Asian and Hispanic communities in parts of the USA. Moreover, birth rate changes can be rapid, as in the case of Ireland, where the birth rate has dropped dramatically while an earlier 'bulge' is still inflating enrolments. In France, there has been decline in primary but rapid growth in student enrolments in prevocational programmes. In the higher technician courses in the second cycle of secondary schooling (years 15 to 18 plus) for example, numbers have more than doubled in ten years. Similar changes are occurring in Britain with a consequent focusing on both generalist and specialist prevocational training from the junior secondary years onwards in the school sector.

The challenge of falling rolls overall, combined with what may be quite substantial sectoral growth reflecting increased participation, now constitutes a serious adjustment problem. Nevertheless this problem is less severe than the grave difficulty foreshadowed some years ago. In the case of Canada, after a rapid decline the rate has levelled off to less than 1 per cent decrease per annum and, at the secondary level, has been counterbalanced by improved retention beyond the compulsory attendance age and dropouts returning to complete high school diploma requirements. In common with most member countries, Canada is experiencing a participation percentage rate 'boom' and the prospect of rates for 17 and 18 years olds in the high eighties and into the nineties is now a real one, given the percentages of the initial school enrollees from the early seventies who are now staying on to year 12 or its equivalent. These levels have already been achieved in Finland, Japan and Germany. In Australia, England and Wales and France, the percentages are in the sixties.

The participation trend is widely and generally upwards and all or practically all countries can expect over the next decade to confront the implications of virtually 100 per cent participation in schooling/ further education throughout the whole period of adolescence and perhaps into early adulthood. Major questions arise, therefore, about the content of the curriculum, teacher–student relations, teaching methods and learning processes, the implications for social life and the transition from school to work/higher education.

No less important than school population size and its sectoral distribution is school population mix. Whereas in Japan this may be relatively easily handled in a very largely (but not entirely) mono-cultural and monolingual population, in Australia, New Zealand, Canada, the United States and, in varying degrees, in the countries of western and northern Europe, it is a very significant factor. Responses vary from comprehensive policies for initial teaching in the mother tongue, and the employment of either nationals as teachers, to the development of system-wide policies for multicultural education, deploying the criteria of social justice, social harmony and economic efficiency. There is, in several countries, an unacceptably wide range of retention rates (and school success) across ethnic groups. In some – New Zealand is a very interesting case in point – indigenous populations ('the people of the land') are the principal target of reform programmes.

These policies are not, however, uncontroversial, and there is evidence – as Australian and Canadian documents demonstrate – of a growing reaction with strong political overtones. The need for curriculum and pedagogy to embrace a wide range of requirements in respect of mother tongue teaching, national language, ethnic related socio-economic disadvantage and cultural pluralism in values and lifestyles is growing not diminishing.

Mention must also be made of gender mix, and the concern being expressed in several countries at the disproportionate male–female enrolments in science and technology courses in the middle and upper years of schooling, and the sex role stereotyping that remain a dominant feature of pedagogy. These concerns are well documented in the OECD report, *Girls and Women in Education*.[8]

Economic factors appear to be dominant in determining at least the context for rhetoric, debate and policy formulation in many countries. These factors include structural changes in the economy as wealth production shifts (albeit unevenly) from agriculture and traditional manufacturing to the service and finance sectors; the oft-repeated need for new forms of technically defined skills in the labour market; governments' emphasis on the role of small business and related entrepreneurial and managerial skills; and changing trade, current account and credit/debt balances. Although there is a considerable debate on these and other factors within and across the OECD countries, and we must recognise that different perspectives result in different interpretations and policies, there is a virtually universal trend towards a renewed analysis of schooling as an instrument of national economic policy. The conclusions and follow-up report from the OECD Intergovernmental Conference on Education and the Economy in a Changing Society demonstrate this in no uncertain terms.[9]

The reasons for this renewed interest in education–economy relations have been substantially documented in OECD literature and may be traced not only to the long-term effects of the oil crisis of the early 1970s, and the subsequent reviews and reductions of public expenditure in most member states, but also to the strong competitive edge in international trading and financial relations. Education is given a classic, Adam Smithian role in wealth production and wealth recovery. While this is most noticeable in the substantial debtor countries (e.g. Australia, the United States) it is not confined to them and indeed has a reciprocal effect. One example is the recent Japanese endeavour, through the Prime Minister's National Council on Educational Reform, to internationalise the curriculum to encourage in Japanese youth a deeper understanding of their country's growing worldwide role and responsibilities.

Financial stringency is having noticeable effects in policies for schooling, in the way it is fuelling such diverse concerns as interest in accountability and other efficiency measures, performance indicators and managerial approaches, training and work preparation in the upper years of secondary schooling and renewed emphasis on basic skills in the early years of primary schooling. There is a strong flavour of the national efficiency movement which has surfaced periodically in several member countries ever since public schooling became a large scale public enterprise.[10]

These very strong current policy motifs could change were there to be a sustained and general uplift of economic activity, but they seem set for several years to come. What is most noticeable in the discussions on this point is the realisation that an integrated, cross-sectoral approach is for educators, economists, social planners, business people and union representatives to get together. This need is recognised in the British movement known as 'The Industrial Society'. That can be more easily achieved at the levels of policy makers, administrators, and representatives of organisations than at the classroom level. Moves are, however, underway in many countries to improve the interaction of teachers with the workplace and with community bodies. By such means there can be a practical integration of economic, social and educational considerations which, at present, are all too often overstated at the global level and underestimated at the level of school practice.

Educators are under considerable pressure to demonstrate that the positive outcomes of schooling are reflected in improved performance in defined, priority areas of the curriculum. Critics and sceptics notwithstanding, national education systems have been remarkably responsive. Consider, for example, France where the number of young people obtaining the Baccalauréat has increased eightfold since 1950. In several systems, including France, Britain and the United States, there is a growing emphasis on those performance indicators which provide the public with information on nationwide standards of student attainment. There are educational and financial costs, as well as benefits, in this drive. Educators need to keep matters in perspective.

The economic criteria of efficient and effective use of public resources are evident in this trend. Although other factors are at work as well, there is no doubt that continuing national assessments of the economy and initiatives by governments to restructure and better manage their economies are having a growing influence on national decisions about school development and the curriculum. They are less evident in pedagogical change, the sphere which is being very largely left to the teachers whose opportunities for innovation are, nevertheless, reduced under continuing financial pressure in many countries.

Mainly in the Anglo-Saxon countries, there are very definite moves towards central control and direction of the broad outlines of the curriculum and of assessment. Recent statements by the Austra-

lian Federal Minister of Employment, Education and Training point
in this direction. But by far the most striking case is the 1988
Education Act in Britain, one of whose effects will be to introduce
(or reintroduce) a national, centrally determined and monitored
curriculum in predefined core subjects and to establish nationwide
testing for all students in government schools at the ages 7, 11 and
14. Economic factors frequently merge into political considerations
and the realm of ideology.

The political and ideological balance of forces in many member
countries is very significantly different in the late 1980s from what it
was in the mid to late 1960s. Most striking, in its implications for
school development and learning, is the emergence of new forms of
political conservatism, including the so-called 'New Right'. Such
conservatism is not confined to the parties traditionally to the right
of the political spectrum and may be taken to indicate a general shift
in electorates towards more caution in adopting widespread social
change and greater attention to core social values. Some commentators have interpreted this as a reaction to the immense range of
social reform movements and rapidity of those introduced since the
1960s combined with what is often claimed to be a relaxation of
society's expectations of youth and young people's standards of
conduct. Others emphasise the worldwide pace and scope of issues
(e.g. genetic engineering, weaponry, pollution, urbanisation). In
cither case there is evidence that the issue of values is becoming
more salient in debates about curricula and pedagogy at all levels
and stages of schooling.

At the extreme right of the political spectrum there is a perpetual
demand for value indoctrination, which might include patriotic
citizenship values or dogmatic socio-religious beliefs and values.
More widespread is a well-balanced debate, as in Norway, between
advocates of traditional ethics, with a definite religious basis, and a
secularist and social issues perspective.

Underlying these tendencies and the debates surrounding them is
a sense of unease at the prospect of social disorder or disharmony,
or just disquiet or dismay at the breakdown of traditional values and
habits of conduct. The latter concern is most evident in the Japanese
Prime Minister's National Council for Educational Reform which
has trenchantly criticised the 'desolation' of modern Japan. It also
finds expression in the United States where values education has
been strongly urged upon schools by the successive political administrations. It is not surprising that schools are experiencing difficulty in finding adequate responses to the challenges they face in
determining an appropriate stance towards values education in the
open, democratic society.

As mentioned, Norway provides an interesting example of continuing, unresolved debates in the realm of norms and values, both

cultural and religious/ethical. This is in the context of a traditionally religious society (and schooling) encountering the full impact of a secularising age. Similarly, there is in Norway a 'back to basics' conservative reaction to the historic broadening and extending of education up to the school leaving age. This reaction is indeed widespread in many member countries including Australia, England and Wales, the Netherlands and, very conspicuously, the United States. In the latter country two recent reports by the Secretary of State for Education, respectively on elementary and secondary schooling, highlight what Mr Bennett describes as a growing national concern about the fundamental values of American life and the role of the school in promoting them.[11] In another case, France in 1986 commenced a new programme of compulsory civic education in the college (junior secondary stage). The amount of attention now given to vocational/work preparation education in the secondary schools of France, Britain and many other countries also carries an important message about values: the values of the work ethic, of skilled performance and the discipline of formal training in highly structured school–work environments.

Closely associated with the 'basics' drive and the endeavours being made to determine key or central values in the curriculum (e.g. disciplined knowledge, persistence, achievement orientation, skilled performance) is a growing emphasis on assessment of performance. Indeed, moves towards a performance assessment in the curriculum almost invariably start with the subject areas of language and mathematics which in practically all countries form the 'core of the core' in primary schooling. From all of this it is but a short step to reviewing and assessing the quality of schooling conceived as measurable outputs – and analysing relations between such output measures and the inputs which are most easily quantifiable in terms of recurrent and capital expenditures: salaries, equipment and materials, buildings.

Who should be in control?

In a broad sense, many of the foregoing concerns are political inasmuch as their focus is control, the criteria against which control will be exercised and the hands in which control will be vested. More generally, the issue is the distribution of power and authority. The trend towards controlling the broad framework of the curriculum in the name of a predefined national interest and through a central authority with political backing is the most pervasive of the current trends. This is true whether the mechanisms are central ministry directives, processes of national consultation or guidelines for local decision makers.

Disentangling the factors of (i) finance and political power from

(ii) the culture of schooling, the structure and organisation of the curriculum and pedagogy (iii) access to and participation in the benefits of schooling and (iv) evaluation and accountability measures is now virtually impossible. This itself is an indication of the extent to which prevailing assumptions about the 'proper' relationships between school and society appear to have overtaken the internal dynamics of the educational system in the change process. Put in a slightly different way, the displacement of the educational professional by the administrator, manager and politician appears to be gathering pace in several member countries.

It is necessary to use the qualifier 'appears' since we must distinguish between, on the one hand, what might be termed public arena discourse on educational policy making and, on the other, the structure, organisation and processes of education itself. Much of the national level public debate and the rhetoric surrounding education typically seem to leave the schools, the teachers, students and even the local communities unaffected. When there are observable effects, they are mediated through the inner dynamics of the school system and through local concerns and interests. Power and control may be consolidated in the discourse of policy but fragmented in the much wider and more diffuse field of educational action in regional and local authorities and the schools themselves. This fact, together with a dearth of research on educational practice, makes it exceedingly difficult to generalise about on the ground changes in school practice.

From another perspective, it may be observed that there are several levels, dimensions or aspects of control. They interact in determining outcomes in action including outcomes in curriculum and teaching practice. Thus 'control' functions at the level of the broadly stated general aim, the subjects that are required to be taught, the resources provided to support that teaching, the training of the teachers and their selection, and the pedagogical and organisational processes of the school. It would be an interesting study to plot each country's position on each of these dimensions in a comparative analysis. That would be, however, only a first move and not a very profound one at that. What has to be explained is the inner dynamics of the different systems. We can observe similarities in these across many if not most member countries.

There is nothing new about the affirmations of a national as distinct from individual or sectoral interest in the curriculum and the outcome of schooling. Every country report refers to this in one way or another and, in every case, there is a discernible stirring at the national level. This in itself opens up the debate on who should control the curriculum. As we shall see below, in some countries the very concepts of education and schooling are historically intertwined with nation building.[12]

A distinction is commonly made between centralised and decentralised decision making to explain differences in action on these different dimensions. But such a sharp and uncompromising distinction is clearly inadequate in the situations we are now addressing.

First, it presupposes a simple dichotomy whereas the reality is one of a range from single national authorities in unitary states to federal arrangements, and mixed systems which involve substantial regional or local authority. Many different examples might be cited but let us consider Canada, where education constitutionally belongs to the provinces and where the federal government exercises certain powers, e.g. in relation to languages and minority groups, and the local school boards exercise authority over the operation and administration of the school systems and the implementation of the curriculum, under delegations from the province.

There is commonly a sharing of roles and responsibilities between a mixture of agencies and institutions both public and private. This reflects the historical legacy as much as it does a formal division of power. Private education arrangements illustrate these points very clearly in the older European societies such as the Netherlands, England and France, but also in Australia where private schooling is not only educationally significant but an important electoral factor.

Third, and of crucial importance in several countries at present, there are changes taking place in the nature of control and influence and the manner in which they are exercised. These cut across administrative and even legal structures. The accountability movement, for example, is no less important for within-school procedures than for the operations of national systems.

As the author of the Finnish report remarks, education is on the move, change is continuous: 'The whole education system is actually on the go, since the message of the necessity for continuous change has been widely accepted in society.' Yet the change, even within Finland, a relatively small and homogeneous country, is not uniform or consistent. The broad structural reform of schooling, achieved in the 1970s, has reached stability and energies are now directed towards content and working methods in schooling and the restructuring of vocational and adult education. Since administration, in that country, is organised at central, regional and local levels and since there is a move to strengthen local roles, Finland exemplifies the point that control is shared and that the centralised–decentralised dichotomy no longer captures the essential features of control and decision making. The situation is similar in New Zealand and in Australia. In France, often held up as a model of centralised control, moves, for example towards elaborate consultative procedures at all levels from the central Ministry to the individual school council and the greater involvement of teachers in the determination of teaching methods and student evaluation, introduce new perspectives into the analysis. We must conclude that

in several countries there is very definitely a shifting pattern
whereby the conventional centralised–decentralised distinction is
breaking down, as both devolution and new forms of concentration
are occurring.

Changes in patterns of control over curriculum and pedagogy
point towards new forms of concentration of power. These changes
help us better to understand an important shift in the inner
dynamics of the education system. A typical observation is that in
the Canadian report, 'the predominant trends in curriculum reform
are toward infusing school programming with a stronger sense of
direction and, concomitantly, subjecting its outcomes to a more
rigorous and systematic assessment'. Whereas, in the 1960s and into
the 1970s, curricular and pedagogical reform were powerfully
influenced from within the subject disciplines, by developmental
and cognitive psychology and to a lesser extent by a newly emerging
sociology of education, and by the expansion and development of
teacher education, the orientation now is much more towards social
policy issues. This represents a profound shift of ethos and values.

In the Netherlands it is well recognised that power and authority
must be shared between home and school and such community
organisations as the churches. This is not to say, however, that there
is a stable balance among these three. There is a lively debate on the
need for schooling to help ameliorate such social problems as
vandalism, drug abuse, violence and sexually related disease,
together with renewed calls for schooling to focus on 'the basics' and
leave more scope to homes and churches for civic and moral
education.

This mix of trends raises questions of priority as well as distribution of authority. It is precisely the need to shape policy for
schooling around priorities that is the nub of a major debate:
governments affirm national or state/provincial needs to which they
wish curriculum decisions to respond; community interest groups,
professional bodies (including teachers) often affirm different
priorities. Countries are recognising a need to be clearer about
which of the many functions or roles of schooling are to receive the
greatest, most urgent treatment and how, and which of the numerous educational tasks that need to be performed can be left to
agencies other than the school.

There is perhaps an undue reliance on the written word, the
guideline, the policy directive, or even the legislative enactment in
sorting out issues such as these. Policy is often formulated through
glossily printed texts issuing from central sources. Thus, a recent
summary of government policy statements and initiatives in the
Australian State of Victoria draws attention to the contribution a
well-planned general education can make to the government's
policy commitment to a Youth Guarantee, and to explicit strategies

to achieve social justice and strengthen the state's economy. Roles of teachers, parents, school boards and central authorities are indicated.[13] But many teachers and school councils do not read such texts. When, as happens, they are translated into guidelines, there is uncertainty about the degree to which a guideline is prescriptive or merely hortatory. An alternative to guidelines is, of course, legislation, together with regulations: common devices for prescribing curriculum in broad terms.

In England, the Secretary of State for Education and Science, in outlining his government's intention to regain control of the curriculum through a national core curriculum, gave weight to the country's needs in an age of acute international economic competition. Opening the Second Reading Debate on the Education Reform Bill in the House of Commons, Mr Baker said: 'Raising the quality of education in our schools is the most important task for this Parliament.' He embellished his speech with a quotation from a nineteenth-century Conservative Prime Minister who, in 1874, informed the Commons that: 'Upon the education of the people of this country the fate of this country depends.'[14] Not to be outdone in the House of Lords, Lord Jenkins, echoing a motion of 1790 from John Dunning, proposed 'that the influence of our Executive is increasing and ought to be diminished'.

Mr Baker argued that in order to achieve all that he sought – which included devolution to headteachers, governors and freedom to parents – to release energies, 'we have to use the central power of Parliament. It is a paradox. But it's one thing to use the powers of central government to take power into the centre, and quite another to use it to devolve power to the citizen.'[15] Mr Baker's Bill nevertheless provoked controversy on a scale not witnessed in British education since the Second World War. The wings of controversy were neatly adumbrated in an editorial in *The Times Higher Educational Supplement*: 'Mr Kenneth Baker's "Great Education Reform Bill", which is unlikely ever to lose its ironic inverted commas, is a contradictory measure. It seeks both to aggrandise the power of the state and to encourage unregulated free market choice.'[16] Unperturbed, Mr Baker in introducing the Third Reading described it as a 'landmark in our educational system' while Prime Minister Thatcher credited her government with introducing 'sweeping reform in the educational system in England and Wales'.[17]

Yet another approach is illustrated in the widely read and vehemently debated American document *A Nation at Risk*, which was assiduously promoted by the US Department of Education and has provided a kind of fundamentalist text on new directions.[18] Such a basic approach to text writing seems necessary if a message is to be clearly and widely disseminated to a large and diffuse population.

But just because the text proclaims a point of view, or a policy, it is all too likely to generate a powerful opposition. This is nowhere better illustrated than in France: the more assertive and incisive the national educational authority the more likely is the reform to fail. This, again, shows up the limitations of the conventional analysis of centralised versus decentralised decision making.

Education and national self-image: the public and its problems

Throughout the 1980s, American reports on the new directions felt to be needed in schooling have underlined a perceived crisis in national economic and social affairs, a crisis moreover which was held by some, in chiliastic vein, to be at the very roots of American culture. This at any rate was a pervasive theme of the core document of the reform movement, *A Nation at Risk*: 'The educational foundations of our society are presently being eroded by a rising tide of mediocrity that threatens our very future.'

It is instructive to compare the American (and to a lesser extent the British) soul searching with that of the other countries that have contributed to this report. The style and tone of Finnish official statements are restrained. They quite systematically treat the curriculum of the elementary and secondary school as an integral part of overall social policies, focusing on educational and social equality, the relationship of knowledge and skill to changing production requirements, democratic citizenship and cultural activities. The approach is measured and there is a sense of steady achievement in addressing national goals and priorities.

The current reform in Japan – consequent on the 1985–87 review, the latest in the regular ten-year cycle – is predicated on widely discussed views about so-called 'school desolation': school violence, bullying, excessive competition, intense pressure on students, resistance by students to the demands of schooling, a decline of moral standards.

It is a matter of debate how far such problems reflect wider concerns, such as socio-cultural problems and the role of the school in addressing them – or not as the case may be – and the industrial and technological revolutions and their impact on the international community in which Japan increasingly sees itself as a major player. Social and cultural concerns were highlighted in the remit to the National Council for Educational Reform which was specially established by the then Prime Minister in September 1986, 'in light of the urgent need to secure an education adapted to the social changes and cultural development of the nation . . . [for the purpose of] designing necessary reforms with regard to government policies and measures . . . and with a view to securing such education as is compatible with the aforementioned changes and development' (law for the establishment of the National Council). It is noteworthy that, in establishing a National Council at all, the Prime Minister affirmed the national importance and scope of the reforms that were needed. In presenting his thoughts about the likely direction of the reform, Professor Michio Okamoto, Chairman of the National Council and therefore a key figure in what promises to be a significant series of developments in national education, saw late twentieth-century educational change as the harbinger of a twenty-first century in which, he said, 'Japan would go out to meet the world'.[19]

In its reports, the Japanese National Council criticised the materialism and conformity of modern society, its neglect of the qualities and needs of individuals and of human values. But education itself must share responsibility: the educators were reproached for failing to keep pace with these changes. From the Japanese perspective, school curricula and pedagogy have a vital role to play in restoring a worthwhile culture. Substantial changes in education are required to equip individuals with the ability to cope with 'social changes in the future'. In the context of the reform proposal this statement refers as much to new attitudes and values (or perhaps the reaffirmation of some established but increasingly taken for granted) values of the culture, alongside a scientific-technological-international mind set, as to the flexibility and adaptability to change so frequently enjoined upon students in Western societies.

The Japanese situation and reform proposals seem to highlight important tensions with parallels in all countries: control, order and direction to meet common and shared social needs, and individualistic and humanistic values to satisfy the aspirations of the individual person; the harnessing of economic growth and technological change in the interests of an enlarged, not a diminished humanity. Since the early days of the European scientific revolution, this has been the dream of the Utopians. It is fascinating to find it at the centre of contemporary policy debates in public education.

Schooling is widely and naturally looked to as a means of creating and recreating the social order. In the Durkheimian words of a former French Director of Education, 'The public education system underpins republican society from generation to generation. Destined from the outset to promote instruction, it continues to do so today.' Yet, he says, it is confronted with the most severe challenges,

in an economy in crisis where qualifications have to be raised, in a country which traditionally welcomes large numbers of refugees to make of them free and responsible citizens, and in a society dominated by the media which put out a great deal of information but little knowledge. In so doing, it emphasises the essential link between knowledge and liberty.[20]

From a curriculum perspective, the perennial questions of what kind of knowledge, who determines it and how it is articulated are of course crucial. When government-proclaimed national priorities and needs are perceived as the chief determinants, the needs and interests of the self-determining individual or sub-group may seem in abeyance. Yet the liberty of the subject, the health of the society – and its economy – and education are inextricably linked. Education is part of the national image. It is in the United States of America that what is referred to in that country's report as 'an integral relationship between effective education' and the country's welfare, is being most vehemently and comprehensively debated at present. As in France, liberty is at stake but the liberty in question has a great deal to do with the nation's declining economic position and the need 'to sustain the American position as world leader'.

Perceptions of the relationship between education and national well being, as the authors of the American report indicate, are not of recent origin. Indeed in that country they have underlain discussions of curriculum and schooling since the time of European settlement on the eastern seaboard early in the seventeenth century. Historically, this relationship has reflected the successive ideological, normative and intellectual waves, of seventeenth-century theocracy, eighteenth-century enlightenment and nineteenth-century republicanism and nationalism. Despite the endeavours of fundamentalists and absolutists of different persuasions, whether religious, ethical, political or whatever, it has been generally understood in modern times that the school aims to foster the individual and at the same time to be an adaptive institution. As such the school adapts to the culture of the society, reinforcing and reproducing it, or in some measure assists in the making and remaking of culture.

These orientations towards schooling are as strong and evident in the USA today as at any previous time in history, and their interrelationships seem as ambiguous as they are necessary. This level of concern may not be quite matched elsewhere but, as mentioned above, the establishment by the Prime Minister of a special National Council for Educational Reform in Japan and the powerful new education legislation in Britain throw into relief the potential if not the actual conflict within the culture – between the declared needs of the state and the proclivities of its citizens, between public and private interests. If not the identity of the nation then at least its underpinnings and its relations with other countries provide governments with ways of challenging education.

International comparisons of performance are popular if frequently of dubious validity. The initiative generally comes largely from central government itself or from central government agencies. While such initiatives are paramount in the United States it should not be forgotten that they are paralleled by an unprecedented outpouring of critiques, reviews, proposals, conferences, colloquies, seminars and meetings organised by numerous non-government bodies.

There is no lack of public engagement with educational issues in a number of member countries. Like the United States of America, Canada has, in recent years, subjected itself to a series of reviews, commissions, evaluations and research studies. For practically every Province there have now emerged curriculum proposals and packages, the majority of them providing for firmer direction, more definite (and obligatory) curriculum frameworks, and more use of assessment, evaluation and accountability measures, in the national or provincial interest. These measures reflect a wide assortment of public concerns as the comprehensive reviews of education at both elementary and secondary education have been completed. There are also very specific instances in Canada of the readiness of sections of the public to address particular problems or issues as they perceive their interests to be threatened (interest groups as a major force in educational policies). Government 'interference' (e.g. the private school issue in France in 1986) is fiercely resisted where strong private sector interests are at stake.

Although in some countries there is little overt evidence of major controversy about the directions of policy for curriculum and school practice there may be, nevertheless, a powerful undercurrent of interest in proposals for change. As the public authorities make more efforts to consult and circulate ideas and proposals for comment and as the media increasingly highlight educational issues, so does the public engage in the politics of educational participation. Several of the country reports provide instances: in Australia, examples include the heightened interest in the skills training role of schools, student choice in the curriculum and performance testing. In the Netherlands, environmental health and moral issues have surfaced. There is ample evidence that education is being taken into the public arena. In many countries, it is now standard practice to issue consultative documents not just to professional groups but widely across the community.[21]

During its three years of existence the Japanese National Council met 668 times, had 14 public hearings in different parts of the country with a total of 5,500 participants and heard the views of 483 experts; its members' ideas and other items were published in a monthly bulletin and collective conclusions and recommendations were embodied in interim reports which, after public debate, were turned into four official reports. In Saskatchewan, the 1984 review of curriculum and instruction attracted some 40,000 written items in the form of completed questions, briefs and letters. Likewise, in New Zealand quite remarkable levels of participation were achieved in the recently completed Review of Curriculum for Schools: 21,500 submissions in response to the committee's invitation to members of the public to make their views known and 10,000 responses to the draft report. There was a similar response to the New Zealand government's Task Force to Review Educational Administration.

Participation as a process has it effects. According to the authors of the New Zealand report, 'The extent and quality of the submissions have influenced developments in the curriculum for schools, even in advance of final acceptance of the document.' Snippets from citizens' comments on public education and proposals for change, published or official documents reveal a wide spectrum of opinion which is extraordinarily difficult to reconcile.

Increasingly, proposals for changing school curricula, teaching and learning procedures and related matters are drafted as texts, suitable for public debate and discussion – and, as we have seen, the public are responding, critically yes, but also positively and constructively. It is necessary to correct an impression that publics in member countries are generally dissatisfied with schooling. Misleading reports in parts of the media have given rise to a myth. Research evidence generally indicates high levels of satisfaction even where specific changes are sought.

In this chapter, the emphasis has been on the response of education and educators to wide changes in society. Educational change, its pervasiveness notwithstanding, is not, however, universal. In some countries there is a high level of satisfaction with the status quo. This may well reflect a desire to keep intact an image of social, economic and educational well being. In others, and the Swiss report outlines the problem, traditional academic values prevail even if there is a strongly felt need to change them.

In West Germany it is reported that there is a standstill in educational policy, there are no new policy initiatives and the period since 1975 has been one combining a cautious educational conservatism ('let us not abandon what we have achieved for the sake of the uncertain benefits of change') with outright scepticism about the results of the reforms of the preceding decade. Germany, and perhaps other German-speaking systems, are exceptional in this degree of caution over educational change. The explanation in Germany may lie as much in nervousness over the economy, political polarisation and the lack of a new political ascendancy (such as exists in Britain and the United States) as in considered responses to what was or was not achieved by way of educational reform between 1965 and 1975. The American and Japanese situations, by contrast, seem more indicative of an emerging international trend of events than is the German one.

A résumé of educational responses

No general overview of trends in policy debates about schooling in member countries can hope to be inclusive. At best, in the foregoing section a sample of directions and trends has been presented largely in the context of ways in which education is responding to social, economic and political change. The terms of the general debate, the directions in which school development and learning are moving, may be briefly summarised:

1 The reforms of the 1950s and onwards in school structures and organisation, leading to improved access and opportunity, comprehensive systems, the common school, the reduction, elimination or modification of selection by examination at different stages of schooling, and to the spread of educational opportunity broadly across the whole age group, are largely accepted and are being consolidated and refined. The German-speaking countries did not generally adopt the comprehensive school but reformed from within. Examinations have changed where they have been retained and there is a revival of interest in them in some countries and a growth of attainment testing.

2 Attention in policy formulation and public debates is turning increasingly towards the content and quality of what is taught, raising standards of achievement (in the sense of comparability of standards across a whole system), responsiveness to defined student, parent and community needs, the conditions of teaching and learning in classrooms and schools, and the efficient and effective management of classrooms to achieve desired learning outcomes. Public accountability is emphasised as is also an insistence that educational structures and practices should fit the present needs of the economic and industrial sphere.

3 While the needs of special groups of students (e.g. special gifts or talents, handicap, ethnic minorities, girls and technical subjects) are widely acknowledged, with specific provision of programmes and resources for purposes of school organisation and curriculum planning, mainstreaming and a common core curriculum are emphasised in many – but not all – countries. The 'neglect' of gifts and talents is seen as a problem in some systems. There is a tension between a common core for all, which is usually grounded in a theory of general education, the vocationally inspired drive towards practical and useful know-

ledge and skills, and those highly individual needs and interests to be found among diverse student groups.

4 Most noticeably in the countries where there is widespread public criticism of or concern about the performance of the educational system, there is considerable progress in defining the characteristics of successful schools. Much scientific effort has gone into evaluation and research studies on the results in schooling of intervention strategies and the conditions needed for successful teaching and learning. Hence the interest in the USA in 'better schools' and 'what works' and in the UK, in 'good practice'. Educational inspectorates, for example in the UK, Sweden and France, are recognised as indispensable indicators in the process of establishing quality in the changing circumstances of schooling.

5 Although there is consistency in the commitment to reform and improvement as a general educational orientation in a period of considerable social, industrial, scientific and technological change, there is little agreement about the fundamental educational rationale for or even the directions to be taken by many of the changes. There have been profound disagreements in several countries, stretching back to the 1960s and earlier, involving child-centred or child-oriented developmentalists, liberal humanists, vocationalists and economic rationalists. Governments having no monopoly of insight into or sensitivity towards educational issues; it is instructive to consult the literature of professional and academic bodies and community interest groups in order to draw out the different dimensions of the debate. Of particular significance is the fact that much of the national level drive towards more work-oriented, efficient, cost effective educational programmes is widely criticised as a form of managerialist technocracy. There is a considerable gap between system managers, policy makers and politicians on the one hand, and leading professional figures and groups on the other.

6 Growing interest in a common core curriculum denotes at least a readiness in countries to search for agreements on a common ground and to focus curriculum priorities. It seems to be very widely agreed that general education should continue throughout the whole period of compulsory schooling, that it should be broad and fundamental but with an increasing orientation towards working and adult life, a high level of (transferable) skills and committed citizenship. There is rather less but still a growing commitment to continuing, lifelong education of which schooling forms the first part.

7 The question of who shall control education, who shall provide the resources and how educational policies and procedures and

the use of resources are to be accounted for is of widespread concern. In most countries, we find mounting evidence of increasing central government intervention, not always directly but through fiscal and financial policies, regulatory procedures, monitoring and evaluating, guidelines and the like.

8 While education is universally recognised as a mechanism of social adaptation and adjustment, by those outside as well as those within the profession, it is mainly the latter who are drawing attention to the need to understand and come to terms with changing student values and lifestyles. In the eyes of some of the critics, some proposals for reform, however, seem to treat the students more as the objects of policies designed to achieve goals of national renewal and development than as human participants and partners in the educative process. Thus the industrial notion of quality control, the preoccupation with adjustment to technological change and the growing interest of ministries of industry, commerce, trade and labour are not always interrelated with personal, developmental models of schooling. The result can be a certain incoherence in overall national policies. This indicates a need both for closer interaction among the numerous interest groups and more sophisticated models of educational, economic and social development. New Zealand and Finland are among the minority of countries that seem to stand apart from many of these trends. After several years of intensive debate and a series of not always well articulated initiatives, in Britain there now seems to be a new coherence and integration of policies and programmes.

9 National level curriculum and pedagogical change cannot be achieved by working on the curriculum and teaching methodologies alone. School organisation, teacher education, terms and conditions of service, school–workplace relations and school–community values impact upon the curriculum and ways of teaching and learning. They are all part of an exceedingly complex picture whose elements are interrelated. Pressures for curriculum and pedagogical change are coming from outside education as well as from within, they are indirect as well as direct and the achievement of change requires, it seems, widespread participation. This, however, often as not, is in the form of a power struggle, not a concerted drive.

10 The educational response to the wide array of changes and trends touched upon in this chapter has been considerable. Educators need, however, to continue to draw them to the attention of those elements in the wider public which remain critical and whose support for educational development is needed. The curriculum responses will be discussed in ensuing chapters. They include: the introduction of new subjects (e.g.

computer science), or the further development of earlier innovations (e.g. primary science, environmental studies), the continual updating of content across the curriculum, numerous attempts to give subject content closer relationships with everyday and working life, attention to values education across the curriculum and student and group centred pedagogical innovation.

Notes and references

1 Berman, P. and McLaughlin, M. W. (1978), *Federal Programs Supporting Educational Change*, Vol. 8, *Implementing and Sustaining Innovation*, Santa Monica, California, Rand Corporation; Huberman, A. M. and Miles, M. B. (1984), *Innovation Up Close. How School Improvement Works*, New York, Plenum Press; Skilbeck, M. (1985), 'Curriculum development – from RDD to RED: review, evaluate, develop', in Nisbet, J. *et al*. (eds), *World Yearbook of Education, 1985. Research Policy and Practice*, London, Kogan Page.

2 Berman, P. and McLaughlin, M. W. (1975), *Federal Programs Supporting Educational Change*, Vol. 4, *The Findings in Review*, Santa Monica, California, Rand Corporation; Kliebard, H. M. (1979), 'The drive for curriculum change in the United States, 1890–1958. From local reform to a national preoccupation', *Journal of Curriculum Studies*, 11, 12, pp. 273–81, and Kliebard, H. M. (1986), *The Struggle for the American Curriculum*, London, Routledge and Kegan Paul; McClure, R. M. (1971), 'The reforms of the fifties and sixties: a historical look at the near past', *Seventieth Yearbook of the National Society for the Study of Education: The Curriculum: Retrospect and Prospect*, Chicago, Ill., The Society, pp. 45–75; Giacquinta, J. B. and Kazlan, C. (1980), 'The growth and decline of public school innovations; a national study of the open classroom in the United States', *Journal of Curriculum Studies*, 12, 1, pp. 16–72; Gammage, P. (1987), 'Chinese Whispers', *Oxford Review of Education*, 13, 1, pp. 95–109; An Roinn Oidachais (1971), *Curaclam Na Bunscoile (Primary School Curriculum)*, Dublin, The Stationery Office, Parts 1 and 2.

3 A recent Australian case study documents the 'rationality' problem. Rizvi, F. and Kemmis, S. (1987), 'Dilemmas of Reform', *The Participation and Equity Program in Victorian Schools*, Geelong, Victoria, Deakin Institute for Studies in Education. See also Kirst, M. W. and Meisner, G. R. (1985), 'Turbulence in American secondary schools: what reforms last?', *Curriculum Inquiry*, 15, 2, pp. 169–86.

4 US Office of Education (1951), *Life Adjustment Education for Every Youth*, Bulletin 22, Washington, DC, Government Printing Office. Controversy surrounded 'life adjustment' education, cf. Scott, C. Winfield and Hill, C. M. (eds) (1954), *Public Education Under Criticism*, New York, Prentice-Hall; Ravitch, D. (1983), *The Troubled Crusade. American Education, 1945–1980*, New York, Basic Books.

5 Kallos, D. and Lundgren, U. P. (1976), *An Enquiry Concerning Curriculum: Foundations for Curriculum Change*, Goteborgs, Pedagogiska Institutionen, Goteborgs Universitet.

6 Her Majesty's Inspectorate (1977), *Curriculum 11–16*, London, Her Majesty's Stationery Office.

7 Papadopoulos, G. (1987), *Proceedings of the Conference of High Level Experts on Education*, Tokyo, Organising Committee for the Conference, p. 11.

8 OECD (1986), *Girls and Women in Education*, Paris, OECD.
9 OECD Reference to Report of 1988 Education and Economy Conference.
10 Callahan, R. (1962), *Education and the Cult of Efficiency*, Chicago, Ill., University of Chicago Press.
11 Bennett, W. J. (1986), 'First Lessons', *A Report on Elementary Education in America*, Washington, DC, US Department of Education; Bennett, W. J. (1987), *James Maddison High School, A Curriculum for American Students*, Washington, DC, US Department of Education.
12 See Curtis, M. (1935), *The Social Ideas of American Educators*, New York, Charles Scribners Sons; Wiggin, G. A. (1962), *Education and Nationalism*, New York, McGraw-Hill.
13 Victoria State Board of Education (1987), *Directions in Curriculum*, Melbourne, State Board of Education.
14 *Hansard*, 3.12.87, Column 771.
15 Baker, K. (1988), 'Tories are not school bullies', *The Sunday Telegraph*, 13 March, p. 11.
16 Editorial, *The Times Educational Supplement* (1987), 'Beyond Mr. Baker', 18 September.
17 *Hansard*, 11.5.88, Column 636.
18 US National Commission on Excellence in Education (1983), *A Nation at Risk*, Washington, DC, Government Printing Office. See also the US Secretary of Education's 'progress report' on the reform movement that ensued, Bennett, W. J. (1988), *American Education: Making it Work*, Washington, DC, Department of Education.
19 *Organising Committee for the Conference Proceedings* (1987), Kyoto, The Committee, pp. 23–30.
20 Cerquiglini, B. (1987), Unpublished Secretariat paper.
21 See, for example, Department of Education and Science/Welsh Office (1987), *The National Curriculum 5–16, a Consultative Document*, London, DES; Department of Education, New Zealand (1988), *Draft National Curriculum Statement*, Wellington, Department of Education.

1.2

Curriculum Traditions

Mike Golby

The curriculum is what school is for. Whatever other functions and purposes the school may serve, what it sets out to teach and what it does teach lies at the heart of its existence. Schools certainly perform the function of keeping children off the streets in the daytime and students off the tally of those looking for work. They certainly serve the purposes of a workforce of teachers and others in providing professional, quasi-professional or other paid occupations. The functions served by schools may be analysed many ways for the education system is deeply implicated in the social fabric. And what is sought by parents, teachers, employers, politicians and others from the schools is also greatly diverse and, often enough, contradictory.

The curriculum, you would think, is at the centre of all this. In view of the many ways school sustains and is sustained by our social and political arrangements and in view of its ubiquity in the life of the people, you would think that what it teaches would be of great moment in the popular debates. But you would be wrong for the curriculum of schools has been generally taken for granted, its structure and rationale unexamined outside the ranks of the education professionals. Regulations for primary and secondary schools up to the Second World War enshrined largely uncontested popular beliefs about what was appropriate. The received grammar school curriculum, marked by subject mindedness for the secondary schools, leavened only by practical and technical concessions for the less clever; the drills and frills of the elementary school tradition for the primary schools lightened by the childhood indulgences of play and discovery learning. Neither the secondary nor the primary school curriculum received fundamental attention to match the institutional changes brought about by the 1944 Act which created these separate phases of schooling.

The national curriculum of the 1988 Education Act likewise stirs no great public controversy except over corporate worship and how far it should be Christian in character. In the postwar period, when expansion and reconstruction of the system consumed all political energies, the teachers talked mainly to themselves about the basis for the curriculum. This detachment from mainstream political and intellectual life is well exemplified in the history of the Schools Council which so conspicuously failed to become the national forum for working out the curriculum that Derek Morrell envisioned. This was a collective failure of the political culture.

The national curriculum of the 1988 Education Act need not be Napoleonic in its protracted implementation up to 1992. It is not inevitable that it will enshrine the undoubtedly conservative, even reactionary, values of its begetters. Examples of legislation whose intent is altered in practice are not hard to find. The political game to play for is the essential spirit in which the national curriculum is to be enacted and which will guide its development. It may therefore be timely to bring to light and examine some of the more obvious and powerful forms of thought that have underlain the curriculum structures and practices out of which a new order must be born. These forms of thinking, or paradigms, are diverse and philosophically competitive. To elucidate them is a service to democracy.

It is therefore the purpose here to identify some influential theories in the interests of greater communication between them. Such communication matters because modern pluralism demands the maximum possible co-existence of values and cultures. It is objectionable that the curriculum of publicly maintained schools should be based on one-sided views of the complexity of curriculum making. To seek connections and to identify contradictions in the thinking which goes into the school curriculum is to inform debate. That is the best purpose of liberal educational theory.

It is axiomatic here that there exists no single unproblematic and overarching curriculum theory to which all disputes about practicalities can safely be referred. Yet there is one tradition, powerful and appealing, which denies this. Utilitarianism by definition seeks to reduce questions of social welfare and questions of individual morality to a calculus of pleasures. Philosophy has for two hundred years charted the progress of this belief and its application to policy making. In the early twentieth century the philosophical triumph of positivism cleared the way for technocracy, the idea that questions of human welfare were soluble through the application of science. So far as the school curriculum is concerned, technocracy enters the scene in the guise of rational curriculum planning.

The technocratic tradition

Curriculum theory is conducted against the pervasive influence of this line of thinking, whose prime exemplars are Bobbitt and Tyler (Bobbitt, 1918, 1924; Tyler, 1949). The idea that decisions about designs for learning can be achieved by recourse to a means–end model of human action is fundamental here. If we are clear about what we wish to teach, and the reasons why, curriculum decisions are to be reached through the specification of clear objectives and the choice of technically apt methods for the achievement of those objectives. Clear objectives entail the specification of outcomes in terms of the learners' abilities at the end of the course or item of instruction. Preferably these outcomes should be stated behaviourally; that is, they should be statements open to no or little interpretation, being value-neutral statements containing verbs of learner behaviour which can be observed to be present. Success in curriculum is to be measured in terms of the learners' status in relation to these behavioural measures. Evaluation, likewise, consists in checks of the *achievement* of the learners against the objectives prescribed for them.

There are a number of significant objections to this account of curriculum theory.

First, it rests on an assumption as to fundamental agreement on the aims and objectives of the programme. In itself it does not provide a means of debating the desirability of the aims and objectives that are to be the starting points for the programme. On the contrary, these are taken as read and curriculum planning is cast as the technical exercise of designing learning to pre-specified ends.

Secondly, it makes the assumption that all learning can be reduced to statements of learner behaviour. Against this, there is the commonsense view that learning, being a mental process, goes on covertly in the mind. Neither of these two extremes is defensible. If there is to be no evidence of learning it is hard to see that we can ever be justified in ascribing the achievement of learning to someone. However, to take *particular evidence* of learning to be necessarily pre-specifiable is to miss the point that an indefinite range of evidence may be appropriate to claims that a learner has had success. This is particularly the case where learning is of an order higher than merely physical performance (where statements of behaviour are not only *evidence for* but also *constitutive of* any objective you could specify) (Hirst, 1965). In higher order learning, whether cognitive or affective in character, finite lists of behaviour are inappropriate because the achievements are so complex that they can only be adjudicated contextually by one who has knowledge both of the area of achievement under consideration and of the learner's relation to it. What is true, however, is that teachers and evaluators must make such judgements and that they do so on the basis of learner performance. The technocratic tradition makes the mistake of misrepresenting educational performance by reducing the range of evidence for it.

Thirdly, it adopts a version of teaching as moulding a learner to a predetermined shape. This view of teaching is not current in all traditions of schooling. It has its home in industrial and military training situations. In other traditions this conception of the teacher's task is broadened to acknowledge the possibility, even the desirability, of learners' transcending the teacher's knowledge during the teaching–learning transaction. The likelihood of this broadening of conceptions of the teaching task increases as subject matter itself becomes more problematic. Thus, in military drill situations for example, it is built in that conformity to behaviourally specified performances is all that is required. There, pre-specified behavioural objectives are entirely suitable descriptions of what is looked for. If we consider physical education, however, it becomes apparent that what is sought is not exhaustively described in physical terms. Qualities of control in movement and attributes such as imagination in movement quickly evade behavioural description. Considering intellectual achievements and achievement in the areas of personal, social, aesthetic, emotional and moral education, we find that descriptions of those achievements are highly elaborate, couched in terms peculiar to those several areas and, when they are manifested, discernible only to those already initiated in the field. That this is so negates one of the major claims for the technocratic tradition, namely that it permits systematic technical evaluation of learning programmes, thereby opening them up to the scrutiny of a public not itself initiated into the forms of thought which are the content of the programme.

Fourthly, the technocratic view casts the subject matter of the curriculum into a subsidiary relationship to the objectives of the curriculum (Stenhouse, 1970). There is here the objection that educational planning demands attention to the logic of subject matter in order to identify what is educationally worthwhile. We can, moreover, acknowledge that this is so without at the same time adopting the fully-fledged version of 'taking a means to an end' that the tradition demands. Educational value, critics such as R. S. Peters have insisted, is implicit in worthwhile activities. Such activities are to be pursued as educational for the procedural principles inherent in them. They are not to be deemed educative only provisionally upon the observable results they happen to bring about in learners. However poorly mastered, they exemplify public traditions of rationality which are entailed in the concept of education itself (Peters, 1966).

That there is some use in the techniques of 'rational curriculum planning' propounded in the technocratic tradition is undoubtedly true. Historically, the movement offered a clear prescription for planners in a situation where there were no clear models. Planners were offered clear guidance on the specification of knowledge, for example (Bloom *et al.*, 1956). For learners, it offered descriptions of their tasks which were in many ways helpful to them and in some cases formed the basis for contractual arrangements between teacher and learner. That the planning model was clear, if flawed, also provided a language of criticism for the public at large. This is not a trifling consideration, bearing in mind the enormous sums the public votes for education. It is in the United States that the movement has had its greatest influence. There, business, industrial and academic work ethics are more closely aligned than in Europe. As an ideological position on the curriculum, therefore, it is not surprising that the technocratic tradition has held sway where a means–end model of human actions is so influential in closely related spheres of social life. In European cultures there has been an historically more distant relationship between the worlds of commerce and industry and education. For that reason, when the theory of the curriculum in its technocratic form crossed the Atlantic it met with considerable resistance.

J. F. Kerr's collection *Changing the Curriculum* (Kerr, 1968) is a representative early attempt to translate the mainly American technocratic tradition into an English idiom. It was paralleled by a number of similar books (Nicholls and Nicholls, 1972; Taylor, 1970; Wiseman and Pidgeon, 1972). The key feature of these transplants is their emphasis on model building as a technique for planning. The orientation is practical curriculum planning and reform based on the principles of rational curriculum planning.

It will be instructive to review Kerr's model and to base our discussion upon it. We should first note, however, a number of important points about model building in general. Models, particularly when diagrammatically presented have a power to beguile with their simplicity. This simplicity is a necessary feature, however, for model making is essentially an attempt to filter out significant from trivial features of a situation. The criteria for significance cannot themselves be represented in a model as they are presuppositions in the model itself. It follows that the use of models demands vigilance for unwelcome presuppositions going toward their construction. In the case of Kerr's model, there is a presupposition that the model is not merely a *description* of curriculum reality but is designed to assist decision making. It is thus a model *for* the curriculum rather than a model *of* the curriculum, an important distinction made by Maccia (1962). It is prescriptive as well as descriptive and the relationship between the two aspects is obscure. This is so because of a confusion that often vitiates curriculum theory, namely a confusion between curriculum as *plan* and curriculum as *process*. A model for planning will clearly differ, though it must be premissed upon, a model for process. A model of the processes of the curriculum would be an attempt to chart the significant occurrences and transactions in schooling: a model for planning must have an implicit theory about how these processes are to be modified. Kerr's model reveals a vacillation between these two conceptions and it shares this defect with many other such model building exercises.

The liberal-humanist tradition

Kerr's book can be seen as the superimposition of a conceptual apparatus and package of planning recommendations upon an existing set of doctrines about curriculum planning. It is noteworthy that the model specifies 'knowledge' as a major section of the curriculum reflecting a traditionally naive acceptance of contemporary school knowledge as 'given' in the curriculum. Moreover, the model goes on to indicate that school knowledge has some tight relationship with 'disciplines', although 'pupils' and 'society' are given apparently equal status as sources for objectives.

Figure 1   *Source:* Kerr, J. F. (1968) *Changing the Curriculum* (London, University of London Press)

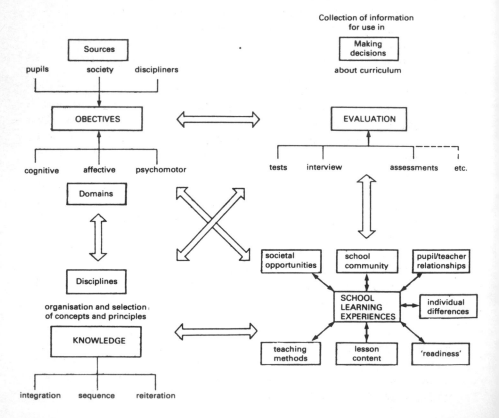

What is significant in Kerr is his implicit compromise with the dominant liberal-humanist view of curriculum as initiation into a settled body of high-status subjects. Liberal-humanists fail to stimulate reflection on what validates these subjects singly and what they add up to as contributions to the educational experience of the young.

The key attempt to undertake this task is that of Hirst (1965) in *Liberal Education and the Nature of Knowledge*. Hirst argues that the knowledge of which mind is 'constituted' consists of a range of 'forms of thought' each of which represents a unique way of experiencing and understanding the world. By a form of knowledge is meant a distinct way in which our experience becomes structured round the use of accepted public symbols. The symbols thus having public meaning, their use is in some way testable against experience and there is the progressive development of series of tested symbolic expressions. In this way experience has been probed further and further by extending and elaborating the use of the symbols and by means of these it has become possible for the personal experience of individuals to become more fully structured, more fully understood. The various forms of knowledge can be seen in low level developments within the common area of our knowledge of the everyday world. From this there branch out the developed forms which, taking certain elements in our common knowledge as a basis, have grown in distinctive ways. In the developed forms of knowledge the following related distinguishing features can be seen:

1 They each involve certain central concepts that are peculiar in character to the form. For example, those of gravity, acceleration, hydrogen, and photosynthesis characteristic of the sciences; number, integral and matrix in mathematics; God, sin and predestination in religion; ought, good and wrong in moral knowledge.
2 In a given form of knowledge these and other concepts that denote, if perhaps in a very complex way, certain aspects of experience, form a network of possible relationships in which experience can be understood. As a result the form has a distinctive logical structure.
3 The form, by virtue of its particular terms and logic, has expressions or statements (possibly answering a distinctive type of question) that in some way or other, however indirect it may be, are testable against experience. This is the case in scientific knowledge, moral knowledge, and in the arts, though in the arts no questions are explicit and the criteria for the tests are only partially expressible in words. Each form, then, has distinctive expressions that are testable against experience in accordance with particular criteria that are peculiar to the form.

4 The forms have developed particular techniques and skills for exploring experience and testing their distinctive expressions, for instance the techniques of the sciences and those of the various literary arts. The result has been the amassing of all the symbolically expressed knowledge that we now have in the arts and the sciences.

For Hirst a liberal education must minimally involve the pupil being initiated into all the 'forms of thought'. Thus he advocates a knowledge-centred curriculum, though not necessarily a curriculum based upon any particular division of knowledge into 'subjects'. For example, he recognises that 'fields of knowledge' also exist, examples of which are theoretical and practical areas of activity such as agriculture, medicine or education itself.

Other theorists in this camp are King and Brownell (1966), who conceive an academic discipline as a 'community of discourse', a group of scholars with a sense of shared concerns, publications and shared identity, and Phenix (1964), who bases his recommendation on a logical analysis of what can be meaningfully said. In Britain writers such as Whitfield (1971) paralleled the Americans Bruner (1960, 1966) and Ford and Pugho (1964) in drawing attention to the importance of structure in subject matter. Structure renders mere information meaningful, provides for readier learning, promotes transfer, reduces the gap between elementary and advanced knowledge in a field.

Pedagogically, a long-standing model of teaching in which a learner is conceived as a postulant to be initiated into the mysteries of a subject by working at it alongside a 'master' (very much a model of traditional university teaching) was developed in the new emphasis on fundamentals of a subject. Oakeshott (1974) expresses the pedagogic point thus:

> All actual conduct, all specific activity springs up within an already existing idiom of activity. And by 'idiom of activity' I mean a knowledge of how to behave appropriately in the circumstances. Scientific activity is the exploration of the knowledge scientists have of how to go about asking and answering scientific questions; moral activity is the exploration of the knowledge we have of how to behave well. And we come to penetrate an idiom of activity in no other way than by practising the activity; for it is the practice of an activity that we can acquire the knowledge of how to practice it.

Liberal humanism as represented by these modern writers is not without challenge. Some doubt that the intellectual demands of such a knowledge-based curriculum could be made accessible to all pupils. Bantock (1971), for example, suggests that the contemporary watered down academic education offered to the mass of children is unsatisfactory and argues, against Hirst, that the basis of the curriculum for the mass of unacademic children should be more concrete, more practical and 'affective-artistic' in orientation. Bantock's view is based on a romantic conception of working-class culture and is, of course, a form of academic elitism. Other critics of the liberal-humanist ideology are found among those who advocate a 'socially relevant' curriculum, particularly in areas of urban decay (Midwinter, 1972). Such a view can be called into question as potentially socially divisive in offering a school experience directly related only to local conditions and not to cosmopolitan problems (Merson and Campbell, 1974). Perhaps more significantly, the liberal-humanist tradition is opposed by a longer-standing protest movement, namely child centred progressivism.

The progressive traditions

If the liberal-humanist takes the structure of knowledge as his starting point for curriculum planning, the progressivist takes subject matter into consideration only insofar as it illuminates the child's world. Growth is the central metaphor. Malcolm Skilbeck outlines some of the major tenets of the Romantic movement that underlies progressivism thus:

1 The movement is a fundamental challenge to Enlightenment confidence in rationality, objectivity, universalism, causality, abstract analysis, and urbanity. It emphasises 'human inwardness', private subjective meanings and symbols, states of consciousness, feeling states, and complex personal motives.

2 Knowledge is yielded by direct experience, intuition, reverie, and by communication in full encounter with persons and things; it is 'wrenched from nature', but not by cold science.

3 Man is a spiritual entity who is nevertheless, in Cervantes's phrase, the 'son of his works', discovering and fulfilling himself through his energetic, active impingement on the external world. He is not a 'factor' in nature, but a free, responsible moral agent.

4 Sincerity, wholeheartedness, self-sacrifice, indomitable will in pursuit of some self-fulfilling cause are all worthwhile; compromise and the 'sell-out' are crimes.

5 Society is organic, plant- or animal-like, interacting with the environment and varying in time and place; it is not a clockwork mechanism following universal laws; history is not 'universal' but a succession of unique, varied particulars; culture and society are diverse, not reducible to a single ideal type; man's cultural life is a life of struggle and conflict.

6 Man's 'natural habitat' is the remote, the colourful, the wild, the elemental; countryside, woodlands, distant islands, unexplored

    territories: urban, industrial society is vicious, depraving, dis-
torting.

7 God, if he exists, is reachable through emotional ritual, or
mystical exercises, including communing with nature. By some
romantics he is seen to exist as the enemy of mankind, a giant
torturer.

8 Art is authentic inasmuch as it expresses the passions and deepest
experience of the individual artist; art is communication between
persons and groups within a culture and in historical time. But art
is not undisciplined: the task is 'to keep one's head in the course
of the storm and to direct one's troops'.

9 The child is father of the man, his own 'best philosopher';
childhood experience is authentic, direct, vivid, penetrating, rich
and fleeting; childhood is a state worthy in itself and not merely as
a prelude to adulthood. (Skilbeck, 1976.)

For the progressivist, pedagogy is opportunistic, sustained by
intimate knowledge of the individual child in a framework of
organised resources. The teacher is seen as expert on child development, learning and classroom organisation. Planning is the provision of opportunities for the following of interests in a secure
emotional framework of 'benign environment' (Fisher, 1972).

The progressive tradition has had its principal impact on primary
education, particularly with the Plowden Report which represented
the high-water mark of progressive thinking in the public domain.
Objections are both theoretical and practical. The individualised
curriculum it seems to imply denies the idea of a stable common
course of study and substitutes instead the quest for personal
meaning. This is in practice likely to be chaotic in all but the most
skilful hands. Research points to its naivety in relation to social
class and gender aspects, practice being liable to quietist conservative assumptions about morality, social order and power (King,
1983; Sharp and Green, 1975). Nevertheless, the force of progressive curricular thinking is seen best as moderating instructional
teaching styles throughout the education system, redressing the
balance between teacher and taught and causing the content of the
curriculum to be considered in relation to the felt interests of the
student. Talk of 'negotiated curricula' in the 14–18 sector and the
movement for profiles and records of achievement, for example, are
very much results of progressive thinking in environments otherwise
saturated by technocratic and, still, liberal humanistic assumptions.

The national curriculum

We may now consider how the foregoing traditions of curriculum
theorising and their associated practices relate to the development

of a national curriculum. In fact, of course, the national curriculum proposals as published in the DES and Welsh Office Consultative Document in July 1987, and as adopted despite the enormous and mainly hostile reception they received, consist of a list of core and foundation subjects directly derived from the 1904 Regulations. In that respect they draw upon the liberal-humanist tradition of the grammar schools with a technical sharpening in the form of craft, design and technology. The fact that this *table d'hote* menu is *for all* extends equality of access beyond that of 1944's tripartism. The idea of testing all children at 7, 11, 14 and 16 relies upon a technology of testing which it is not available off the shelf and over which there will certainly be both technical and ideological struggles. In particular, the hopes of teachers for formative, educational testing and parental memories of the stress of exams of one kind and another will certainly complicate the introduction of testing as well as the form in which results are published.

We have then a national curriculum in train which draws upon liberal-humanistic and technocratic assumptions. It does this without explicit rationale, what justification there is being a mix of assertions about the national economic performance, parental expectations and the elusive idea of standards. Progressive thinking is entirely absent. Those curriculum developments which most expressed progressive thinking, such as the prevocational movement, aspects of TVEI (Technical and Vocational Education Initiative) and cross-curricular work such as health education find no place in the proposed new order.

Now of course the fudging has to begin. Proposals have to be enacted. Not only technicalities are at stake, since practice can also reveal new philosophical possibilities. It is fortunate then that there exists a further tradition of curriculum thinking which offers help.

The cultural analysis tradition

Technocracy renders curriculum making into a technical exercise, failing to account for the sources of educational values. It thus delivers itself up to the powers that be. Liberal humanism for all its emphasis on the rational mind fails likewise to consider its social and historical context. Progressivism locks itself into the here and now with a vague hope for a happy ever after. By contrast, a view of curriculum as a cultural artefact emerging from a social negotiation between generations and classes offers hope of intellectual grasp at a time when education patently is a matter of struggle between the perspectives of professional educators and their political masters. Chitty identifies a contest over curriculum between bureaucratic and professional ideologies, where the bureaucrats (the DES) advocate

a curriculum based on the 1904 Regulations while professionals (HMI) assert a curriculum for understanding a complex society offered as an entitlement of all children (Chitty, 1988).

To trace the heritage of this view and to recognise that this view is itself ideological in that it takes a definite line on the role of school in relation to cultural and political structures we have to return to American sources. Dewey saw school knowledge as validated by its contribution, pragmatically, to democratic cultural development (Dewey, 1899). Smith, Stanley and Shores summarise and epitomise a long line of thinking that takes the school as a socialising institution, whose function is to transmit to the next generation those things within the culture that are most valued, including ideas, ideals, beliefs, skills, tools, aesthetic discernment, methods of thinking and institutions (Smith, Stanley and Shores, 1950). School is thus an institution concerned to centralise experience around what is valued universally. What is more, a society that respects minorities will expect school also to represent subcultures in its curriculum. Determining what is most generally valued, what are the identifiable subcultures in a pluralistic society, how cultural universals and cultural specialities (Linton, 1936) are to be educationally mediated, becomes the focal problem for curriculum design.

The school curriculum is seen as the meeting place of a large number of legitimate interests, for example those of pupils, teachers, parents, employers, trade unions. The curriculum needs to accommodate as many such interests as possible. The central problem of curriculum is therefore to develop mechanisms for the expression of those interests and clearer conceptions of the rights and duties of the parties concerned. The spirit of this approach is seen in practice in the Schools Council's Working Paper 53, *The Whole Curriculum, 13–16* in which an 'educational covenant' is suggested between interested parties (Schools Council, 1975). The pivotal position of teachers in this dispensation is obvious. It is also obvious that teachers are ill-equipped for the task of mediating conflict, setting up dialogue at an ideological level (for questions of curriculum design are ultimately profoundly ideological) and developing curricula that are more than uneasy compromises, having a coherent design that identifies shared values and makes room for legitimate dissent. Indeed, MacIntyre has concluded, pessimistically for the tradition, that in a period characterised by lack of a public life of reason teachers are 'the forlorn hope of the culture of Western modernity' (MacIntyre, 1987). There can be little doubt in the longer run, however, that technocratic, liberal-humanist and progressive traditions need to be encompassed in some larger view such as that here sketched as prolegomenon to a future curriculum theory.

References

Bantock, G. H. (1971), 'Towards a theory of popular education', *Times Educational Supplement*, 12 and 19 March.

Bloom, B. S. *et al.* (1956), *Taxonomy of Educational Objectives: I, The Cognitive Domain*, London, Longman.

Bobbitt, F. (1918), *The Curriculum*, Boston, Mass., Houghton Mifflin.

Bobbitt, F. (1924), *How To Make A Curriculum*, Boston, Mass., Houghton Mifflin.

Broudy, A. S., Smith, B. O., and Burnett, J. R. (1964), *Democracy and Excellence in American Secondary Education*, Chicago, Ill., Rand McNally.

Bruner, J. (1960), *The Process in Education*, Cambridge, Mass., Harvard University Press.

Bruner, J. (1966), *Towards a Theory of Instruction*, Cambridge, Mass., Harvard University Press.

Chitty, C. (1988), 'Two models of a national curriculum. Origins and interpretations', in Lawton, D. and Chitty, C. (eds), *The National Curriculum, Bedford Way Paper 33*, London, Institute of Education, University of London.

Dewey, J. (1899), *The School and Society*, Chicago, Ill., University of Chicago Press.

Fisher, R. J. (1972), *Learning How to Learn: The English Primary School and American Education*, New York, Harcourt, Brace Jovanovich.

Ford, G. W., and Pugho, L. (eds) (1964), *The Structure of Knowledge and the Curriculum*, Chicago, Ill., Rand McNally.

Hirst, P. H. (1965), 'Liberal education and the nature of knowledge', in R. D. Archanbauld (ed.), *Philosophical Analysis and Education*, London, Routledge and Kegan Paul.

Kerr, J. (ed.) (1968), *Changing the Curriculum*, London, University of London Press.

King, A. R. and Brownell, J. R. (1966), *The Curriculum and the Disciplines of Knowledge*, New York, Wiley.

King, R. A. (1983), *All Things Bright and Beautiful? A Sociological Study of Infant Classrooms*, Chichester, Wiley.

Linton, R. (1936), *The Study of Man*, New York, Appleton-Century-Crofts.

Maccia, E. (1962), *The Conceptions of Model in Educational Theorizing*, Columbus, Ohio, Bureau of Research and Service, Ohio State University.

MacIntyre, A. (1987), 'The idea of an educated public', in Haydon, G. (ed.) *Education as Values*, Institute of Education, University of London.

Merson, M. W., and Campbell, R. J. (1974), 'Community education: instruction for inequality', *Education for Teaching*, Spring.

Midwinter, E. (1972), *Projections: An Educational Priority Area at Work*, London, Ward Lock Educational.

Nicholls, A. and Nicholls, H. (1972), *Developing a Curriculum: A Practical Guide*, London, Allen and Unwin.

Oakeshott, M. (1974), *Rationalism in Politics and Other Essays*, London, Methuen.

Peters, R. S. (1966), *Ethics and Education*, London, Allen and Unwin.

Phenix, P. (1964), *Realms of Meaning: A Philosophy of the Curriculum for General Education*, New York, McGraw-Hill.

Schools Council (1975), *The Whole Curriculum 13–16*, London, Evans/Methuen Educational.

Sharp, R. and Green (1975), *Education and Social Control*, Routledge.

Skilbeck, M. (1976), *Culture, Ideology and Knowledge*, Open University Course E203, Unit 3, Milton Keynes, Open University Press.

Smith, B. O., Stanley, W. O., and Shores, J. H. (1950), *Fundamentals of Curriculum Development*, New York, Harcourt, Brace and World.

Stenhouse (1970), 'Some limitations of the use of objectives in curriculum research and planning', *Pedagogica Europaea*, 6, 73–83.

Taylor, D. H. (1970), *How Teachers Plan Their Courses*, Slough, NFER.

Tyler, R. W. (1949), *Basic Principles of Curriculum and Instruction*, Chicago, Ill., University of Chicago Press.

Whitfield, R. (1971), *Discipline of the Curriculum*, Maidenhead, McGraw-Hill.

Wiseman, S. and Pidgeon (1972), *Curriculum Evaluation*, Slough, NFER.

SECTION 2

The Politicisation of the Curriculum

Introduction

> I am concerned on my journeys to find complaints from industry that new recruits from the schools sometimes do not have the basic tools to do the job that is required.

With this, Prime Minister James Callaghan begins, in his Ruskin College speech (Appendix 1), to catalogue the failings of an education system. It is a theme his successor Margaret Thatcher took up with some energy. At the end of her second and beginning of her third administration in 1987 to 1988 radical policy proposals transformed the British education scene. The 1987 consultation document on the national curriculum, in an unusual but politically adept move, makes a cross-party reference to the Ruskin speech.

In this section a number of different strands in the debate of the 1980s are brought together. Sheila Lawlor criticises from the right government proposals for a national curriculum, while Oliver Letwin sets out the view that the idea of a school aim to train for jobs is noxious. For the Institute of Economic Affairs, curriculum prescription undervalues the market principle and this, above all, should determine provision, a view not shared by John Tomlinson, a representative, *par excellence*, of an educational establishment over which right-wing advisers and politicians poured such scorn during the mid-1980s.

John Quicke examines some of the tensions and contradictions within, and between, policies advocated by groups on the right. The pattern of legislation reflects some of these disagreements. John Raynor explores the nostalgia factor, the revival of English nationalism. He sees an apparently unproblematic reassertion of patriarchy and traditional values as having 'excluding appeal' with important consequences for those who belong to excluded groups.

2.1

A National or a Nationalist Curriculum?

John Raynor

The word nationalism is, in some ways, an indelicate word in the late twentieth century. We have long moved on (we like to think) from the eighteenth and nineteenth centuries when the achievement of sovereignty and national identity were seen as desirable and rational political ends to be sought and fought for. But war and talk of war; the rise of international agencies and of international capital; the severing of old colonial ties and the achievement of national status by former colonies of the old European empires, would seem to suggest that it is not only a political ideal that has been superseded, but one that in today's complex world appears irrational and irrelevant.[1] And yet, despite the rival claims of internationalism or the rival claims by advocates of class war on the other (both seeing nationalism as an irrelevance) nationalism, as an ideology, still retains a powerful hold on the political and personal imagination and is always likely to reassert itself when the political and economic base begins to crumble or the prevailing ideology loses its grip – as we appear to be witnessing in Eastern Europe currently. It can reassert itself too, in distinctively non-democratic ways in xenophobia, in racism and in authoritarianism.

The argument I wish to offer is that in what has been termed the 'Thatcher Revolution' we are witnessing a revival of English Nationalism – a kind of 'Little Englandism' which, by sleight of hand, is translated into *British* nationalism. It is a nationalism which has organised itself around forms of patriarchy and cultural and national identity with an appeal to a kind of commonsense and unproblematic view as to what are believed to be traditional British values. It is an appeal that is popular, but for many groups, it is an *excluding* appeal and for that reason could become a source of contest for those groups who in the highly diverse British nation state define themselves by quite different territorial, linguistic, religious or cultural appeals. The notion of *Englishness* is not unproblematic and could become a source of contest for those groups who insist on cultural diversity as legitimate goals.

The reaffirmation of nationalism

Whether the ten years of Thatcherism has provided us with a genuine revolution or not, time alone will tell. Certainly, there has been a transformation through the modification of the economic base (greater share ownership, privatisation of industry and of housing, the elimination of uneconomic industries, etc.). There has been too, a reform of the superstructural elements such as institutional, professional and trade union power blocks. And, finally, there is taking place a replacement of the older liberal fraternal ideology by one dominated by *economism* and by a form of domestic *nationalism*. A quite new group has come to dominate both political debate and action which if nothing else at least helps confirm the old Marxist-Leninist proposition that all nationalism is *bourgeois*.[2]

Whether or not the last ten years has provided a permanent re-ordering of the political and economic culture, is difficult to gauge as one is swept along on the roller-coaster of change. Certainly, Thatcherism appears to be genuinely revolutionary in that it consists of a political movement (embracing many groups), a political programme (if not a blueprint) and has given priority to the creation of a kind of 'civic religion' in which it has sought a consensus of shared values in which the appeal to the *nation* is a central element. The reasons that have contributed to this reaffirmation of nationalism stem from the interrelated issues of what has been called the 'crisis in culture' and the 'crisis of the state'.

Since the war Britain has been a politically and culturally unsure nation – unsure of destination, unsure of foot. Unsure about our post-imperialist role, and our client-status *vis-à-vis* the United States. Unsure of our future as our industrial decline continued and indeed, unsure of unity itself in the face of Celtic nationalism and of civil war in Ulster. Accompanying this has been the deep unease about the changing nature of our civil society, about its ethnic pluralism, about the threats to its patriarchal traditions and the anxieties about the non-orthodox in society, who have been traditionally outside the mainstream – women, blacks, gays, cultural rebels – and who have become in the last twenty years more articulate, vociferous and organised.

In the 1960s and 1970s this unease was expressed over the insularity of our culture and our limited native intellectual traditions, dominated since before the Second World War by the intellectual legacy of white central European émigrés – Wittgenstein, Popper, Hayek, Namier.[3] Today, cultural dominance belongs to the more limited views of the 'New Right' while the Left struggles towards an understanding of living in a new era, in 'New Times'.

Associated with this has been those concerns over the inadequacies of the modern state. Whether there is a 'crisis of legitimacy' or not, sets of disaggregated complaints have been voiced which have centred on the effectiveness of our political and administrative institutions, the inadequacies of the constitution, the lack of protection of the rights of individuals and groups, as well as the invasion of our privacy, have been increasingly voiced. There has been in public life a general complacency (most prominent in the Trade Union movement) and a constipated and sedimented form of ancestor worship, which even Margaret Thatcher is not allergic to. We have veered between a belief in Podsnappery ('the most favoured of all nations') and an inverted Podsnappery, best articulated by Perry Anderson and Tom Nairn.[4] And critically (and affecting all political parties) has been the power of ethno-nationalism, with its assertion of a national identity in Scotland, Wales and Northern Ireland, countered by appeals to the unity of the United Kingdom.[5]

What the Thatcher years have done is to attempt to fill the cultural vacuum, and in this process few prisoners have been taken. The ideology of *economism* has asserted the primacy of the economic base as having priority over reform of political institutions – the hallmark of postwar old Tory and Labour administrations. In addition there has been the process of historical revisionism which has put the work of both Labour and Tory administrations (Butler, Macmillan and Heath) into the rubbish-bin, to be replaced by a no-nonsense, self-confident and moralistic voice – what has been called 'morality without bourgeois guilt'.

Between the hazardous extremes of disintegration and coercion, and in a world economy complicated by the presence of supranational trading units such as the EEC and by the part played in the domestic economy by transnational corporations and international capital, we are led not towards a greater internationalism but paradoxically towards the strengthening of domestic nationalism, as evidenced by Margaret Thatcher's speech at Bruges. In that search for the certainties that bind together, the national curriculum can be seen as having a crucial part to play.

The National Curriculum

It is interesting to note that the word *national* in respect of education was first employed at the turn of the twentieth century, when a national inquest into education was called for then, as it was late in the twentieth century. The national inquest then coincided with one of those periodic phases of self-examination and doubt which we frequently go through in Britain and which goes under the convenient heading of 'the state of the nation'. The parallels are interesting to note: anxiety about our decline as a national power and our competitiveness economically; domestic anxieties about the power of 'the mob' (C. F. Masterman); about religious doubts; about dislike of capital and international capital coupled to xenophobia about foreigners and Jews (Belloc and Chesterton), and a reassertion of Little Englandism.

The curiosity is that now, late in the twentieth century in establishing a National Curriculum we have, as Aldrich has pointed out, produced one more or less identical to that legislated for in 1904.[6]

The newly established national curriculum is curious on two counts. It is not simply the mismatch between the *'economism'* of Thatcherism which has called on education to meet the needs of establishing a well-trained workforce to meet the requirements of industry and commerce by means of a very traditional curriculum, it is that in addition the curriculum chooses to be unrelated to the changing society in which it is expected to take place. In a Europe and in a Britain whose demographic and cultural make-up has so clearly changed, the part to be played by the curriculum in sustaining a specific view of the nation has to be placed under close scrutiny.

When instructions go out to, say, the Working Parties on the curriculum they are couched in an appeal to the commonsense notion of traditional English values. It is an appeal which is essentially non-problematic. When speaking about the English language Mr Baker puts it like this:

> I want to talk about the English language, our mother tongue. Next to our people, the English language is our greatest asset, it is the essential ingredient of the Englishness of England. Its role [sic] in our national life is probably more important today than ever before. You will notice I am speaking about English and the English. Fascinating things could be said about English in relation to other parts of the UK.[7]

Now the rest of the lecture is both clever and not unpersuasive and yet it rests on a restricted view of the language experience of so many children in British schools. How does that view connect to the 150 or more language groups found in London schools, for example?

Again, in Mr Baker's terms of reference for the newly appointed History Curriculum Working Group, we see greatest emphasis being placed on national history, 'The programmes of study should have at the core, the history of Britain, the record of its past and, in particular, its political, constitutional and cultural heritage'.

In fairness, the terms of reference do go on to suggest that they 'take account of Britain's evolution as a European, Commonwealth and world power'. The difficulty being that the starting point is essentially a mono-cultural and nationalistic one, whereas it is the very diversity of the nation over time, its connectedness with the rest of the world and the nature of the histories of its diverse constituent groups which together make up the nation and who are likely to find themselves included only insofar as they help to define English nationality. And as with history and English, so with the reaffirmation of the centrality of Judeo-Christian tradition in England as evidenced in the Education Bill, despite the decline in religious faith in Britain and the growth of a multi-faith society.

Of course, much rests on the reports of the different Working Groups and their reports to the Secretary of State. And here, on the evidence of the Maths, Science and English 5–11 Working Groups they are resisting some of the worst excesses and taking note not only of good professional practice but, in addition, recognising wider intercultural perspectives.

Conclusion

It would be disingenuous to argue that the classical curriculum of European countries has never placed a high degree of importance on the teaching of the national language, national history and national culture; they are measures, common to many nations, whose aim is to ensure political continuity if not nationalistic ambition. It is rather the degree to which we are being persuaded to embrace a particular vision of English nationalism as a kind of cement to bind together the parts, which is the cause for concern. It is a response to a kind of moral panic. As the problems of the nation are tackled economically, so, too, they have to be accompanied it seems by measures which seek to re-establish what is supposed to be distinctive about the English nation so that once again we can be bound together into a whole. That process contains the danger of policing of the boundaries of knowledge.

A curriculum based on a narrow vision of the mono-cultural state will be an impoverished curriculum; there are too many languages and too many histories of the people in the British Isles. To deny their voice and their history and to expect them to become passively assimilated (and, if not, marginalised) will, if nothing else, rob us of major contributions to the strength of the nation.

The national curriculum cannot be seen simply as an internal affair; the world continues to exist both within and outside our frontiers. To try to pin down the curriculum as though it were unconnected to the outside world is perverse. The English language does not belong exclusively to the English – least of all the British – and neither does the right to define the history of Britain belong exclusively to the English either.

The plurality of languages, religious belief, culture and family structures do pose crucial questions which we find difficult to adjust to, and it would be foolish to underestimate the difficulties. But the majority of populations in Britain and Europe are being called on to accept people with different ideas and cultural patterns with which they are unfamiliar, and all this against a background of vast political and economic change, of which the Single European Act in 1992 is but one example.

The challenges can be ignored but if so, we expose ourselves to a kind of chilling nationalism which has, in the past, allowed authoritarianism, racism and narrow xenophobia to prosper. A more positive response would be through the adoption of a genuine intercultural curriculum.[8] It may help us to avoid the excesses of the past and their tragic consequences.

Acknowledgment

I would like to thank Crispin Jones, Jagdish Gundara and Keith Kimberley of London University, Institute of Education for their comments on earlier drafts of this paper.

Notes

1 Hobsbawm, E. (1977), 'Some reflections on *The Break-Up of Britain*', *New Left Review*, 105.
2 Marx, K. and Engels, F. (1972), on Proletarian Internationalism [anthology], Moscow, Progressive Books.
3 Anderson, P. (1969), 'Components of the national culture', in Blackburn (ed.), *Student Power*, London, Pelican Books.
4 See, for example, Edward Thompson (1977), 'The peculiarities of the English', in *The Poverty of Theory and Other Essays*.
5 See Nairn, T. (1977), *The Break-Up of Britain: Crisis and Neo-Nationalism*, London, New Left Books.
6 Aldrich, R. (1988), 'The national curriculum: an historical perspective', in Lawton, D. and Chitty, C., *The National Curriculum*, London, Bedford Way Papers.
7 Alan Palmer lecture given by the Education Secretary, Kenneth Baker, at Pangbourne College, Berkshire on Friday, 7 November 1986.
8 See, for example, Council of Europe, *Intercultural Education: Concept, Context and Curriculum Practice*.

2.2

Curriculum and the Market: Are They Compatible?

John Tomlinson

The Education Reform Bill is designed to be a radical break with the past. Once it is in place, the principles underlying the provision of public education in England and Wales will be fundamentally different from those of the 1944 settlement and earlier.

The objectives are to create a 'social market' in education, establish a national curriculum and testing system, make education more responsive to economic forces and attract more non-public funding. It is asserted that if achieved these mechanisms would raise standards, increase consumer choice and make the whole system, including higher education, more accountable.

To establish a social market in education it is necessary to break down the notion and system of a publicly planned and provided education service. The local education authorities which now have this duty to provide education have interpreted it within the tradition developed since 1870. They have seen access to educational opportunity as a right of citizenship rather than a privilege conferred or constrained by accident of birth, geography, class, sex or race. In so doing they were reflecting the intentions of Parliament: the new Education Act 'will have a very big social effect apart from educational. It will weld us into what Disraeli described as "one nation"', as R. A. Butler put it in 1944 (quoted in the *Listener*, 1988). Education has been seen as one of the processes by which more and more individuals and groups in society might be enfranchised and drawn into full membership of that society.

A market, however, works on different principles. Education needs to be seen as a commodity to be purchased and consumed. There must be significant differences between goods on offer to make choice apparent. The consumer (the parent for the child) must be assumed to know his or her best interest. Hence different kinds of school need to be created, to replace free, universal provision and access based on principles of equity. Hence also 'objective' information for parents, regular monitoring and a complaints procedure must replace the professional–client relationship and its overtones of producer control.

The means by which the duty of the LEA to provide (now characterised as a monopoly) is to be replaced by the market are: open enrolment, financial and managerial delegation to schools, grant-maintained schools ('opting out'), city technology colleges and the assisted places scheme. Were all these mechanisms to be effective to the extent evidently intended there would be no sense in which the local education authority could any longer be held responsible for the strategic planning of educational provision in its area. The responses necessary to meet demographic change (such as the response to the recent impact of falling rolls), economic cycles and changes of educational policy would be effectively in the hands of 'the market', that is, the schools themselves, organised as semi-autonomous, competitive units, and of the macro-financial policies of government. The responsibilities for the variety and quality of provision would have been shifted also – from the elected LEA to the appointed governing bodies and the central government.

Will this radical departure in the way school education is provided achieve the objectives intended? Is it likely, for example, that there will be more choice, higher standards and more accountability? The many contradictions to be found in the Bill, especially between ends and means, must raise serious doubts.

Consider the objective of a national curriculum. The idea of a broad but differentiated curriculum being the entitlement of all children has general political and professional support. Its attraction lies in the implied promise of continuing the attempt to improve equality of opportunity. However, the market will offer different kinds of school. Markets are about differences. The LEA-maintained schools and the 'opted-out' schools will have to 'deliver' the national curriculum. The city technology colleges will have to 'have regard' to it. But it will not apply to independent schools or to pupils in them supported by public funds. It seems an inescapable conclusion that different categories of school will attempt to differentiate themselves by what they offer beyond the national curriculum, and that a hierarchy of status will emerge, backed by additional funding from parents and industry and differential selection policies. A national curriculum and a market in education cannot be compatible in any logic we understand. Perhaps the national curriculum is meant as a safety net for the least favoured maintained schools; or perhaps it is a façade behind which differences can multiply. In either case it becomes a curriculum for other people's children.

Even within the proposal for the national curriculum itself there are contradictions. As Sheila Browne, a former Senior Chief Inspector, put it:

> If only one could be sure that, in the Bill, the over-riding sub-clause 1(2) would dominate. This reads:
> 'The curriculum for a maintained school satisfies the requirements of this section if it is a balanced and broadly based curriculum which (a) promotes the spiritual, moral, cultural, mental and physical development of pupils at the schools and of society; and (b) prepares such pupils for the opportunities, responsibilities and experience of adult life.'
> That is light-years away from Clause 2 with its itemized requirements for attainment targets, programmes of study and assessment arrangements (Browne, 1988).

The consultation document spoke with the same two voices, the one that understood the need to set a framework within which individuality and innovation could flourish, and the other which went into self-defeating detail. No justification is offered for expressing the curriculum in subject terms or for the choice of subjects. No acknowledgement is made of the differences in teaching and learning between primary and secondary education. Perhaps most worrying of all, Clause 9 of the Bill apparently forbids all innovation without the express approval of the Secretary of State, and that by a cumbersome procedure.

Is it likely that the proposals will widen choice, at least for more than a few? Within the LEA, the present rules will continue to apply, that if a school other than the nearest to the home is chosen, the difference in the cost of transport is met by the parent. So choice in that sense will be no wider and still available only for those able and willing to pay the extra cost. Moreover, surveys suggest that, within those constraints, more than 90 per cent of parents already get their first choice of secondary school. At grant-maintained schools and city technology colleges the governors will control entry. Again, choice will be available only for the few, and those only in areas where such schools appear – another unknown factor. The very act of choice will, of course, affect the schools chosen or avoided. Unpopular schools will continue to serve many, while declining in resources and morale. Those choosing a popular school may find its character changing as it gains in size. (It is noticeable that established independent schools do not as a matter of policy choose to oscillate in size.) Thus the choices made by the few in the market may affect the educational opportunities of most, themselves included. A more ominous aspect is that parental and community choice may come to be exercised on grounds of social and racial prejudice. 'Ghettoisation' is the ugly word applied to this ugly prospect (Campbell, Little and Tomlinson, 1987).

It must also be open to question whether the new-style governing bodies and the responsibilities to be devolved upon them will be attended with the success necessary to achieve the Bill's objectives. The delegation to governors of powers of staff appointment and dismissal is problematic (especially while retaining the LEA as employer). The consequent loss of opportunity for strategic deployment of teachers by the LEA is unproven as a better way to optimise the use of scarce human resources. And the prospect of school appointments being decided at the scale of the parish pump is not encouraging. The retreat from such procedures has been part of the development of the LEA this century. The schemes of devolved financial management remain to be constructed still less implemented and proved. The procedures and systems needed to support grant-maintained schools do not yet exist and those for city technology colleges are yet elementary.

Parents are being asked to adopt a significantly new and different role in their relations with teachers. Research over the last generation has shown the advantages to children's education of their parents being involved as collaborators with teachers. That insight is slowly, through a realignment of relationships, being used in schools. Under the new proposals parents are being asked to adopt the role of inquisitor and monitor of teachers and schools, and to use the new complaints procedures, all in the exercise of consumer sovereignty. It remains uncertain, if we are also to try to continue to pursue the advantage of partnership and collaboration, how many parents and teachers will find it possible to assume the two roles simultaneously and avoid the inherent conflict. Alongside this sits the uncertainty as to whether the larger number of school governors, each bearing greater financial and managerial responsibility, can be recruited from the economic and social communities around the schools. The Bill's ambitions in this respect imply the existence of a 'political nation' whose actuality remains to be proved.

These uncertainties deriving from so much novelty need to be set in the context of a significant redistribution of existing powers and the attribution of many new powers – estimated to total 182 – to the Secretary of State. In the transfer of so much responsibility, from the LEA to the school governing body and the Secretary of State, the loser is the local government. That must mean that the structure of elected representative government will be weakened. No discussion of this issue was invited in the consultation documents, and at first its significance was denied by the Government; however, in January 1988 the Secretary of State entitled his address to the North of England Education Conference, 'The Constitutional Significance of the Education Reform Bill'. He argued there was none that mattered. Yet the change in the intentions and in the language of government is stark. It is necessary to go back only as far as March 1985, to the Government's White Paper *Better Schools*, to see the differences. That considerable State paper opened: 'The quality of school education concerns everyone. The Government has reviewed, together with its partners, its policies for school education in England and Wales. This White Paper sets out its conclusions' (DES, 1985). Fifteen months and a general election later the talk of partners had disappeared and the conclusions were radically different.

The anxieties raised by the consultation documents and the Bill remain. Is it reasonable to expect the reforms to achieve their putative aims in the light of the internal contradictions of the Bill and the incompatibility of a market approach with a national curriculum? Is the degree of institutional and political innovation likely to be capable of realisation? And, if the answers to these questions must be in doubt, can the slide into authoritarianism be justified? Behind all these questions lies the fundamental issue for a democracy: how the power of the State should be directed so far as the public funding and provision of education are concerned. Should it be directed towards a secular process of enfranchisement, or to reinforce and widen differences? Most of all, if a decision has been made to move from the former objective to the latter, should not that be the true subject of public debate, rather than the rhetoric about choice and standards?

References

Baker, K. (1988), Address to the North of England Education Conference, Nottingham, 6 January 1988.

Browne, S. (1988), Presidential Address to the North of England Education Conference, Nottingham, 4 January 1988.

Campbell, R. J., Little, V. and Tomlinson, J. R. G. (eds) (1987), 'Public education policy: the case explored', *Journal of Education Policy*, 2, 4.

DES (1985), *Better Schools* (Cmnd 9469), London, HMSO.

Listener (1988), 7 January, p. 27.

Tomlinson, J. R. G. (1986), 'Public education, public good', *Oxford Review of Education*, XII, 3.

2.3

Curriculum and the Market

Institute of Economic Affairs

The debate over a Government-imposed national curriculum is regrettably diverting attention from what really matters in the Government's current proposals, that is devolved management to schools.

The most effective national curriculum is that set by the market, by the consumers of the education service. This will be far more responsive to children's needs and society's demands than any centrally imposed curriculum, no matter how well meant. Attempts by Government and by Parliament to impose a curriculum, no matter how 'generally agreed' they think it to be, are a poor second best in terms of quality, flexibility and responsiveness to needs than is allowing the market to decide and setting the system free to respond to the overwhelming demand for higher standards. The Government must trust market forces rather than some committee of the great and good.

Uniformity between schools is not only unnecessary, it is potentially damaging. The picture of children constantly roaming the country, changing schools frequently, is a false one. To the extent that an enforced change of school interrupts a child's education, that will always be so, with or without a centrally imposed national curriculum. Any attempt to prescribe the curriculum in such a detailed way is the very strait-jacket that the government professes to want to avoid. It would actually reduce standards in the best schools, while doing little or nothing for the poorer ones.

It is a fallacy to suppose that setting a crowded curriculum of worthy subjects will crowd out the unacceptable peace studies, homosexual studies and the rest. It is naive to suppose that the bad teacher and the bad LEA will cease to introduce such dangerous nonsense into the classroom just because Parliament has legislated a national curriculum. If they have a mind to abuse children in such a way, they will continue to do so, whether in the period marked history or in that called health education.

Section C outlining the provisions of the Bill portrays a frightening degree of secondary legislation and bureaucracy for years ahead. Such detailed control would set the curriculum in stone for twenty years or more, not even responsive to the higher standards of skill and knowledge which the Government itself expects will be seen in future generations of children. Such legislative detail is a lawyer's dream but a teacher's nightmare. The Government must start treating the teachers, or most of them, as professional people.

By what right do national curriculum subject working groups impose their views upon the teaching profession and upon the consumer market of parents and children? One historian's view will prevail against that of another merely because the one was chosen by the Secretary of State to serve on a committee while the other was not. All the Government needs to do is to issue an updated and improved version of *Better Schools* and to say that, henceforth, inspections and judgements on schools registering and deregistering by HMI, will use these criteria. They would soon become the norm, but they could at least be constantly updated. If the Government wants to impose its view, and we doubt that it should, it does not need legislation.

2.4

Correct Core

Sheila Lawlor

The problem

The most marked characteristic of Mrs Thatcher's Governments is the way in which they have changed the nature and premises of political debate. This has been particularly true in economic and industrial policy. Here a set of assumptions had developed since the Second World War and become an orthodoxy. But so successful has the challenge been that even the Labour Party has come to accept many Thatcherite premises.

The challenge has been extended to other orthodoxies which inhibited the exercise of individual freedom. For example, in local government and housing the imbalance of power exercised by the State, its agents, and a variety of vested interests has been corrected in favour of the individual. Greater freedom and responsibility will be further enhanced by the reform of local government finance to make authorities more accountable. Here also the Labour Party has shifted its position.

But the orthodoxies which have dominated education policy have been challenged in one respect only – by tilting the administrative balance away from the monopolies of the state and its agents, the LEAs and education establishment, slightly in favour of the parents and the schools themselves. They have not been challenged when it comes to the content of education. Even while introducing limited measures of administrative reform, successive Conservative Secretaries of State have continued to subscribe to the recent orthodoxies and have even introduced new ones.

The national curriculum proposed in the new Education Reform Bill presents an opportunity for change but the danger exists that far from tackling the orthodoxies, it will further entrench them. If the content of the proposed national curriculum merely reflects the views of members of the 'education service' – teachers, their unions, LEAs, education theorists and worst of all Her Majesty's Inspectorate (HMI) – then the national curriculum, instead of serving to raise standards, will lower them.

The proposed national curriculum recognises English, Mathematics and Science as its three 'core' subjects. What are the assumptions which dominate thinking about these subjects within the 'education service'?

The most recent and comprehensive exposition of them can be found for English in the Bullock report *A Language for Life* (HMSO, 1974), and for maths in the Cockcroft report *Mathematics Counts* (HMSO, 1982).[1] Their recommendations have been summarised and promulgated by HMI in *English from 5 to 16* and *Mathematics from 5 to 16* – pamphlets intended to guide teachers and LEAs in what and how to teach.[2] In science there is no equivalent report, although the HMI document *Science 5–16: A Statement of Policy* (HMSO, 1985), shows how many assumptions behind science teaching are similar to those of the Bullock and Cockcroft reports.[3] They all assume:

1 that individual subjects are a thing of the past and can usefully be approached 'across the curriculum';
2 that pupils should not be expected to master much information or knowledge beyond their immediate experience and that concentration on – or memorising – information, facts and principles should be discouraged;
3 that pupils should master complicated and sophisticated concepts more appropriate to academic research;
4 that there can be no external standards set to which pupils might be taught; rather, what is taught must be relative to each pupil and his ability, and restricted accordingly;
5 that oral work and discussion matter as much as written work;
6 that learning must take place without effort and in the guise of games, puzzles and activities;
7 that teaching is akin to salesmanship; what is taught, and how it is taught, needs to 'continue to catch the pupil's interest and imagination';
8 that pupils must not be allowed to experience failure; and
9 that the purpose of teaching is as much social as academic, in order to reflect the issues 'with which pupils will have to come to terms' such as 'multicultural' society, 'a greater diversity of personal values', and 'the equal treatment of men and women . . . which needs to be supported in the curriculum'.[4]

The official reports
English: The Bullock report

The assumptions on which Lord Bullock based his report on English teaching are evident in its title: *A Language for Life*. English should not be regarded as a subject; it 'does not hold together as a body of knowledge which can be identified, quantified and then transmitted'. Rather, English lessons should be regarded as one opportunity among others for the learning of 'language'; and this language learning must be closely connected with 'life'. 'Language competence', the report explains, 'grows, incrementally, through an interaction of writing, talking, reading and experience, the body of resulting work forming an organic whole'.

Moreover, competence in language is not seen as very much to do with an ability to write correct Standard English. Bullock does not accept the concept of correctness in English, but prefers to talk of 'appropriateness'. Prescriptive approaches to grammar, spelling and punctuation are dismissed by the report, not so much with contempt as with amusement.

Not surprisingly, therefore, Bullock does not favour traditional methods of English teaching. The teaching of formal grammar, and the setting of exercises designed to inculcate a given point of grammatical practice, is not to be encouraged as a normal method of instruction. Comprehension exercises and spelling tests are of little value. Rather, children should 'learn about language', as Bullock puts it, 'by experiencing it and experimenting with its use'. Emphasis must be put on spoken language just as much as on writing; and writing should always be for a purpose and for a particular audience. Spelling should not be taught from lists, but based on the pupil's needs. Restriction of study material to books would be unduly limited: 'press clippings, photographs, printed extracts and all manner of ephemeral material' should be used; while high quality recording, film and videotapes are also desirable parts of the English teacher's equipment.[5]

Mathematics: The Cockcroft report

The Cockcroft committee published its report, *Mathematics Counts*, in 1982. The report reflects how the recent emphasis has shifted away from teaching pupils specific facts; and away from expecting them to master quickly the basic numerical and arithmetical skills. Instead, pupils were, from a young age, to be introduced to complex and sophisticated mathematical concepts without necessarily mastering, or even being expected to master, the basic skills and knowledge on which these rest. In Cockcroft's view, maths had an aim at once vague and ambitious. Maths was 'a powerful means of communication [and this provided] . . . the principal reason for teaching maths to all children'.

Although Cockcroft did not urge the elimination of computational skills, he warned that there must not be narrow concentration upon them. Indeed, for Cockcroft, numeracy involved an acquaintance with, rather than a mastery of, numbers: an 'at homeness' with them and 'some appreciation and understanding of information which is presented in mathematical terms, for instance, in graphs, charts or tables'.

Cockcroft's view of mathematics is as a 'means of communication', rather than as a subject with a clear body of knowledge and techniques – as is evident in his recommendations to teachers: they should promote 'good attitudes'. The pupils should enjoy the activity: be encouraged by being given puzzles. But Cockcroft did not allow that clear and correct knowledge assisted 'understanding'. Instead, he seemed to deprecate the ability to solve a problem correctly, because it did not prove a pupil's 'understanding' – the development of which he saw as a thing apart from training. Mathematics must be relevant to the pupil's experience; and it should not 'be necessary in the learning of mathematics to commit things to memory without at the same time seeking to develop a proper understanding of the maths to which they relate'.

The thrust of Cockcroft's argument was therefore against the mastering of knowledge, or techniques, whether for their own sake or as a base on which to build. Committing to memory, or seeing that pupils concentrated on their weaker areas, was discouraged. There was to be greater emphasis on practical work and discussion between teacher and pupils and among pupils themselves.

These aims and methods of maths teaching were to be pursued from the start. At the primary school, maths was not to be seen as the teaching or learning of skills and techniques nor solely as preparation for the next stage. Rather, it should 'enrich children's aesthetic and linguistic experience'. The emphasis should be on practical work, which was 'essential'; and, though numbers and computation should be tackled as one of six topics, Cockcroft insisted that the learning of number facts needed to be based on understanding. Moreover, young children ought not to move too quickly to written work in maths, for forming a figure was a 'skill' and the report opposed a premature start on formal arithmetic.[6]

Science 5–16

The teaching of science has not been the subject of a recent committee of inquiry, as English and maths have been. But the way in which science teaching has developed, and may continue to develop, can be gauged from the DES document *Science 5–16: A Statement of Policy* (HMSO, 1985) which draws on an earlier DES document *Science Education in Schools: A Consultative Document* (HMSO, 1982) and the responses to it.

Like the Bullock and Cockcroft reports for English and maths and the HMI series, the thrust of *Science 5–16* is away from the teaching or mastery of a body of factual information and abstract principles, in favour of what is seen as 'relevant' science. It emphasises practical and investigative work. Yet it also recommends that science education should be seen as a 'continuum' and that even young pupils should be introduced to sophisticated concepts.

Science 5–16 stated that the essential characteristic of a science education is that pupils should be introduced to the methods of science which constitute scientific competence; and not expressly to scientific knowledge and principles. Pupils ought to develop certain abilities – such as making observations, carrying out experiments, conducting investigations. In respect of the acquisition of knowledge (not accorded especial significance), the suggestion was that 'facts' should be selected and taught only in so far as they were relevant to the wider world. Just what knowledge of facts and principles should be taught was for 'continued review'; but in any case, knowledge should be approached 'through practical work and otherwise'.

Science teaching did not, therefore, specifically involve the mastery of scientific principles and knowledge either as an end in itself, or as a base on which to build. Rather, as *Science 5–16* expressly sets out, the characteristics to be emphasised in science teaching were to be:

1 a balance between acquisition of knowledge and practice of method;
2 relevance to everyday experience and suitability to different abilities;
3 the introduction of a wide range of concepts and cross-curricular links;
4 its practical nature, with emphasis on science as an investigative and problem-solving activity; and,
5 assessment should be designed to test skills and processes as well as the ability to reproduce and apply scientific knowledge, and to test, not what pupils ought to know, but simply what they do.

Pupils, from an early age, should become accustomed to processes and appropriate work should begin in infant classes. Secondary science education should be determined by considerations of 'breadth', 'balance' and 'relevance'. Teaching should be closely related to everyday and industrial applications of science. Full weight should be given to the development of scientific skills and processes as well as to knowledge and understanding. A reduction in the overall amount of factual knowledge was 'unavoidable'.

Pupils should balance their studies of biological and physical sciences up to the age of 16. 'Balance', again, between the different components of science education, including the development of skills, should be kept. In addition, science should have relevance to the daily lives of those who learned it. It was thought that too much time was spent accumulating facts and principles which had little apparent – or real – relevance. Topics should be included on the basis of such relevance to pupils' future working lives; there must be differentiation in the science course to allow for all abilities, and there should be equal opportunities for girls and boys to benefit from balanced courses – with special attention paid to girls' expectations and attitudes.[7]

Theory into practice
HMI directives

In its two pamphlets *English 5 to 16* and *Mathematics 5 to 16*, HMI echoes the ideas of the Bullock and Cockcroft reports. These pamphlets helped in practice to make their recommendations and views mandatory. This was not unwelcome, seeing that they reflected (and reflect) prevailing views; and seeing that the HMI were inspecting, and would continue to inspect, teaching on their basis.[8]

Although *English 5 to 16* contained some apparently traditional recommendations about teaching grammar, the general tenor of the document, as its author emphasised, was far from traditional. It suggested that the objectives of teaching English are less clear than those of other subjects. It encouraged teaching based not on the acquisition of information and the mastery of rules and skills, but an 'understanding' of the use of English 'for the transactions of our everyday lives' and 'for personal and social relationships'. Tasks should be set which require 'communication for real or realistic purposes'. It advised that social factors, as well as different abilities, must be taken into account; and it was not appropriate to teach by setting out 'objects in ascending scale of difficulty, or by defining a limited range of skills that most pupils should be able to master, and then adding others which are suitable only for the able.[9]

Mathematics 5 to 16 explains that the main reason for teaching maths is as a means of communication. What it refers to as the 'mere manipulation of numerical and algebraic symbols' is of secondary importance. Maths itself, indeed, is not important, but the result is. And it warns that pupils preoccupied with trying to master the details might not appreciate the relationship within mathematics. Neither should maths involve an imposed body of knowledge, nor be too solitary an activity; rather, thinking, discussion and mutual refinement of ideas contribute to mathematical development. No pupil should be so extended that his principal feeling is of failure. 'In depth' mathematics should be encouraged, not through in-depth teaching, but through salesmanship; enthusiastic teaching; surveys of people's opinions; attractive resource materials; investigative activities; games, puzzles, television material.[10]

The interim reports

Once it was decided to institute a National Curriculum, the Secretary of State for Education appointed two working groups in maths and science to make recommendations. No working party was appointed for English, but it is possible that the report of the Kingman Commission, which had already begun its investigation of English Language teaching in schools, will be used to determine the curriculum. From the interim reports of the maths and science working parties, and from remarks made by members of the Kingman Commission, it is becoming clear that misgivings about the form which the National Curriculum will take are not unjustified.

Mathematics Working Group

The Maths *Interim Report* failed to set specific targets for pupils at given ages. Nor did it consider which areas of mathematics should be given priority, nor recommend that any particular attention be paid to the pupil's need to master numerical and arithmetical skills.

The authors of the report did not challenge the developments in, and assumptions behind, maths teaching as propagated by Cockcroft. Indeed, they were 'much influenced by' the Cockcroft report. They welcomed its consequences for developments in the classroom – such as 'more practical, problem-solving and investigative work'. They saw their task as building on 'existing good practice'.

Instead of setting out clearly defined topics and targets to be reached by a given age, the report suggested that attainment targets should be grouped into three categories, which it describes as 'personal qualities', 'mathematical strategies for problem solving' and 'areas of mathematics'.

When the report was published in December 1987, Professor S. J. Prais, FBA, a member of the working group (who has since resigned), published a critical *Note of Dissent*. He considered that the committee had not tackled the problems of mathematical attainment – of raising it or of narrowing the wide gap between high and low attainers. Nor did it address itself to such issues as which areas of maths were important at which age, the question of school organisation, or the implications of the proposed system of testing. Prais argued that it was wrong to take maths teaching in England as practised now as a satisfactory base from which to build. He pointed out that the mathematical attainments of school-leavers in this country compared badly with those of our European competitors and of Japan; and that this had consequences for further education, for industry and for Britain's competitiveness. Prais insisted that not enough attention had been paid to basic arithmetic, the skills of which should be mastered mainly at primary school; many difficulties at the secondary level were due to poor foundations laid at the primary level. Even if, in later life, calculators were to be used, it was important as a child to carry out pencil and paper work, and drill and rote learning. Nor had it yet been shown that the substitution of other topics for numerical practices at earlier ages tended to improve ultimate attainments. The Germans and the Japanese place greater emphasis than we do on such things; and they restrict the use of the calculator.[11]

Science Working Group

The *Interim Report* from the Science Working Group makes its proposals within the framework of the DES statement *Science 5–16*. Like the Mathematics Group, it professed an intention to build on 'existing good practice'. It held that development of practical skills and attitudes was as important as knowledge which, in any case, should be of a relevant and practical nature.

Science teaching should be 'broad' (covering social, economic, personal and ethical implications); 'balanced'; 'relevant' to today's world; differentiated (to be accessible to all, irrespective of ability, race, gender or social and cultural background). And it should also have cross-curricular links.

The *Interim Report* saw science learning as having three principal constituents, none of which was more important than the other: knowledge and understanding; skills; and attitudes. It was to the development of these that science at school should be directed – and on which pupils might be assessed.

The authors of the report claimed that the 'teaching of pure or formal science by itself can lead to ineffective learning by many pupils'. Yet they also had ambitious aims for pupils which even research scientists develop only with mastery of their subject. The report expected all pupils, not only 'to learn and to use scientific methods of investigation' but:

> to develop the skills of imaginative but disciplined enquiry which include systematic observation, making and testing hypotheses, designing and carrying out experiments competently and surely, drawing inferences from evidence, formulating and communicating conclusions in an appropriate form and applying them to new situations.[12]

Pupils should come to learn how to gain access to, and use selectively and appropriately, published scientific knowledge.

The Kingman Commission

The Kingman Commission, the terms of reference and members of which were announced in January 1987, has not yet produced its report on English Language teaching. Its members are now bound to silence by the Official Secrets Act. Comments to the Press at an earlier stage in its deliberations suggest that the report may not deviate far from the views and presumptions dominant in the 'education service': 'appropriateness' of language rather than correctness in standard English should be the aim; and exercises in spelling, punctuation and syntax should remain things of the past.

Although some members of the Commission – writers and journalists as distinct from professional educationalists – have had doubts, they appear not to have felt able to sustain their views against experts whose acquaintance with linguistics and educational theory gives their comments apparent weight and cogency.[13]

Mistaken assumptions

The preceding pages have shown the set of presumptions on which it is all too likely that the content of the proposed national curriculum will be based. The theory is that there should be no absolute standards; that teaching is not a matter of passing on a body of knowledge; that what is taught must be relevant to the child's world; that practical and investigative work is as important as other work – as also is discussion and talking; that teaching should not be confined to narrow subjects, but should be across the curriculum; that education has a 'social role'; and that learning should be promoted through games, puzzles, enjoyment.

Such assumptions in the recent past have not led to higher standards. On the contrary, many pupils leave school today illiterate and innumerate. They are unable to write simple, correct English; do elementary arithmetical calculations; or satisfy employers understandably disillusioned with levels of competency. There may indeed have always been a shortage of educated and trained school-leavers, as theorists are quick to affirm. But these shortages occurred when most pupils left school with little or no secondary education. Yet today, although all pupils are obliged to attend secondary school until 16, the deficiencies are very great, as is attested not only by employers' organisations but even by the reports of HMI.

The case of mathematics shows with particular clarity how standards in English schools are too low, in comparison with those of Europe and Japan. This is particularly true of mathematical pupils in the lower range of ability. Surveys by the International Association for the Evaluation of Educational Achievement reveal that Britain has a larger spread between top and bottom attainment than any other country covered in its enquiries – due to the 'long tail' of low achievers. This is particularly evident when we contrast arithmetical attainment in this country with that of Germany; and the basic aptitudes of pupils in vocational schools in France and

Germany with those in our Further Education Colleges.[14]

The presumptions discussed in this chapter have not, then, led to higher standards. So why should they be accepted? Consider the opposite case:

1 Without learning a body of knowledge, pupils will flounder. They cannot master a discrete subject; and they will not – without sure, detailed knowledge and a framework – have the substance on which to reflect, or a basis on which to develop, analytical powers.

2 Standards can be maintained only if they are evident. Pupils need to have clear targets to which to work; and most teachers need some externally imposed level to be set as a target if they are to teach effectively. Only the exceptional teacher can in practice ensure that each child reaches his 'own' top level.

3 Teaching only what is 'relevant' amounts to teaching merely what an adult deems to be 'relevant'. It reflects the adult's world and his experience of 'everyday', not that of the child. Unlike the adult the child is delighted to learn 'irrelevant' information. His interest is in what is relevant to the subject, not to the 'everyday' world. Moreover, what is 'relevant' today will not necessarily be 'relevant' when the pupil leaves school. Far better that he master the principles so that whatever the nature of the problem, he can apply them.

4 The emphasis placed on practical and investigative work has become an end in itself, instead of a means towards acquiring knowledge. Without adequate instruction, practical work is a poor and time-consuming means of teaching. Pupils – of all ages – want, and need, to master a framework and body of knowledge. It is for teachers and schools to decide the best methods; but the curriculum should not contain any requirement for every school to follow a given method.

   And why should greater emphasis be put on pupils discussing among themselves and with the teacher (as opposed to more formal questions-and-answers)? It is not clear. There is no reason to imagine that pupils learn from talking. Indeed, they may not want to talk. They may have nothing to say. If it is a matter of building confidence, then the best way to do so is through building their knowledge.

5 The emphasis on cross-curricular teaching makes it difficult for pupils to acquire knowledge and techniques in any given area as a necessary first step. Although a cross-curricular approach might be suitable at a higher level, at school it merely imposes an adult's over-sophisticated approach on pupils who are not ready for it.

6 The 'social role' of education, often deemed to be as important as the academic content, is no more than a crude attempt at social conditioning. This should not be the task of any school.

7 Teaching should not be a form of salesmanship; and pupils will not necessarily learn through games and puzzles, or without hard and conscious effort. Very many things in life – at school and later – including the acquisition of knowledge, require effort and concentration.Unless pupils are trained to concentrate and make the effort to master knowledge they will suffer in two ways: they will not necessarily master the required information and they will not become trained to cope with the demands of adult life.

The curricula for English, maths and science, Part 2 avoid these presumptions and propose for each subject a solid basis of knowledge and fundamental techniques. This is the proper function of a national curriculum: one which will really enable standards to be raised.

Notes and references

1 *A Language for Life*. Report of the Committee of Inquiry appointed by the Secretary of State, Department of Education and Science under the Chairmanship of Sir Alan (now Lord) Bullock, FBA; HMSO (1974). (Hereafter referred to as the Bullock report.) *Mathematics Counts*. Report of the committee of inquiry into the teaching of mathematics in schools under the Chairmanship of Dr W. H. D. Cockcroft; HMSO (1982). (Hereafter referred to as the Cockcroft report.)

2 *English from 5 to 16* (Second Edition incorporating responses); *Curriculum Matters 1*; an HMI series; HMSO (1986). (Hereafter referred to as *English 5 to 16*.) *Mathematics from 5 to 16* (Second Edition incorporating responses); *Curriculum Matters 3*; an HMI series; HMSO (1987). (Hereafter referred to as *Mathematics 5 to 16*.)

3 Department of Education and Science, Welsh Office; *Science 5–16: A Statement of Policy*; HMSO (1985). (Hereafter referred to as *Science 5–16*.)

4 *The School Curriculum*, DES, Welsh Office; HMSO (1981); 7th impression (1985), also made the general case for a curriculum to be relative to the pupil's world, for continuity in learning for each pupil (rather than set absolute standards), and for an approach 'across the curriculum' (rather than concentration on individual subjects), the titles of which were described as 'a kind of shorthand'; see *The School Curriculum*.

5 Bullock report, see especially pp. 5, 7, 169–70, 171, 173, 234–5, 515.

6 Cockcroft report, see especially pp. 1, 11, 61, 70, 71, 92.

7 *Science 5–16*; and *Science Education in Schools: A Consultative Document*; HMSO (1985). For the characteristics of, and priorities within, science education, see *Science 5–16*, pp. S–5. For science in secondary education, ibid., pp. 12–18. For recommendations on science in primary schools, ibid., pp. 6–11; see also *Science in Primary Schools*, a discussion paper from the HMI Science Committee; HMSO (1984). For changes proposed to the existing science curriculum, see *Science Education in Schools: A Consultative Document*; DES and Welsh Office (1982); pp. 6–28.

8 *English 5 to 16*, pp. 5–43; *Mathematics 5 to 16*, pp. 67–81; *English our English*; CPS (1987); pp. 13–16, 39–40.

9 *English from 5 to 16*, pp. 3–4.

10 *Mathematics from 5 to 16*, pp. 2–3, 5–7.

11   National Curriculum Mathematics Working Group, *Interim Report*; DES and Welsh Office; December 1987; pp. 1–3, 13–78. See the statement issued by the Secretary of State for Education and Science, 17 December 1987, DES Press Release 382/87. For Prais' comments, National Curriculum Mathematics Working Group, *Interim Report, Note of Dissent*; S. J. Prais, FBA; 17 December 1987.

12   National Curriculum Science Working Group, *Interim Report*; DES and Welsh Office; pp. 6, 8, 10–13, 15–16, 25; see chapter 3 which develops the 'three essential elements'.

13   Membership and terms of reference of the Kingman Commission were announced in January 1987, Hansard, 21.1.87, cols 555–6. They were asked to recommend 'a model of the English language, whether written or spoken, which would: (i) serve as a basis of how teachers are trained to understand how the English language works; (ii) inform professional discussion of all aspects of English teaching'. *The Daily Telegraph*, 13 May 1987.

14   For example, 58 per cent of Japanese 14 year olds, but only 22 per cent of British 14 year olds knew the answer to the following question: what is the value of 'x' if $5x + 4 = 4x - 31$? For other examples and discussion, see: *The Times*, 18 February 1988; S. J. Prais, National Curriculum Mathematics Working Group, *Interim Report, Note of Dissent*, 17 December 1987; *National Institute Economic Review*, May 1985, February 1987; M. Cresswell and J. Gubb, *The Second International Mathematics Study in England and Wales*; NFER, Nelson (1987). International comparisons are not possible in English teaching, but evidence has been assembled in *English our English*, pp. 6–7, to show that here, too, standards are unacceptably low. For this year's IEA report on Science, see *TES*, 14 March 1988.

2.5

Grounding Comes First

Oliver Letwin

I maintain that the strict duty of every school is to ensure that, by the end of their school days, every pupil has what I shall call a grounding. By this, I mean an understanding of those things which it is necessary to understand in order to take a properly independent part in the life of our society. To be such an independent actor, people must be able to read and comprehend information of divers sorts; otherwise, they are unable to make properly independent choices about their jobs, their houses, their everyday purchases, their travel and so forth. They must also be able to make sense of the newspapers, and the spoken words of public life, since how else can they hold independent, informed attitudes about their governors, and the political system? It is essential, too, that people should grasp enough mathematics to see the simple effects of their decisions upon their lives, since otherwise they are constantly at the mercy of others, who will use their ignorance as an opportunity for themselves. And, perhaps most important of all, people must be able to express themselves with sufficient clarity both on paper and in speech, to make themselves fairly understood, since they are otherwise virtually unable to cope with the choices which are the stuff of an independent life in our society, or to be recognised by others as possessors of an independent voice, worthy of being heard in its own right. A person who lacks such a grounding, and is therefore unable to take an independent part in the life of our society, clearly represents a failure on the part of the school or schools which he attended. If we care at all about living in a liberal democracy, in which people are permitted to make choices for themselves, then we are duty-bound to provide everybody with tools which enable them to make and express such choices, on the basis of understanding what is being chosen, rather than as mere arbitrary leaps in the dark. This involves enforcing schooling upon all potential citizens; but it also involves providing, in school, the grounding that validates such compulsion. A person who fails to receive a grounding represents a paradox, because he has been the subject of compulsory schooling which would be justifiable only if the life of our society is somehow dependent upon his having attended school; yet he has not received what would have justified such compulsion.

Grounding involves acquiring both a range of skills and a certain amount of knowledge – at a level where knowledge and skill are almost indistinguishable from one another. Reading and writing, understanding simple mathematics, and expressing oneself clearly, are of course skills: one has to know how to do them instead of merely knowing that something or other is the case about them. But, in the course of learning, one inevitably acquires certain specific items of knowledge. One learns that certain words refer to certain objects and activities, that 2+2=4, probably also (on the way) that the moon is not made of cheddar cheese, and a number of other items of sheer information. Whether the skills are taught by teaching the information, or whether the information is acquired through teaching the skills, is a matter of teaching practice, rather than of teaching aim – or indeed, simply a matter of luck. But about the aim, the duty, there is no room for disagreement. Every child needs, by whatever method, to have acquired the combination of knowledge and skill which enables him to live in a liberal, democratic society.

The provision of such a grounding is, I believe, the only absolute duty of a school.

Many people concerned with education – and certainly almost all the present educational establishment – would deny this, to the point of finding it outrageous. They would argue that such a concept of schooling is hopelessly narrow, and that any school which provides its pupils with no more than a rudimentary grounding is failing miserably in its duty.

These arguments fail to recognise the extent of the opportunities which are opened up for someone who has a grounding. An individual is, in a most fundamental sense, someone who makes decisions for himself rather than having them made for him by others – someone who has sufficient access to the fruits of civilisation to enable him to understand something of what is on offer and to develop real preferences. That is just what a grounding enables a person to do. Like the working man at the Workers' Educational Association, and the audience at the improving lectures of the last century, a person with a grounding can go to the library and read, go to lectures and listen, ask questions and apprehend any answer that is given in clear English. A person with a grounding has what nobody without one can ever have – a basis upon which to build an understanding of the world.

Of course, a grounding is not the crowning achievement of a school in relation to the encouragement of individuality. A school which provides only a grounding has no right to claim that it has done all that could be done for its pupils' capacity to make independent judgements. That would be to suggest that individuality is an open and shut affair – which it most certainly is not. A person is not simply capable of individual judgement or simply incapable of it. Some people are more capable of it than others. As a person's understanding of his world, of the possibilities within that world, becomes larger, his range of choice widens: he becomes aware of possibilities which his imagination was previously unable to furnish. This is a product not of grounding, but of true education. The two aims of schooling, the essential duty to provide a grounding and the larger, hoped-for goal of enabling pupils to become educated both contribute – at different levels – to the encouragement of individuality.

Many educational theorists, and among them many who count themselves as conservatives of one sort or another, will no doubt argue that it is both wrong and dangerous to describe the aims of schooling in this very general and abstract way. They will complain that these aims make no mention of the teaching of English history, of scripture, of the encouragement of artistic creativity and musical ability, of training for jobs. Above all, they will complain that no mention is made here of the need for schools to teach sound morals to their pupils. But these omissions are intentional. Contrary to the prevailing fashion, it is neither safe nor right to lay down, from the pulpit or from Whitehall, a whole range of specific skills and items of information that should be taught by every school. Beyond a grounding, which is the indispensible prerequisite for playing an independent role in our society, there is no specific skill which needs to be acquired by every pupil: schools which fail to teach their pupils how to conduct physical experiments or how to speak French or how to play the piano may nevertheless be adequate or even very good schools. In some narrowly religious schools, for example, none of these things are taught. But still the pupils receive a grounding and (in some cases) emerge as educated people through their study of sacred texts, the languages of their own community and the traditions which are attached to these languages. On what basis has anyone the right to object if children are, by the choice of their parents, provided with a schooling so manifestly suited to their way of life and so clearly justified by its social results?

The idea that a school's aim is to train people for jobs is equally noxious. Acquiring a grounding is probably as important for most jobs that are now done, as it is for living as a citizen in a liberal democratic society; but there are still many jobs that can be filled adequately without any grounding; and there are many more that can be done well by people who are in no sense educated. This is an utter irrelevance from the point of view of schooling; if both grounding and education were unnecessary for every job in the world, that would not detract in the slightest degree from their importance. Jobs are done to provide those who do them and their customers with economic benefits which have some human value because they contribute to a civilised existence. Schooling, both in providing a grounding and in attempting to yield educated people, is making a direct contribution of its own to the sustenance of a civilised existence. It is therefore on a par with, not subservient to, economic work.

The teaching of sound morals is a much more delicate issue. The instilling of moral principles and practices is a prime aim of a school, in the sense that everything done in a school, not only in the classroom but also on the sports field and in the example set by the teachers should obviously encourage pupils to become better rather than worse people. In the days when it was taken for granted that every school had a duty to provide its children with a grounding, this moral aim could be stressed without danger. When Tom Brown was told that his moral education mattered more than any deep learning he might acquire, that was perfectly sensible, because it was assumed by his father that he would receive a decent grounding as a matter of course. But things are different now. It is not taken by any means for granted that every school will aim to provide a grounding for its pupils by the time that they leave school. Instead, a large number of teachers and 'educationalists' take the view that the provision of a grounding is unimportant so long as the children emerge as nice, compassionate, sensitive, socially progressive people. This is as dangerous as any educational doctrine that has been perpetrated during the last forty years. The pupils who attend schools dominated by this doctrine may emerge with delicate consciences; but they are likely to be so unsuited to play an independent role in society, that they will soon turn into embittered, miserable adults. Moral training is not therefore a substitute for providing a grounding. It is something that ought to go on through, rather than in addition to, the specific activity of teaching and learning.

2.6

The 'New Right' and Education

John Quicke

Introduction

The intervention of the 'New Right' in education can be seen as part of a broader hegemonic project to construct a political discourse through which the authority of the state and traditional social values can be restored. In education, the main outlines of the project have been sketched in various publications, but the simplest and most compact statement is the Hillgate Group's 'radical' manifesto *Whose Schools?* The group, consisting of a number of teachers and academics like Roger Scruton, Lawrence Norcross and Caroline Cox, claims not to be presenting a manifesto of a political party; but, writing several months before the general election of June 1987, they aimed clearly to reinforce and extend their influence in the Conservative Party.

Like all hegemonic projects, it uses the language of crisis to persuade people that something needs to be done urgently and that the moment is opportune due to the breakdown of consensus – in this case the liberal and social democratic consensus which has allegedly dominated the educational establishment. By such means, the impression is conveyed that a reconstruction is not only necessary but possible.

Central to their analysis is a view about parents' trust in the education system. Parents who rely on state education are said to

no longer have confidence that their children will acquire the learning and skills which will prepare them for membership of society. They have less and less assurance that moral standards, religious understanding and a respect for British institutions will be communicated to their children. They cannot be sure that their children's talents will be fully encouraged, or that they will have the best possible chance to proceed either to a career or to higher education, or to an employment that is suited to their needs and abilities. In short, in many cases trust in Britain's educational system is breaking down; and with reason.[1]

This lack of trust has been brought about because LEAs and teachers, like all producers in a monopolised industry, have ceased to respond to the demands of the consumers and have abused their power. The ideology they have propagated – characterised schematically as 'curriculum reform', 'relevance' and 'child-centred learning' – has been destructive of traditional educational values with no obvious benefit to the child. Egalitarian propaganda 'working through a system of bureaucratic patronage [has] encouraged a false philosophy of education' (see Note 1, The Hillgate Group, p. 3) in which education is seen in instrumentalist, social engineering terms rather than as an end in itself.

The solution is to give more power to the parents by giving them the right to choose the education which they feel is the most suitable for their children; and to lessen the power of the LEAs and their self-appointed 'experts' and other educationists 'engaged in the second order study of the process of learning' (see Note 1, The Hillgate Group, p. 10). Schools should be made self-governing; education differentiated 'to cater for the many and diverse gifts of the nation's children' (see Note 1, The Hillgate Group, p. 11); and a national curriculum established. There should also be a national examination system which was exacting, objective, rigorous, fair and free from 'local corruption'.

As far as influence on the Conservative Party is concerned, the Hillgate Group can undoubtedly claim some success. Their mark can be clearly seen on the flood of consultative documents on education produced by the incoming Conservative Government in its first few months of office: documents on the national curriculum 5–16, on the admission of pupils to maintained schools, on the financial delegation to schools and on grant maintained schools. The consultative document on the curriculum lays out the government's plans for a national curriculum consisting of a core of three subjects – English, Maths and Science – and a number of other foundation subjects comprising a foreign language, Technology, History, Geography, Art, Music and Physical Education. The core would take up 30–40 per cent and together with the foundation subjects 80–90 per cent of curriculum time. Apart from Technology, all these are traditional subject disciplines. New areas like Health Education are not ruled out, but would be incorporated under Biology. These subject descriptions are strikingly traditional and almost identical to those advocated by the Hillgate Group. As in *Whose School?* there is no mention of integrated subjects like humanities or environmental studies, or of the 'pastoral curriculum' or personal and social education, or of 'newer' subjects like psychology, sociology, politics or economics.

The consultative document lays great emphasis on assessment. Nationally moderated tests will measure attainment levels in the various core and foundation subjects at 7, 11, 14 and 16 and these will be based on the knowledge, skills and understanding expected of pupils at each stage and specified in some detail in programmes of work. The principle that assessment should be national, exacting and objective is also stressed in *Whose Schools?* although there clearly would be some disagreement with the Government over detail. For instance, the Hillgate Group see the GCSE as a dangerous innovation. The new exam, however, is not nearly as radical as they imagine. Pupils will still be publicly examined and by and large the criteria will be as 'academically' rigorous as anything that went before.

The other discussion documents are all designed to lessen the control of LEAs over schools. The paper on financial delegation to schools contains a paragraph which, though only incidental to the aim of local financial management, seems to be designed to remove the power of appointment of headteacher and teaching staff from LEAs. Paragraph 12 proposes that 'the Secretary of State envisages that the selection of headteachers, teachers and other staff would be a matter to be delegated to the governing body'.

Under the grant maintained system schools will be able to opt out of LEA control. The proposal to allow schools to recruit up to their physical capacity will be extremely disruptive of LEA plans to cope with falling rolls. The consequences for their efficiency and thus credibility among parents and the community are predictable. Apart from City Technology Colleges, the Government does not as yet seem to favour an extension of the ownership of schools by trusts, advocated by the Hillgate Group on page 13 of *Whose Schools?*; but this does not greatly detract from the accord between them on the importance of removing schools from LEA control.

However, despite its influence in high places, the 'New Right's' success is not total. Opposition has come from a variety of quarters, not least from within the ranks of the Conservative Party itself. The Bow Group, which is thought to have the support of up to a hundred Conservative MPs, has criticised the proposal to create a network of grant maintained schools. The Conservative leader on the Association of County Councils' education committee and the 'wet' Conservative Education Association have also expressed their reservations. According to a *TES* report, 'the unease of the Tory Left and Centre is further fuelled by their conviction that the radical Right has a powerful ally in the Prime Minister.'[2]

'Taking over' the commanding heights of the Conservative Party is clearly not enough to establish hegemony. A 'new consensus' has to be achieved and this has to be worked for, which the Hillgate Group seem quite prepared to do. In fact in some ways they want to move at a slower pace than the Government whose commitment to genuine consultation is doubtful. As Scruton points out in a response to his critics in the *TES*: 'We are doing our best to stimulate debate without which no national curriculum can be anything better than a one-sided edict . . .'.[3] As is the case with all good Gramscians – and the borrowings from the conceptual framework of this Marxist Italian theoretician have been noted[4] – the aim is to conquer hearts and minds via a slow drip feed into the nation's consciousness. The role of intellectuals is crucial to this process. They are chiefly responsible for formulating the redefinitions and reconstructions which contest existing theories and assumptions and which 'shape practical ideologies and penetrate the level of common sense, mixing and mingling with ideological practices more spontaneously generated'.[5]

The nature of the 'New Right'

In seeking to illuminate this project we need first of all to examine the political philosophy of the 'New Right'. A useful starting point is to elaborate the distinction between neo-conservatism and neo-liberalism. Numerous writers[6] have pointed out that what is known as the 'New Right' ideology consists of an amalgam of these contrasting philosophies. In general terms Belsey[7] has summed up the difference between them as follows. Neo-liberalism prioritises freedom of choice, the individual, the market, minimal government and *laissez faire* in contrast to neo-conservatism, which prioritises notions of social authoritarianism, the disciplined society, hierarchy and subordination, the nation and strong government. What they have in common is the general aim of securing a free economy, but as Gamble points out their priorities are different: 'Neo-liberals put the objective of a free economy first; the strong state is a means of achieving this. The state is not valued in itself. Just the opposite is true for neo-conservatives.'[8]

For the latter it is a question of creating a free economy so that the authority of the state can be secured and with it the authority of institutions throughout civil society, like the family and schools. The free economy will act as a discipline in economic institutions and the authority restored there will be generalised throughout society.

However, both agree that the authority of the state has been severely weakened and that radical measures are required to restore it which will necessitate a break with the postwar consensus on what is politically achievable (see Note 1, The Hillgate Group, p. 22). Both assume a crisis of hegemony whereby state authority has been weakened in four areas: representativeness, due to the decline of Parliament and the rise of corporate representation; the management of the economy, due to poor economic performance; public finance due to 'overloading'; and social order due to the spread of permissiveness (see Note 1, The Hillgate Group, p. 23). Restorative aims in these areas clearly underpin the Government documents referred to above and the Hillgate Group's radical manifesto.

The 'new consensus': the critique of politicisation

In education, however, it seems to be the neo-conservative rather than the neo-liberal wing who have taken the lead in controlling the debate and constructing the framework for a 'new consensus'. The main intention seems to involve a generalisation of the inherent tensions within the 'New Right' into the broader sphere of the liberal educational establishment with a view to focusing discussion on the opposition between, but ultimate unification of, the central concepts of 'freedom' and 'the nation'. In engaging with liberal educationists, the neo-conservatives' strategy has been to highlight those elements they have in common with all forms of liberal education and to contrast the value they jointly espouse with those underpinning the radical, left of centre ideologies allegedly dominant in educational bureaucracies, particularly at local level. They point to the politicisation of the curriculum as an example of the illiberalism and indoctrinating tendencies of the left in education, and defend the traditional curriculum as the only one based on genuinely educational principles. Antiracist and antisexist education, peace studies, world studies and various other 'newer' subjects are the centre pieces of this politicised curriculum which reflects the politicised world-view of its proponents. There is an intrinsic connection between this view and indoctrination. As Scruton, Ellis-Jones and O'Keeffe explain, there is a distinction between the 'politicised' world-view and the 'political' world-view. The latter 'recognises social goals as multifarious and conflicting and politics as no more than a limited process, whereby differences are recognised and, where possible, accommodated or resolved'. The former leads to a 'politics of goals' whereby all social action and institutions are seen as facilitative of or, alternatively, barriers to the attainment of an overriding set of political goals. This results in intolerance because there is a 'lack of respect for all independent purposes' and a lack of respect for objective truth since all 'truth' is seen as ideological. For those who hold such a view the only thing offered is 'unending "struggle" a ceaseless process of violent change in pursuit of a state of "social justice" whose characteristics are never explained . . .'.[9] The characteristic pedagogy of such a view is indoctrination distinguishable from education by its methods, which prevent the 'exercise of those critical faculties which education sets out to develop'.[10]

The waywardness of the curriculum is not only reflected in 'newer' subjects but also in the way established subjects are treated. Thus according to Partington history teaching has been subverted and ideologised by various radical pressure groups[11] and Barcan refers to the downgrading of traditional English resulting in a 'plurality of styles' reflecting 'deteriorated-liberal, Marxist and progressive perspectives', all of which sought to replace liberal humanism as the dominant form.[12] These authors seek alliances with the liberal centre and the 'old left'. They both contribute to a book of readings, published by the Social Affairs Unit, which is clearly intended to mobilise opinion around commonalities between leading neo-conservatives like Roger Scruton and prominent liberal educationists like Frank Palmer. The 'right' have produced such publications before (e.g. the Black Papers) but what is unprecedented is the breadth and sharpness of its critique of recent curriculum reforms and its characterisation of the 'left' as alien interlopers beyond the pale of 'normal' educational discourse.

The latter's marginalisation as ideologists and indoctrinators is made even more explicit in *Antiracism: An Assault of Education and Value*, edited by Frank Palmer.[13] The antiracist curriculum, like all 'antisms', is said to be based on a denigration of the cultural heritage and therefore a deprecation of the very framework of tolerance which permits radical critique of existing British institutions. It is anti-educational and illiberal, and based on the fashionable notion that Britain is a society where racism has been institutionalised. The 'New Right' vehemently deny the truth of this notion and provide countless historical and contemporary illustrations to support their view.[14]

Palmer's contribution is a most eloquent and erudite statement of the liberal wing of the 'New Right'. He is critical of the notion of institutionalised racism because it locates 'goodness' and 'badness' in the consequences of our actions rather than in our intentions, a position which, for him, leads to an emphasis on behavioural change and the proposed remedy that children and teachers be drilled and conditioned via racism-awareness courses. For Palmer, education is not about this. Racism having been freely chosen must be freely renounced. The antiracist curriculum cannot facilitate this because it does not permit moral argument. What is required to combat racism – and Palmer does not deny that racism exists – is not antiracist training, but a traditional academic education which emphasises the 'pursuit of truth' and a sound moral education involving the examination of prejudice and the making of choices.

A similar point is made about current fashions in English teaching. He bemoans the fact that English teachers now have to work in an anti-academic environment, where skills-based learning underpinned by the assumptions of behavioural psychology and popularised by the pastoral system is 'destructive of the notion of unique persons' and 'neglects the complexity of human agency'.[15]

A unity of opposites

However, the potential shakiness of the 'new consensus' because of pressures arising from internal contradictions can be demonstrated by comparing Palmer's writings with those of Roger Scruton. It is scarcely surprising that liberals and neo-conservatives have different educational philosophies but the way this difference is expressed in this instance is particularly interesting. Both would contrast the indoctrination of, say, the antiracist curriculum with the 'freedom of choice' and respect for persons endemic to liberal education, but here the similarity ends. For Palmer 'freedom' is clearly the dominant principle. His emphasis is on choice, rationality, open 'transactions' and 'negotiation' between generations, and he castigates all 'antisms' for not permitting moral argument. For Scruton, critical thinking and questioning of traditional beliefs is allowed but only 'if the activity of questioning is contained within the recognised limits of cultural stability'[16] and 'freedom' as a value seems to play second string to the imperative of 'cultural survival'. For Palmer there is clearly more chance to disengage with the past and more opportunity to challenge the existing system. Although he clearly respects 'British culture', his educational philosophy seems to imply a great willingness to criticise it.

The attitude of each to the existentialist writings of Jean Paul Sartre is revealing. Scruton's main target is Laingian doctrine but Sartre is included in the 'great body of myth' behind this doctrine and he refers to his St. Genet as one of a number of works in the 'theology of modern satanism'.[17] What appalls him is the characterisation of the paternalism and authority of the bourgeois family as 'oppressive' and the subversiveness of the doctrine which calls for individuals to 'actualise their existential possibilities' by freeing themselves from this alienating and dehumanising institution. However, Palmer's critique of Sartre is muted and his general attitude towards him more positive. Although he thinks 'Sartre is renowned for exaggerating the nature and extent of human freedom',[18] he concedes that this criticism is merely a caveat rather than wholesale. For him Sartre is clearly on the side of the angels; Scruton casts him down into hell.

In fact Scruton is so hostile to liberalism that it is quite remarkable how he has managed to collaborate with any one even remotely associated with it. In his book *The Meaning of Conservatism* he characterises the philosophy of liberalism as the 'principle enemy of conservatism' and is scathing about liberal notions of individual autonomy and the 'natural' rights of man. His view of a conservative is one who

> seeks above all for government and regards no citizen as possessed of a natural right that transcends his obligation to be ruled. Even democracy can be discarded without detriment to the civil well being as the conservative see it.[19]

The notion of 'freedom' espoused by neo-conservatives is therefore not an individualistic liberal one but more akin to the 'willing subordination to God' (or in this case the nation) proposed by traditional religious authorities.[20]

Nevertheless, the welding together of these polar opposites under the arch of an agreement about the restoration of state authority and the celebration of value in British culture has been successfully accomplished in the various publications referred to above. In contrast to the old consensus which was based on an alliance between social democracy and liberalism, the new consensus, if achieved, would forge a unity between the liberal centre and the radical right.

The appeal of the 'New Right'

The populist appeal of the 'New Right' should certainly not be underestimated. That local bureaucracies have frequently been undemocratic and patronising in their attitude to consumers is scarcely controversial. Many local education authorities now recognise the need for more devolution and consumer participation. It is widely acknowledged that services have been delivered in the patronising manner of Fabian social engineering, on the basis of assumptions about local needs made by administrators and experts at some distance from the grass roots. Moreover, some bureaucracies have generated sectional interests based more on concerns for organisational survival than 'serving the people'. Some experts and officials have indulged in monopolistic practices, carving out territories for themselves and encouraging dependence behaviour on the part of clients. Like its enemy the 'New Left', the 'New Right' has responded to criticism of service delivery with its own version of a popular programme – 'more power to parents'.

It is also probably true that many teachers and parents are concerned about innovations like antiracist and antisexist curricula for similar reasons to the 'New Right'. Many object to what they see as the politicisation of the curriculum and the illiberalism of certain teaching methods, although they may not express it in these terms. It would be imprudent to dismiss this as the knee jerk reaction of those already themselves indoctrinated by media hype. There is clearly, in certain instances, some truth in Scruton and O'Keeffe's assertions about the politicisation of the curriculum, although perhaps a more accurate description of what they object to is 'reductionism'. The causes of discrimination against black people, for example, clearly cannot always automatically be reduced to one all-pervading factor called 'racism' without grossly oversimplifying the motivational structures of so-called racist individuals and thereby in a sense dehumanising them. It is also true that there are dangers in adopting a position which is always 'anti' something without ever clearly stating 'what one is for'. According to Palmer, antiracism (and indeed 'antism' generally) starts from a position of weakness by positing a 'big evil' – racism, assuming its pernicious influence can be detected in every nook and cranny of social life, and perceives morality solely in terms of the fight against it. This kind of thinking leads to an emphasis on moral training rather than the cultivation of critical awareness and encourages a 'rooting out' mentality which conceives of all members of dominant groups as 'contaminated'. Its influence can be detected on some racism awareness courses which seem to be more about 'training' than 'education', and in the authoritarian pedagogical styles of those who claim to be raising consciousness.

Also many on the 'New Left' would sympathise with criticisms of their 'hard line' colleagues that they are obsessed with 'struggle' and that they rationalise their refusal to outline a vision of the just society with the flawed argument that such visions are merely utopian daydreaming or 'blue-printism'. Nor can this criticism be readily dismissed as the ravings of a few diehards of a particular sect. As Lukes argues, the Marxist tradition generally has failed to address important questions about the essential features of its vision of community and emancipation.[21] The link between moral philosophy and social theory remains underdeveloped in this tradition although its theoretical framework is not inherently incapable of making such a link.[22]

'New Right' criticisms of other fashionable trends are also pertinent. In its romantic, individualistic form there is little doubt that the notion of child centred learning has led to some confused and absurd practices, mostly stemming from the failures to distinguish between empirical and moral claims.[23] And the skills based curriculum is indeed sometimes 'mindless' and overly influenced by a crude behavioural psychology.

Consequences

What are the likely consequences of the 'New Right's' policies? Even in its own terms, it seems unlikely that a genuinely academic curriculum will be provided for most pupils: that is, a curriculum which reflects the controversies and arguments within traditional subjects, and which is constructed and taught in a manner which connects with the culturally located experiences of pupils. Such a curriculum could not possibly be delivered in a climate where pedagogical innovation was constrained by teachers having to work to pre-specified objectives and where there was so much emphasis on 'bench marks'. The flowering of critical thinking – and surely this must be one of the central aims of the genuinely academic curriculum? – demands that the freedom to experiment is taken seriously, as a guiding principle for teaching and learning.

A further consequence is that the educational system is likely to become more instrumentalist in orientation. Even for 'bright' pupils the aim will continue to be to get through exams rather than learning for its own sake. 'Relevance' will be conceived in various ways, but it will always be a dominant concept. However, 'relevance' is what the 'New Right' say they are opposed to. Their attitude here needs further examination.

For Scruton the aims of education are internal. 'In education a child learns to pursue things which must be pursued for their own sakes.' Its values are not expressed in the pursuit of ends but in the 'capacity to embody social meaning'.[24] In general the consultation document's emphasis on the traditional curriculum is compatible with this view, but there is another strand of rhetoric in this document which does not fit so easily into the education-for-itself philosophy. There are references to curricula 'which will help to develop [pupils'] capacity to adapt and respond flexibly to a changing world' (p. 3) and on page 2 a reference to the 1976 Ruskin speech of Sir James Callaghan which refers to 'challenges of employment in tomorrow's world'. Clearly the authors of the consultative document are attempting to incorporate elements of the 'new vocationalism' which has undoubtedly, until recently, spearheaded the Government's attempt to reconstruct education. The fact that the only new subject in the foundation curriculum is technology is an obvious reflection of its influence. Within the Conservative Party the main support for the new vocationalism comes not from liberal-humanists associated with the 'New Right' but from another group of liberals described by Dale as 'industrial trainers'.[25] For Room there are the political liberals who are committed to the idea that industrialism can itself produce a more meritocratic and harmonious society.[26] Such liberals 'will tolerate a higher level of state provision in so far as it fosters meritocracy through the development of human capital and the opening up of opportunities for all who merit them'.[27] In the previous Conservative Government the influence of this group could be seen in the Technical and Vocational Education Initiative which was the main strategy at that time for circumventing the power of the LEAs. Channelling funds through the MSC was intended to ensure that monies were spent as the Government wished although, as Dale has pointed out, what TVEI was in any particular school or LEA was always the outcome of the interplay between MSC requirements and the existing pattern of practice.[28]

But it is interesting that, in the consultation document, TVEI is seen as having to fit in with a curriculum structure which is derived from an educational philosophy markedly different from that of the 'new vocationalism'. Rather than the centre piece of a new curriculum the document proposes that 'Curriculum development programmes such as the Technical Vocational Education Initiative . . .

[will] build on the framework offered by the national curriculum' (p. 11), thus ensuring that the central pillars of the academic curriculum are intact before further innovation is contemplated. While it is true that one of these pillars is 'technology', this seems if anything to be counter to the main methodological and cross-curricular concerns of TVEI which are thereby reduced to those which can be accommodated within a single discipline.

However, despite its being alien to their philosophy, TVEI and the new vocationalism, apart from a few barbed comments about social and life skills, is never really subjected to extended criticism by the academics of the 'New Right'. Why should this be? Perhaps there are basically two reasons. The first is a tactical one. This particular initiative threatened to weaken the grip of the LEAs and, therefore, it would be logical for the 'New Right' not to oppose it, even if they did not give it their wholehearted support. A more important reason may be to do with the way they perceive the future of education and other institutions. They are happy to see a non-educational state institution like the MSC facilitate the 'autonomous' development of privatised, employer based training schemes and eventually draw off from schools those who, in the 'New Right's' view, cannot and indeed do not wish to be educated. Such pupils will be graded by profiling – a remnant of the 'pastoral curriculum'. Those who drop on to a 'vocational' track may have various options in their final years at school but one of them will *not* be 'education'.

Intentions

Differentiation along these lines may be intended by the Government, but in the process it seems to envisage that all pupils will at least have had an opportunity to partake of the national curriculum. All pupils will be expected to take GCSE in core and some foundation subjects. However, in reality it is unlikely that the opportunity to become 'educated' will exist for most pupils, and this is precisely what is intended by the neo-conservative wing of the 'New Right'. Unlike liberal-humanists and other potential supporters of the 'new consensus', neo-conservatives actively oppose the idea of universal education and are increasingly less afraid to make this explicit. Scruton actually states:

> It is not possible to provide universal education. Nor indeed is it desirable. For the appetite for learning points people only in a certain direction; it siphons them away from those places where they might have been contented.

As for the liberals' cherished hope of 'equality of opportunity':

> Such a thing seems to be neither possible nor desirable. For what opportunity

does an unintelligent child have to partake of the advantages conferred by an institution which demands intelligence?[29]

Despite references to 'intelligence', however, there is no crude individualist notion of ability underpinning this philosophy. A central feature of the neo-conservative position is that it opposes individualism. For instance, Scruton's emphasis on 'naturalism' is embedded in a sociological paradigm which recognises 'cultural meanings'. For him such meanings run deep in people's personalities, so deep in fact that for him it would be odd if they did not somehow reflect natural inclinations. Nevertheless, culture and personality are understood through 'meanings', whatever the economic, social and biological determinants of behaviour. For Scruton, society is made up of a number of autonomous institutions or communities of meaning the 'flowering' of which the state facilitates, provided they do not represent an alien or dysfunctional social force; that is, one which acts as a disease to the body politic. To participate in education is to become aware of a community – an educational community – which is one of the autonomous institutions through which people are able to define themselves and 'to discover the language in which to express their common essence'.[30]

If this sense of community is strong and gives rise to social structures accepting of state authority then there is no need for a concept of rights, like the right to education for example. However, from the neo-conservative viewpoint, such a state of affairs does not exist at the moment and it is largely because it doesn't that there is a crisis. Waldegrave comments on the decline of community and the 'atomised society of individuals faced with the growing institutions of the state'[31] (p. 108). The aim should be to stop the state's expansion by filling the gap between the state and the alienated individual with communities. This of course does not mean that the state becomes weaker. Just the opposite in fact, because in order to establish the conditions for the development of communities within the embrace of its authority it has to be strong enough to take on and dismantle those institutions which are in decline, subversive or 'contagious to the social organism' and which impede the autonomous growth of new and 'healthy' communities.

For neo-conservatives then the concept of 'community education' means something rather different from when it is used by educational radicals. It is only those who are 'intelligent' enough to tune into its meanings that education will mean becoming a member of an educational community which can confirm and develop an individual's sense of identity. For many, perhaps the majority, education is not for them; other institutions with different selection criteria are more suitable.

The sting in the tail, of course, is that it just so happens that educational institutions in addition to bonding people into community, also confer privileges outside those institutions. For the neo-conservative this is just a fact of life and there is not much you can do about it. Although non-educational institutions should have comparable authority, many of them 'will not confer the social mobility and the social power that is conferred by education'.[32] Social stratification is therefore inevitable – it is a natural and inevitable outcome of institutional autonomy.

Once it is generally accepted that education is for a minority only and that this is based on facts about the nature of the social organism then the 'New Right's' hegemonic project in education will have been completed. Authority will have been restored to an elitist and selective system of education. People can have few complaints about a system which legitimately reproduces inequality and those who see it otherwise can be justly labelled subversive.

Conclusion

In this article I have attempted to illuminate the 'New Right's' position on education and the nature of its hegemonic project. Their strategy involves appeals to populist critiques of curriculum reform, professionalism and bureaucracy, and attempts to establish alliances with liberals around a 'new consensus'. The success of the project can be measured in terms of its influence on Government policy as reflected in the consultative documents issued by the Conservative Government in its first few months of office.

Resistance is likely to come from the so-called liberal/social democratic establishment and there are also elements within the Conservative Party who will counsel the Government to adopt a more pragmatic line. Despite his stated enthusiasm for change, Kenneth Baker does not appear to be a complete convert to 'New Right' thinking. But there is no doubt that the current proposals represent a distinct shift to the right and there is little wonder that Rhodes Boyson regards them as the first step on the road to vouchers.

In the light of the foregoing analysis, it is unlikely that an effective challenge can be mounted by arguing against the traditionalism of the 'New Right' purely from a liberal individualist perspective. Emphasising the relative neglect of the autonomy principle in itself is not really to challenge the 'new consensus' at all. The debate which emerges from this is precisely the one which the 'New Right' has set out to construct. The radical left in education is attacked for its illiberalism, but once they have been ruled out of court and 'seen off', then a discussion can take place around the concepts of 'freedom' and 'the nation'. Nor is there much point in rallying around the 'new vocationalism' as the only credible opposition, because, as I have demonstrated, the 'New Right' seems to be willing and able to accommodate this movement, despite its differences with it.

A genuine challenge is likely to come from a perspective which contests the neo-conservatives' interpretation of the social givens lodged in the 'British personality' and in the meaning of national culture. In education, the traditional 'academic' curriculum can be questioned because of its divisiveness and destruction of community and culture. It is not, in the words of the Hillgate Group, a 'sensible and tried curriculum' but is one that has proved to be for most people an alien form imposed upon them from above which has invalidated rather than refined or enhanced their experiences. In the struggle against that tradition, an alternative tradition has to be remembered and celebrated – a tradition which values equality and universal education as well as the joy of learning, and the pursuit of human excellence.

References

1 The Hillgate Group (1986), *Whose Schools? A Radical Manifesto*, London, The Hillgate Group, p. 1.
2 Times Educational Supplement, 21 August 1987.
3 Times Educational Supplement, 13 March 1987.
4 G. Seidel (1986), 'Culture, Nationalism and "Race" in the British and French New Right', in R. Levitas, *The Ideology of the New Right*, Cambridge, Polity Press.
5 R. Sharp (1980), *Knowledge, Ideology and the Politics of Schooling*, London, Routledge and Kegan Paul, p. 102.
6 For example, R. Levitas (1986), *The Ideology of the New Right*, Cambridge, Polity Press.
7 A. Belsey (1986), 'The New Right, social order and civil liberties', in R. Levitas, op. cit.
8 A. Gamble (1985), 'Smashing the State: Thatcher's Radical Crusade', *Marxism Today*, p. 22.
9 R. Scruton, A. Ellis-Jones and D. O'Keeffe (1985), *Education and Indoctrination*, Harrow, Middlesex, Education Research Centre, p. 12.
10 Op. cit., p. 16.
11 G. Partington (1986), 'History: re-written to ideological fashion', in D. O'Keeffe, *The Wayward Curriculum*, Exeter, Social Affairs Unit.
12 A. Barcan (1985), 'English: two decades of attrition', in D. O'Keeffe, op. cit.
13 F. Palmer (ed.) (1986), *Anti-Racism: An Assault on Education and Value*, London, The Sherwood Press.
14 T. Hastie (1986), 'History, race and propaganda', in F. Palmer, op. cit.
15 F. Palmer (1983), 'English: Reducing Learning to Short-cut "Skills",' in D. O'Keeffe, op. cit., pp. 43 and 47 respectively.
16 R. Scruton (1985), 'The Myth of Cultural Relativism', in F. Palmer, op. cit., p. 132.
17 R. Scruton (1980), *The Meaning of Conservatism*, Harmondsworth, Penguin, p. 36.
18 F. Palmer, op. cit., p. 160.

19 R. Scruton, op. cit., p. 16.
20 R. Levitas, op. cit., p. 92.
21 S. Lukes (1985), *Marxism and Morality*, Oxford, Clarendon Press.
22 See R. Bocock (1986), *Hegemony*, Chichester, Horwood/Tavistock.
23 See H. Entwistle (1970), *Child-Centred Education*, London, Methuen.
24 R. Scruton, op. cit., p. 148.
25 R. Dale (1985), *Education, Training and Employment*, Milton Keynes, The Open University.
26 G. Room (1979), *The Sociology of Welfare*, London, Martin Robertson.
27 T. Edwards, M. Fulbrook and G. Whitty (1984), 'The state and the independent sector: policies, ideologies and theories', in L. Barton and S. Walker, *Social Crisis and Educational Research*, London, Croom Helm, p. 129.
28 R. Dale, op. cit.
29 R. Scruton, op. cit., p. 157.
30 Op. cit., p. 155.
31 W. Waldegrave (1978), *The Binding of Leviathan*, London, Hamish Hamilton, p. 108.
32 R. Scruton, op. cit., p. 160.

SECTION 3

Issues for the Curriculum

Introduction

The debate over measured achievement has continued unabated throughout the last decade. Harry Torrance discusses the origins and developments of mental testing and the inheritance they have left in the assessment policies of the 1990s. Caroline Gipps outlines the terms in which debates about standards and assessment have developed in England and Wales. Resolving the tension between the political imperative for new and simple forms of assessment and the technical difficulties of producing reliable valid systems and procedures is likely to be one of the most controversial aspects of curriculum debate through to the end of the century.

Gender, race and disability have become major areas of concern for curriculum reformers. An extensive literature has developed in both fields, in many instances providing linked theoretical perspectives. Barry Troyna provides a historical overview of the way radical forms of education have been conceptualised by policy makers and educationists and he sets out his own agenda for the enactment of non-racist criteria in various educational settings.

Catherine Manthorpe explores the 'girls and science' debate which, whilst attracting the interest of policy makers, remains controversial in terms of policy implementation. Dena Attar's historical analysis of home economics, an interesting contrast with the policy issues raised by science, also relates directly to issues raised by the centrally prescribed national curriculum for England and Wales. (Home economics has been excluded, a decision which Dena Attar would seem to approve.) She teases out the assumptions, mostly hidden or unnoticed, where policy has been made and where the consequences can be assessed; a grounded context which if developed in other areas could provide a new stimulus to policy formulation.

Finally an extract is included from the London research on primary school effectiveness. 'School Matters', although not directly addressed to curriculum policies, has significant implications for the relationship between curriculum and pedagogy. The project posed a number of key questions and the tentative answers given are directly relevant to curriculum policy making at all levels. The school effectiveness movement, as it has come to be known, has developed alongside mainstream curriculum development work. The links are tenuous but likely to develop as curriculum policies respond increasingly to newer and sharper forms of public and political evaluation.

3.1

The Origins and Development of Mental Testing in England and Wales

Harry Torrance

The last quarter of the nineteenth century had brought considerable disquiet about the commonly perceived stagnation of Britain's economic growth and the better performance of international trading rivals, which was thought, at least in part, to be linked to their education programmes. Discussion was stimulated about the direction of future technological progress and the education system which was needed to promote and complement such progress. The case for a new kind of secondary education – a technological education – as opposed to a marginalised and purely vocational post-elementary training (in addition to, but distinct from, academic science) began to be put forcefully (for a discussion of this see Banks, 1955). However the grammar tradition triumphed with the 1902 Education Act and then the 1904 Secondary School Regulations supporting an academic curriculum. Fees were set high by the 1902 Act with some free places or scholarships. Pressure, by the National Union of Teachers among others, brought significant concessions in 1907 with regard to the availability of free places in existing schools.

But the total number of free places depended on the number of schools and in fact the percentage of each age group gaining free grammar school places only rose from 1 per cent in 1894 to 5 per cent in the 1930s (Morris, 1961). And these free places had to be competed for of course. So although the development of 'objective' tests over the first three decades of the twentieth century was considered at the time to be a progressive move (fairer than essay tests, or interviews, see for example Valentine, 1932 and Brereton, 1944) the fact remains that testing to assess attainment and predict future performance came to be introduced to help distribute the very small number of *free* secondary school places. Similarly, it must be remembered that the development of a unified system of primary and secondary education and the testing that went with it took place

within the context of a traditional class-based view of what education was for and who should benefit from it. Theories of education
continued to be implicitly informed by nineteenth-century views
long after the structures which had produced such views had
undergone significant (but not fundamental) change and long after
the overt expression of such views, at least in educational circles,
had been frowned on.

A brief review of some government reports might clarify these
points. The Taunton Commission (Schools Inquiry Commission,
1868), interestingly enough in view of Karier's interpretation of
American schooling, made frequent reference to Prussia as an
excellent model. The report proposed three distinct types of schooling: 'first grade', 'second grade' and 'third grade' schools, to prepare
the sons of the aristocracy and landed gentry, the sons of business-
men and manufacturers, and the sons of artisans and tradesmen,
each for their separate stations in life. Attendance would be to age
18, 16, and 14 respectively, with curricula to match. Elementary
education was separate again, to age 12, for the children of the
labouring poor. In the words of the report: 'It is obvious that these
distinctions correspond roughly . . . to the gradations of society';
and 'The three grades do not lead into one another, but should
stand side by side . . . leading to different ends' (Schools Inquiry
Commission, 1868, pp. 15–16, 94–5). In fact the Taunton Report
was not implemented as it stood, but the idea of a class-based –
elementary and grammar – system of education was. The Hadow
Report (Board of Education, 1926) attempted to rationalise and
control the dual system by recognising what was happening in many
areas and recommending it generally: the end-on joining of
elementary and grammar to form primary and secondary education.
Psychological evidence was quoted in support of this. But education
to suit each 'type' of child was the successor to education to suit each
social class; these essentially comprised the 'non-academic' – to be
catered for in 'Modern schools', and the 'academic' – to continue
going to 'grammar schools' with selection at age eleven. Selection
was to be based on a written examination. Also: 'A written
psychological test might also be specially employed in dealing with
borderline cases, or where a discrepancy has been observed between the result of the written examination and the teacher's
estimate of proficiency' (Board of Education, 1926, p. 178).

Two later government reports, Spens (Board of Education, 1938)
and Norwood (Board of Education, 1943) leading up to the 1944
Education Act, selected and made explicit some of the theories of
intelligence implicit in Hadow. The section of the Spens Report
dealing with mental and emotional development was 'based on a
memorandum prepared for the Committee by Professor Burt'

(p. 120). The recommendations drew heavily on this evidence and argued for example that:

> Intellectual development during childhood appears to progress as it were governed by a single central factor, usually known as 'general intelligence', which may broadly be described as innate all round intellectual ability . . . Our psychological witnesses assured us that it can be measured approximately by means of intelligence tests . . . We were informed that, with few exceptions, it is possible at a very early age to predict with some degree of accuracy the ultimate level of a child's intellectual powers . . . (pp. 123–4).

Both reports recommended differentiation according to 'type' – interests, abilities, motivation of the individual. In many ways of course this is an idea that one would not wish to fault, but in practice Spens' and Norwood's recommendations hark back to the Taunton Report and involved fitting students into three styles of schooling still closely reflecting 'the gradations of society' rather than developing schooling for the benefit of the individual. Thus Spens recommended three kinds of schools, Grammar schools, Technical schools, and Modern Schools, and Norwood endorsed this, for: 'The pupil who is interested in learning for its own sake . . . the pupil whose interests and abilities lie markedly in the field of applied science or applied art . . . the pupil [who] deals more easily with concrete things than with ideas (Board of Education, 1943, pp. 2–3).

However, as well as presenting psychological evidence, Hadow, Spens and Norwood also repeatedly paid tribute to numerous innovations and experiments up and down the country, and when it suited them discounted the need for psychological backing. For example, general ideas of individual development and individual interests were adopted and the term 'child-centred education' used frequently. The specific future structure of education would continue to be based, as Norwood reported, on 'general educational experience'. Now for a new concept – 'general intelligence' – to be used to reproduce so directly the social divisions of the Taunton Report, seventy years previously, is indeed to make use of 'general educational experience', but it is to legitimate that experience rather than prove that it had been correct. The argument here is not about some great conspiracy, but rather that eminent scholars and educators, entrusted with reports of great importance and wary of a new discipline – psychology – used it partially, to give weight to continuing practice and prevailing currents of opinion; and adopted its vocabulary to articulate those opinions.

Indeed, Burt himself took issue with the Norwood Report. In a specific response to the report (Burt, 1943) he repeated his arguments that 'individual differences in intelligence can be observed and assessed at a much earlier age [than eleven]' (p. 133), but was unhappy with the all too idealist 'type of mind' theorising. Burt thought administrative convenience the main force behind selection at eleven, but he endorsed selection as such, in effect saying that the right policy had been adopted but not for exactly the right (i.e., his) reasons.

The development of secondary education in England then, was largely independent of psychological testing, but not of psychology, and the idea of innate differences in intellectual ability. The immediate precursor to the introduction of psychological language into these general government surveys and reports was the 'Report by the Consultative Committee on Psychological Tests of Educable Capacity' (Board of Education, 1924) while the idea of innate and heritable differences in intellectual ability had its roots in the British eugenics movement and particularly in the thought of Francis Galton. Several papers by Norton (1978a, b, 1979) and MacKenzie (1976, 1978) have sketched out the history of the British eugenics movement, its social context, and the symbiotic relationship it enjoyed with the development of mental testing and early statistical techniques. Very briefly, Norton, and especially MacKenzie, argue that the research that various individuals in the field of Biology, Mathematics and Psychology engaged in had a sufficiently common theme and direction for it to be viewed as deriving from both certain intellectual traditions and an emerging class interest. Searle (1978) has argued that it is precisely because eugenics did not articulate the class interests of the emerging professional groups in England that it faded so quickly, but it does seem that for a certain decisive period of time in post-Darwinian Victorian and Edwardian England research into differences between individuals developed in different disciplines along very similar lines and with very definite political implications.

Essentially Galton's theory was that 'natural ability' could be taken, as was physical stature, to follow a normal curve of distribution, and that those individuals who were eminent in society must be those with the highest endowment of 'natural ability'. Further, this ability was heritable. (It might be noted at this point that Galton himself was an excellent example of the new intellectual/business elite, having close family ties with the Wedgwoods and the Darwins.) Despite not taking serious account of the existing distribution of wealth and power, of differential access to entrepreneurial and professional opportunities, i.e. despite its serious flaws, Galton's theory attracted supporters who virtually devoted their lifes' work to attempting to demonstrate its efficacy empirically. The connections stretch personally and intellectually from Galton, through Charles Spearman (Professor of Psychology at University College, London), Karl Pearson (the first Galton Professor of Eugenics at UCL), and others to Cyril Burt, whose father was actually the

Galton family physician (Burt met Galton as a boy) and who eventually succeeded Spearman as Professor of Psychology at UCL in 1932. Burt's biographer, L. S. Hearnshaw, states unequivocally that 'the influence of Galton on Burt was undoubtedly a decisive one' (Hearnshaw, 1979, p. 24). Spearman was the first person to put forward the idea (in 1904) that intelligence comprised specific abilities underlain by a general factor – 'g'. He introduced statistical methods into psychological theory in order to try to isolate and measure 'g'. Pearson was concerned to develop statistical procedures to facilitate research into heredity, to study the relationships between two populations connected by heredity. Burt pursued research among groups of schoolchildren, to verify the existence of innate and heritable ability, and to develop tests to measure it.

What these men had in common, it can be argued, was professional as opposed to aristocratic or entrepreneurial status. They belonged to a certain faction of the middle classes, increasingly powerful, but nevertheless in need of a legitimating ideology. Against a background of economic stagnation, even more public city squalor and poverty, and the setbacks of the Boer War a little later, the idea of a governing elite of the (heritably) able became a powerful one. Concern for the future of the nation was expressed in a number of ways and in a number of contexts. The National Council for Public Morals commanded significant attention and produced a series of reports for the government in the 1920s (e.g. NCPM, 1923). Rather later the Scottish Council for Research in Education engaged in two investigations of the 'Intelligence of Scottish Schoolchildren' (SCRE, 1933, 1949) with the expectation (not confirmed) that the intelligence of the population was falling. Policy implications deriving from this perspective included the notion of intervention in reproduction (as opposed to *laissez faire* reproduction: the market (natural selection) will decide who is fittest and who therefore survives) to control the numbers of the 'fit' (i.e. the middle classes, especially professionals) *vis-à-vis* the 'unfit' (i.e. the labouring poor). Such thinking seemed to span the continuum from Fabian Socialism (state planning by 'experts', encouraging birth control for example, for the benefit of the masses) to extremely right-wing interventionist strategies. It provides a backcloth against which to view and assess the pursuit of research into individual differences.

Also worth noting at this point is Sutherland's (1977) observation that 'In England . . . a preoccupation with identification and separate treatment of [subnormal] children considerably ante-dated the development of sophisticated diagnostic tools'; and 'The development of mental testing had a reinforcing rather than an innovative effect' (pp. 138, 140). Thus scientific research was following in the wake of prevailing social attitudes, reflecting and reinforcing them.

Indeed the development and reworking of Galton's theory, with its nebulous and illusory terminology – 'natural ability', 'eminence' – being sharpened up to objectively measurable 'g' and 'IQ', with the concomitant claims to knowledge thus implied, parallels the Taunton-to-Norwood development remarkably.

Burt, of course, must be *the* major figure in a review of the development of secondary education and testing in England. We have already noted his contribution to the Spens Report. Called on during the First World War to work on a government statistical committee concerned with the supply of munitions (Hearnshaw, 1979, p. 40), Burt moved on to contribute evidence to the National Council for Public Morals and a whole chapter (on the history of mental testing) plus a great deal of expert evidence to the 'Report . . . on psychological tests of educable capacity', mentioned above. The report itself attempts fairly inconclusively to define intelligence (see pp. 67–71), what intelligence tests measure, and whether they can be of use in educational selection. But Burt's (and Spearman's) influence is clear: 'What intelligence tests measure . . . is inborn, allround, intellectual ability' (p. 71). Of the tests reproduced in the report's appendices, the committee wrote that 'the more effective' tests had been omitted because they 'cannot be explained to those unacquainted with psychological procedure without a lengthy technical description' (p. 199). Those tests that the committee did see fit to reproduce demonstrate in fact that what intelligence tests were measuring was learned mental agility and reasoning, heavily dependent on a high level of linguistic sophistication. For example the London Revision of the Binet-Simon scale (Burt's work) required that a child:

Age XI

49. Explains three absurdities out of five, e.g. 'I have three brothers, Tom, Jack and myself.'
50. Answers three out of five harder questions, e.g. 'Why should we judge a person by what he does, not by what he says?'
51. Give sixty words in three minutes.
52. Repeats seven numbers.
53. Builds one sentence with three words in one minute (same words as for Test 47) (p. 202).

Cross out plainly the 'extra' word in each of the following lines:

charity	kindness	benevolence	revenge	love
square	circular	oblong	hexagonal	triangular
needle	tack	nail	knife	pin
coal	bread	coke	wood	paper
bran	wool	cotton	hemp	jute
hair	feathers	wool	grass	fur (p. 214)

It is probably worth noting in passing that while Burt was by far the most influential psychologist of his day in terms of official attention, Thomson had most impact on the local authorities in terms of the tests which they bought and used.

The main point I want to make here, however, is not that the tests were or were not testing what it was claimed that they tested, but rather that the report as a whole represents official recognition of the discipline of psychology, and the efficacy of psychometry; of the objective existence of innate mental differences and the language with which to describe and discuss them. A major contributor to this recognition (always remembering the social and historical context in which he operated) was Burt, a man whose work Hearnshaw describes as marked by 'inadequate reporting and incautious conclusions' (p. 30) and which Kamin concludes is 'not worthy of our current scientific attention' (p. 71). Future reports had this one to guide them. They took their lead from it, built on it, and turned to Burt again (the Spens Report for example) for further advice on the problem which he himself had defined for them.

As regards the assertion of the testers that their products measured innate ability, we can see clearly enough that this is suspect. Also we might expect that such a claim would involve the use of some independent and objective yardstick, but in fact the accuracy of psychological tests was measured against prevailing notions of ability, and teacher estimations of rank order – thus an acceptably accurate test would be one which reproduced the teacher rank order.

Burt undertook a series of surveys when appointed Psychologist to the Education Department of London County Council in 1913. These he reported in various memoranda, collected and published in 1921. New editions have remained substantially unaltered (see Burt, 1962, 4th edn). Burt writes that his formal instructions involved the development of methods of identifying special children: 'subnormal' and 'super-normal'. He devoted a large amount of his time to evaluating and developing existing mental tests emerging from France – the Binet-Simon tests. Burt revised their tests by comparing the results from such tests with teachers' rank orders of children in their school: 'In nearly every case the observational judgements of the pupils' own teachers provided the original basis of comparison by means of which our tests were first validated' (Burt, 1962, p. XXII); and 'There is no standard of comparison which can surpass or supercede the considered estimate of an observant teacher, working daily with the individual children over a period of several months or years. This is the criterion I have used' (Burt, 1962, p. 249).

One is left to wonder what counts as 'the considered estimate of an observant teacher'. That aside it must be noted that Burt felt this comparison to be both progressive and vital to the cause of developing accurate tests. Burt also stressed that testing was but a small part of educational assessment, though his instructions for rank ordering were narrow enough – what teachers themselves thought the child's innate ability to be. The main points to emerge however must be, first, that Burt's encouragement of the use of tests along with his personal example of concentrating his attention on psychometry meant the importance of testing and its attendant language growing ever greater at the expense of other forms of assessment; secondly, that any comparison with teacher judgements and subsequent development of tests to achieve a higher correlation with teachers' rank orders means that such development would be in the direction of confirming existing realities. Thus the resultant tests may have produced accurate rank orders of intellectual ability as defined by certain teachers at a certain point in time, but cannot be called 'objective' measurements of any real and unchanging entity.

The argument then, is that with the incorporation of a variety of educational practices into the vocabulary of 'academic' and 'non-academic', Victorian attitudes to education came to be reproduced and institutionalised in different forms. Now on both sides of the Atlantic mental testing derived from a concern with the 'quality' of the population, and in effect developed to protect and sustain class interests; but it would appear that class and cultural bias in the use of testing and in the tests themselves varied from the obvious and explicit to the subtle and implicit. Such variation would seem to stem from both the prevailing social conditions and the organisation of schooling. In America social change on an unprecedented scale provoked blunt definitions of what was, or was not, acceptably 'American'. In England a more gradual challenge to existing patterns of economic and social life was met with a more subtle educational response. The curriculum was broadened but kept within the confines of an academic tradition, access was expanded but for the most part only to low-status secondary education.

In bringing this review to a close it is interesting to note that while testing, despite probably even more severe criticism in the United States than in this country, continues apace in the US, the formal and public articulation of testing theory in England – the eleven plus – came under attack and started to be dismantled almost as soon as it was nationally instituted. Research by the National Foundation for Educational Research in the late 1940s and throughout the 1950s soon began to undermine the certainties of Spens and Norwood.

Originally conceived of as a fact-finding exercise to discover how different local authorities were operating the selection procedures necessitated by the 1944 Education Act, the research began to reveal unequal provision of grammar school places around the country. It was reported by Yates and Pidgeon (1957) that some

LEAs could provide grammar school places for only 10 per cent of their primary school leavers while others could provide places for as many as 45 per cent. Vernon (1957) reported as little as 9 per cent in Gateshead right up to 60 per cent in Merioneth. These findings, along with discoveries about how different local authorities used tests in different ways, gave rise to public concern about the selection process in general: some LEAs used tests rigidly, others favoured primary school records or a combination of tests and records, still others asked schools to pre-select the 'best' candidates for the test.

But even more important, both for the public of the day and our argument here, were reports about the effects of coaching and practice on test results. NFER reports clearly stated that coaching and practice could increase IQ scores(Watts, Pidgeon and Yates, 1952 and Yates, 1953). Gains depended on a multitude of interacting variables: qualities of the coaching, the length of practice time, the curriculum and general ethos of the school, but gains there certainly were. The debate about coaching was conducted in *The Times Educational Supplement* and beyond, as well as in the scientific journals. Here then, was refutation of the idea of an innate and immutable property which some individuals possessed while others did not.

Such was the debate in the light of these findings and publications such as Brian Simon's *Intelligence Testing and the Comprehensive School* that the British Psychological Society set up a Working Party chaired by Philip Vernon, Professor of Educational Psychology at the University of London Institute of Education. Obviously rattled by the many and various attacks on the eleven plus, and by implications on the emerging profession of educational psychologist, the BPS set out to re-establish psychologists as rational and apolitical experts who could be relied upon to put their own house in order: 'In view of the . . . spate of misleading and often emotionally-toned writing on the topic, the British Psychological Society has decided that it would be in the public interest to set down what is known on the various aspects of the problem . . .' (Vernon, 1957, p. 8).

The report reviewed early work as just that – early and therefore not surprisingly mistaken at times (as opposed to deliberately misleading or 'incautious'). Nevertheless it did contradict the 'truths' which informed government policy only fifteen years previously. The report reviewed work on test design, reliability and validity, on the effects of coaching, and drew attention to the statistical manipulation engaged in by testers:

It should be noted that . . . scoring involves an assumption . . . that intelligence . . . is 'normally distributed' . . . no conclusive proof that intelligence is so distributed can be adduced, and . . . the distribution of the scores or the IQs we actually obtain from most tests approximate to 'normal' type simply because of the manner in which the tests are constructed (Vernon, 1957, pp. 91–2).

The report attempted an interactive definition of intelligence, essentially claiming that we learn to act intelligently (as opposed to 'inborn, all round, intellectual ability') although intelligence cannot be taught: 'by intelligence we mean more general qualities of comprehending, reasoning and judging . . . which have been picked up without much specific instruction . . . not . . . innate ability' (Vernon, 1957, pp. 107–8). The report also looked at work on pupil record cards and teacher estimates of ability, concluding (again in direct contradiction of Burt's assertions regarding the 'considered estimate of an observant teacher') that such estimates could not be relied upon and that teachers: 'may unwittingly be influenced by the child's cheekiness, bullying or delinquent tendencies, dirtiness, troublesomeness in class, and their opposites' (Vernon, 1957, pp. 138–9). Selection was still practised of course, and for the most part the psychologists still held that IQ tests were the best predictors of academic success. However sociological work which paralleled the psychologists' research began to challenge the nature of the prediction. Also the few individuals who passed the eleven plus because of the IQ tests when they may have failed on an attainment test began to be dismissed as irrelevant, compared to the vast fluctuations in opportunity across the country caused by discrepant provision, and by changes in pupil numbers from year to year within an authority (see, e.g. Halsey and Gardner, 1953; Floud and Halsey, 1957; Halsey, 1958).

Psychologists themselves were prepared to recognise the weaknesses of selection and statements recommending comprehensive secondary education did come to be made. Watts *et al.*, for example, wrote in 1952 that:

> The results of our work would seem to imply that we should think less in terms of sharply differentiated types of secondary school and more in terms of the principle that children whose abilities and needs are similar should be given similar courses of education, irrespective of the type of school to which they may have been allocated (p. 33).

While the BPS held that: 'On psychological grounds, then, there would seem to be more to be said in favour of comprehensive schools than against' (Vernon, 1957, p. 50). It is clear then, that while this new generation of psychologists were still interested in both laying claim to, and making use of, the position of 'expert', carved out over fifty years, they did so in a very different social and historical context compared to their predecessors. The 1950s was a decade of reconstruction and expansion, with the emphasis on access to educational opportunity and the need to make the most of our 'talent'. Conversely the ultimate logic of the eugenicists' argument had been seen in Hitler's Germany. All the while sociological evidence suggested equality of opportunity was not aided by testing – the original 'progressive' *raison d'être*.

More than this however, education in England had always had its humane element, and the criticism of the eleven plus started as soon as it was realised that the 1944 Act meant subjecting very young children to a selection process with immense consequences, often preceded by months or even years of narrow coaching. As the BPS report put it: 'it seems to us more important to ensure that maximum justice should appear to be done than to take a rigid stand on statistical findings' (Vernon, 1957, p. 155). In similar vein, Ben Morris, Director of the NFER in the 1950s, later wrote: 'The psychology of mental measurement, through failure to scrutinise adequately its presuppositions developed into a technology . . .' (Morris, 1966, p. 156). A new generation of psychologists had come to terms with the fact that they were dealing with people.

Acknowledgments

I would like to acknowledge comments and advice from David Hamilton, Barry MacDonald and Nigel Norris, who read an earlier version of this paper. Gillian Sutherland has also been most helpful, and both she and Bernard Norton supplied me with papers that I would not otherwise have seen.

References

Banks, O. (1955), *Parity and Prestige in English Secondary Education*, London, Routledge and Kegan Paul.

Block, N. J. and Dworking, G. (eds) (1976), *The I.Q. Controversy*, New York, Pantheon.

Board of Education (1924), *Reports of the Consultative Committee on Psychological Tests of Educable Capacity*, London, HMSO.

Board of Education (1926), *Report of the Consultative Committee on Education of the Adolescent*, London, HMSO.

Board of Education (1938), *Report of the Consultative Committee on Secondary Education*, London, HMSO.

Board of Education (1943), *Curriculum and Examinations in Secondary Schools*, London, HMSO.

Bowles, S. and Gintis, H. (1977), 'Capitalism and education', in Young, M. and Whitty, G. (eds) (1977), *Society, State and Schooling*, Eastbourne, Falmer Press.

Brereton, J. L. (1944), *The Case for Examinations*, London, Cambridge University Press.

Burt, C. L. (1943), 'The education of the young adolescent: the psychological implications of the Norwood Report', *British Journal of Educational Psychology*, 13, pp. 126–40.

Burt, C. L. (1962), *Mental and Scholastic Tests*, 4th edn, London, Staple Press.

Callahan, R. E. (1962), *Education and the Cult of Efficiency*, Chicago, University of Chicago Press.

Drost, W. H. (1967), *David Sneddon and Education for Social Efficiency*, Wisconsin, University of Wisconsin Press.

Floud, J. and Halsey, A. H. (1957), 'Intelligence tests, social class, and selection for secondary school', *British Journal of Sociology*, 8, pp. 33–9.

Haller, J. S. and Haller, R. M. (1974), *The Physician and Sexuality in Victorian America*, Illinois, University of Illinois Press.

Halsey, A. H. (1958), 'Genetics, social structure and intelligence', *British Journal of Sociology*, 9, pp. 15–28.

Halsey, A. H., Floud, J. and Anderson, C. A. (eds) (1961), *Education, Economy and Society*, New York, Free Press.

Halsey, A. H. and Gardner, L. (1953), 'Selection for secondary education and achievement in four grammar schools', *British Journal of Sociology*, 4, pp. 60–75.

Halsey, A. H. and Karabel, J. (eds) (1977), *Power and Ideology in Education*, Oxford, Oxford University Press.

Hearnshaw, L. S. (1979), *Cyril Burt: Psychologist*, London, Hodder and Stoughton.

Joncich, G. (1968), *The Sane Positivist: a biography of Edward L. Thorndike*, New York, Wesleyan University Press.

Kamin, L. J. (1977), *The Science and Politics of I.Q.*, Harmondsworth, Penguin.

Karier, C. J. (1972a), Liberalism and the quest for orderly change; (1972b), Testing for order in the corporate liberal state; (1973), Business values and the educational state; reprinted in: Dale, R., Esland, G. and MacDonald, M. (eds) (1976), *Schooling and Capitalism*, London, Routledge and Kegan Paul and Open University Press.

Karier, C. J., Violas and Spring, J. (eds) (1973), *Roots of Crisis*, New York, Rand McNally.

MacKenzie, D. (1976), 'Eugenics in Britain', *Social Studies of Science*, 6, pp. 499–532.

MacKenzie, D. (1978), 'Statistical theory and social interests: a case study', *Social Studies of Science*, 8, pp. 35–83.

Morris, B. (1966), 'The contribution of psychology to the study of education', in Tibble, J. W. (ed.), *The Study of Education*, London, Routledge and Kegan Paul.

Morris, N. (1961), 'An historian's view of examinations', in Wiseman, S. (ed.) (1961), *Examinations and English Education*, Manchester University Press.

National Council for Public Morals (1923), *Youth and Race*, London, Kegan Paul, Trench, Trubner.

Norton, B. J. (1978a), 'Karl Pearson and statistics: the social origins of scientific innovation', *Social Studies of Science*, 8, pp. 3–34; (1978b), 'Psychologists and social class', paper presented to the *Past and Present Society Conference*, 29 September 1978; (1979), 'Charles Spearman and the general factor of intelligence: genesis and interpretation in the light of socio-personal considerations', *Journal of the History of the Behavioural Sciences*, 15, pp. 142–54.

Schools Inquiry Commission (1868), *Report of the Commissioners*, London, HMSO.

Scottish Council for Research in Education (1933), *The Intelligence of Scottish Schoolchildren*, University of London Press.

Scottish Council for Research in Education (1949), *The Trend of Scottish Intelligence*, London, University of London Press.

Searle, G. R. (1978), 'Eugenics and class', paper presented to the *Past and Present Society Conference*, 29 September 1978.

Simon, B. (1953), 'Intelligence testing and the comprehensive school', reprinted in

Simon, B. (1978), *Intelligence Psychology Education*, London, Lawrence and Wishart.

Spring, J. (1972), *Education and the Rise of the Corporate Liberal State*, Boston, Beacon Press.

Sutherland, G. (1977), 'The magic of measurement: mental testing and English education 1900–1940', *Transactions of the Royal Historical Society*, 5th series, 29, pp. 135–53.

Tyack, D. (1974), *The One Best System*, Boston, Harvard University Press.

Valentine, C. W. (1932), *The Reliability of Examinations*, London, University of London Press.

Vernon, P. (ed.) (1957), *Secondary School Selection*, London, Methuen.

Watts, A. F., Pidgeon, D. A. and Yates, A. (1952), *Secondary School Entrance Examinations*, London, Newnes.

Yates, A. (1953), 'Symposium on the effects of coaching and practice in intelligence tests. An analysis of some recent investigations', *British Journal of Educational Psychology*, 23, pp. 147–54.

Yates, A. and Pidgeon, D. A. (1957), *Admission to Grammar Schools*, London, Newnes.

Young, M. F. D. (ed.) (1971), *Knowledge and Control*, London, Collier MacMillan.

3.2

The Debate Over Standards and the Uses of Testing

Caroline Gipps

Introduction

In this paper I want to concentrate on the notion of standards in education, to look at how testing is used in the school system and whether, or how, testing can raise standards.

The first thing to say is that concern over standards is not the prerogative of the third quarter of the twentieth century. Both the Bullock Report and the Cockroft Report quoted complaints about standards in reading and maths from 60 and 100 years ago respectively.[1] In the USA standardised examinations were being used to *maintain* standards in the 1840s.[2] The interesting thing, of course, is the way standards are nearly always thought to be falling. Public concern over standards comes in waves and is often triggered off by activities outside the world of the classroom. When a cause for poor economic or technological performance is sought, the school system is an easy target.

What do we mean by standards?

'Standards' is a term which is probably more loosely used than any other in education. When we talk about standards we may be referring to levels of attainment in basic skills such as reading and maths, or levels of attainment in a much wider range of school activities; we may be talking about standards of provision, e.g., the number of teachers and books per child, or we may be talking about levels of behaviour, dress and other social phenomena. Thus, in the narrowest sense, standards can mean levels of performance on a test, and in the widest sense can encompass notions of social and moral behaviour and discipline as well as educational attainment. It is when defined most widely, moving into the area of general values, that it is most prone to subjective and anecdotal use. The link between the narrow and wide uses of the term is tenuous, but one that is often made. In the minds of the general public, a decline in standards of dress and 'moral' behaviour, which may well be due to changing social and cultural conventions, is likely to be linked with a perceived decline in educational standards. The fact that many members of the public seem to feel that educational standards are falling (despite evidence to the contrary from, e.g. the DES School Leavers Survey)[3] is one to which educationists must face up. In the current climate, when consumerism is the dominating educational ideology,[4] parents', employers' and politicians' opinions about standards are vitally important.

History should have warned us that the view that standards are declining would provide politicians with the impetus and rationale for the setting of approved standards (in the form of levels of test performance) in order to ensure quality control. First there was Sir Keith Joseph's objective for GCSE: to bring 80–90 per cent of all 16 year old pupils *at least* (his emphasis) up to the level now associated with that grade of CSE whch is currently achieved by average pupils. Now we have Kenneth Baker's benchmarks accompanied by testing (and a national curriculum).

The Director of Education for Croydon has a lot to say on standards:

> The establishment of standards, which must be consistent with international expectations, is a necessary condition of the restoration of the commitment to excellence missing from many parts of the education service. In the absence of external standards, pupils and teachers have no alternative but to establish their own. Understandably, these standards are all too often too low . . .
>
> Standards will make the education service truly accountable to parents . . .
>
> They will also provide the public with a means of measuring the effectiveness of the education system . . .
>
> Standards will enable administrators to target their budgets where improvements are needed, instead of, as now, in ways unrelated to any sense or expectation of educational performance: there is little point in comparing levels of expenditure – unit costs, pupil-teacher ratios or class sizes – if no one knows how effectively the money is used . . .
>
> The introduction of a national curriculum and universal standards would guarantee equality of opportunity to the pupil, accountability to parents and the public, intellectual rigour to the programme of learning, and enable the education service to be managed in ways which relate financial output to educational output . . .[5]

Not only do his comments make the 'establishment of standards' seem immensely sensible, they bring up the difficult issue of how to get a measure of value for money within the educational system. Anathema though such a concept may be to many professionals, it is another issue which we cannot afford to ignore in the 1980s and 1990s. The thorny question is: How do we know that we are getting value for money unless we have some assessment of standards of performance?

As this preamble has indicated, 'standards' always come back in some way to pupil performance, which is in turn assessed by exams or tests. The current debate assumes that testing will somehow raise standards but this is an assumption which needs some discussion. The current talk about benchmarks and national testing programmes makes it sound as though, public examinations apart, there is little testing within the system and certainly that testing children at 7 and 11 would be a new development. We have, however, evidence to show that this is simply not true; there is a considerable amount of testing going on in schools at 7, 9 *and* 11 and one of the major purposes of this testing has been to monitor standards. We have carried out two surveys which relate directly to this issue and I shall outline the findings in the next section.

The extent of testing in LEAs

In 1981 we carried out a survey of all LEAs asking about any testing programmes they had, that is, standardised tests of reading, maths, etc. given routinely to all or part of an age group.[6] We discovered that testing was widespread, with at least 79 per cent of LEAs doing some kind of testing. The breakdown of LEAs which test is given in Table 1.

Table 1　*Number of LEAs with testing programmes in 1981*

	London	Metropolitan Boroughs	County Councils	Total No.	Total %
Testing	18	29	35	82	78.8
Not testing	3	3	7	13	12.5
No information	0	4	5	9	8.7
Total	21	36	47	104	100%

Table 2 gives a picture of what subjects are being tested and at what ages.

We can see from Table 2 that testing at 7–8 is, or was, fairly common. Testing at 11+ is even more common than at either 7 or 8, and it is at this age that verbal reasoning tests are most used. There was little testing of this sort at 14, though no doubt school exams featured in the lives of this age group. The testing at 13 was often for the purpose of aiding option choice.

Towards the end of 1983 we sent another questionnaire to all LEAs, this time asking specifically about screening programmes, that is, tests or checklists given routinely to all or part of an age

Table 2   *Number of LEAs testing at different ages in 1981*

	Infant			Junior				Secondary				No. LEAs testing each subject
	5	6	7	8	9	10	11	12	13	14	15	
Reading	1	30	41	15	12	36	2	10	5	2		71
Maths			3	14	7	11	21	3	4	2	3	36
IQ[1]			3	12	5	5	34	1	3			40
English				3	4	5	8	1				10
Test Batteries[2]				2	1	1	2	2	1			4
Spelling							2					2
Infant Checklists	4	5	2									10

Notes
[1] IQ tests include verbal and non-verbal reasoning tests.
[2] Batteries include the Richmond Tests and the Cognitive Abilities Test.

group with the purpose of identifying children with special educational needs.[7] Again, testing was widespread with 71 per cent of all LEAs having at least one such programme (see Table 3).

Table 3   *Number of LEAs with testing programmes in 1983*

	London	Metropolitan Boroughs	County Councils	Total No.	%
Screening	16	24	34	74	71.1
Not screening	4	5	7	16	15.4
No information	1	7	6	14	13.5
Total	21	36	47	104	100%

Although this might look like a relative decline in the level of testing since 1981 we cannot make this assumption, since in the two surveys we were asking different things: in the second survey we were asking specifically about screening programmes. These tend to be used at younger ages (see Table 4) and to involve reading tests more exclusively.

Table 4   *Number of LEAs screening at different ages in 1983*

	Infant				Junior			Secondary			
	5	6	7	8	9	10	11	12	13	14	15
Number of LEAs	18	22	37	36	11	13	28	4	5	0	0

Yet again, the evidence shows that there is a great deal of testing particularly in the 7 and 8 year old groups.

The uses of testing

In our earlier study we asked LEAs why they had these testing programmes and to what uses they were put. The reasons LEAs gave us for introducing testing programmes can be grouped broadly into three categories – political, organisational and professional. *Political* reasons included the atmosphere in the mid to late 1970s at the time of the Great Debate, the Black Papers and the William Tyndale affair, resulting in pressure from members of Education Committees and a desire by some Chief Education Officers to be fore-armed in the event of questions over standards. *Organisational* factors included the ending of the 11+, school reorganisation and LEA reorganisation, all leading to a demand for information particularly relating to primary/secondary transfer. Lastly, *professional* reasons included concern over the numbers of children being referred for remedial help – both too large and too small – and concern over, for example, reading standards following publication of the Bullock Report and identification of children with special needs following Warnock. Clearly, apart from the identification of slow learners, 'standards' are and were a prime mover.

These three categories result in testing programmes for three purposes: monitoring, transfer and screening. In this paper I shall concentrate on monitoring programmes, since these relate specifically to the standards theme.

Monitoring is the business of examining *group* scores, where the groups may be classes, school age-cohorts or authority-wide age-cohorts, with a view to making comparisons. A total of 50 LEAs out of 82 from which we obtained information gave monitoring as the sole, or one, reason for one or more of their testing programmes.

There are predominately *two kinds of monitoring*: monitoring of

Table 5   *The purpose of LEA testing*

Purpose	No. of LEAs	No. testing schemes
Screening only	7	23
Monitoring only	5	22
Transfer only	2	11
Record keeping only	1	10
Allocation of resources only	0	4
Screening+Monitoring+/−other	43	81
Screening+other	16	23
Monitoring+other	2	16
Other	3	13
Total	79	203
No information	3	5

LEA authority-wide results, which involves comparison with national norms 'to get a general picture of standards', and monitoring of school results which involves comparing schools.

Monitoring does not necessarily imply any particular testing plan and it is not necessary to test all children; comparisons can be made using samples. Indeed most people, with the APU in mind, probably think of monitoring strictly in terms of sampling, or *light sampling* as it is called. In practice, however, most LEAs which claim to be monitoring engage in blanket testing, partly, or perhaps mostly, because they wish to screen at the same time, and also because light sampling of the order of 10 per cent is not thought to provide enough information on which to base inter-school comparisons. This latter feeling is not confined to LEA officers. The head-teachers in schools being tested often prefer to have *all* the relevant age group tested.

The way in which the test results of individual schools are used tends to be private and informal. Commonly each school will receive its own test scores together with those of the LEA as a whole or divisions within the LEA. There may be a visit from the adviser/inspector to discuss the school's results, or there may be discussion at a Heads' meeting. However, our research in schools showed the use of formal meetings to be infrequent.

So we know that LEAs use tests quite extensively to monitor standards in schools, but tend to use the results 'professionally', which means privately.

Public exam results

By contrast, public exam results are now analysed rather more publicly, particularly in the wake of the 1980 Education Act which requires schools to produce their results for the benefit of parents. The DES analyses these exam results. The English School Leavers Survey – essentially a statistical analysis of exam results – says: 'Taken over the six years (1977/8 to 1983/4) the qualifications of school leavers have shown modest but steady improvement.'[8] But of course this is not proof that 'standards' are rising. Statistics of this kind are virtually meaningless because GCE grading is largely norm-referenced (when grades are awarded on the basis of how a student fares in comparison with other candidates) rather than criterion-referenced (where there is an attempt to compare a student's performance with some 'absolute' standard). If this is the case, the number of passes will increase automatically as the number of candidates rises (to keep the proportion of passes stable) even if the overall performance of candidates does not rise. Nevertheless, the accusation that, for example, A levels are wholly norm-referenced is vehemently denied by the senior examiners who play the key role of carriers of standards from year to year.

Another problem is that the content of exams is different from year to year and this reflects changes in the syllabus. A Schools Council study of the feasibility of comparing standards of grades awarded in 1963 and 1973 in A Level English literature, mathematics and chemistry (basically by getting 1973 examiners to mark 1963 scripts) concluded that changes in syllabuses and methods of examining over the period made it impossible to draw conclusions about changes in standards.[9] These conclusions effectively disqualify public examination results from being used to make statements about general levels of educational performance.[10] So public exam results are analysed publicly, but cannot be used to comment on standards accurately.

Will the GCSE be any better at telling us whether 'standards' are going up or down? It can only do that, of course, if it becomes a true criterion-referenced examination. Since the development of grade related criteria is causing many problems at the moment, it seems a long way off.

The Assessment of Performance Unit (APU)[11]

We do, of course, have a national assessment programme which was set up with a brief to monitor standards. The APU is a unit within the DES which supervises the national assessment of performance in maths, language, science, modern languages and design for technology. Although the APU was set up at a time of concern over the education of minority children and has as one of its tasks to identify 'under-achievement', in reality its main task, as far as the DES was concerned, was to operate as an indicator of educational standards and to give ministers information on whether, and by how much, these were rising or falling.[12]

The APU has made little progress on its task of providing information on standards and how these are changing, because there is a major technical problem in measuring changes in performance on tests over time. That is, changes large enough to be meaningful will only be detected over a number of years, at least four or five, and any serious monitoring of performance would go on over a longer period than that. For example, the NFER national reading surveys ran from 1948–72.

The problem is that the same test used over that sort of period becomes dated. The curriculum changes, teaching changes, and society changes, thus affecting, for example, our use of language. Thus the test becomes harder and standards will seem to fall. To make the test 'fair' it is necessary to update it, but then you cannot compare the results on the modified version of the test with the results on the original form because it is not a true comparison.

> The problem here is that various statistical techniques are needed to calculate comparable difficulty levels and there is no consensus on which of them is satisfactory. It seems that 'absolute' measures of change over time are difficult if not impossible to obtain and, at most, we can only hope to measure 'relative' – between group – changes.[13]

In the early 1980s the APU had to drop the controversial Rasch technique of analysing difficulty levels of test items and admit that it could not comment on trends over time, i.e., 'standards'. What it does do, however, is use a pool of common items which it deems not to have dated and looks at performance on those over the four years of the original surveys. This gives some guide to what is happening to levels of performance, but the pool will, however, decrease over time.

What the maths work has shown is that, on these items, there has been a small but significant increase in the percentage of children passing at both 11 and 15 between 1978 and 1982. More interestingly, perhaps, what they have also shown is that some sex differences in mathematics performance which are thought to appear at adolescence are, in fact, present at 11. At 11, boys are ahead of girls on measures but behind on computation, while, at 15, boys are ahead on both. The 11 year old finding has not shown up before because standard maths tests usually combine the two elements and report a single score.[14] The reporting of a single score is something the APU teams have by and large avoided on the grounds that there is far more useful information to be gained in looking at performance in different sets of skills or areas of the curriculum. Of course, the problem is that this sort of detailed information is much more difficult to digest and to handle; what many politicians and members of the public would like is a single figure, like the old reading quotient.

We can see that what the APU is doing, therefore, rather than making comments about overall levels of performance or standards, is comparing the performance of sub-groups at points in time, for example, boys and girls, regions of the country and children with different levels of provision of science equipment, laboratory accommodation, etc. This has been one of the main activities of the APU over the last 4–5 years, and could be described as looking at 'relatively low performance', which is the unit's working definition of under-achievement.

Although the APU can only make the most tentative comments about changes in levels of performance in the way that the general public, if you like, would expect, its results can be used to give hard facts about what children of 11 and 15 can do in certain subjects. For example, when the Chairman and Chief Executive of

Jaguar Cars claimed that of the young people applying for apprenticeship a third 'couldn't even add up six plus nine', the Deputy Director of Education for Coventry responded by pointing out the disparity between this comment and the findings of the APU. After all the APU had reported that 94 per cent of 15 years olds could add two *four-digit* figures.[15] The same article reported the Minister for Information Technology as saying 'Schools are turning out dangerously high quotas of illiterate, innumerate, delinquent unemployables'. The appraisal of the findings of the APU Language Team reported, however, that 'No evidence of widespread illiteracy was discovered. On the contrary the evidence is that most pupils have achieved a working literacy by the age of 11' and 'No collapse of standards was discovered. Over the five years of the surveys, improvements in the performance of primary pupils was evidenced, while secondary performance remained "fairly static".'[16] There is, of course, always room for politicians to ignore the data if it does not suit them, and for educationists to argue over its meaning.

To try and sum up this section, we must conclude that, although there is a great deal of testing and examining in the school system, it can only provide us with limited information on standards of performance. This is for a number of reasons: at LEA testing level because of the limited number of subjects covered, and private/ professional use of results; at public exam level because of the norm-referenced approach which does not permit measure of 'absolute' standards; at national level because of the difficulties in analysing tests which have to change in content over extended periods of time. However, the current emphasis of the Government seems to be to use tests to *set* (and raise) standards rather than to measure them.[17]

Using tests to set standards

The idea that tests can measure standards in education is one thing. The idea that testing can raise standards is quite another, yet this has received even less critical attention. The implicit belief among some of those who are concerned about standards is that introducing a testing programme will raise standards. The publication of exam results was seen as being one way of maintaining standards, an argument foreshadowed in a leaflet produced by the National Council of Educational Standards.[18] This essay suggests 17 ways of 'improving standards in our schools' including monitoring through tests, exams, and HMI full inspections, the results of which should all be made public. The connection between testing and improved performance is, however, rarely made explicit. The stimulus (testing) is applied and the outcome (improved test performance) hoped for, but the process linking the two remains largely undiscussed; it is the 'black box' metaphor.

There are, however, various hypotheses about how the introduction of testing might result in improved test performance. At a general level there is the possibility that accurate estimates of performance levels will stir reaction (and reform) that will in turn lead to higher levels of performance.[19] This reaction may take several forms:

1 It may result in teaching to the test, which is quite likely to result in improved performance on the test, as an American newspaper quote illustrates below, but if test results rise as a consequence of teaching to the test rather than as a consequence of some other change in the classroom process, what is such a rise worth?

2 It can focus attention on the subject area being tested. At the primary level we do know that in some cases heads have insisted on reading being timetabled for the fourth year classes, because LEA tests have been introduced for this age. We also know that, in an authority which tests maths at 11 using items from a bank, some teachers are quite open about spending more time on maths than they would otherwise choose to/or and of making certain that they cover the specified areas. But the latter could also be true, of course, of LEAs which have maths guidelines – it is not necessarily a consequence of testing programmes.

3 Curriculum backwash may occur: that is, test content may have an impact on teacher practice. We know that advisers choose certain tests because they want teachers to move their teaching in a certain direction. For example, the Edinburgh Reading Tests have been chosen by some LEA advisers, not only because of their diagnostic element, but also because they promote a wider view of reading which advisers would like to see their teachers embrace. Also, some advisers we have spoken to are frankly delighted with the content of the APU maths and science tests and wish them to affect the curriculum of their teachers, as did some of the headteachers in our sample. This is an example of what we would call 'positive backwash'. The received notion has been that backwash is bad, mostly on the grounds that tests concentrate on only a small part of the curriculum and the danger is that too much time can be spent in preparing for them. But the message we have also received from advisers and heads is that, sometimes, tests can be used as an engine of covert curriculum reform in order to enrich the curriculum, and certainly some of the APU test developments seem to have had this effect.[20]

4 Knowledge of results can have an impact. We know that it is common practice where results are analysed centrally for heads to receive their school's mean score each year together with the

authority or division mean score. If their mean score on a test is very different from that of the authority as a whole or from their own score last year, the head may well encourage staff to direct more attention to that subject, and we do know that this happens.

Two quotes from both sides of the Atlantic illustrate some of the problems which can be associated with testing. The first is from a local paper in California, the second from the Cockroft Report.

> *'Teaching to Test' Credited with Improvements in Basic Skills.* Students in San Diego County public schools scored better this year on every phase of the state's annual battery of basic skills tests, especially in districts gearing their curriculum to fit the exams . . . The lesson many school districts have drawn . . . is that if a school system wants to score high it should 'teach to the test'. 'That doesn't mean they're cheating', said Pierson (pupil services director) 'But they are moulding their curriculum to fit what the CAP tests'.[21]

> The availability of tests, however well-constructed, would not of itself lead to the increase of mathematical understanding . . . we seek. We are well aware of the dangers of subjecting pupils to more, and more frequent, testing and we accept that the combination of certain kinds of testing and teaching could produce results which are the opposite of those we desire.[22]

Thus the introduction of testing, whether LEA programmes such as those that already exist or new programmes to assess benchmarks, will not of itself bring about raised levels of performance, short of teaching to the test. It needs to be coupled with other moves to encourage enhanced performance, for example changes in teaching methods or content, or the provision of extra resources.

Current developments

At the local level the London Borough of Croydon is a particularly interesting example. Children there are tested on maths and reading at 7, 9 and 11 with non-verbal reasoning tests at 9 as well. This testing programme was introduced in 1985 with much opposition from the teaching unions. The LEA's parents guide 'Primary Education in Croydon' sets out aims and objectives for primary schools. The guide states that the children are given the tests so that 'their performance can be measured against set standards'.[23] Ultimately the LEA plans to introduce tests in other subjects areas, linked closely with curriculum guidelines, in order to produce a profile of each child in all areas of the curriculum at 7, 9, 11 and 14.

However, for the moment schools are judged on this limited range of performance and each school's results reported to the Education Committee. Each (named) school is given a profile including the number and percentage of pupils scoring above or below the Croydon mean. On this basis year-by-year comparisons are made within a school and between schools. Any school which has interesting scores – that is particularly high or low, or which vary considerably from those of neighbouring schools – is visited by the inspectorate.

This then is the new form of LEA testing programme and it differs in a number of significant respects from those we observed five years ago. First, although the tests are the same – short, standardised and only covering the basic skills – they are linked to defined (albeit loosely) objectives for different ages. Secondly, there is the intention to link the assessment with detailed curriculum guidelines, rather than to let them 'float free'. Finally, named school results are presented to the Education Committee and selected schools are followed up by formal visits from inspectors.

There are those who see in this a reductionist approach to education which limits the teacher's professional role and imposes an unacceptable burden of testing on young children; while there are others who see it simply as good sense, good management and the best way of providing accountability to parents.

The effect of this assessment and curriculum package on schools and children will be keenly observed, not least by the parents and teachers in Croydon. It is too soon yet to know how it will turn out or how many other LEAs will adopt a similar approach. Interestingly, the London Borough of Brent announced in 1986 that they were going to set attainment targets in the basic skills for their primary children because of concern about under-achievement. The LEA will then draw up guidelines setting out what should be achieved in teaching basic skills.[24] Thus we have two London Boroughs, Croydon and Brent, which are politically very different, but making similar moves.

However, many LEAs may be holding back from developing new assessment programmes until it is clear what the DES intends to do about benchmarks and their assessment.

In October 1986 Mr Baker, Secretary of State for Education, said that he wished to see attainment targets for children of different ages developed on the grounds that they would help pupils to achieve the best performance they were capable of.[25]

Mr Baker's comments can be foreshadowed in Eric Bolton's (Senior Chief HMI) comments in November 1985:

Much of the work on assessment and evaluation to date is biased towards the secondary phase. We lack broad agreement about how to describe and scrutinise the primary curriculum. The absence of clarity and agreement about what children should be capable of at various stages of their primary education leads to a distinct lack of information about standards of pupil achievement in individual primary schools and a consequent difficulty of establishing any standards of achievement as a basis for an assessment of performance.[26]

The blue-print for a national curriculum now includes attainment targets which take account of the need to differentiate between pupils of diverse abilities and aptitudes.[27] As Lawton points out:

> an essential feature of the Baker plan is to have age-related benchmark testing. This has all sorts of bureaucratic advantages in terms of presentation of statistics and making comparisons between teachers and schools. But age-related testing makes it very difficult to avoid normative procedures, norm-related criteria, and judgements based on the expectations of how a statistically-normal child should perform.[28]

There has been a considerable amount of concern voiced over the effect of testing children and labelling some as failures. Mr Baker does not seem concerned about this however:

> In his conference speech he poured scorn on the non-competitive schooling advocated by Left-led Labour authorities . . . 'It has become rather unfashionable to give tests to children today because there is the belief that that segregates the winners from the losers,' he said. Parents knew such an approach was bogus.[29]

It is not at all clear what form the assessment of attainment targets – or as they are now more commonly called benchmarks – will take, particularly since some HMI now seem concerned about whether benchmarks would be helpful, and about the dangers of introducing a national testing programme. To add to the confusion the former chief HMI for primary education, who thinks that widely accepted benchmarks would be helpful, has said that they do not need to be followed by mechanical testing.[30]

Murphy has considered the implications of assessing a national curriculum[31] and I have already covered much of the ground in this paper. However, in addition to the concerns over teaching to the test and narrowing the curriculum to what is testable, I believe one of the most worrying aspects of the attainment targets plan is the suggestion that they be differentiated. No doubt this is meant to reduce the amount of failure young children will be exposed to. But the implication is that children will be categorised (and streamed?) from the age of 7 and this will have profound implications, not only for the children, but for the nature of primary education.

Conclusion

To summarise, attainment targets, benchmarks and their assessment, are in the melting pot at the moment. It is hard to predict their eventual form, or what LEAs will do to set up their own testing programmes, but clearly testing is firmly on the agenda to set and raise standards. What I hope to have made clear in this paper is that to use testing to set, raise, or measure standards is not as straightforward a task as some would have us believe.

Acknowledgments

I should like to thank Harvey Goldstein and Richard Pring for their helpful comments on a draft of this Chapter.

References

1 *Education*, 2 July 1982.
2 D. P. Resnick (1980), 'Educational policy and the applied historian: testing, competency and standards', *Journal of Social History*, June.
3 *Times Educational Supplement*, 27 June 1986.
4 D. Lawton (1987), 'The role of legislation in educational standards', *NUT Education Review*, 1, 1.
5 *Sunday Times*, 12 April 1987.
6 C. Gipps, S. Steadman, T. Blackstone, and B. Stierer (1983), *Testing children: standardised testing in Local Education Authorities and schools*, London, Heinemann Educational.
7 C. Gipps, H. Gross and H. Goldstein (1987), *Warnock's 18%: Children with special needs in the primary school*, Lewes, Falmer Press.
8 *Times Educational Supplement*, 27 June 1986.
9 T. Christie and G. M. Forrest (1980), *Standards at GCE A-level: 1963 and 1973*, London, Macmillan Educational Books.
10 H. Goldstein (1986), 'Models for equating test scores and for studying the comparability of public examinations', in D. Nuttall (ed.), *Assessing Educational Achievement*, Lewes, Falmer Press.
11 Some of this section is taken from the author's paper 'The APU: monitoring children?', *NUT Education Review*, 1, Spring.
12 C. Gipps and H. Goldstein (1983), *Monitoring children: An evaluation of the Assessment of Performance Unit*, London, Heinemann Educational Books.
13 H. Goldstein (1983), 'Measuring changes in educational attainment over time: problems and possibilities', *Journal of Educational Measurement*, 20, 4, Winter.
14 Cambridge Institute of Education (1985), 'New perspectives on the mathematics curriculum: an independent appraisal of the outcomes of APU mathematics testing 1978–82', London, HMSO.
15 *Times Educational Supplement*, 16 May 1986.
16 G. Thornton (1986), 'APU language testing 1979–1983: an independent appraisal of the findings', London, HMSO, pp. 71 and 78.
17 *Times Educational Supplement*, 10 April 1987.
18 V. Bogdanor (1979), *Standards in Schools*, National Council for Educational Standards.
19 H. Acland (1981), 'Beliefs about testing: the case of the NAEP', University of Southern California, unpublished paper.
20 C. Gipps (1987), 'The APU: from Trojan Horse to Angel of Light', *Curriculum*, 8, 1.
21 San Diego Union, California (1982), 'County Students Improve CAP Scores', 2 December, p. B-1.
22 W. H. Cockroft (ed.) (1982), *Mathematics counts: Report of the committee of inquiry into the teaching of mathematics in schools*, London, HMSO, para. 552.
23 Croydon LEA (1985), 'Primary Education in Croydon', Croydon LEA, p. 9.
24 *Times Educational Supplement*, 1 August 1986.
25 *Times Educational Supplement*, 3 October 1986.
26 *Times Educational Supplement*, 22 November 1985.

27 SCDC (1987), 'Towards a national curriculum: a response to initiatives on the need for a national curriculum', SCDC, March.
28 *Times Educational Supplement*, 1 May 1987.
29 *Daily Telegraph*, 9 February 1987.
30 *Times Educational Supplement*, 20 February 1987, 8 May 1987, and 21 April 1987.
31 R. Murphy (1987), 'Assessing a national curriculum', *Journal of Educational Policy*, Autumn.

3.3

Reflections on the Scientific Education of Girls

Catherine Manthorpe

Introduction

This Chapter was first given as a talk to the ASE Anglia Region meeting held to celebrate the fiftieth anniversary of the inauguration of the Cambridge and District Branch of the Association of Women Science Teachers (AWST). It begins with a consideration of the origins and work of the AWST and goes on to reflect on some of the issues raised by the present concern to ensure that all girls receive a balanced science education.

The AWST and science education

In 1951, Miss Mary Sutton, as President of the AWST, in her Presidential Address, spoke of the Association as 'quite the nicest body of women I have ever had any contact with, and I value immensely . . . the many friends I have made among its members'.[1] As a 'body of women' working predominantly in girls' schools, the Association was in an excellent position to give voice to what it regarded to be the most appropriate form of science education for girls. Indeed, the origins of the Association in 1912 lay in the perception of a group of women science teachers that girls' science education was facing a 'crisis'. These teachers, all members of the science section of the London Branch of the Association of Assistant Mistresses, felt that the formation of an Association of Science Teachers[2] was necessary because, as expressed in the early minutes of the Association,

> At the present time the science teaching in schools was passing through a critical period and that for the present at any rate it was useful for science teachers to band themselves together as a corporate whole and not to have their influence weakened by the votes of members who are not and have not been engaged in science teaching.[3]

The 'critical period' to which these minutes referred was the contemporary discussion on the introduction of domestic science as an alternative to traditional science in the girls' schools. The reasons for this interest related to public fears at the beginning of the twentieth century about the degeneracy of British society and the British race evidenced by the 1904 report of the Inter-Departmental Committee on Physical Deterioration. This report drew attention to:

> the extremely low standards of living and fitness apparent in the congested central districts of larger towns and cities. In accounting for these conditions, the authors of the report laid heavy emphasis on the habits and domestic organization of the inhabitants. Women in particular were blamed for their ignorance of household affairs, hygiene and nutrition, their diminished sense of maternal obligation and their wrong-headed notions of infant care.[4]

Attention was focused on the need for education in domestic subjects for all girls in all types of schools, including the girls' secondary schools. While the public elementary schools had included domestic economy in the curriculum for girls since the 1870s and before, hygiene and domestic economy were not centrally established – if present at all – in the curricula of the secondary schools for girls. Another reason for the interest in domestic science was the concern to reform what was regarded to be the overly formal and academic science curriculum and to make it more relevant to 'the chief business of girls' lives'.[5] Thus, it was felt that domestic science could at one and the same time, reform the traditional science curriculum for girls, quell anxieties about the level of domestic skill in the female population *and* reduce pressure on the overcrowded timetable found in the girls' schools. The AST opposed this move on the grounds that the replacement of traditional courses of physics and chemistry by domestic science would downgrade the intellectual advantages of the study of science, disrupt its logical sequence and have adverse consequences for those girls hoping to specialise in science or medicine at university. Such views coincided with those of other members of the female teaching profession who argued that 'the intellectual birthright must not be sold for skill in making puddings'.[6]

From those early beginnings the Association was concerned with the *access* of girls to science education and the *content* of that education. It repeatedly furnished official bodies with reports and memos about the difficulties of teaching science in girls' schools because of shortage of time, teachers, equipment and so on. The list of dissatisfactions sent to the Norwood Committee in 1942 is a representative example of the type of problems the members of the Association faced:

1 Too few good teachers of science.

2 Lack of appreciation by the Headmistresses of the need of time for science mistresses to prepare practical work, and a tendency to put non-science lessons into laboratories, thus further hampering preparation.
3 Large classes.
4 Lack of laboratory accommodation, inadequate buildings and equipment in some schools.
5 Lack of sufficient laboratory assistants.

A sixth complaint, reflecting perhaps something of the status of science in girls' schools was 'of the tendency, growing less but still prevalent, to ignore the cultural aspects of science, this is sometimes shown by the too great emphasis upon the study of languages'.[7]

In its efforts to improve the teaching of science the Association also spent long hours in deliberations over syllabuses, examination questions and the like. As well as drawing up its own syllabuses, the Association responded to what it perceived to be the male bias of the existing science syllabuses, by commenting, for example, on the amount of time devoted to mechanics and electricity and the way in which they were introduced. It was not that the Association thought that the study of mechanics or electricity was unimportant for girls, but as it stated in its response to the Science Masters' Association (SMA) general science syllabus, the way these subjects were introduced were 'thought to be better adapted to the needs of boys than of girls'. By contrast, the syllabuses of the AWST stressed the everyday, practical uses of mechanical and electrical knowledge, suggesting that fuses, electric irons, electric bells, light, telegraph and telephone could be used to illustrate the subject matter. Such criticisms are not unknown in relation to contemporary science syllabuses and are being taken up in some current curriculum initiatives.

Throughout its lifetime the Association was the professional association to which official bodies turned for opinion and advice on the scientific education of girls. From our current perspective, with the concern that has been expressed over the last decade about the so-called 'underachievement' of girls in science and technology it seems a little ironic that the AWST amalgamated with the SMA when it did. Of course, at that time, in 1963, it might have seemed the obvious thing to do. The integrity of an identifiable female science teaching profession was being eroded by several developments of postwar Britain. For example, the single sex, graded educational system was fast giving way to a co-educational, comprehensive system. Not only did this mean that the network of girls' schools – what might be called the 'institutional base' of the AWST – contracted, but also that the women's teaching profession lost some of its former power. Headmistresses were more likely to become deputy heads when a single sex school went co-educational than *vice versa*. The general shortage of scientists was felt in the schools by a shortage of science teachers and, in the girls' schools, this was exacerbated by the trend towards earlier marriage and the rapid turnover of part-time teachers. As one member regretfully stated in the 1950s, 'spinsters are a dying race', and with that went the time and commitment that single women could give to professional associations. Some girls' schools even had to employ science masters for the first time. By the late 1950s it seemed to many that the existence of an association which spoke for the needs of the scientific education of girls as opposed to all pupils was something of an anachronism.

Interestingly however, that period also brought the first murmurings of what has become a contemporary problem. By the late 1950s, with the increasing shortage of scientists and engineers, girls had been discovered to be, in the words of journalists, politicians and industrialists 'an untapped pool', 'wasted', 'a largely neglected source of recruitment', 'the biggest untapped source of scientists and engineers'. This cry was taken up even more strongly at the end of the 1970s and has continued throughout the present decade with the activities of the 1984 'Women into Science and Engineering' (WISE) year being the most recent major initiative. These concerns of state and industry are clearly concerns about the shortage of trained personnel rather than with women's education as such, and one can expect that when we no longer have a shortage of scientists and engineers this focus on the scientific education of girls will diminish. However, other voices have been raised in the past decade over this issue. Those who believe in equal opportunities for boys and girls have been concerned that girls' lack of scientific qualifications has meant that they are severely disadvantaged when it comes to future career opportunities. A more radical view has suggested that the under-representation of girls in science is evidence of a fundamental disharmony between the pursuit of science and being female. This view has added fuel to the growing feminist critique of the assumptions, structures and practices of contemporary science.

A third perspective has come from science educators who, from the early 1970s, began to express concern that girls were 'opting out' of the physical sciences. Their concern has been related not only to the instrumental values of science education but also to the belief that science is a particular and distinct form of knowledge which should not be absent from a balanced education. This concern has led to a wide variety of 'affirmative action' projects which have aimed to encourage more girls to study science at school.[8]

After more than a decade of concern for the scientific education of girls it is time to 'take stock' of what has been achieved, what has been learnt and what remains to be done. In what follows I propose to take issue with some aspects of the current debate and reclaim for the historical record some of the work of the AWST which sadly has been forgotten.

The historical legacy

First of all, I fear that what has often not been considered in the contemporary discussion of why girls don't choose science at school is the historical legacy of the present situation in which boys generally follow the physical sciences and girls the biological sciences. In our recent history, as noted above, girls' schools were less materially well off and consequently less able to provide the full range of sciences to their students. The girls' schools that did offer the full range of sciences were exceptional to the majority of schools for girls, and later mixed schools, which perhaps encouraged the study of botany or approached the study of science through the study of domestic economy, hygiene and later biology. Even as late as 1973 it was found that in some schools girls and boys were being offered different science options. It is interesting to go back even earlier to the period before formal schooling was institutionalised in a systematic way in the mid- to late-nineteenth century to examine the functions scientific knowledge served in the education of girls, and the significance this had for the later development of school science education for girls. It is not possible, however, to speak of the functions of scientific knowledge without first a brief discussion of the social context in which it was introduced. This must necessarily be a mere sketch with rather broad generalisations.

The period of the late eighteenth and early nineteenth centuries was one of conservative reaction and retrenchment following reform agitation and Jacobinism inspired by the French revolution. Such conservative sentiments left their legacy in the social and cultural spheres in the 'revolution of manners and morals' effected by an alliance between Evangelicalism and Utilitarianism. Large sections of the English upper and middle classes, shaken by the revolutionary fervour in France, turned to the revivalist church for what has been called 'a spiritual re-ordering of society'. Jacobinism was conceived as a 'moral malady' which could only be cured by a stiff dose of 'vital religion' – a 'practical Christianity' in which 'godliness, cleanliving and patriotism were inescapably joined'. For women it was this 'revolution' which had profound and lasting effects, promoting as it did a specific notion of femininity which was expressed most fully in the Victorian concept of the 'perfect lady' and the complementary sexual attitudes. Science became the perfect leisure time activity for these classes conforming as it did to the stipulation that amusements should be moral, private, cheap, quiet and non-sensual. What better than the study of botany to show up the order of God's universe?[9]

For girls these religious and moral aspects of science were deemed particularly beneficial. As one writer, Maria Edgeworth, stated in her book *Letters for Literary Ladies* in 1795:

> Botany has become fashionable, in time it may be useful if it be not already. Chemistry will follow botany. Chemistry is a science well-suited to the talents and situation of women; it is not a science of parade, it affords occupation and infinite variety; it demands no bodily strength; it can be pursued in retirement; it applies immediately to useful and domestic purposes; and whilst the ingenuity of the most inventive mind may in this science be exercised, there is no danger of inflaming the imagination because the mind is intent upon realities, the knowledge that is acquired is exact and the pleasure of the pursuit is the reward of the labourer.[10]

Similarly, Priscilla Wakefield in her *Introduction to Botany* of 1798, wished that the study of botany:

> become a substitute for some of the trifling, not to say pernicious objects that too frequently occupy the leisure of young ladies of fashionable manners, and by employing their faculties rationally act as an antidote to levity and idleness.[11]

With a slightly different emphasis, Jane Marcet, author of the famous *Conversations on Chemistry*, which was addressed particularly to 'the female sex', believed that:

> A woman may obtain such a knowledge of chemistry as will not only throw an interest on the common occurrences of life but will enlarge the sphere of her ideas and render the contemplation of nature a source of delightful instruction.[12]

Scientific knowledge for girls then, was seen as a way of improving their manners and morals. Any sense of the *application* of such knowledge was limited strictly to the domestic sphere. A turning point for the higher education of girls was the publication of the report of the Schools Inquiry Commission in 1868 which had included in its terms of reference girls' schools. Not only did this reveal what little provision there was for girls, but also that some schools for girls were providing quite a good education in science. Two headmistresses – the famous Miss Beale of Cheltenham Ladies College and Miss Buss of the North London Collegiate School for Girls – gave evidence to the Commission. For Miss Beale, the study of science appeared to be undertaken for the same reasons as earlier in the century. In her words, 'not for pride of intellect but a subduing sense of the great responsibility which all God's gifts involve'. For Miss Buss, however, who was actively involved in the campaign for the higher education of women it may be inferred that science had a firm place in the curriculum because of her desire that girls' education should be the same as boys'. Later, as noted above, another reason for teaching science to girls also developed during the latter years of the nineteenth century and this was connected to the role it could play in ensuring girls' efficiency in housewifery and social arts.

What happened in the development of the girls' high school was that alongside courses in physics, chemistry and botany, sometimes taught in purpose-built laboratories, were courses in hygiene, physiology and later domestic science – courses which were not to be found in the corresponding boys' schools.

In spite of the diversification of educational provision in the early years of the twentieth century, the philosophy behind science education in the girls' high schools lasted at least until the 1960s. This philosophy, in the words of Sophie Bryant, headmistress of the North London Collegiate School for Girls (1895–1918) was that science education was primarily an intellectual pursuit 'calculated to develop each one in accordance with his proper end as a moral, rational and serviceable being'.[13] Professional opportunities which may have derived from the study of science were, of course, not ignored, and were an added advantage, but the place of science in the curriculum was consistently justified on these intellectual, cultural and 'civic minded' grounds. Given its base in the girls' high schools, the AWST was also a strong advocate of this view of science education.

Of course, only a minority of girls were educated in the girls' high schools and some account should be given of the functions of science education in the schools which catered for the majority of children. In the nineteenth century these were the elementary schools which in the twentieth century developed into the primary schools and the various forms of secondary education. In these schools, the historical evidence suggests that the most common route to a science education for girls was through domestic economy, hygiene, physiology, 'laws of health' and later biology and domestic science. As in the earlier part of the nineteenth century the scientific knowledge was by no means an end in itself but served the purpose of giving girls the knowledge they would require for the role in life it was assumed they would fulfil – motherhood – and those professions which were most closely linked to this role, such as nursing. Thus, in 1962 out of 115 secondary modern schools questioned, only eighteen offered physics and chemistry to girls, twenty-five offered general science and two offered zoology in the sixth form, the remaining seventy only offered biology. Apart from the shortage of science teachers this was explained by:

1 'Girls' traditional interest in living things'
2 'The link with the preparation for nursing'

3 'Time table difficulties in mixed schools where science groups may often be filled with boys'.[14]

The point I am really making with these historical examples is that until girls were 'discovered' to be 'an untapped pool' of scientific talent in the 1950s and again in the 1970s educational attitudes and institutions, with the exception of the girls' high schools, had encouraged different courses for boys and girls on the grounds that their needs, interests and future lives would be different. In this the contemporary differences in the science choice between boys and girls must be seen not simply in terms of defective attitudes of girls, or girls' unwillingness or inability to take up the opportunities given to them, but rather more as a *social* problem related to how the functions of schooling have been defined for girls and boys in the past and how these definitions might still be operating, albeit at a more subtle level, in the present time.

Girl-friendly science?

The second point I wish to make is related to this. I am beginning to fear that in our concern to remedy the imbalance between boys and girls pursuing the sciences we may unintentionally reinforce the very differences we wish to abolish. In the past few years there have been the Girls Into Science and Technology (GIST) and Girls and Technology Education (GATE) projects, three international Girls and Science and Technology (GASAT) conferences and the WISE year. I support these initiatives and have worked with some of them, but the emphasis which they make on girls and science and technology, while influential in raising awareness of an important problem, also can lead to the problem being conceived in terms of one for, and about, girls rather than a problem for, and about, science education. There's no easy solution to this conundrum. As Margrit Eichler has noted: 'it is a general paradox of critical thought that a critique remains antithetically tied to what it criticises'.[15] Thus following her example of the atheist who, while trying to prove that God does not exist continues to emphasise the importance of God, it might be said that while trying to prove that girls are as capable at science as are boys we continue to emphasise that the issue is open to doubt.

I am fully in sympathy with those who coined, and use, the phrase 'girl-friendly science' to mean a science education which:

builds on girls' as much as boys' interests
stresses the social and human applications of science in everyday life
ensures girls' participation in science lessons as much as boys'
makes no distinction between girls and boys choosing science.[16]

However, I have reservations about how the term is received outside what might be called the 'girls and science' community. As one enthusiast of the term herself recognised, although the suggestion of a 'girl-friendly science' is 'not to produce girl-friendly science for girls and to leave the traditional boy-friendly science for boys' but to reform the science education of all, 'there is always a danger that teachers will use it in this way'.[17] This is one way in which a strategy which aims to reduce sex differences in science may actually produce an opposite effect. Another might be to attempt to reduce sexism in science textbooks. Geoffry Walford asks, do we go for short-term objectives – that is an increase in the number of girls studying science at school – or long-term objectives – changing the nature of gender role socialisation and the sexual division of labour in scientific work. He argues that some recent initiatives involving changing the representation of science in textbooks by including images that are more stereotypically feminine and which appeal more strongly to girls' interests (interests which he contends are the product of a particular socialisation process) meet these short-term goals, but by consolidating already existing gender differences do nothing for the longer-term objectives of changing the sex bias to be found in scientific occupations.[18] As with the suggestion that we should 'feminise' science education by including more activities with which girls might be more familiar, there is a danger that the wrong message is received not only by girls and boys but the teachers themselves.

These problems point to the possibility that there is a danger of treating girls' achievement in science as somehow distinct from the question of science education in general. Yet as Roy Schofield said more than a decade ago: 'If we are concerned that girls are not taking the opportunities afforded them to study science, it is very important that we critically examine the justifications we propose for having the subject as part of the curriculum for anybody.'[19] I wonder if it isn't time to change the terms of the debate away from girls' 'failure' or 'underachievement' in science and ask instead, 'what is science education *for*?'. Similarly, instead of asking why *girls don't* choose science we could ask why *boys do* choose science. This opens a whole new perspective on the issue.

To take the first question first – 'what is science education for?' – it becomes clear that the answer that we give – or that has been given in the past – has strong implications for what is in the science curriculum and thus can affect who chooses to pursue the subject. For example, if it is said that we teach science to ensure an adequate supply of trained scientists and technologists for our society and its international competitive standing and so on (and it is now commonplace to cite the launch of the Sputnik rocket in the 1950s as the catalyst for reform in American and British school science education) then, first, in a society in which there is a fairly clear sexual division of occupations and in which the scientific is linked (with notable exceptions) to the 'male sphere' we can hardly expect girls either to rush into the subject or be interested in the content of the curriculum, conversely boys, if only for pragmatic, instrumental reasons *will* be attracted to the subject. Second, such a rationale would mean that the science curriculum would be geared to training future scientists rather than to the scientific education of all, and this could easily lead to a narrowness of approach appealing only to the most scientifically gifted and committed.

If, however, it was said that science was to be taught in schools because it is an important aspect of human knowledge and culture without an understanding of which no child's education would be complete, then it would seem that a different approach would have to be taken to the construction of the science curriculum. Such an approach might be less academic than current science courses, based on social relations and absolutely relevant to modern interests and applications. It could involve some science history and be child centred rather than subject centred. It might aim for a balance between pure and applied science, individual practical work and demonstrations, theory and practice. Subjects relating to 'everyday life' would be used throughout the course. All types of audio-visual aids would be used as well as visits to places of scientific interest along with visits from outside speakers for lectures and discussions.

These proposals are nothing new and in fact are drawn from the AWST Interim Report on Reconstructional Problems in Post-Primary Science Education of 1944. The topicality of these proposals – with their hint of 'girl-friendliness' – is perhaps both measure of the broad-ranging approach of the AWST to science education and of the resistance that continues to exist to change in a professionally-oriented science curriculum. Of course, our society does need scientists and technologists but so does it need a scientifically literate population which both understands the science and technology which plays such a central part in contemporary life and has a sense of responsible control over that science and technology. It is a great cause for concern if girls are disadvantaged more than boys in both these aspects of science education, but the question must be, as Schofield says, whether we *impose* scientific failure on girls – and some boys – through our choice of science curriculum, and whether by examining the reasons and justifications for science education we cannot find different ways of approaching the 'girls and science' problem.

Education or training?

My third, and final point, is that I am beginning to wonder how far in our concern for the scientific education of girls we also perhaps overemphasise the importance of science education to the detriment of the humanities and the arts – (is it no more than a coincidence that girls tend to excel in these areas?). There are two possible consequences to this overemphasis. The *first* is that it can contribute to the growing belief that the only legitimate knowledge is that which is measurable, statistically significant or the product of 'data'. Conversely, thinking, feeling, dreaming – in other words the emotional and affective sphere, as well as those areas of knowledge which rely as much on perception and judgement as quantitative analysis – are correspondingly delegitimised and human thought and action becomes dangerously impoverished. *Secondly*, in all the discussion of girls' underachievement in science, little has been said of the 'underachievement' of boys in other areas of the curriculum. From statistics of examination entries it is clear that not only is human biology to boys what physics is to girls, but art, music, French, German and English literature are similarly to boys what mathematics and chemistry are to girls. Isn't this side of 'underachievement' also an educational and social problem about which we should be concerned? And, what effect will it have on relations between the sexes if one half of the population develops in one direction and one half in the other?

Of course, science educators may well retort that it is not up to science education either to effect social change or to ensure that all pupils develop all aspects of their 'humanness' – that is the function of the school curriculum as a whole. But, the question which still needs to be addressed is how far and in what ways should science education relate to the total school curriculum. Again, this is not a new question, but one which, in an age of early specialisation, has perhaps become obscured. What the 'girls and science' problem indicates is that this is a question which needs to be revived, and here, the hopes for science education expressed by a former president of the AWST are still relevant for science educators today:

> We must not let ourselves forget that our function in schools as science teachers is to educate, not just fit, girls for the narrow groove of some particular branch of pure and applied science . . . Scientific training in schools should form part of a general education. Through it the child should come to see that science forms part of our culture. We as science teachers must share with our colleagues on the arts side the task of trying to develop balanced human beings as well as helping to give potential scientists a broad and sturdy foundation on which to base their future work and so become better scientists.[20]

Notes and references

1 Quoted in Layton, D. (1984), *Interpreters of Science: A History of the Association for Science Education*, John Murray/ASE, p. 63.
2 The Association for Science Education (AST) changed its name to the Association of Women Science Teachers (AWST) in 1922.
3 AST (1912), *Minutes of the General Meeting*, 23 November.
4 Dyhouse, C. (1977), 'Good wives and little mothers – social anxieties and the schoolgirls' curriculum', *Oxford Review of Education*, 3, (1), 22.
5 Smithells, A. (1906), 'School training for the home duties of women', *Annual Report of the British Association for the Advancement of Science*, p. 781.
6 Quoted in Milburn, J. (1969), *The Secondary School Mistress: A Study of Her Professional Views and their Significance in the Educational Developments of the Period, 1895–1914*, unpublished PhD thesis, University of London, p. 243. For a more detailed discussion of domestic science see Manthorpe, C. (1986), 'Science or domestic science? The struggle to define an appropriate science education for girls in early twentieth-century England', *History of Education*, 15 (3), 195–213.
7 AWST, *Minutes of the Meetings of the Executive Committee*, 17 April 1942.
8 See for example, Harding, J. (1983), *Switched Off: The Science Education of Girls*, Longman for Schools Council; Whyte, J. (1986), *Girls Into Science and Technology*, Routledge and Kegan Paul.
9 Kitteringham, G. S. (1981), *Studies in the Popularization of Science in England, 1800–30*, unpublished PhD thesis, University of Kent; Taylor, B. (1983), *Eve and the New Jerusalem*, London, Virago, pp. 12–14.
10 Edgeworth, M. (1814), *Letters for Literary Ladies*, 4th edn, Johnson and Co.
11 Wakefield, P. (1798), *An Introduction to Botany*, 2nd edn, E. Newbery.
12 Marcet, J. (1806), *Conversations on Chemistry*, 6th edn, Longman and Co.
13 Bryant, S. (1898), 'The curriculum of a girls' school', *Special Reports on Educational Subjects*, 2, 99–132.
14 Gurr, C. E. (1963), *Modern School Girls*, Middlesex County Council, p. 38.
15 Eichler, M. (1980), *The Double Standard – a Feminist Critique of Feminist Social Science*, Croom Helm, p. 13.
16 Whyte, J., op. cit., p. 91.
17 Kelly, A. (1985), 'The construction of masculine science', *British Journal of the Sociology of Education*, 6, (12), 133–54.
18 Walford, G. (1983), 'Science textbook images and the reproduction of sexual divisions in society', *Research in Science and Technology Education*, 1, (1), 65–72.
19 Schofield, R. (1975), 'Teaching science: alternative justifications', in *Girls and Science and Technology – Cause for Concern?*, Chelsea College, Centre for Science Education, p. 25.
20 Raeburn, J. K. (1955–56), 'Presidential Address', *AWST Annual Report, 1955–56*, p. 11.

3.4

Now You See It, Now You Don't: the History of Home Economics – a Study in Gender

Dena Attar

The history of home economics is unique in many respects. Taught almost exclusively to girls, under various names, for over a century it is both one of the oldest and one of the most recently reconstructed of school subjects. Its existence originated and maintained gender differentiation within the curriculum (Purvis, 1985; Turnbull, 1987), and its effect on girls' education as a whole, whether or not they actually studied it, has been incalculable and largely deleterious. The importance and value claimed for it by its supporters over the years can hardly be exaggerated. One 1878 schoolbook informed girls that their study of domestic economy was divinely ordained; in 1988 campaigners hoping for its inclusion in the national curriculum argued that it was as vital to the quality of life as the three 'Rs', and that its neglect would lead to an increase in child abuse (Attar, forthcoming). On the other hand the claim that it is a valuable and useful subject has never been seriously tested and its actual content has been given little attention, the most likely reason being the low status associated with its identity as a girls' subject.

There have been two historical periods when home economics teaching was seen as controversial, although in both cases the content of the subject was less at issue than the question of to whom it should be taught. The traditional ground of opposition has been equal opportunities: girls made to study domestic subjects were effectively, and often explicitly, being denied access to other areas of the curriculum offered to boys. It is no coincidence that disputes about home economics teaching occurred when wider campaigns for women's equality were being waged, and died down alongside them when they lapsed.

Between the last years of the nineteenth century and the First World War, the controversy centred on girls in secondary rather than elementary schools, who were middle class rather than working class. The quality and content of domestic economy teaching in elementary and secondary schools did have its critics and there were attempts to make it more of a science (Manthorpe, 1986; Waring, 1985), but its place in the education of working-class girls was not questioned. Prompted by the infant mortality rate, the Board of Education even suggested that the subject be expanded to include more on infant care (Campbell, 1910), although at the same time the secondary schools attended by middle-class girls were successfully able to resist attempts to replace science with domestic science and were able to minimise the time spent on domestic subjects (Dyhouse, 1981; Manthorpe, 1986).

More recently, during the decade from approximately 1975 to 1985, the debate has centred on equal access, which in practice has meant the extent to which girls were either forced to take home economics rather than craft, design and technology or were under pressure to opt for it when they had a notionally free choice. The absence of boys from home economics has not been similarly viewed as cause for much concern, although the greatest gender imbalance among examination entries is still seen in home economics (DES, 1988). Despite the 1975 Sex Discrimination Act which made it illegal for schools to exclude boys from home economics, and the national criteria for GCSE which since 1986 have prohibited gender bias in examinations and syllabuses, the sex ratio has not altered much. Ten girls took O level or CSE home economics in 1975 for every boy; in 1985 there were nine girls for every boy (DES, 1988). Home economics has made a tortuous transition from a thoroughly gendered subject to one which is now claimed to be, or to be in the process of becoming, gender free (Wynn, 1983). This recent transformation raises large questions, and overshadowing them all is the question of its identity as a coherent subject area within the curriculum now that it is no longer in theory (however much it may be in practice) a girls' subject.

Home economics began its career as a school subject soon after the 1870 Education Act. Under one of its former names – domestic economy – it was made a compulsory subject for girls in elementary schools in 1878, although needlework had been obligatory since 1862 and girls could opt to be examined in domestic economy from 1875. At that time the syllabus was centrally controlled and defined quite inflexibly, in accordance with the 'Revised Code' of 1862 and with subsequent government Codes. These provided for school grants and hence, teachers' wages, to be paid in accordance with school attendance figures and with the results of examining the pupils – the notorious 'payments by results' system. School textbooks explicitly addressed girls as future wives and mothers, and occasionally too as prospective domestic servants. A working paper by the Home Economics Committee of HM Inspectorate in 1978 provided the following account of the subject's development:

> Home Economics was introduced into the curriculum of the secondary school in the nineteenth century and its aim at that time was to improve the living standards of the poor. Pupils were given instruction in cooking nutritious economical meals, making and caring for clothes and household articles, and observing the rules of hygiene. Cookery, sewing, housewifery and laundry work were seen as essential elements of the curriculum for girls.

This version of events is misleading in several respects, but it does suggest the confidence with which domestic economy teachers once went about their trade. Domestic economy is portrayed as having an aim which can be clearly and succinctly defined. 'Pupils were given instruction' in various techniques. Most importantly, it was simply 'essential' for elementary school girls to learn all four branches of domestic economy.

Domestic economy teaching in schools had its critics from the start, although they were not all in agreement about its faults (Attar, 1987). One traditional view was that such teaching was not the province of schools but belonged in the home – mothers ought to teach their own daughters. Some parents were opposed to their daughters undertaking heavy, dirty work, either on the grounds that such work would be beyond them at a young age, or because it was thought degrading and they wanted their children to escape such drudgery. There was also a well-founded suspicion that working-class girls were being taught domestic economy for the ultimate benefit of the middle classes who were anxious for better trained servants. The authors of one domestic economy textbook published in 1894 wrote that teachers should advise mothers to encourage their daughters into domestic service in preference to other occupations (Newsholme and Scott, quoted in Attar, 1987). Lastly, and most influentially for middle-class pupils, there were objections from feminist pioneers in the field of education who wanted to ensure that girls had access, as far as possible, to the same curriculum which was offered to boys (Dyhouse, 1981).

Advocates of domestic economy teaching defended themselves by pointing out the need to improve living standards in working-class homes, which were supposedly so bad because of the incompetence of working-class women. There was an urgent need for improvement, and they claimed the answer was to teach girls how to be better housewives, attacking those who objected as anti-progressive. Ailsa Yoxall (1913), in a history of domestic economy teaching written for the Association of Teachers of Domestic Science (ATDS), referred to the 'prejudices' of mothers who thought cookery classes a waste of time, and who were even more strongly opposed to laundrywork lessons. A much fairer account of

working-class parents' case against domestic subjects was presented
by Augusta Webster (1879) in an essay on the second Domestic
Economy Congress of 1878. She wrote:

> As to teaching household processes in the elementary schools, for elementary
> education it certainly is an evil that girls whose only opportunities of intellectual
> training are those given them at these schools, and whose school career is
> necessarily timed to terminate while they are still children, should have a large
> portion of their school hours appropriated to household arts which could be
> better learned with household practice.

Despite doing justice to parents' objections in a way Yoxall did
not, Webster saw the 'evil' of domestic economy appropriating so
much of girls' school time as a necessary one, because the 'evil' of
bad housekeeping in working-class homes was even worse. She
argued that although girls might learn little of use at school, they
would acquire the wish to learn more and would go willingly into
domestic service to complete their training. Better trained servants
would 'rehabilitate' domestic service, continuing a process which
would end, at last, with better housewives who would be capable of
passing their domestic skills on to the next generation themselves.

The message was that domestic life, for girls, took priority, even
though working-class women were much more likely than middle-
class women to be employed outside their homes. Provided girls
learned this lesson, it did not matter too much if schools were
unable to teach practical skills with any great measure of success.
Turnbull (1987) has shown that for needlework, similarly, motives
for teaching the subject were put forward which were moral rather
than educational – 'needlework as sedative'. Digby and Searby
(1981) argue that in this context the elementary schools were acting
as agents of social control, since 'bourgeois aspirations and middle-
class ideas of domestic respectability were presented to the working-
class schoolgirls in their elementary-school domestic instruction.'

I would add that the schools acted as agents of social control in
another way, since the existence of domestic economy teaching in
schools was based on the idea that working-class families lived in
poverty, disease and squalor because of the ignorance and deficient
skills of the average working-class woman. One speaker at the 1878
Domestic Economy Congress (quoted in Weddell, 1955) offered a
fairly typical view of the deplorable state of the homes of the
'labouring poor': 'it is not the low rate of wages, or the tyranny of
masters, or the greed of landlords which is the real root of their
miseries, but thriftlessness on the one hand, and intemperance on
the other, are the evil geniuses of our English households'.

The convenient argument that poverty and its consequences are
the fault of the poor was of course not new in 1878, nor has it
disappeared since. Yet barely transformed, this notion of the

irrelevance of economic conditions and the all-importance of unpaid female labour in determining the material circumstances of the poor was taken to justify the wholesale teaching of domestic economy. To paraphrase Augusta Webster, girls might not actually learn many practical skills, but they would at least learn the importance they ought to attach to the subject. In other words, they would learn to blame themselves for their domestic miseries, rather than any external agency.

In 1909 some members of the Fabian Women's Group set out to combat this view of the unthrifty, unskilled working-class woman by examining in minute detail the daily lives and weekly budgets of working-class families in Lambeth. They did not seek out the poorest households, but compiled their evidence from accounts provided by women trying to manage their homes and families on 'round about a pound a week', the title of the book written by Maud Pember Reeves (1913) to record their findings. The Fabian women wanted to prove the need for women to be paid, direct, a 'mother's allowance'. The survey disproved the middle-class belief that all except the feckless could live adequately on such incomes, and also showed that the status of women within the family had to be taken into account. Women could not organise the family budget in the most economical way and cook cheap nutritious meals when their husbands, as wage earners, assumed the right to dictate how their meals were cooked and to have a major share of the family's resources allocated to themselves.

Home economics teaching was not only unable to improve the diets and housing conditions of the poor while it overlooked the constraints on women which resulted from their economic dependence, but it was also often so impractical it was seen, even by some of its teachers, as largely useless. The elementary school syllabus was divided into three stages, as follows:

Stage I. Food; its composition and nutritive value. Clothing and washing.
Stage II. Food; its functions. The dwelling, warming, cleaning, and ventilation.
Stage III. Food; its preparation and culinary treatment. Rules for health; the management of a sick room.

Many pupils could not afford to pay for ingredients for cooking, and many schools had no facilities for practical work. As with other subjects, much teaching was by rote, and pupils were encouraged to memorise the textbooks on which examination questions were set. It is easy to exaggerate the difference in content between the syllabus offered to working-class and to middle-class girls. While it is true that working-class girls were being prepared for domestic futures as housewives or servants, and middle-class girls were expected to fulfil a somewhat different domestic role since they would employ servants (Purvis, 1985), teaching in the elementary schools was theoretical as well as practical, and there was sometimes little scope for the teaching of manual skills. Partly because it replaced science teaching for girls in elementary schools to an extent (Waring, 1985) and partly because it was taught as a theoretical subject, the domestic economy syllabus was a mixture of prescriptive advice and vaguely scientific explanation. In contrast some books addressed to middle-class pupils which assumed they would have servants to organise were mainly lists of instructions on various aspects of housekeeping (Attar, 1987).

Between 1880 and 1914 domestic economy gradually changed into domestic science. (Ehrenreich and English (1979) give a precise date of 1879 for the launch of 'domestic science' in the United States.) The tendency to base domestic instruction on some sketchy 'scientific' explanations was well established in domestic economy textbooks, and in other domestic manuals, well before 1887. As early as 1859 Isabella Beeton plagiarised Liebig – or more likely a secondary source – for the section on the composition of foods which went into *Household Management*. Earlier still, Robert Kemp Philip's *The Housewife's Reason Why* of 1857 purported to afford 'the manager of household affairs intelligible (i.e. scientific) reasons for the various duties she has to perform' (Attar, 1987). There were a range of forces poised to make domestic work a promising field for scientific intervention and general discussion including the movements for public health and for infant welfare, along with fashionable ideas about utility and thrift.

As several commentators have noted (Dyhouse, 1981; Purvis, 1985; Manthorpe, 1986) the secondary schools, not the elementary schools, were the site of the struggle between feminists opposed to the intrusion of domestic economy or domestic science into the curriculum for girls and those who advocated it, and this was related to the issue of what courses in science girls ought to follow. To a lesser extent a similar argument waged over higher education: shortly after a course in 'home science and economics' for women opened at King's College, London, to a cool welcome from feminists trying to secure access to higher education generally for women, Alice Ravenhill and Catherine Schiff published a collection of essays entitled *Household administration/its place in the higher education of women* (1910), which included the proposal that housewives should learn economics, bacteriology and 'sanitary science' purely in order to become more efficient at housework. While appearing to endorse further and higher education for women, Ravenhill, Schiff and others like them could not envisage or approve of any alternative purpose in female education beyond fitting women for domesticity.

In 1909 a new regulation for secondary schools stated 'Provision should be made in the case of girls for instruction of a practical character in the elements of housewifery. For girls over 15 years of age an approved course in domestic subjects may be taken instead of science'. Yoxall (1913) praised those headmistresses who linked 'the teaching in cookery with that of the science classes', but of those schools which instructed only the 'backward girls' in domestic arts she complained 'the whole principle of it was wrong and based on the fallacy that neither special aptitude nor much brain power is necessary for a good housewife'. Yet clearly secondary schools could only teach domestic subjects to girls at 15-plus if they stopped teaching them science, and secondary headmistresses who were still pioneers in the field of girls' education, ambitious for their schools and their pupils, would hardly have chosen to curtail their science teaching.

The ATDS in 1911 published 'Suggestions on the teaching of housecraft in secondary schools offered by the special committee appointed to consider this subject'. It recommended that 'a course of housecraft should form an essential part of a woman's education' and should be taught to all secondary school girls – no more opting out for the high-flyers. In their view 'the teaching of housecraft should always be preceded by an elementary course of practical science', with housecraft instruction postponed to the last two years of a girl's school life. The science and housecraft mistresses were urged to confer with one another, and to 'correlate their scheme of instruction as far as is practicable'. It is easy to see the benefits such a scheme would bring to the status of domestic subjects and their teachers, and their acceptability in secondary schools. For the science subjects, to correlate physics and chemistry teaching with the girls' forthcoming lessons on cookery, laundrywork and home management was hardly going to enhance their status and the 'elementary science' syllabus the ATDS proposed was predictably narrow and restricted. The only purpose in studying physics was apparently to learn about heat transference in a way which could be applied to cooking methods, while in chemistry girls would learn about air in connection with house ventilation, water in connection with washing, and about a few basic chemicals used in the home. The movement for more domestic science in secondary schools met determined opposition from science teachers particularly, and by 1918 it had evidently failed (Manthorpe, 1986).

Even among domestic subjects teachers themselves, there had been some resistance to the treatment of cookery, laundrywork and housewifery as branches of experimental science. The author of *Homecraft in the classroom* (Hill, 1914, quoted in Attar, 1987) wrote of her lessons: 'The work was always approached as some aspect of home-life, *never* as so-called "Domestic Science", which, alas, is frequently very doubtful science with nothing "domestic" about it at all.'

The resources for teaching domestic subjects as practical preparation for 'home-life', rather than as a science substitute, were gradually made available, particularly to girls in technical and secondary modern schools. The Hadow Report in 1926 urged local education authorities to expand provision for practical subjects, and include accommodation for them in all secondary schools, a directive followed up by the 1944 Education Act which stated that practical subjects had to be included in secondary education.

Girls in grammar schools were often still able to escape much domestic science teaching, although they were usually required to take needlework which inevitably displaced other curricular possibilities and ensured that gender differentiation was everywhere maintained. Newsom (1948), surveying the state of affairs in domestic science teaching, complained that while in secondary modern schools girls learnt 'often elaborate skills in cookery and laundry-work' in well-equipped classrooms, the grammar school girl was 'far too busy doing her homework and trying to discover the difference between a common and amorphous phosphorus to get down to such a sordid subject as Boeuf Bourguignonne or a Creme Caramel'. Leaving aside Newsom's extraordinary notions of what the grammar school, in other words middle-class, girl ought to learn in domestic science, it is interesting how closely his argument resembled the one put forward decades earlier by such defenders of domestic subjects as Yoxall, Ravenhill and Schiff. He conceded that practical teaching in school might be ineffective; the secondary modern schoolgirl forgot her 'elaborate skills' before she needed to use them. Nevertheless he ridiculed the idea of an exclusively academic curriculum for girls, and proposed that degree courses, as well as the entire secondary school curriculum, should be adapted to make them more relevant to what he saw as girls' inevitable destinies as housewives. According to Newsom, girls' education should not be like that of boys, but should be moulded in as many ways as possible to fit them to be wives and mothers.

In practice a minority of girls went to grammar schools, their numbers often kept down further than selection at 11+ would anyway have ensured in order to provide 'equal' access for boys who tended to do less well in the selection tests (Thom, 1987). The majority in secondary modern or technical schools were indeed provided with a very different, and domestically oriented, education. As Thom (1987) has noted, the postwar debate about intelligence testing and the inequalities of selective schooling skated over the whole question of gender differentiation. Technical education really meant manual skills training for boys, and the concept of a specific group of pupils who could be selected for their technical aptitude was arguably quite inconsistent when applied to girls, since all girls were supposed to have a domestic vocation and technical education for girls meant, in practice, yet more domestic education (McCulloch, 1985).

In the 1950s and 1960s the stress was on providing realistic conditions for housecraft teaching, as it was then known. This not only meant providing schools with model flats where pupils could practise their skills, a feature of provision referred to approvingly in the Newsom Report of 1963, but also entailed teaching the different branches of the subject in relation to each other. Pupils were not only taught craft skills, but were taught how to 'dovetail' their work, as Enid McIntosh, Chairman of the ATDS, explained (1955):

> It did not, then [after the Second World War], seem either sensible or practical to continue to teach girls to spend hours doing a simple task which, in their own homes, would have to be done quickly, if all the other work was to be fitted in. This led to a linking of all branches of housecraft into one field of activity so that the girls could learn to dovetail the work in the same way as would be done at home.

A new problem of relevance began to trouble teachers in the 1960s: how appropriate were the craft skills they taught to girls growing up in the late twentieth century? Clark (1970), wrote that 'one of the few parts of home economics that cannot, so far, be taken over by any other department, is our teaching of basic skills and their development'. Yet a considerable part of her book on cookery teaching was devoted to criticising the 'basic skills' most often taught – pastry and cake making. These were taught because they were popular and pupils – or their parents – were willing to pay for the basic ingredients. It is also likely that they featured so prominently in examination papers because the results were relatively easy to assess, in comparison with other products. A cake either rose or it didn't. Pupils learnt prescribed methods for various kinds of cake making and pastry making which kept practical cookery within orderly bounds. Clark was anxious that teaching should correspond more closely to patterns of good nutrition, and to the patterns of girls' future lives (she assumed throughout that pupils were invariably female). She also tried to address what was seen as the problem of 'multiculturalism', the subject of a number of articles in the ATDS journal *Housecraft* in the early 1970s, although it was a decade later before serious consideration was given to the question of cultural bias in assessment, and such bias has arguably not disappeared from home economics teaching materials (Attar, forthcoming).

The effect of the Sex Discrimination Act which became law in 1975 was that, even if nothing much actually changed in the classroom, teachers and examination boards had to prepare for change. Over 90 per cent of the pupils opting for home economics were still girls, but it could no longer be described officially as a girls' subject.

Contrasting statements from the 1980s about the teaching of home economics with earlier documents, the most striking change is that the confidence has gone. In other respects not only has surprisingly little changed, but with the introduction of the GCSE examination a greater degree of central government control has moved the subject closer towards the definitions of the last century, after a few decades of straying away. The latest redefinition of home economics has been the most difficult for its practitioners. In the past, it could be taught to girls simply as 'essential', an often repeated word, for their future lives as housewives. As a science, it had never quite managed to establish itself, and as a set of craft skills the traditional syllabuses made it difficult to teach and assess within a multicultural setting.

Recent writing on home economics is preoccupied with these issues even though the question of gender is rarely raised explicitly. The new definitions are often curiously hard to read, tending to avoid concrete subjects as much as possible (to avoid gender and cultural bias) and giving wide-ranging, vague and abstract explanations of the purpose of home economics. Starting in 1975 with the change in the law, the Schools Council set up a three-year research and development project with the title 'Home economics in the middle years'. It had a fairly wide brief, but its main purpose apparently lay in the first of its aims, 'to reconsider the place of home economics in the curriculum of 8 to 13 year-old pupils of *both* sexes' (my emphasis). Hutchinson (1979) explained that the team were especially concerned to adjust the focus of home economics, and their conclusion, which they took as their fundamental premise, was that 'the focus of home economics is the home and family'.

Thus with a neat shift, gender disappeared: the housewife and mother who was the previous focus of home economics teaching vanished into 'the home and family'. A problem remained with the actual content of home economics, once its focus was re-established. It was obvious what unified the domestic subjects of cookery, laundrywork, household management, and needlework in the past – they were all women's work. Now that bond could no longer be acknowledged, the project team found that 'much of the content of home economics was presented in too fragmentary a form'. Their solution was that a new set of definitions had to be found. As Hutchinson put it: 'The team concluded that a framework of key concepts related to the focus was an essential basis for further development.'

The team duly offered five concepts: nutrition, protection, development, interdependence and management. These were not to be taught alone, but as interrelated. The problem of reconciling separate subject specialisms such as needlework and cookery within a single curriculum area, without acknowledging the gender link, was addressed rather differently by Vaines (1979). Her solution was the 'unified field approach', which assumed that home economists could be specialists of some kind, but that 'there are common themes which bind the whole of the social system of home economics'. There are remarkable echoes of McIntosh's field of related activities here, but the inability to acknowledge the most obvious 'common theme' of gender presented Vaines with an almost insuperable problem. Taking six pages to define home economics which she described as 'still struggling to define its identity', she was finally unable to explain what unified the field of home economics, or precisely what the common themes were.

The HMI Home Economics Committee (1985) subsequently issued its own suggestions for categorising home economics in three main areas: home and family, nutrition and food, and textiles. The 'objectives' of home economics were presented under three headings: values and attitudes, knowledge and concepts, and skills. The work of the Committee and of the Schools Council paved the way for the GCSE National Criteria (1986), which used much the same language and laid down officially how home economics was to be taught for pupils between 14 and 16, without gender or other bias.

The first obvious feature of the document setting out the national criteria is its length: seventeen pages, with two appendices. In contrast, the national criteria for biology, to take but one example, is less than a third the length. The space was needed to explain what home economics is, as it is no longer self-explanatory, and to show how the various themes, aspects and essences interrelate. The document begins with a definition of home economics as: 'a study of the interrelationships between the provision of food, clothing, shelter and related services, and man's [sic] physical, economic, social and aesthetic needs in the context of the Home'.

This could be rewritten as 'a study of the best way to service a man in his own home'. It carefully avoids mention of who is doing the servicing, as does the document as a whole. The focus, pace Hutchinson, is still on home and family while 'family' is taken (in a footnote) to mean 'any household group'. The subject is divided into four major 'aspects', Family, Food, Home, Textiles.

The published criteria for home economics is the second version, for the first version submitted by a working party failed to meet the approval of Sir Keith Joseph, then Secretary of State for Education. Sir Keith's intervention, emphasising home and family rather than allowing textiles or food to be studied as entirely separate individual subjects, was in keeping with his known views on the 'cycle of deprivation' and the poor quality of child-rearing which he considered was to be found in the lowest social classes. At his insistence,

GCSE candidates were obliged to study whichever 'aspect' they chose as their main study area in relation to all the other aspects – the original working party thought this would make the subject impossible to teach and wanted pupils to be freer to specialise (Christian-Carter, 1985; Higgins, 1985). But the essence of home economics, the final document insists, is 'the interrelationships which unify the study of these major aspects'. Further, the essence amounts to not one common theme but seven: human development, health, safety/protection, efficiency, values, aesthetics, and interaction with environment.

At this point a concrete example is surely needed, and the authors of the *Guide for teachers* which accompanied the National Criteria helpfully provided one. A pupil whose main study area was 'home and family' or 'textiles and family' would be able to make a project on washing machines relevant to all four 'aspects', as required, by considering the common themes of interaction with the environment, efficiency, values and safety. As for incorporating the aspect 'food', 'the removal of food-stains and the position of the washing machine relative to other equipment could provide relevant links'. The *Guide* continues hopefully, 'you could, no doubt, suggest others'.

In another example, assuming the main study to be 'textiles', the common theme 'human development', in relation to the 'aspects' a pupil could study the effect of diet on body shape, the effect of body shape on self-image and relationships, and body shape in relation to design. Apart from the fact that fitting the subject to the syllabus has become virtually an end in itself here, there are disturbing features of this proposed study. Given that almost all the pupils studying GCSE textiles courses are adolescent girls, it is depressingly likely that this 'study' would serve as a means of reinforcing messages directed at women from innumerable sources outside school about the need to be slim.

The point of teaching home economics, other than its preservation at all costs as a school subject, now lies in the emphasis on service. The problem of how to set and mark a cookery paper which pupils from any background could do has been circumvented by switching the emphasis from *how* to cook to *who* to cook *for*: the interrelationship of needs and services. In order to keep gender out of home economics, questions about whose needs are being serviced by whom have to be suppressed. Many specimen assignments present pupils with short summaries of a situation which places them as the provider of a service to, for example, a physically handicapped child, or a sibling. The end results of these assignments could only be marked in a culturally neutral manner if examiners proposed to ignore the content of pupils' answers and mark communication skills alone. However much they attempt to be open, they cannot ultimately evade the fact that cooking, caring for children and other 'domestic' occupations are cultural activities. The neutrality they strive for is not finally possible, unless anything is allowable, but in an examination with a mark scheme it must be assumed that the examiners' openness stops somewhere. Pupils are expected to deliver an appropriate service, without doubting that there is an appropriate service and without asking why.

In the 1980s meanwhile the old craft skills teaching and the new orientation towards service, which fitted in well with a government philosophy of returning to 'care in the community' (usually meaning by women, unpaid), met and meshed with the 'new vocationalism', with the result that for post-16 pupils home economics teaching fragmented into a variety of courses. While the titles were new, the contents of these courses supposedly designed to equip pupils, particularly those who would otherwise add to the rising total of youth unemployment, with marketable skills were a familiar combination of domestic skills teaching coupled with the rhetoric of 'service'. The schedule for one CPVE 'services to people' course even listed housewife, nanny and mother's help among the occupational roles it was geared towards – revealing evidence of how substantially similar the aims of some course providers were to those of their nineteenth-century counterparts.

Millman (1985) found that TVEI was not in fact providing girls with equal opportunities, in spite of an avowed intention to do so; girls were still concentrated within traditionally female subject areas, 'training' for work which was an extension of the domestic, caring role within the home. Skeggs (1988) noted that girls on 'caring'-type courses were often critical of the course content, but although they expressed scorn for activities such as bathing dolls – 'that doll crap' – they appeared to be affected by the course emphasis on secure family life, and its link with efficiency in child-rearing and home-making practices. Skeggs described such courses as being virtually 'domestic apprenticeships', more effective in socialising girls away from the labour market than in preparing them for it.

The 1988 Education Act presented home economics teachers with their most serious threat to date. The national curriculum, a combination of grammar school nostalgia and hard-headedness, not surprisingly had no room for the new incarnation of home economics. The National Association of Teachers of Home Economics (NATHE) campaigned for the inclusion of their subject, sending a delegation to Kenneth Baker, the Secretary of State, and declaring in an open letter to him that home economics was the only subject to teach 'health and safety at home, responsibility, self-reliance, survival, management of life perpetuating resources, protection against hazards to life, skills in analysis and problem solving,

technological awareness and skills, preparation for life in general'
(NATHE, 1988). The Minister apparently did not heed this wildly
inflated claim, and the national curriculum recommendations for
science teaching also disappointed those teachers who had pinned
their hopes on home economics becoming once again a species of
science (Attar, forthcoming). Eventually the two fundamental craft
skills within home economics, often referred to by teachers as the
only elements of their subject which might not be taught at least as
well elsewhere, found a logical home as components of design and
technology, a development broadly welcomed by the NATHE
(National Curriculum Design and Technology Working Group,
1988; NATHE, 1989).

After the plethora of material explaining why any study of food or
textiles had to be linked to home and family, the Design and
Technology group's recommendations are like a breath of fresh air.
The inclusion of the food and textiles branches of home economics
was influenced by a perceived need to make design and technology
more 'girl-friendly', at least as much as by NATHE and their
supporters. There is still a danger that the implementation of this
aspect of the national curriculum will lead to more girls doing more
cooking and sewing, although the working party issued a clear
warning against allowing pupils to narrow the focus of their work to
a domestic context. The emphasis on design at least gives pupils the
possibility of working with food in ways seldom allowed within
home economics, where they have frequently been expected simply
to follow instructions, and produce dishes from a restricted reper-
tory.

There are other implications for home economics as a subsection
of design and technology. Home economics teachers, virtually all
women, are likely to find the integration of their subject with CDT,
taught overwhelmingly by men who have a tendency to hold
somewhat traditional views (Grant, 1983) presents them with new
status problems. With practical work now the province of design
and technology, the future of other areas of home economics
teaching also looks uncertain.

The doctrine of separate spheres on which home economics
ultimately rests has not disappeared but at least it has not been
enshrined in the national curriculum. It is now more apparent than
ever that anything useful in home economics lies in areas which
could be covered by other subjects with more depth and a more
critical approach. The 'assess and evaluate' assignments designed to
make GCSE home economics appear as a challenging, open-ended
and relevant subject recall the worst aspects of the last century's
domestic science. While girls (and a few boys) wasted their time on
a pseudo-scientific assignment reminiscent of a television commer-
cial which required them to 'plan a comparative study' of a 'wide

range of products available for cleaning in the kitchen' (Midland Examining Group, 1986) they were clearly missing opportunities to learn the scientific principles which would eventually enable them to analyse cleaning materials – should they ever wish to do so.

The creators of GCSE home economics tried to deflect attention from the ideological core of their subject by concentrating on process rather than content, but the newer insistence on content has called their bluff. Without the glue of gender, the claim that home economics constitutes a unified field of study may finally become impossible to sustain.

References

Attar, D. (1987), *A Bibliography of Household Books Published in Britain 1800–1914*, London, Prospect.

Attar, D. (forthcoming), *Wasting Girls' Time*, London, Virago.

B/TEC (1985), *The Certificate of Pre-vocational Education: Core Competences and Vocational Module Specifications*, London, B/TEC.

Campbell, J. (1910), *Memorandum on the teaching of infant care and management in public elementary schools*, London, Board of Education.

Christian-Carter, J. (1985), 'A brave new world?', *Times Educational Supplement*, 19 April.

Clark, M. (1970), *Teaching Cookery*, Oxford, Pergamon.

Department of Education and Science (DES) (1988), *Statistical Bulletin 13/88*, London.

Digby, A. and Searby, P. (1981), *Children, School and Society in Nineteenth-Century England*, London, Macmillan.

Dyhouse, C. (1981), *Girls Growing Up in Late Victorian and Edwardian England*, London, Routledge and Kegan Paul.

Ehrenreich, B. and English, D. (1979), *For Her Own Good: 150 Years of the Experts' Advice to Women*, New York, Anchor.

Evans, J. and Davies, B. (1988), 'The rise and fall of vocational education', in Pollard, A., Purvis, J. and Walford, G. (eds), *Education, Training and the New Vocationalism*, Milton Keynes, Open University.

Goodson, I. (ed.) (1985), *Social histories of the secondary curriculum*, Falmer, Lewes.

Grant, M. (1983), 'Craft, design and technology', in Whyld, J. (ed.), *Sexism in the secondary curriculum*, London, Harper Row.

Her Majesty's Inspectorate (1985), *Home economics from 5 to 16: Curriculum matters, 5*, London, HMSO.

Her Majesty's Inspectorate Home Economics Committee (1978), *Curriculum 11–16: Home Economics*, London, Department of Education and Science.

Higgins, P. (1985), 'Don't be a dinosaur', *Times Educational Supplement*, 19 April.

Holland, J. (1988), 'Girls and occupational choice: in search of meanings', in Pollard, A., Purvis, J. and Walford, G. (eds), *Education, Training and the New Vocationalism*, Milton Keynes, Open University.

Holt, M. and Reid, W. A. (1988), 'Instrumentalism and education; 14–18 rhetoric and the 11–16 curriculum', in Pollard, A., Purvis, J. and Walford, G. (eds), *Education, Training and the New Vocationalism*, Milton Keynes, Open University.

House of Commons Education, Science and Arts Committee (1981), *The Secon-*

dary School Curriculum and Examinations, Second Report, Vols I and II, London, HMSO.

Hunt, F. (1987), 'Divided aims: the educational implications of opposing ideologies in girls' secondary schooling, 1850–1940', in Hunt, F. (ed.), *Lessons for Life: the Schooling of Girls and Women 1850–1950*, Oxford, Blackwell.

Hutchinson, V. G. (1979), 'Focus on home and family', *New Trends in Home Economics Education*, 1, Vol. 1, UNESCO.

McCulloch, G. (1985), 'Pioneers of an alternative road? The Association of Heads of Technical Schools 1951–1964', in Goodson, I., op. cit.

McIntosh, E. (1955), 'The teaching of housecraft in the schools of today', in Weddell, M., *Training in home management*, London, Routledge and Kegan Paul.

Manthorpe, C. (1986), 'Science or domestic science?', *History of Education*, 15, 3.

Midland Examining Group (1986), *Home economics: home studies GCSE syllabus for 1988*.

Millman, V. (1985), 'The new vocationalism in secondary schools: its influence on girls', in Whyte, J., Deem, R., Kant, L. and Cruikshank, M. (eds), *Girl Friendly Schooling*, London, Methuen.

NATHE *National Foundation Curriculum* (1988), open letter to Kenneth Baker, London, NATHE.

NATHE (1989), *Initial response to the interim report of the design and technology working group*, letter circulated with *Modus*, 7, 1.

National Curriculum Design and Technology Working Group (1988), *Interim Report*, London, Department of Education and Science and the Welsh Office.

Newsom, J. (1948), *The Education of Girls*, London, Faber and Faber.

Oliver, S. (1984), *Assessment in a multicultural society: home economics at 16+*, Longman/Schools Council.

Pember Reeves, M. (1979), *Round About a Pound a Week*, first published 1913, reprinted London, Virago.

Purvis, J. (1985), 'Domestic subjects since 1870', in Goodson, I., op. cit.

Rice, E. E. (1885), *Text-book of domestic economy*, London, Blackie.

Secondary Examination Council (1986), *Home Economics GCSE: A guide for teachers*.

Skeggs, B. (1988), 'Gender reproduction and further education: domestic apprenticeships', *British Journal of Sociology of Education*, 9, 2.

Thom, D. (1987), 'Better a teacher than a hairdresser', in Hunt, F., op. cit.

Turnbull, A. (1987), 'Learning her womanly work: the elementary school curriculum 1870–1914', in Hunt, F., op. cit.

Vaines, E. (1979), 'Home economics: a unified field approach', *New Trends in Home Economics*, 1, 1.

Waring, M. (1985), '"To make the mind strong, rather than to make it full": elementary school science teaching in London 1870–1904', in Goodson, I., op. cit.

Webster, A. (1879), *A Housewife's Opinion*, London, Macmillan.

Weddell, M. (1955), *Training in Home Management*, London, Routledge and Kegan Paul.

Wynn, B. (1983), 'Home economics', in Whyld, J. (ed.), *Sexism in the Secondary Curriculum*, London, Harper and Row.

Yoxall, A. (1965), *A History of the Teaching of Domestic Subjects*, first published 1913, Bath, Cedric Chivers.

3.5

Beyond Multiculturalism: Towards the Enactment of Antiracist Education in Policy, Provision and Pedagogy[1]

Barry Troyna

Racial forms of education: some conceptual frameworks

There is now a growing body of literature dealing with the ways in which social scientists and others have interpreted the relationship between the UK educational system and black students[2] and how these have been translated into substantive policy statements and provision. Some of this literature has been confined to historical narrative, showing how policy approaches have altered since the presence of black students in UK schools first began to make an impact on policy making in the 1960s (Tomlinson, 1983). Others, however, have been concerned with summarising these changes in conceptual terms. At the risk of over-simplification, there would seem to be three dominant conceptual frameworks available for this purpose. In this opening section I want to provide a brief résumé of these approaches. I want then to outline the nature of the current and prevailing 'racial forms of education', to use Chris Mullard's phrase (1984); namely, multicultural and antiracist education. Here I will argue strongly that these are irreconcilable conceptions of educational change. Finally, I want to suggest ways in which the principles of antiracist education might be enacted in a range of educational settings in the UK.

The first of the conceptual frameworks which I want to discuss has been associated particularly with the work of Rosalind Street-Porter (1978), Eric Bolton (1979), Mullard (1982) and Troyna (1982). Essentially, the analytical tools which they use are drawn from the sociology of race relations and specify ideological and policy approaches in terms of assimilation, integration, cultural pluralism and, most recently, antiracism. These phases are periodised from the mid-1960s through to the 1980s, although they are not intended to imply a neat and regular progression. Nor are they intended to denote practices on the 'chalk face'. Rather, their intention is to characterise prevailing ideologies as they are reflected in official rhetoric and policy on education at the level of the local and national state. Each ideological concept embodies a specific 'racial form of education'. As Mullard suggests, the assimilation, integration and cultural pluralism phases were dominated and exemplified by 'immigrant', 'multiracial' and 'multicultural' forms of education respectively (1984, p. 14). Most significantly, as both Mullard and I have argued, the move towards multicultural definitions of education did not entail any significant departure from the assumptions and principles which underpinned assimilationist concepts. That is to say, although representing a more liberal variant of the assimilationist model, multicultural education continued to draw its inspiration and rationale from white, middle-class professional understandings of how the educational system might best respond to the perceived 'needs' and 'interests' of black students and their parents. Thus, whichever of these paradigms was in the ascendancy, the power relationship between black and white citizens remained unchallenged. The focus of concern was cultural differences and the extent to which these were regarded as inhibiting the educational careers and experiences of black students. Notably absent from the policy approaches which these paradigms gave rise to was a consideration of the impact of racism on black students' differential access to, experiences in and rewards from the educational system.[3]

A second analytical approach to this issue was developed by David Kirp in his controversial book *Doing Good by Doing Little* (1979). Kirp dichotomised ideological and policy responses into 'racially inexplicit' and 'racially explicit' formulations. These terms comprised both descriptive and evaluative elements. To begin with, he characterised the approach in the UK as 'radically inexplicit' to distinguish it from policy formulations in the USA where, since 1954, 'race' had been a salient feature of the educational policy agenda.[4] Since then, Kirp argued, racial inequality has constituted a fulcrum around which policy interventions in the USA have operated. He noted that this contrasted sharply with the way in which policies had been oriented in the UK. Writing in 1979, Kirp suggested that with the conspicuous exception of policies relating to the dispersal of black students in some LEAs, race related issues had not figured explicitly as policy concerns. Instead, their significance had been diffused through a range of 'racially inexplicit' categories such as language provision, educational disadvantage, cultural deprivation and cultural adjustment. It was within these broadly conceived categories that policymakers had decided to tackle the problems associated with black students. At a substantive level, Kirp's account could not be faulted. What gave cause for concern was his evaluation of the approach adopted by UK policymakers. For him, this deliberately inadvertent strategy could be regarded as 'doing good by stealth'. He insisted that such an approach had much to commend it because it did not contravene the principles of universalism and individualism which underpin social policy in the UK. What is more, by embedding race related issues within this broader framework for intervention, policymakers preempted the possibility of a 'white backlash'. As he put it 'one helps non-whites by *not* favouring them explicitly. The benefits to minorities from such an approach are thought to be real if invisible – or better, real because invisible' (Kirp, 1979, p. 51, original emphasis). Kirp's commitment to the ideology of doing little has been criticised for its failure to recognise how 'inexplicitness', by its very nature, precludes any engagement with the impact of racism on black students' experiences.

After all, it presumes that existing categories which define modes of policy intervention are capable of capturing and dealing with the full range of disadvantages experienced by young blacks. This is a facile and sanguine interpretation of issues which denies the significance of racism on the lives and opportunities of these youngsters. The fundamental weakness of Kirp's appraisal is that it fails to conceive the education system as a site in which the reproduction of racism is confirmed and achieved. As such it does not engage with the most obvious of the demands expressed by black groups in the UK; that policymakers develop approaches and forms of provision which acknowledge and tackle racism and the practices which stem from it. To characterise this 'inexplicit' approach as 'good' is to disregard the voice of the black communities and help legitimate an educational system which contributes to their continued oppression and enforced inequality.

The third approach to understanding policy formation was developed in *Racism, Education and the State* which Jenny Williams and I wrote (Troyna and Williams, 1986). It emerged from our reservations about the explanatory power of existing conceptual tools of analysis. Without discarding the assimilation, integration, cultural pluralism framework, we suggested that the development of ideological and policy approaches might best be understood with reference to the deracialisation/racialisation process. Here we drew heavily on Frank Reeves' (1983) definition of these concepts and their application to British racial discourse. We argued that those policies which embraced assimilation, integration or cultural pluralism as their paradigm were classic exemplars of deracialised discourse. By this we meant that policymakers who had framed their policies along these lines had deliberately eschewed overt reference to racial descriptions, evaluations and prescriptions in preference to apparently more legitimate educational imperatives. Thus, we argued that:

> the processes of resocialisation, language tuition and correction and dispersal could be argued for on the seemingly 'good' educational grounds that the culture, language and spatial concentration of black students not only impeded their educational advancement but also had the potential to affect negatively the educational progress of their white classmates (Troyna and Williams, 1986, p. 13).

Following on from this we suggested that policy formulations – whether embedded in the ideological framework of assimilation, integration or cultural pluralism – were premissed on the assumption that the priority was the *management* of problems thrown up by the presence of black students rather than the mitigation of problems which they encountered precisely because they were black citizens living in a racist society. Thus, the package of reforms introduced in the 1970s concentrated on trying to ensure that the schooling experience of black students were made more palatable. They were geared towards a representation of their (presumed) lifestyles in curriculum design and teaching aids. What they ignored were the formal and informal racist processes which constrained the educational opportunities available to these students. This, we concluded, was discrimination by proxy.

We contrasted these deracialised forms of discourse and intervention with the (benign) racialisation of educational policy and debate. Again, following Reeves, we suggested that there were certain contexts where explicit use was made of racial evaluations and categorisations and that these contexts might be benign or malevolent. For example, ethnic record keeping in education would be designated as 'malevolent' if used by the National Front for avowedly racist aims, or 'benign' if used, say, by the Commission for Racial Equality for explicitly antiracist intentions.

We contended that the current trend towards the publication of antiracist education policies at local education authority (LEA) level represented a *benign* form of racialisation in that they reflected a growing awareness of and indignation at racial injustice. In consequence then: 'Racial evaluation and prescription is directed at refuting racism and eliminating racialist practices' (Reeves, 1983, p. 175). For Jenny Williams and I, the deracialisation/racialisation framework provided the most appropriate lens through which to observe and interpret the changing nature and focus of LEAs' ideological and policy positions on race-related matters.

Since we completed the book (in July 1985) the racialisation of educational policy seems to have accelerated. Indeed, when confronted with many of the recent advertisements in the national and specialist press the ubiquitous visitor from Mars might well conclude that the overwhelming majority of policies and practices of local authorities and their education departments have been racialised in a benign form. The publication of LEA policy statements which centralise concepts such as 'racism', 'equality', 'rights' and 'justice', the range and nature of newly created posts associated with policy initiatives in Authorities such as Berkshire, Brent, Haringey, the Inner London Education Authority (ILEA) and Manchester, and the apparent increased participation of black professionals and non-professionals in the determination and allocation of service provision imply that antiracist conceptions of educational reform constitute the prevailing orthodoxy at the level of the local state. The visitor from Mars might also be tempted to infer a parallel development at the level of the national state from the tenor of the Swann Committee's report, *Education for All* (DES, 1985), and the speech presented to the HMI Hospitality Conference in March 1986 by the then Minister of State for Education, Chris Patten. In the former, Lord Swann and his colleagues drew attention to the 'insiduous evil' of racism, outlined how its persistence contributed to the '*mis*-education' of students and recommended that all LEAs declare a commitment 'to countering the influence of racism' (1985, p. 770). Although slightly more circumspect in his endorsement of antiracist teaching, Chris Patten drew attention to the value of explicit interventions along these lines to combat the influence of fascist organisations in both urban and rural settings. As he put it:

> Some pupils as a result of a variety of influences seem to develop negative attitudes towards other ethnic groups . . . A discussion focussing directly on race relations may be particularly desirable if . . . schools have been the subject of leafleting by extremist organisations whose sole deplorable aim would appear to be the undermining of good race relations (Patten, 1986).

Of course, none of these developments should be construed as exemplary of a consensus around the racialisation of educational discourse and policy. The populist appeal which Honeyford (in Bradford) and Savery (in Bristol) attracted in their opposition to this trend alongside the critiques mounted from the right (Flew, 1984; Joseph, 1986; Palmer, 1987) and liberal (Craft, 1986; Jeffcoate, 1984) wings of the educational community provide a salutary reminder of the struggle in which antiracist educationists are engaged.

Nonetheless, the scenario I have sketched above would suggest that the main imperative for educational policymakers in the mid-1980s is to develop practices which focus on the racist underpinnings and operation of white dominated institutions (LEAs, colleges, schools) rather than ethnic minority cultures and lifestyles, and which aim to remove those obstacles which impede the educational advancement of black students.

While this is undoubtedly the rationale underlying the policy orientation of certain LEAs it remains, nevertheless, a muted response. For the overwhelming majority of LEAs which have eschewed 'racially inexplicit' approaches in favour of multicultural education, the context continues to be 'them' rather than 'us'. In short, they persist with a deracialised set of imperatives informed more by cultural pluralism than antiracism. In the following section I want to consider more fully the relationship between multicultural and antiracist forms of education.

Multicultural and antiracist approaches in education

It is important to emphasise that both multicultural education (MCE) and antiracist education (ARE) are diffuse conceptions of educational reform and it would therefore be misleading to depict either formulation as embracing a single trajectory or motivating force. Indeed, writers such as James Banks (1986) and Brian Bullivant (1986) insist that MCE subsumes within its concerns a consideration of those issues which are prioritised by the ARE perspective. At the same time, multiculturalists such as Robert Jeffcoate (1984) and Maurice Craft (1986) distance themselves emphatically from ARE and the political ideology which underpins it.

Despite the efforts of Banks, and others, to generate an inclusive definition of MCE which takes on board some of the concerns of ARE, it is my contention that the two perspectives are irreconcilable. They imply a different view of the nature and processes of racism which, in turn, prompts the development of different frameworks within which specific priorities for action are embedded. Of course, it is true that some LEAs have racialised their educational policies in so far as racism is now acknowledged as a constituent of the barriers which impede systematically black advancement. Similarly, as I mentioned earlier, the Swann Committee noted the insidious influence of racism in educational settings. The difference, however, lies in the way racism is conceived within MCE and ARE perspectives. In the former, racism is understood primarily as the product of ignorance and perpetuated by negative attitudes and individual prejudices. A critical reading of the Swann Committee's chapter on racism illustrates this point (Carter and Williams, 1987; Troyna, 1986). Those favouring ARE, on the other hand, while accepting the persistance of stereotypes and prejudices, demand that a thorough analysis of their origins must derive from an interrogation of the social and political structure. These fundamentally different conceptions of racism and the strategies which they give rise to have been dealt with in Mullard's recent work (1984). He characterises MCE as *microscopic* in that its advocates tend to focus narrowly and intently on issues relating to culture. They are concerned with formulating policies to eradicate ignorance of other cultures, undermine the prejudice and discrimination which stems from ignorance, and develop greater understanding and tolerance of members of minority ethnic and cultural groups. The site of change is the school: the nature of change concerns the removal of ethnocentric material from the curriculum and teaching materials and their replacement by more culturally sensitive and appropriate educational aids and stimuli. Most recently, pedagogical considerations have been identified as important to the MCE model and the 'prejudice reduction' movement (King, 1986; Lynch, 1987).

In contrast, ARE had been defined by Mullard as *periscopic*, that is to say it deliberately seeks to make 'a connection between *institutional* discriminations and inequalities of race, class and gender' (Mullard, 1984, p. 37, emphasis added). Here it is possible to see a link between Mullard's depiction of ARE and Stuart Hall's prescriptions for teaching 'race' which he outlined in his article for *Multiracial Education* in 1980. Both imply that ARE is intended to probe the manner in which racism rationalises and helps perpetuate injustice and the differential power accorded to groups in society. Both also suggest that for the aims of ARE to be realised the issues of 'race' and racism cannot be abstracted from the broader political, historical and social processes of society which have institutionalised unequal power. In specific terms, this calls for the development of general theories of oppression and inequality within which the specificity of racism is not obscured. What is more, it implies the forging of alliances between groups both within and beyond the school gates and the identification of school staff and students as responsible for combating manifest forms of racial, class and gender inequalities. In sum, then, and going further than Mullard, I would suggest that MCE focuses mainly on individual conversion. Moreover, when multiculturalists do take on board the notion of institutional racism, they propose reforms in cultural pluralist terms. ARE, on the other hand, prioritises collective action and conceives strategies for change in explicitly political terms which lead to challenges of existing power relations. However, before elaborating on the ARE agenda for reforms, I want to spend some time engaging critically with MCE. This is important if we are to prepare the ground for the legitimation of ARE.

The central tenets of MCE

Despite the gradual move towards ARE, the MCE movement both in the UK and elsewhere has been remarkably resistant to change, except for the occasional genuflection towards racism as an issue to consider. Its central tenets also remain impervious to criticism, perhaps because they appeal to liberal commonsense notions. However, as Stuart Hall has pointed out, the role of social science is to 'deconstruct the obvious' (1980, p. 6). This is my goal in this section.

Despite the various inflections of MCE I would suggest that from the following statements (selected from a range of influential sources), it is possible to distil the main tenets of MCE. I want to analyse critically their status in order to demonstrate the impoverished nature of the MCE argument.

> Our society is a multicultural, multiracial one, and the curriculum should reflect a sympathetic understanding of the different cultures and races [sic] that now make up our society (DES, 1977, p. 41).

> For the curriculum to have meaning and relevance for all pupils now in our schools, its content, emphasis and the values and assumptions contained must reflect the wide range of cultures, histories and lifestyles in our multiracial society (Home Office, 1978, p. 6).

> ... the curriculum in all schools should reflect the fact that Britain is both multiracial and culturally diverse ... the intention of multicultural education is simply to provide all children with a balanced education which reflects the nature of our society (Rampton Report; DES, 1981, p. 27).

> Education for diversity and for social and racial harmony suggests that the richness of cultural variety in Britain, let alone over the world, should be appreciated and utilised in education curricula for all students in widening cultural awareness and in developing sensitivity towards the cultural identity and practices of various groups (CNAA, 1985, p. 1).

> Cultures should be emphatically described in their own terms and not judged against some notion of 'ethocentric' or 'Euro-centric' culture (Schools Council, cited in DES, 1985, p. 329).

It seems to me that the essence of these statements crystallises around four central (and admittedly seductive) propositions. In each of the passages they are presented as unproblematic; however, like the oft-repeated phrase 'multicultural education is synonymous with good practices in education' (Duncan, 1986, p. 39), their commonsense appeal conceals their tenuous status in political, theoretical and philosophical contexts. They are:

1 Britain is a multicultural society
2 the curriculum should reflect that substantive fact
3 learning about other cultures will benefit all students
4 cultural relativism is a desirable and tenable position.

Let us take each of these in turn. The first would seem to be uncontentious. However, at least one writer has questioned the legitimacy of the epithet 'multicultural' in the UK context. Brian Bullivant (1986) has suggested that the assertion demands empirical scrutiny. In his view, distinctive minority cultural groups comprise around 4 per cent of the UK population, tend to originate from three parts of the world (Africa, Asia, the Caribbean) and include a substantial number born and brought up in Britain. For Bullivant, then, the term *tricultural* might be a more accurate description (op. cit., p. 38). The validity or otherwise of this argument does not concern me here. The point I want to stress is that it is a plausible corrective to the taken-for-granted and most basic premise of MCE. Similar reservations might be expressed about the second proposition. After all, whether or not the school curriculum should reflect cultural diversity is an open question. What we tend to find, however, is a clear example of the philosophical device known as the naturalistic fallacy: that is, deriving an 'ought' from an 'is'. The proposition, in other words, needs to be argued cogently rather than asserted.

The claim that learning about other cultures will benefit all students is also open to question. It is based on two assertions. First, that black students will benefit academically from learning about their own ethnic and cultural lifestyles. This was encapsulated in one school policy on MCE which insisted: 'Multicultural education is a whole curriculum which also involves an attitude to life. It aims to promote a positive self-image and respect for the attitudes and values of others. Such an education will improve academic attainment' (Birley High School, 1980, p. 2). Following the same line of argument, the Rampton Report presumed that increased knowledge of their ethnic and cultural origins would help black students achieve equality of opportunity in the search for jobs (see Troyna, 1984, for discussion). Quite clearly, this formulation conflates the presentation of lifestyles with the enhancement of life chances and, in the process, obscures the determining impact of racism on the school and post-school experiences and opportunities of black students. To suggest that MCE (as presented in this third proposition) has emancipatory properties which might overcome the debilitating effects of racism in education and occupational contexts is misleading and empirically spurious (Troyna and Smith, 1983; Eggleston, *et al.*, 1986).

But what impact might learning about other cultures have on the perceptions and attitudes of white students? Again, the conventional wisdom would lead us to believe that 'prejudice reduction' would be a logical and inevitable outcome. However, Amir's (1969) review of literature on the theme of 'contact hypothesis in ethnic relations' demonstrates the wishful thinking nature of this proposition. Indeed, as Connor has pointed out, increased knowledge of other groups might in fact enhance feelings of 'differentness' and reinforce identification with one's own group. As Connor indicates: 'Minimally, it may be asserted that increasing awareness of a second group is not certain to promote harmony and is at least likely to produce, on balance, a negative response' (Connor, 1972, p. 344). This is an especially important caveat given the priority accorded this tenet in the canons of MCE.

Finally, we come to the recommendation that cultures should be empathetically treated in their own terms, a position which the Swann Committee advocated strongly, as Steve Harrison has noted (1986, pp. 184–5). Taken to its logical extreme, of course, it implies that 'everything and anything goes' provided it has been legitimated in one or more cultural contexts. More likely, however, it presumes the existence of what James Lynch (1983) terms 'rational universals' so that any practices at variance with these criteria would be proscribed. But this does not greatly assist the teacher wishing to debate, say, the position of women in certain fundamentalist Muslim societies. Indeed, to debate this issue might, in itself, mean a contravention of Islamic principles. This principle also raises the critical issue of the appropriateness of relativist interpretations. Caroline Ramazanoglu sums up the dilemma in the following passage:

> There is great difficulty in steering interpretations of these arguments between the Scylla of cultural relativism (Muslim women cannot be judged to be oppressed when they are simply celebrating the Muslim way of life – the Western concept of autonomy is irrelevant to their culture) and the Charybdis of positive truth (we know Muslim women are oppressed, even if they do not, because we possess universal criteria of oppression, external to Islam, which identify veiling, the celebration of motherhood and cliterodectomy as oppressive) (Ramazanoglu, 1986, p. 259).

This determination to represent cultures empathetically could also lead to an emphasis on broadly sketched caricatures and a corresponding neglect of more individual impulses for change. In other words, there is a danger of lapsing into reductionism along the lines of those drawn by Philip Walkling and Chris Brannigan in their discussion of Muslim girls in the UK education system. Briefly, Walkling and Brannigan (1986) juxtaposed the 'transformative' nature of state schools with the 'transmissionist' imperatives of Muslim culture and schools and suggested that this represented a clash between the goals of antisexist education (emancipating women from their oppression) and ARE (complying with the demands of minority communities). In our response, Bruce Carrington and I have criticised Walkling and Brannigan for their tendency to reproduce cultural stereotypes and their neglect of young Asian women's involvement in the determination of their destinies (Troyna and Carrington, 1987).[5]

I have argued that each of the central tenets of MCE is erected on dubious political, theoretical or philosophical foundations. Despite

evidence to the contrary, however, they continue to assume importance in the justification for MCE models of reform. The need for
antiracists to challenge the veracity of the multicultural/cultural
pluralist paradigm should be self-evident. Its continued adoption,
after all, forecloses the possibility of advancing and legitimating
antiracist forms of educational, social and political change and
provides the rationale for the continuing pre-eminence of what
Mullard defines as 'ethnicism' in contemporary debates and policy.
The resulting trajectory of policy initiatives and related forms of
action has been identified by Mullard in a recent paper:

> As the cultural representation of the ideological form of racism, ethnicism then
> constitutes a set of representations of *ethnic* differences, peculiarities, cultural
> biographies, histories and practices, which are used to justify specific courses of
> action that possess the effect of institutionalising ethnic/cultural differences. In
> doing this ethnicist policies and practices also tend to obfuscate the common
> experiences, histories and social political conditions of black and (ethnic)
> minority groups and hence the degree of communality of experience that might
> exist between these and certain white class groups in society (1986, p. 11,
> original emphasis).

However, the retention of MCE as a viable and prevalent
paradigm in educational policy and debate draws our attention to
the failure of social scientists to engage directly and critically with its
presumptions and pretentions. This is a point which Geneva Gay
addressed when she noted the failure of social scientists and
educationists 'to produce hard evidence of its efficacy' (1983,
p. 563).

But similar criticisms might be directed towards ARE perspectives and modes of practice. Commentators such as Banks, though
broadly sympathetic to ARE, insist that its proponents are 'vague
and ambitious when they propose strategies for school reform'
(1986, p. 224). Jenny Williams and I were also critical of the lack of
specificity in the ARE perspectives and suggested a number of
reasons for this which I will deal with briefly here. First, policymakers tended to operate with an inadequate grasp of the nature of
racism and institutional racism, especially as these operate within
educational settings. For instance, institutional racism, we argued,
tended to be defined by its consequences so that the phrase became
a catch-all formulation for almost all the inadequacies within school
which touched on the lives of black students. We insisted that this
reductionist approach was over-simplistic and generated an impoverished analysis of the school's role in the reproduction of
inequalities. Secondly, we pointed to the absence of a coherent,
overarching framework within which policymakers might encourage
teachers to operate a locally consistent strategy to combat racial,

gender and class inequalities. Thirdly, we suggested that policymakers were reluctant to confront directly the allocative and selective function of schooling and were concerned with the more limited aim of ensuring a more equitable distribution of students throughout the school hierarchy, based on racial, gender or class origins. Finally, we noted that policymakers were hesitant in declaring their support for forms of political education which might expedite a clearer understanding of the ways in which racism was reproduced in local and national contexts (Troyna and Williams, 1986, pp. 95–109). These criticisms should not be taken to mean that supporters of ARE have not pinpointed specific strategies. Among others, Madan Sarup (1986) and Mullard (1984) have indicated some of the ways in which their own particular definitions of ARE might be translated into action. This is not the place to comment directly on their proposals. Instead, I want to conclude by pointing to two major and recurrent omissions from the ARE agenda, as formulated by academics, practitioners, community activists and policymakers, to provide justification for their enactment and give some initial cues as to how this might be achieved.

ARE: some possible ways forward

The progressive development of racial forms of education from immigrant to antiracist education has been accompanied by a growing awareness of the need to implicate all educational institutions in these changes. This, of course, constituted the essential theme of the Swann Committee's final report and informed the principle of *Education for All* which it commended to the Secretary of State for Education in March 1985. It also forms the leitmotif of most LEA policy documents. Despite this, empirical surveys continue to highlight the reluctance of schools with few black students to engage in changes, other than in the most perfunctory manner (Troyna and Ball, 1985). Perhaps one of the reasons is that policymakers and educationists, in general, simply have not given enough thought or emphasis to how the principles of ARE might be implemented in these settings.[6] My current research in the further education sector, for instance, has revealed how, despite their impressive policy commitments, the Further Education Unit (FEU), Commission for Racial Equality (CRE) and the National Association of Teachers in Further and Higher Education (NATHE), when provided with the opportunity to exemplify their philosophy in practice fail to do so. This criticism must also be directed at Godfrey Brandt and his book, *The Realisation of*

Antiracist Teaching (1986). There, after a formal and elaborated construction of antiracist principles and pedagogy we find that his observations and comments on antiracist teaching are drawn exclusively from ethnically mixed schools. His insistence that he 'specifically attempted to find "ordinary" teachers in "ordinary" schools' (Brandt, 1986, p. 148) is discrepant with the fact that the 'majority of Britain's population does not live in inner cities, nor is it in regular contact with non-white people' (Taylor, 1984–85, p. 1).

Following on from my earlier argument, I want to suggest that the strategy of intervention in these (and other) settings might be constructed around forms of political education. It is a strategy which takes as its starting point the view that racism constitutes one of the ways in which an individual might account for the way things are. It may provide a readily intelligible and plausible explanation for her/his view of the world. For instance, Raymond Cochrane and Michael Billig (1984) found in their interviews with white working-class school students in the West Midlands that they conceived of their limited life chances in terms of (unfair) racial competition. Another example might be Honeyford's (1984) explanation of the rise of heroin use in Britain in terms of increased contact with Pakistan (see Foster-Carter, 1987, for further discussion). In each case 'social reality' is perceived and interpreted through a racial frame of reference. If these conceptions of reality are to be challenged effectively then it is essential to provide superior and more plausible explanations of these phenomena. This cannot be done if the issues of 'race' and ethnic relations are considered in isolation; rather, they need to be seen and considered as pertinent aspects of the social structure along with, say, class and gender. This demands a more broadly based approach, the rejection of pre-packaged 'teaching about race relations' materials and the generation of key concepts around which teaching sessions might be based. The aim is to ensure that students not only recognise the specific nature of racial inequality but the nature of the inequalities they themselves experience and share with black people as girls, students, young people or as members of the working class. It is an approach which identifies empathy with rather than sympathy for the oppression of black people as a goal. Further, it concedes that informed collective action constitutes the most effective challenge to racism. The intention, then, is to replace divisions and scapegoating with alliances. Research into this mode of intervention might facilitate the development of models which build upon the principles of ARE.

Another major omission in the formulation of ARE regards the issue of pedagogy. Here I agree with Chris Richards (1986) that 'pedagogy is a priority and not an issue to be tackled only after getting a definition of anti-racism . . .' (p. 74). However, pedagogical considerations rarely appear on policy statements (either at LEA or individual school/college level). Indeed, its significance is belittled to the extent that its continued absence from policy agendas is not even commented upon by those who have claimed to scrutinise critically policy statements (see Dorn, 1983; Mullard, *et al.*, 1983). But as Gordon Allport noted more than 30 years ago:

> If segregation of the sexes or races prevails if authoritarianism and hierarchy dominate the system, the child cannot help but learn that power and status are the dominant factors in human relationships. If, on the other hand, the school system is democratic, if the teacher and child are each respected units, the lesson of respect for the person will easily register. As in society at large, the *structure* of the pedagogical system will blanket and may negate the specific intercultural lessons taught (Allport, 1954, p. 511, original emphasis).

More recently, Patricia White has picked up this point and emphasised the need for congruence between the formal and hidden curriculum in the pursuit of social justice, participatory democracy and egalitarian values:

> Guidelines for teaching and the organisational structure of the school are equally necessary, not least since the child acquires a considerable amount of her political knowledge in an informal way through her membership of the educational institution. It would be foolish to have carefully worked out content guidelines whilst leaving teaching procedures and particularly the structure of the school unregulated (White, 1983, pp. 84–5).

If an explicit goal of ARE is to challenge the practices and history which support racial injustices and unequal power and, at the same time, to contribute to the development of collective action then didactic approaches in the classroom, the reliance on teacher exposition, the stress on individualism and support for an achievement oriented ethos all need to be replaced by forms of cooperative learning within a non-competitive environment. In short, the move towards ARE needs to be accompanied closely by greater emphasis on student centred learning. Naturally, the nature of relationships within student-centred learning contexts, the degree of autonomy accorded students and the impact of these approaches on institutional change need to be examined empirically in a range of educational contexts, if we are to avoid replacing one set of untenable propositions with another.

It should now be clear that ARE, unlike its competing ideology, MCE, constitutes a radical exemplar of political education for it demands a critical examination of those explanations and practices which misinform and oppress people. What is more, it calls for collaboration and cooperation in the process of examination; it also demands greater recognition of students' rights. All of this is likely to threaten established modes of behaviour and relationships within educational institutions. As Francis Dunlop points out, the introduction of more democratic forms of organisation into the educational context must presage a range of challenges to the cultural tasks of education: 'the passing on predominantly by example of values, unformalised skills, appreciations, ways of behaving and so on' (Dunlop, 1979, p. 53). The logical enactment of ARE principles cannot and should not circumvent these matters.

Notes

1 This article was prepared originally for the conference, *Third World Perspectives and Social Policy in Contemporary Britain* which was organised in December 1986 by the ESRC International Affairs Committee. A revised version was presented at a seminar at the Centre for Race and Ethnic Studies at the University of Amsterdam in March 1987. I am grateful to participants at both venues and Bruce Carrington, Richard Hatcher and Jenny Williams for their constructive comments on the earlier versions.

2 By 'black' I am referring to people of Afro-Caribbean and South Asian origin.

3 The concept of 'culture', as it has appeared in the debate on multicultural education, has generally focused on life styles. That is to say, multiculturalists have tended to concentrate on the expressive and historical features said to represent particular culture groups. Translated into imperatives for curriculum reform this has often resulted in the pre-eminence of what I have termed the Three Ss Approach: Saris, Samosas and Steel Bands (Troyna, 1983; Troyna and Williams, 1986). More elaborate critiques of this use of the term culture in the debate have been provided by Bullivant (1986) and Burtonwood (1986).

4 This was the year when the US Supreme Court ruled that segregated education was unconstitutional and in violation of the Fourteenth Amendment.

5 Walkling and Brannigan do not agree with our criticism and have replied to us in the same issue of the *Journal of Moral Education*, 16, 1, 1987.

6 Jenny Williams and I were also guilty of this as we admitted in the conclusion to *Racism, Education and the State*: 'Our approach, even in skeletal form, leaves a number of questions unresolved not least the fact that it is not immediately appropriate for those students in all-white schools or areas' (Troyna and Williams, 1986, p. 123).

References

Allport, G. (1954), *The Nature of Prejudice*, London, Addison-Wesley.

Amir, Y. (1969), 'Contact hypothesis in ethnic relations', *Psychological Bulletin*, 71, pp. 319–42.

Banks, J. (1986), 'Multicultural education and its critics: Britain and the United States', in S. Modgil, *et al.* (eds), *Multicultural Education: the interminable debate*, pp. 221–31, Lewes, Falmer Press.

Birley High School (1980), *Multicultural Education in the 1980s*, Manchester, Manchester Education Committee.

Bolton, E. (1979), 'Education in a multiracial society', *Trends in Education*, 4, Winter, pp. 3–7.

Brandt, G. (1986), *The Realization of Anti-Racist Teaching*, Lewes, Falmer Press.

Bullivant, B. (1986), 'Towards radical multiculturalism: resolving tensions in curriculum and educational planning', in S. Modgil, *et al.* (eds), op. cit., pp. 33–48.

Burtonwood, N. (1986), *The Culture Concept in Educational Studies*, Slough, NFER-Nelson.

Carter, B. and Williams J. (1987), 'Attacking racism in education', in B. Troyna (ed.), *Racial Inequality in Education*, pp. 170–83, London, Tavistock.

CNAA (1985), *Notes on Multicultural Education and the Preparation and Inservice Development of Teachers*, London, CNAA.

Cochrane, R. and Billig, M. (1984), 'I'm not National Front myself, but . . .', *New Society*, 17 May, pp. 255–8.

Connor, W. (1972), 'Nation-building or nation-destroying?', *World Politics*, 24, pp. 319–55.

Craft, M. (1984), 'Education for diversity', in M. Craft (ed.), *Education and Cultural Pluralism*, Lewes, Falmer Press, pp. 5–25.

Craft, M. (1986), 'Multicultural education in the United Kingdom', in J. Banks and J. Lynch (eds), *Multicultural Education in Western Societies*, London, Holt, Rinehart and Winston, pp. 76–97.

DES (1977), *Education in Schools: a consultative document*, Cmnd 6869, London, HMSO.

DES (1981), *West Indian Children in Our Schools*, Rampton Report, Cmnd 8273, London, HMSO.

DES (1985), *Education for All*, Swann Report, Cmnd 9543, London, HMSO.

Dorn, A. (1983), 'LEA policies on multi-racial education', *Multi-Ethnic Education Review*, 2, 2, pp. 3–5.

Duncan, C. (1986), 'Developing a multicultural approach to the curriculum: the role of the headteacher', in R. Arora and C. Duncan (eds), *Multicultural Education: towards good practice*, London, Routledge and Kegan Paul, pp. 36–46.

Dunlop, F. (1979), 'On the democratic organisation of schools', *Cambridge Journal of Education*, 9, pp. 43–54.

Eggleston, J. *et al.* (1986), *Education for Some*, Stoke-on-Trent, Trentham Books.

Flew, A. (1984), *Education, Race and Revolution*, London, Centre for Policy Studies.

Foster-Carter, O. (1987), 'The Honeyford affair: political and policy implications', in B. Troyna (ed.), *Racial Inequality in Education*, pp. 44–58, London, Tavistock.

Gay, G. (1983), 'Multiethnic education: historical developments and future prospects', *Phi Delta Kappan*, 64, pp. 560–3.

Hall, S. (1980), 'Teaching race', *Multiracial Education*, 9, pp. 3–12.

Harrison, S. (1986), 'Swann: the implications for schools', *Journal of Education Policy*, 1, pp. 183–95.

Home Office (1978), *The West Indian Community: observations on the Report of the Select Committee on Race Relations and Immigration*, Cmnd 7186, London, HMSO.

Honeyford, R. (1984), 'Education and race: an alternative view', *Salisbury Review*, Winter, pp. 30–2.

Jeffcoate, R. (1984), *Ethnic Minorities and Education*, London, Harper and Row.

Joseph, Sir K. (1986), *Without Prejudice: education for an ethnically mixed society*, unpublished speech, 20 May.

King, E. (1986), 'Recent experimental strategies for prejudice reduction in American schools and classrooms', *Journal of Curriculum Studies*, 18, pp. 331–8.

Kirp, D. (1979), *Doing Good by Doing Little*, Berkeley, Calif., University of California Press.

Lynch, J. (1983), *The Multiracial Curriculum*, London, Batsford.

Lynch, J. (1987), *Prejudice Reduction and the Schools*, London, Cassell.

Mullard, C. (1982), 'Multiracial education in Britain: from assimilation to cultural pluralism', in J. Tierney (ed.), *Race, Migration and Schooling*, pp. 120–33, London, Holt, Rinehart and Winston.

Mullard, C. (1984), *Anti-Racist Education: the three Os*, Cardiff, National Association for Multiracial Education.

Mullard, C. (1986), *Pluralism, Ethnicism and Ideology: implications for a transformative pedagogy*, Centre for Race and Ethnic Studies, University of Amsterdam, Working Paper 2, Amsterdam, CRES.

Mullard, C. *et al.* (1983), *Local Education Authority Policy Documents: a descriptive analysis of contents*, Working Paper 2, Race Relations Policy and Practice Research Unit, London, Institute of Education, University of London.

Palmer, F. (1987), *Anti-racism: an assault on education and value*, London, Sherwood Press.

Patten, C. (1986), *Swann in the Shires*, unpublished speech, 5–6 March.

Ramazanoglu, C. (1986), 'Gender and Islam – the politics of Muslim feminism', *Ethnic and Racial Studies*, 9, pp. 258–63.

Reeves, F. (1983), *British Racial Discourse*, London, Cambridge University Press.

Richards, C. (1986), 'Anti-racist initiatives', *Screen*, 27, 5, pp. 74–9.

Sarup, M. (1986), *The Politics of Multiracial Education*, London, Routledge and Kegan Paul.

Street-Porter, R. (1978), *Race, Children and Cities*, Unit E361, Milton Keynes, Open University Press.

Taylor, B. (1984–5), 'Multicultural Education in a Monocultural region', *New Community*, 12, pp. 1–8.

Tomlinson, S. (1983), *Ethnic Minorities in British Schools*, London, Heinemann.

Troyna, B. (1982), 'The ideological and policy response to black pupils in British schools', in A. Hartnett (ed.), *The Social Sciences in Educational Studies*, pp. 127–43, London, Heinemann.

Troyna, B. (1983), 'Multicultural education: just another brick in the wall?', *New Community*, 10, pp. 424–8.

Troyna, B. (1984), 'Multicultural education: emancipation or containment?' in L. Barton and S. Walker (eds), *Social Crisis and Educational Research*, pp. 75–97, Beckenham, Croom Helm.

Troyna, B. (1986), '"Swann's song"; the origins, ideology and implications of Education for All', *Journal of Education Policy*, 1, pp. 171–81.

Troyna, B. (1987), *Racial Inequality in Education*, London, Tavistock.

Troyna, B. and Ball, W. (1985), *Views from the Chalk Face: school responses to an LEA Policy on multicultural education*, Policy Papers in Ethnic Relations (1), Centre for Research in Ethnic Relations, University of Warwick.

Troyna, B. and Carrington, B. (1987), 'Antisexist/antiracist education – a false dilemma: a reply to Walkling and Brannigan', *Journal of Moral Education*, 16, pp. 61–5.

Troyna, B. and Smith, D. I. (eds) (1983), *Racism, School and the Labour Market*, Leicester, National Youth Bureau.

Troyna, B. and Williams, J. (1986), *Racism, Education and the State: the racialisation of education policy*, Beckenham, Croom Helm.

Walkling, P. and Brannigan, C. (1986), 'Antisexist/antiracist education: a possible dilemma', *Journal of Moral Education*, 15, pp. 16–25.

White, P. (1983), *Beyond Domination: an essay in the political philosophy of education*, London, Routledge and Kegan Paul.

3.6

School Matters

Peter Mortimore

The key question

A major question addressed by the Junior School Project concerned the factors which contributed to school effectiveness. We found that much of the variation between schools in their effects on pupils' progress and development was explained by differences in policies and practices, and by certain given characteristics. By investigating the interconnections between the many factors linked with school effects on pupils' progress and development, we have been able to identify some of the mechanisms by which effective junior schooling is promoted. In particular, we have shown that the given features of schools and classes are closely related to many aspects of policy and practice. Moreover, effective school policies are associated with the adoption of more effective teaching strategies within the classroom.

The many disparate findings [of the Project on 'mechanisms of effectiveness' have been grouped] into twelve key factors. However, it must be emphasised that these factors are not purely statistical constructs. They have not been obtained solely by means of quantitative analyses. Rather, they are derived from a combination of careful examination and discussion of the statistical findings, and the use of educational and research judgement. They represent the interpretation of the research results by an interdisciplinary team of researchers and teachers.

Key factors for effective junior schooling

[The Project examined the effect of] a variety of factors and processes upon pupils' educational outcomes. Many of these factors had an impact on a range of different outcomes. Similarly, features of the school and the classroom frequently were related to each other and, through a detailed investigation of these links, we have developed a framework of key factors that we believe contribute to effective junior schooling. This framework, however, is not intended to be a blue-print for success. Inevitably there were aspects of school life which we could not examine during the course of the Project. Furthermore, schools, like all institutions, are perpetually changing. Our survey was carried out between 1980 and 1984, and it was not possible to take full account of all the changes (particularly in approaches to the curriculum) that were evolving in schools and classrooms during that period. Nonetheless, a large number of factors were related consistently to effective junior schooling. Those factors which come under the control of the head, the staff or the class teacher we have grouped together under twelve headings. Before examining these factors over which schools and teachers can exercise control, we shall [look] briefly [at the] less flexible characteristics of schools [. . .] – the school and class givens. It is clear that certain of these given features make it easier to create an effective school.

Key given factors

Schools that cover the entire primary age range, where pupils do not have to transfer at age seven, appear to be at an advantage, as do voluntary aided schools. Even though voluntary schools tend to have more socio-economically advantaged intakes than county schools, we still found that voluntary schools tended to be more effective. Smaller schools, with a pupil roll of around 160 or fewer, also appear to benefit their pupils. Research by Galton at Leicester University has also suggested that smaller schools tend to be more effective. Class size is also relevant: smaller classes (with fewer than 24 pupils) had a positive impact upon pupil progress and development, especially in the early years, whereas in classes with 27 or more pupils the effects were less positive.

Not surprisingly, a good physical environment, as reflected in the school's amenities, decorative order and immediate surroundings, was a positive advantage. Extended periods of disruption, due to building work and redecoration, can have a negative impact on pupils' progress. This was in line with Rutter et al.'s (1979) findings concerning the care of school buildings. The stability of the school's teaching force is also an important factor. Changes of head and deputy headteacher, though inevitable, have an unsettling effect upon the pupils. Every effort, therefore, should be made to reduce the potentially negative impact of such changes. Similarly, where there is an unavoidable change of class teacher during the school year, careful planning will be needed to ensure an easy transition, and to minimise disruption to the pupils. Where pupils experience continuity with one class teacher through the whole year, progress is more likely to occur. It is, however, not only continuity of staff that is important. Although major or frequent changes tend to have negative effects, schools were less effective where the headteacher had been in post for a long time. In the more effective schools, heads had usually been in post for between three and seven years.

It is clear, therefore, that some schools are more advantaged in terms of their size, status, environment and stability of teaching staff. Nonetheless, although these favourable given characteristics contribute to effectiveness, they do not, by themselves, ensure it. They provide a supporting framework within which the head and teachers can work to promote pupil progress and development. However, it is the factors within the control of the head and teachers that are crucial. These are the factors that can be changed and improved.

The 12 key factors described below are not arranged in any order of importance. However, we have grouped them into factors that concern school policy (1 to 4), those that relate to classroom policy (5 to 9), and, finally, aspects of relevance to school and class policy (10 to 12).

The twelve key factors

Purposeful leadership of the staff by the headteacher.
The involvement of the deputy head.
The involvement of teachers.
Consistency amongst teachers.
Structured sessions.
Intellectually challenging teaching.
The work-centred environment.
Limited focus within sessions.
Maximum communication between teachers and pupils.
Record keeping.
Parental involvement.
Positive climate.

1   Purposeful leadership of the staff by the headteacher
Purposeful leadership occurred where the headteacher understood the needs of the school and was involved actively in the school's work, without exerting total control over the rest of the staff. In effective schools, headteachers were involved in curriculum discussion and influenced the content of guidelines drawn up within the school, without taking complete control. They also influenced the teaching strategies of teachers, but only selectively, where they judged it necessary. This leadership was demonstrated by an emphasis on the monitoring of pupils' progress, through teachers keeping individual records. Approaches varied – some schools kept written records; others passed on folders of pupils' work to their next teacher; some did both – but a systematic policy of record

keeping was important. With regard to in-service training, those heads exhibiting purposeful leadership did not allow teachers total freedom to attend any course: attendance was encouraged for a good reason. Nonetheless, most teachers in these schools had attended in-service courses.

Thus, effective headteachers were sufficiently involved in, and knowledgeable about, what went on in the classrooms and about the progress of individual pupils. They were more able to feel confident about their teaching staff and did not need to intervene constantly. At the same time, however, they were not afraid to assert their leadership where appropriate.

2   The involvement of the deputy head

Our findings indicate that the deputy head can have a major role to play in promoting the effectiveness of junior schools. Where the deputy was frequently absent, or absent for a prolonged period (due to illness, attendance on long courses, or other commitments), this was detrimental to pupils' progress and development. Moreover, a change of deputy head tended to have negative effects. The responsibilities undertaken by deputy heads also seemed to be significant. Where the head generally involved the deputy in policy decisions, it was beneficial to the pupils. This was particularly true in terms of allocating teachers to classes. Thus, it appears that a certain amount of delegation by the headteacher, and the sharing of responsibilities, promoted effectiveness.

3   The involvement of teachers

In successful schools, the teachers were involved in curriculum planning and played a major role in developing their own curriculum guidelines. As with the deputy head, teacher involvement in decisions concerning which classes they were to teach, was important. Similarly, we found that consultation with teachers about decisions on spending was associated with greater effectiveness. It appears that schools in which teachers were consulted on issues affecting school policy, as well as those affecting them directly, were more likely to be successful. We found a link between schools where the deputy was involved in policy decisions and schools where teachers were involved. Thus, effective primary schools did not operate a small management team – everyone had their say.

4   Consistency among teachers

We have already shown that continuity of staffing had positive effects. Not only, however, do pupils benefit from teacher continuity, but it also appears that consistency in teacher approach is important. For example, in schools where all teachers followed guidelines in the same way (whether closely or selectively), the impact on progress was positive. Where there was variation between teachers in their usage of guidelines, this had a negative effect.

5   Structured sessions

The Project findings indicate that pupils benefited when their school day was given some structure. In effective classes, pupils' work was organised in broad outline by the teacher, who ensured that there was always plenty of work to do. We also found that the progress of pupils benefited when they were not given unlimited responsibility for planning their own daily programme of work, or for choosing work activities, but were guided into areas of study or exploration and taught the skills necessary for independently managing that work. In general, therefore, teachers who organised a framework within which pupils could work, and yet encouraged them to exercise a degree of independence, and allowed some freedom and choice within this structure, were more successful. Children developed and made progress particularly in classrooms where most pupils were able to work in the absence of constant support from their teachers. Clearly, when pupils can work autonomously in this way the teacher is freed to spend time in areas she or he considers a high priority.

6   Intellectually challenging teaching

Not surprisingly, the quality of teaching was very important in promoting pupil progress and development. Our findings show clearly that, in those classes where pupils were stimulated and challenged, progress was greatest. The content of teacher–pupil classroom talk was vitally important. Progress was encouraged where teachers used more higher-order questions and statements, when they encouraged pupils to use their creative imagination and powers of problem solving. Additionally, in classrooms which were bright and interesting, where the context created by the teacher was stimulating, and where teachers communicated their own interest and enthusiasm to the children, greater pupil progress occurred. In contrast, teachers who frequently directed pupils' work without discussing it, or explaining its purpose, were less effective.

A further important feature was the expectation in the more effective classrooms that pupils could manage independently the tasks they were engaged upon. In such classes teachers only rarely intervened with instructions and directives, yet everyone in the class knew what to do and could work without close supervision.

7   Work centred environment

In schools where teachers spent more of their time discussing the content of work with pupils, and less time on routine matters and the maintenance of work activity, the effect was positive. Time devoted to giving pupils feedback about their work also appeared to be very beneficial.

The work centred environment was characterised by a high level of pupil industry in the classroom. Pupils appeared to enjoy their work and were eager to commence new tasks. The noise level was low, although this is not to say that there was silence in the classroom. In fact, none of the classes we visited were completely silent. Furthermore, pupil movement around the classroom was not excessive, and was generally work related. These results receive support from the views of pupils. Even in the third year over 40 per cent of pupils reported that they had difficulty in concentrating on their work most of the time. Where levels of noise and movement were high, concentration seems to be more difficult to maintain. Work centred classrooms, therefore, had a business-like and purposeful air, with pupils obviously enjoying the work they were doing. Furthermore, where classrooms were work centred, lessons were found to be more challenging.

8   Limited focus within sessions

It appears that pupils made greater progress when teachers tended to organise lessons around one particular curriculum area. At times, work could be undertaken in two areas and also produce positive effects, but, where the tendency was for the teacher regularly to organise classroom work such that three or more curriculum areas were running concurrently, then pupils' progress was marred. This finding is related to a number of other factors. For example, pupil industry was lower in classrooms where mixed-activities occurred, noise and pupil movement were greater, and teachers spent less time discussing work and more time on routine issues and behaviour control. Thus, such classrooms were less likely to be work-centred. More importantly, in mixed activity sessions the opportunities for communication between teachers and pupils were reduced (see key factor 9 below).

A focus upon one curriculum area does not imply that all the pupils should do exactly the same work. On the contrary, effects were most positive when the teacher geared the level of work to pupils' needs, but not where all pupils worked individually on exactly the same piece of work. It seems likely that, in mixed curriculum sessions, the demands made upon the teachers' time, attention and energy can become too great for them to ensure effective learning with all groups. Furthermore, it becomes more difficult in such sessions for the teacher to call the class together should the opportunity arise to share an interesting point that may emerge from the work of a particular group or pupil. We recognise that there are many occasions when teachers may wish to diversify the work in the classroom, and beyond, into more than one curriculum area. Sometimes such diversification is unavoidable, perhaps through the constraints of timetabling or because of the nature of the work in progress, but, for the reasons cited above, we would urge the utmost caution over the adoption of a mixed-curriculum methodology as a basis for teaching and learning.

9   Maximum communication between teachers and pupils

We found evidence that pupils gained from having lots of communication with the teacher. Thus, those teachers who spent higher proportions of their time not interacting with the children were less successful in promoting progress and development. The time teachers spent on communications with the whole class was also important. Most teachers devoted most of their attention to speaking with individuals. Each child, therefore, could only expect to receive a fairly small number of individual contacts with their teacher. In fact, as we described earlier, for each pupil the average number of such contacts over a day was only eleven. Given that some children demand, and receive, more attention than the average from their teachers, this means that others have very few individual contacts per day. By speaking to the whole class, teachers increased the overall number of contacts with children, as pupils become part of the teacher's audience more often in such circumstances. Most importantly, higher-order communications occurred more frequently when the teacher talked to the whole class.

We are not, however, advocating traditional class teaching. Our findings did not show any such approach to be beneficial for pupils and, in fact, we found no evidence of readily identifiable teaching styles at all. We feel that teaching is far too complex an activity for it to be categorised in this way. On the contrary, our results indicate the value of a flexible approach, that can blend individual, class and group interaction as appropriate. Furthermore, where children worked in a single curriculum area within sessions (even if they were engaged on individual or group tasks), it was easier for teachers to raise an intellectually challenging point with all pupils. Such exchanges tended to occur when teachers were introducing a topic to the class before pupils were sent off to work individually or in groups. Class discussions were also a popular forum for gathering all pupils together, as was storytelling. These activities offered teachers a particular opportunity to challenge and stimulate their pupils.

10   Record keeping

We have already commented upon the value of record keeping in relation to the purposeful leadership of the headteacher. In addition, it was also an important aspect of teachers' planning and assessment. Where teachers reported that they kept written records of pupils' work progress, in addition to the Authority's Primary

Yearly Record Summary, the effect on the pupils was positive. The keeping of records concerning pupils' personal and social development was also found to be generally beneficial. Furthermore, in many effective schools, teachers kept samples of pupils' work in folders to be passed on to their next teacher.

11   Parental involvement

Our findings show parental involvement in the life of the school to be a positive influence upon pupils' progress and development. This included help in classrooms and on educational visits, and attendance at meetings to discuss children's progress. The headteacher's accessibility to parents was also important; schools operating an informal open-door policy being more effective. Parental involvement in pupils' educational development within the home was also clearly beneficial. Parents who read to their children, heard them read, and provided them with access to books at home, had a positive effect upon their children's learning. Curiously, however, formal parent–teacher associations were not found to be related to effective schooling. Although the reasons for this are not clear it could be that some parents find the formal structure of such bodies to be intimidating and are thus deterred from involvement, rather than encouraged. We also found that some parents feel that PTAs tend to be run by small cliques of parents. We would not wish to advocate, of course, that schools disband their PTAs, but if a school has an association and is not involving parents in other ways it would perhaps be worth considering how parent–school relationships could be opened up.

12   Positive climate

The Junior School Project provides confirmation that an effective school has a positive ethos. Overall, we found the atmosphere to be more pleasant in the effective schools, for a variety of reasons. Both around the school and within the classroom, less emphasis on punishment and critical control, and a greater emphasis on praise and reward was beneficial. Where teachers actively encouraged self-control on the part of pupils, rather than emphasising the negative aspects of their behaviour, progress and development were enhanced. What appeared to be important was firm but fair classroom management. The class teachers' attitude to pupils was also important. Positive effects resulted where teachers obviously enjoyed teaching their classes, valued the fun factor, and communicated their enthusiasm to the children. Their interest in the children as individuals, and not just as learners, also fostered progress. Those who devoted more time to non-school chat or small talk increased pupils' progress and development. Outside the classroom, evidence of a positive climate included: the organisation of lunchtime and

after-school clubs for pupils; involvement of pupils in the presentation of assemblies; teachers eating their lunch at the same tables as
the children; organisation of trips and visits; and the use of the local
environment as a learning resource.

It is important to note that the climate in effective schools was not
only positive for the pupils. The teachers' working conditions also
contributed to the creation of a positive climate. Where teachers
had non-teaching periods, the impact on pupil progress and development was positive. Thus, the climate created by the teachers
for the pupils, and by the head for the teachers, was an important
aspect of school effectiveness. This further appeared to be reflected
in effective schools by happy, well-behaved pupils who were friendly towards each other and outsiders, and by the absence of grafitti
around the school.

Links with other studies

Many of the key factors have been identified in the results of other
studies or reports and we will describe some of the links between
our study and the findings of other research here. However, it must
be stressed that the selection of studies is not intended to be
exhaustive. A more detailed and thorough discussion of the results
of many of the major studies of school effectiveness, particularly
those undertaken in the United States, has been provided by Purkey
and Smith (1983). Reviews by Cuttance (1980a, 1980b, 1986),
Rutter (1983), Grosin (1985) and Reynolds (1985), and the contributions of Rowan, et al. (1983) and Taylor (1985), provide further
information about school effectiveness research. A summary of
major findings on effective learning and teaching is given by the
United States Department of Education (1986).

Positive leadership

A number of other studies have pointed to the importance of the
headteacher's leadership in promoting school effectiveness. For
example, Weber (1971), in an American study of four inner-city
schools recognised as 'exemplary', identified 'strong leadership' as
one of eight school-wide characteristics that influenced pupils'
reading achievement. Trisman, et al. (1976), likewise, noted the
importance of strong 'instructional leadership' in their study of
schools which were unusually effective in promoting reading progress. Work by Armor, et al. (1976) examined schools which had
been especially successful in promoting the reading achievement of
minority children. They concluded that schools where the principals
achieved a balance between a strong leadership role for themselves

and maximum autonomy for teachers were more effective.

Brookover, *et al.* (1979) compared matched pairs (in terms of intakes) of elementary schools which were differentiated by the achievement of their pupils, and concluded that one of seven important factors which led to higher pupil achievement was the leadership role of the principal. Similarly, the Californian State Department of Education (1980) compared schools where pupils' reading scores were improving with those where reading scores were decreasing. This study also confirmed the value of positive leadership, and noted that such leadership was more effective when it included the sharing of responsibility for decision making and planning. Our results support this conclusion. Tomlinson (1980) and Levine and Stark (1981) have also drawn attention to the importance of the principal's leadership in effective schools. In the British context, Rutter, *et al.* (1979), in a major study of secondary schools in inner London, noted the importance of the headteacher's leadership in the promotion of school effectiveness. More recently, the Thomas Report (1985) which examined ways of improving primary schools in the Inner London Education Authority, commented on the necessity for clear and sensitive leadership by the headteacher.

The involvement of the deputy head

This finding is in accordance with the suggestions of Plowden (1967) and Coulson and Cox (1975) that deputies should be more involved in decision making. [The Project noted that] it was often the duty of the deputy head to take charge of the day-to-day organisation of schools and to ensure that everything ran smoothly. Furthermore, many deputy heads had a particular pastoral role in the school, relating both to pupils and other teachers. Finally, they placed great emphasis on their role as a link between the head and the rest of the staff, a role of which many headteachers were also aware.

Far less attention has been paid to the role of the deputy head in previous studies of school effects. There is evidence, however, that the sharing of responsibility for decision making and planning is an important aspect of effective leadership by the head (see the study by the California State Department of Education, 1980). Our findings indicate clearly the value of involving the deputy head in such decision-making and planning. Similarly, in the Thomas Report (1985) it is stated 'we believe that many primary schools would benefit from increased delegation of responsibilities to members of staff' (p. 66). This report also argued that the deputy should be involved in staff leadership and the formulation of school policies.

The involvement of teachers

Staff involvement is, therefore, related to the first factor, the headteacher's purposeful leadership. An authoritarian style of leadership will not encourage staff participation and involvement in decision making. The study by the California State Department of Education (1980) pointed to the importance of sharing the responsibility for decision-making and planning with other staff. Glenn (1981) conducted case studies of four urban elementary schools. Among other factors, she suggested that school effectiveness was enhanced where there was joint planning by the staff. Levine and Stark (1981) also emphasised the importance of 'grade-level decision making' which encouraged collaborative planning among teachers. Moreover, the conclusions of the Thomas Report (1985) noted the value of staff involvement in decision-making in primary schools. The authors state 'it is a matter of high priority that each school should have a sense of wholeness. That can be achieved . . . after the adjustments that inevitably follow staff discussions arranged to consider proposals' (p. 66).

Consistency among teachers

Glenn's study (1981) also pointed to the benefits of consistency amongst teaching staff, particularly in the use of through-the-grades reading and mathematics programmes. Edmonds (1979a, 1979b) emphasised the importance of school-wide policies and agreement among teachers in their aims. Similarly, Levine and Stark (1981) found that coordination of curriculum, instruction and testing to focus on specified objectives achieved through careful planning and staff development, was of value. Tomlinson (1980) also suggested that it was important for teachers to have a common purpose and clearly agreed goals. In the secondary sector, Rutter, et al. (1979) found that consistency among teachers promoted effectiveness, and noted that staff consensus on the value and aims of the school as a whole was related to greater success in promoting pupils' educational outcomes.

Structured sessions

Structure was also shown to be important by Traub, et al. (1976) who found that higher pupil performance in basic skills occurred where there was an emphasis on a more structured approach to learning in which students did not have complete freedom to decide their programme of activities. Similarly, Stallings (1976), in a study of pupils' progress in reading and mathematics in elementary classrooms, found that one of the factors related to higher achievement was the teachers' use of 'systematic instructional patterns'. In a review, Rosenshine and Stevens (1981) also noted the importance of order, structure and purposefulness in the classroom, in promoting pupils' progress. Similarly, Solomon and Kendall (1976) found that excessive pupil choice and responsibility for planning their own work was disadvantageous for pupil achievement and self-esteem. These authors argued it was not a choice between teacher control and pupil control, rather a question of teacher control versus lack of control of learning activities.

Intellectually challenging teaching

Many studies [. . .] have indicated that high expectations of pupils are beneficial (see research by Weber, 1971; Armor, et al., 1976; Trisman, et al., 1976; Rutter, et al., 1979, California State Department of Education, 1980; Glenn, 1981; and reviews by Brophy, 1983 and Pilling and Kellmer Pringle, 1978). Evidence of the value of intellectually challenging teaching is also provided in the study of junior pupils conducted by Galton and Simon (1980). In addition, Levine and Stark (1981) have noted that effective elementary schools emphasised the development of higher-order cognitive skills such as reading comprehension, and problem solving in mathematics.

Work centred environment

Weber's (1971) study also emphasised the importance of an atmosphere of order, purposefulness, and pleasure in learning. Work by Rosenshine and Berliner (1978) has indicated that, where academic engaged time was higher, pupil progress in basic skills was promoted. Brookover and Lezotte (1979), in an analysis of factors which differentiated schools in which pupils' reading scores increased from those where scores were decreased, found that a greater amount of teacher time spent on direct instruction was a characteristic of improving schools. Brookover, et al. (1979) also noted that more time spent on instruction was related to effectiveness.

Work in junior schools in Britain has also shown that the amount of teacher time spent communicating with pupils about their work was related positively to pupil progress. Galton and Simon (1980) noted 'all three groups of successful teachers had more task interactions than the typical teacher in the sample' (p. 196). In addition, Tomlinson (1980) stressed the importance of the efficient use of classroom time. Fisher, et al. (1980), in a study which examined the characteristics of good schools, found that academic learning time was increased, while Glenn's (1981) work has noted the importance of efficient, coordinated scheduling and planning of activities.

Our findings also support those of Armor, *et al.* (1976), which demonstrated that an orderly atmosphere in schools was associated with greater effectiveness. Rutter, *et al.* (1979) also indicated that strategies of classroom management which kept students actively engaged in learning activities had a beneficial effect on pupils' educational outcomes.

Limited focus within sessions

We have found no references in published studies of school effectiveness to the identification of a limited focus as defined in our research being an important aspect of effectiveness. This is likely to reflect the absence in past studies of data about the way teachers mix different curriculum activities.

Maximum communication

Work by Galton and Simon (1980) similarly found that the amount of teacher–pupil contact was important. They noted for all three groups of successful teachers 'the most striking and perhaps the most important feature was that the teachers all achieved above-average levels of interactions with their pupils' (p. 186). Our results demonstrate that one of the ways teachers were able to increase the level of communication with pupils was by the use of a balance of class and individual contacts. Galton and Simon (1980) also found that one of their groups of more successful teachers were the 'class enquirers', who combined whole class teaching with individual work. As with our Project, these authors also found a positive link between the use of higher-order questions and statements and maximum communications.

The Thomas Report (1985) also noted that teacher communication with the whole class could be valuable. Thus, the authors commented 'Here and there our visits to classrooms coincided with an intensive piece of work by a teacher using exposition and discussion with a group of children or the whole class. Almost always this teaching brought a sense of eagerness and involvement to the work that was less often apparent when children were working on their own' (p. 32). They also noted that arrangements for individual work on any large scale frequently break down 'because teachers find it impossible to give sufficient individual attention to children and have to engage children too much in work that is simply time-filling'. Galton and Simon (1980) similarly found that where teachers devoted most of their time to communicating with individuals, the children of necessity spent most of their time working on their own.

Record keeping

A number of previous studies of effectiveness have also noted the importance of school-wide systems for the monitoring and evaluation of pupil progress. Thus, Weber's (1971) work noted the value of careful evaluation of student progress. Edmonds (1979a, 1979b, 1981) found that the frequent monitoring of pupil progress was related positively to effectiveness. Levine and Stark (1981) also emphasised the need for schools to adopt simple procedures for tracking student and class progress and achievement. The California State Department of Education study (1980) noted the necessity for teacher accountability for pupil performance, and the provision of accurate information on that performance. Dean (1980) also reported that 'record-keeping is an essential ingredient in making education continuous' (p. 14).

Parental involvement

Studies conducted in the United States have also suggested that parental involvement is an influential aspect of school effectiveness. Thus, Armor, *et al*. (1976) noted the value of high levels of parent–teacher and parent–headteacher contact. In Britain, work by Hewison and Tizard (1980) has demonstrated a link between parental involvement and reading attainment for junior pupils. Mortimore and Mortimore (1984) provide a review of research which has examined the impact of parental involvement. Hargreaves (1984) and Thomas (1985) have also noted the value of increasing parental involvement in secondary and in primary schools. Thus, the Hargreaves Report notes

> For very many years we have known, both from well established research findings as well as from common sense, that parental commitment is a cornerstone of the school's success. If parents are interested in their children's schooling, if they are supportive of the school's endeavours, if they act in partnership with teachers, then the children will achieve more in school (p. 14).

Positive climate

Other studies have reached similar conclusions concerning a positive climate. As Purkey and Smith (1983) noted, the literature indicates that a student's chance of success in learning cognitive skills is heavily influenced by the climate of the school. Trisman, *et al*. (1976) found that more effective schools tended to have a good school atmosphere including student–teacher rapport. Work by Moos (1978) noted the importance of a positive classroom climate. Brookover, *et al*. (1979) found the quality of the school's social climate was related positively to the promotion of pupil achievement. Edmonds (1979a, 1979b) and Edmonds and Frederiksen (1979) have also reported that a school climate conducive to learning was necessary to promote achievement. In Britain, Rutter, *et al.*'s (1979) work provides evidence of the significance of the characteristics of schools as social institutions. The Rutter study indicated that the school ethos was influential in determining effectiveness. It also noted the importance of praise and of the emphasis on rewards rather than punishments.

Summary

It is clear, therefore, that there are many links between the factors identified as important in the Junior School Project, and those found to contribute to school effectiveness in previous research. Nonetheless, some factors have received less attention in past studies; in particular, the key role of the deputy head, and the value of a limited focus in the classroom. Although a few studies have noted the value of maximising communication between teachers and pupils, in general, this aspect has received only limited attention in most analyses of school effectiveness.

The twelve key factors point to effective schools as being friendly, supportive environments, led by heads who are not afraid to assert their views and yet are able to share management and decision making with the staff. Class teachers within effective schools provide a structured learning situation for their pupils but give them freedom within this framework. By being flexible in their use of whole class, group and individual contacts, they maximise communications with each pupil. Furthermore, through limiting their focus within sessions, their attention is less fragmented. Hence, the opportunities for developing a work centred environment and for presenting challenging work to pupils are increased.

Whilst the twelve key factors we have outlined may not constitute a recipe for effective junior schooling, they can provide a framework within which the various partners in the life of the school – headteacher and staff, parents and pupils, and governors – can operate. Each of these partners has some role to play in fostering the overall success of the school, and when each makes a positive contribution, the result can be an increase in the school's effectiveness.

References

Armor, D., Conry-Oseguera, P., Cox, M., King, N., McConnell, L., Pascal, A., Pauly, E. and Zellman, G. (1976), 'Analysis of the School Preferred Reading

Program in selected Los Angeles Minority Schools' (Report No. R-2007-CAUSD), Santa Monica FA, The Rand Corporation.

Brookover, W. B., Beady, C., Flood, P. and Schweitzer, J. (1979), *School Systems and Student Achievement: Schools Make a Difference*, New York, Praeger.

Brookover, W. B. and Lezotte, L. W. (1979), *Changes in School Characteristics Coincident with Changes in Student Achievement*, East Langing, Institute for Research on Teaching, Michigan State University.

Brophy, J. (1983), 'Research on the Self Fulfilling Prophecy and Teacher Expectations', *Journal of Educational Psychology*, 75, 5, pp. 631–61.

California State Department of Education (1980), 'Report on the Special Studies of Selected ECE Schools with Increasing and Decreasing Reading Scores', Sacramento, California, Office of Program Evaluation and Research.

Coulson, A. and Cox, M. (1975), 'What do deputies do?', *Education 3–13*, 3, 2, pp. 100–3.

Cuttance, P. F. (1980a), 'Coleman, Plowden, Jencks and now, Rutter: An Assessment of a Recent Contribution to the Debate on School Effects', *Scandinavian Journal of Educational Research*, 3, pp. 191–205.

Cuttance, P. F. (1980b), 'Do Schools Consistently Influence the Performance of their Students?', *Educational Review*, 32, 3, pp. 267–80.

Cuttance, P. (1986), 'Effective Schooling: A Report to the Scottish Educational Department', Centre for Educational Sociology, University of Edinburgh.

Dean, J. (1980), 'Continuity', in C. Richards (ed.), *Primary Education: Issues for the Eighties*, London, A. and C. Black.

Edmonds, R. R. (1979a), 'Effective Schools for the Urban Poor', *Educational Leadership*, 37, 1, pp. 15–27.

Edmonds, R. R. (1979b), 'Some Schools Work and More Can', *Social Policy*, 12, 2, pp. 56–60.

Edmonds, R. R. (1981), 'Making Public Schools Effective', *Social Policy*, 12, pp. 56–60.

Edmonds, R. R. and Frederiksen, J. R. (1979), 'Search for Effective Schools: The Identification and Analysis of City Schools that are Instructionally Effective for Poor Children', ERIC Document Reproduction Service No. ED 170 396.

Fisher, C. W., Berliner, D. C., Filby, N. N., Marliave, R., Cahen, L. S. and Dishaw, M. M. (1980), 'Teaching behaviours, academic learning time, and student achievement: an overview', in C. Denham and A. Lieberman (eds), *Time to Learn*, Washington DC, Department of Education.

Galton, M. and Simon, B. (1980), *Progress and Performance in the Primary Classroom*, London, Routledge and Kegan Paul.

Glenn, B. C. (1981), *What Works? An Examination of Effective Schools for Poor Black Children*, Cambridge, Mass, Center for Law and Education, Harvard University.

Grosin, L. (1985), Theoretical Considerations and Strategy for Investigations of School Process and Pupil Outcome in the Swedish Comprehensive School. Paper presented to the British Educational Research Association Conference at the University of Sheffield, August 1985.

Hargreaves, D. (1984), *Improving Secondary Schools*, London, ILEA.

Hewison, J. and Tizard, J. (1980), 'Parental Involvement and Reading Attainment', *British Journal of Educational Psychology*, 50, Part 3, pp. 209–15.

Levine, D. U. and Stark, J. (1981), *Extended Summary and Conclusions: Institutional and Organizational Arrangements and Processes for Improving Academic Achievement at Inner City Elementary Schools*, Kansas City, Center for the Study of Metropolitan Problems in Education, University of Missouri-Kansas City.

Moos, R. H. (1978), 'A typology of junior high and high school classrooms', *American Educational Research Journal*, 15, pp. 53–66.

Mortimore, P. and Mortimore, J. (1984), 'Parents and school, Education special report', *Education*, 5 October.

Pilling, D. and Kellmer Pringle, M. (1978), *Controversial Issues in Child Development*, National Children's Bureau, London, Paul Elek.

Plowden Report (1967), *Children and their Primary Schools*, London, HMSO.

Purkey, S. C. and Smith, M. S. (1983), 'Effective schools: a review', *Elementary School Journal*, 83, 4, pp. 427–52.

Reynolds, D. (ed.) (1985), *Studying School Effectiveness*, London, Falmer.

Rosenshine, B. and Berliner, D. C. (1978), 'Academic engaged time', *British Journal of Teacher Education*, 4, 1, pp. 3–16.

Rosenshine, B. and Stevens, R. (1981), 'Advances in Research on Teaching', unpublished manuscript, University of Illinois, May 1981.

Rowan, B., Bossert, S. T. and Dwyer, D. C. (1983), 'Research on effective schools: a cautionary note', *Educational Researcher*, 12, 4, pp. 24–31.

Rutter, M. (1983), 'School Effects on Pupil Progress: Research Findings and Policy Implications', *Child Development*, 54, 1, pp. 1–29.

Rutter, M., Maughan, B., Mortimore, P. and Ouston, J. (1979), *Fifteen Thousand Hours*, London, Open Books.

Solomon, D. and Kendall, A. J. (1976), *Final Report: Individual Characteristics and Children's Performance in Varied Educational Settings*, Chicago, Ill., Spencer Foundation Project.

Stallings, J. A. (1976), 'How instructional processes relate to child outcomes in a national study of follow through', *Journal of Teacher Education*, 27, 1, pp. 43–7.

Taylor, W. (1985), The Task of the School and the Task of the Teacher. Paper presented to the DES conference on Better School Evaluation and Appraisal for Both Schools and Teachers, University of Birmingham, November 1985.

Thomas, N. (1985), *Improving Primary Schools: Report of the Committee on Primary Education (The Thomas Report)*, London, ILEA.

Tomlinson, T. M. (1980), Student Ability, Student Background and Student Achievement: Another Look at Life in Effective Schools. Paper presented at the Educational Testing Service Conference on Effective Schools. New York, May 1980.

Traub, R., Weiss, J. and Fisher, C. (1976), *Openness in Schools: An Evaluation, Research in Education: Series 5*, Toronto, OISE.

Trisman, D. A., Waller, M. I. and Wilder, C. A. (1976), *A Descriptive and Analytic Study of Compensatory Reading Programs: Final report*, Princeton, NJ, Educational Testing Service.

United States Department of Education (1986), *What Works: Research About Teaching and Learning*, Washington, United States Department of Education.

Weber, G. (1971), *Inner-City Children can be Taught to Read: Four Successful Schools*, Washington, DC, Council for Basic Education.

SECTION 4

Changing the Curriculum

Introduction

Curriculum change has provided the focus for some of the most interesting analytical work in recent years. It is the area where links with the schools effectiveness studies are most close. Both are characterised by a pragmatic approach to generating theory and both have considerable potential for policy formulation and implementation.

Michael Fullan's work, based primarily on work in North America and Canada, has been increasingly acknowledged since the publication in 1982 of his seminal work, *The Meaning of Educational Change*. The extract included in this section establishes very clearly the complexity of the change process. Jean Rudduck, building on extensive experience, emphasises the importance of developing shared understanding among the workers (teachers and pupils) involved in any curriculum development project, a view supported by Sue Johnston, who explores the nature of collaborative models of curriculum development. She develops a social strategies model of implementation that avoids seeing innovation as a belief that conservative, entrenched and obstructive teachers must be conquered.

Derek Hodson pursues the same theme in a critical examination of top-down political/administrative models of curriculum reform. He argues that teachers can and should acquire the skills necessary to plan, design, implement and evaluate curriculum. For Richard Elmore it is the sharp point of implementation, the classroom teacher, which should provide the starting point for policy development. In this way the emphasis is placed not on the policymaker but on someone with immediate proximity to the problem. The connecting point between the problem and the closest point of contact (for example, a classroom teacher) becomes, therefore, the most critical stage of analysis.

Mary Simpson and Bob Moon explore the territory between centralised prescription for curriculum and what happens in schools and classrooms. The Scottish Health Studies development, piloted on the basis of school based initiative, was transformed by central bureaucratic controls at the point of more widespread adoption. Mary Simpson, in looking at the tensions generated when aspects of school based developments are introduced into a centrally controlled system, suggests ways of resolving conflicts. Bob Moon questions the assumptions upon which policies for curriculum change are linked to the structure of particular national systems of education. Despite the political rhetoric about centralised or decentralised controls he suggests that more powerful forces, having established the right conditions, can easily override formal systems of decision making. Curriculum decision makers, for example, need to understand the significance of pressure groups politics and the processes by which influence is achieved.

4.1

Planning, Doing, and Coping with Change

Michael Fullan

For the growing number of people who have attempted to bring about educational change, 'intractability' is becoming a household world. Being ungovernable, however, is not the same as being impervious to influence. And the inability to change *all* situations we would ideally like to reform does not lead to the conclusion that *no* situation can be changed. (To complicate matters even further – to conclude that a situation can be changed in a certain way does not mean that it should be.)

The picture of change which has been evolving needs to be considered from the point of view of what, if anything, can be done about it. To do this, I treat four major aspects of the problem of planning educational change: 'why planning fails', 'success is possible', 'guidelines for planning and coping', and 'scope of change'.

Why planning fails

Understanding why most attempts at educational reform fail goes far beyond the identification of specific technical problems such as lack of good materials, ineffective in-service training, or minimal administrative support. In more fundamental terms, educational change fails partly because of the assumptions of planners and partly because some 'problems' are inherently unsolvable. These two issues are explored in the next two subsections.

Faulty assumptions and ways of thinking about change

In a word, the assumptions of policy-makers are frequently *hyperrational* (Wise, 1977, 1979). One of the initial sources of the problem is the commitment of reformers to see a particular desired change implemented. Commitment to *what should be changed* often varies inversely with knowledge about *how to work through a process of change*. In fact, as I shall claim later, strong commitment to a particular change may be a barrier to setting up an effective process of change, and in any case they are two quite distinct aspects of social change.[1] The adage 'Where there's a will there's a way' is definitely not an apt one for the planning of educational change. There is an abundance of wills, but they are *in* the way rather than pointing to the way.

Lighthall's (1973) incisive critique of Smith and Keith's (1971) famous case study of the failure of a new open-concept elementary school provides strong support for the hypothesis that leadership commitment to a particular version of a change is negatively related to ability to implement it. Lighthall states, as I do throughout this Chapter, that educational change is a process of coming to grips with the *multiple* realities of people who are the main participants in implementing change. The leader who presupposes what the change should be and acts in ways which preclude others' realities is bound to fail. Lighthall describes Superintendent Spanman's first speech to the Kensington school faculty:

> Spanman's visit to Kensington School was to make a 'presentation' to the twenty-one member faculty. It was not for the purpose of discussing with them their joint problems of creating a whole new kind of education. His purpose was to express to the faculty parts of his reality; it was not to exchange his for theirs. Inasmuch as it was the faculty who were to carry the educational goals and images of his reality into action, that is to make much of his reality their realities too, and inasmuch as no person responds to realities other than his own, Spanman's selection of a one-way form of communication was self-defeating. In order for his reality to become part of theirs he would have to have made part of theirs his (Lighthall, p. 263).

Innovators who are unable to alter their realities of change through exchange with would-be implementers can be as authoritarian as the staunchest defenders of the status quo. This is not to say that innovators should not have deep convictions about the need for reform or should be prepared to abandon their ideas at the first sign of opposition. It is to say that innovators need to be open to the realities of others: sometimes because the ideas of others will lead to alterations for the better in the direction of change, and sometimes because the others' realities will expose the problems of implementation which must be addressed and at the very least will indicate where one should start.

Lighthall clearly documents how the superintendent and principal at Kensington continually imposed only their own realities and how their stance led in a relatively short time to disastrous results. Lighthall observed:

> The tendency is widespread for problem solvers to try to jump from their private plans to public implementation of these plans without going through the [number of realities] necessary to fashion them in accordance with problems felt by the adult humans whose energy and intelligence are needed to implement the plans (Lighthall, p. 282).

Sarason (1971, p. 29) states it another way: 'An understandable but unfortunate way of thinking confuses the power (in a legal or organisational chart sense) to effect change with the processes of change.' In short, one of the basic reasons why planning fails is that planners or decision makers of change are unaware of the situations which potential implementers are facing. They introduce changes without providing a means to identify and confront the situational constraints, and without attempting to understand the values, ideas, and experiences of those who are essential for implementing any changes.

But what is wrong with having a strong belief that a certain aspect of schooling should be changed? Is it not appropriately rational to know that a given change is necessary, and to make it policy, if one is in a position to do so? Aside from the fact that many new programmes do not arise from sound considerations, there are other more serious problems. The first problem is that there are many competing versions of what should be done, with each set of proponents equally convinced that their version is the right one. Forceful argument and even the power to make decisions do not at all address questions related to the process of implementation. The fallacy of rationalism is the assumption that the social world can be altered by seemingly logical argument.[2] Sarason comments on the experiences of social scientists when they attempt to apply their knowledge to social action:

> The social scientists who entered the world of social action after World War II, armed with their theories and scientifically tested knowledge, found a world that would not bend to their paradigms. They had entered a world governed by values, not facts, where persuasion and power were in the service of different definitions of age old questions. . . . Many social scientists reacted either with petulance or bewilderment. They had not been content to study and explain the social world; they had wanted to change it. They fared poorly (1978, p. 370).

Wise (1977) also describes several examples of excessive rationalisation, as when educational outcomes are thoroughly prescribed (as in competency-based education) without any feasible plan of how to achieve them. Wise characterises the behaviour of some policy makers as wishful thinking:

> When policy makers require by law that schools achieve a goal which in the past they have not achieved, they may be engaged in wishful thinking. Here policy makers behave as though their desires concerning what a school system should accomplish, will, in fact, be accomplished if the policy makers simply decree it (p. 45).

Wise goes on to argue that even if rational theories of education were better developed – with goals clearly stated, means of implementation set out, evaluation procedures stated – they would not have much of an impact, because schools, like any social organisation, do not operate in a rational vacuum. Some may say that they should, but Wise's point is that they do not, and wishing them to do so shows a misunderstanding of the existing culture of the schools (see Sarason, 1971; Lortie, 1975).[3]

The other faulty approach alluded to above is that planners (whether they be policy makers or developers of innovations) have not been sensitive to the need for a theory of *changing*. We could have at our disposal the best expert in the world in the field of reading – one who is clear about the goals of reading and how to teach to achieve them. We can leave aside the fact that we do not have enough such experts to go around, and the fact that different teaching strategies will be needed in different classrooms. These problems notwithstanding, our expert would fail, if he or she did not possess knowledge and theory about the process of social change – knowledge which is entirely independent of his or her curriculum expertise. More specifically, effective educational planners and policy makers have to combine some expertise and knowledge about the direction or nature of change with an understanding of and an ability to deal with the factors in action which characterise the processes of adoption and implementation.

Unsolvable problems

More disturbing is the conclusion reached by several people who have attempted to understand or combine theory and practice in their daily work: that some problems are so complex that in the final analysis and final action they are simply not amenable to solution.[4] This is not to say that our efforts to solve them cannot be improved. But let us admit the hypothetical possibility that some social problems in a complex diverse society contain innumerable interaction 'causes' which cannot be fully understood. Nor can we necessarily change those factors which we do understand as causes.[5]

Wise refers to the ways in which statements of goals for education frequently ignore this more basic question of whether the goals can be attained:

> To create goals for education is to will that something occur. But goals, in the absence of a theory of how to achieve them, are mere wishful thinking. If there is no reason to believe a goal is attainable – as perhaps evidenced by the fact that it has never been attained – then a rational planning model may not result in goal attainment (Wise, 1977, p. 48).

Social science is not natural science. As sophisticated and impressive as natural science has become in regard to some problems, it is not dealing with objects which have hidden motivations and diverse values which are constantly being activated and frequently change in unpredictable ways. It *is* easier to put a person on the moon than to attain the goal of raising reading levels across the country, because the factors keeping reading at its current levels are innumerable, different in different situations, constantly changing, and not conducive to altering on any wide scale. In solving educational problems, it is not just the number of factors to be understood but the reality that these factors sometimes change during the process: for example, people's attitudes change. Sarason reviews the expectation for social science:

> Just as the natural sciences had developed laws about the nonhuman world, the social sciences would seek the laws of human society, not only for the purposes of explaining the workings of society but for controlling it. They would be the embodiment of Plato's philosopher kings. Apparently, they were not impressed with the fact that Plato saw the problems of social living as so difficult to understand and cope with, requiring of philosopher kings such a fantastic depth of learning and wisdom that one could not entrust social responsibility to them until they were well along in years (Sarason, 1978, p. 375).

Of course, Plato's solution was a 'theory of change' which claimed that the world would be better off *if* we could develop and install philosopher-rulers with certain characteristics. It was not a theory of *how* to arrive at and maintain such a state.

Lindblom (1959) also claims that it is patently impossible to manage social action by analysing all possible alternatives and their consequences:

> Although such an approach can be described, it cannot be practical except for relatively simple problems and even then only in a somewhat modified form. It assumes intellectual capacities and sources of information that men simply do not possess, and it is even more absurd as an approach to policy when the time and money that can be allocated to a policy problem is limited, as is always the case (Lindblom, p. 156).

There are two issues running through the above comments. The first is that with complex social problems the total number of variables (and their interactive, changing nature) is so large that it is logistically infeasible to obtain all the necessary information, and cognitively impossible for individuals to comprehend the total picture even if the information is available (see Schon, 1971, p. 215).[6] The second is that even if some experts were able to comprehend the total picture themselves, our theories and experiences with meaning and implementation suggest that they would have a devil of a time getting others to act on their knowledge – partly because others will not easily understand the complex knowledge, and partly because the process of implementation contains so many barriers which have nothing to do with the quality of knowledge available.

In sum, to return to the opening paragraph of this section, planning fails partly because of the assumptions of planners (policy-makers, developers) and partly because the problems may not be solvable. In a perverted twist of Greek mythology the hubris of the change agent becomes the nemesis of the implementers and others affected by new programmes. The first form of hubris occurs when policy makers assume that the solutions that they have come to adopt are unquestionably the right ones. We have seen that those solutions are bound to be questioned on grounds of competing values or technical soundness.

The second and related form of hubris, which compounds the problem, occurs when planners of change introduce new programmes in ways which ignore the factors associated with the process of implementation – factors which are only partly controllable, but which are guaranteed to be out of control if ignored. The more the planners are committed to a particular change, the *less* effective they will be in getting others to implement it if their commitment represents an unyielding or impatient stance in the face of ineluctable problems of implementation. Commitment to a particular programme makes it less likely that they will set up the necessary time-consuming procedures for implementation, less likely that they will be open to the transformation of their cherished programme and tolerant of the delays which will inevitably occur when other people begin to work with it. If we react to delays and transformations by assuming that they arise from the incompetence or bullheadedness of those implementing the programme, we will add one more major barrier to the considerable number already operating. The solution is not to be less committed to what we perceive as needed reforms, but to be more sensitive to the possibility that our version of the change may not be the fully correct one, and to recognise that having good ideas may be less than half the battle (compared to establishing a process which will allow us to use the ideas).

Success is possible

Recognising the limitations of planning is not the same thing as concluding that effective change is unattainable. But in order to conclude that planned educational change is possible, it would not be sufficient to locate situations where change seems to be working. We would need to find examples where a setting has been *deliberately transformed* from a previous state to a new one which represents clear *improvement* on some *criteria*. We need to know about the causes and dynamics of how change occurs.

There are several good examples of how school districts radically transformed and improved the quality of education through a process of deliberate change. Berman and McLaughlin's (1979) description of Lakeville district (pseudonym) represents a concise but comprehensive account of how major changes transpired over a several-year period. Among the reasons: hiring a new superintendent, creating a new role for central district personnel, transferring school principals and establishing new expectations and training for the role of principals, creating incentives and opportunities for teachers to obtain resources for changes which they proposed, establishing a teachers' centre and other activities to stimulate teacher interaction and professional development, obtaining added resources through federal innovative programmes.

The school effectiveness research shows why some individual schools are quite successful in the face of some of the most intransigent educational problems. This research demonstrates that schools and classrooms have a positive impact on student learning in situations where (1) there is strong programme leadership in the school on the part of the principal; (2) administrators and teachers make instruction a high priority and there is a high proportion of 'time on task' by students; (3) administrators and teachers expect (believe) that virtually all children can improve their achievement; (4) the school's atmosphere or climate is orderly and supportive of instructional emphases; and (5) there is a means to monitor pupil progress through diagnostic data collection and use of data for instructional improvement (Edmonds, 1979; Denham and Lieberman, 1980; Lezotte, et al., 1980; see also D'Amico, 1980). There is also a growing body of research which indicates that programmes for parents can be implemented and can produce significant results.

The point of all this is that successful change is possible in the real world, even under difficult conditions. And many of the reasons for the achievements can be pinpointed. By and large, the reasons for success relate to the fifteen factors analysed elsewhere (see Fullan, 1982, ch. 5). I am not by any means implying that these factors can be inserted like pieces in a puzzle. However, there are classrooms, schools, communities, and districts which have altered the conditions for change in more favourable, workable directions. Not every situation is alterable, especially at certain periods of time, but it is a good bet that many situations are amenable to constructive change.

The central, practical question is how best to plan for and cope with change in settings which are not now enjoying success. This takes us into the vicissitudes of a theory of changing and contingency theories in which improvement rather than resolution is the name of the game.

Planning and coping

We have come to the most difficult problem of all. When all is said, what can we actually do to plan for and to cope with educational change? This question is pursued in the following subsections. First,

I introduce the topic by indicating some of the basic issues and by noting that advice will have to vary according to the different situations in which we find ourselves. Secondly, I provide some advice for those who find that they are forced to respond to and cope with change introduced by others. Thirdly, the bulk of the section is addressed to the question of how to plan and implement change more effectively. Three interrelated sets of issues are investigated: What assumptions about change should we know? What knowledge and skills will be necessary? What guidelines for action can be formulated?

Change is full of paradoxes. Being deeply committed to a particular change in itself provides no guidelines for attaining it, and may blind us to the realities of others which would be necessary for transforming and implementing the change effectively. Having no vision at all is what makes for educational band-wagons. In the final analysis, either we have to give up and admit that effective educational change is impossible, or we have to take our best knowledge and attempt to improve our efforts. We do possess much knowledge which could make improvement possible. Whether this

Figure 2   *Change situations according to authority position and relation to the change effort*

		Authority position	
		I Planner (e.g., policy-maker)	II Planner (e.g., developer)
Relation to change effort	Initiator or promoter		
	Recipient or responder	III Coper (e.g., principal)	IV Coper (e.g., teacher)

knowledge gets used is itself a problem of change, part of the infinite regression which, once we have gained some knowledge of the process of change, leads us to ask how do we get that knowledge – of the process of change – used or implemented.

A framework for planning and/or coping with educational change has been implicit throughout this book. It does not lead to an optimistic scenario, because there are too many deep-rooted factors keeping things the way they are. I do not think that a detailed technical treatment on how to plan for change is the most profitable route to take, although such a treatment may have some benefit.[7] The most beneficial approach consists in our being able to understand the process of change, locate our place in it, and act by influencing those factors which are changeable and by minimising the power of those which are not. All of this requires a way of thinking about educational change which has not been characteristic of either planners or victims of past change efforts.

In general, there are four logical types of change situations we could face as individuals. These are depicted in Figure 2. There are many different specific roles even within a single cell which cannot be delineated here, but people generally find themselves in one of the four situations depending on whether they are initiating/ promoting a change or are on the receiving end and whether or not they are in authority positions. I start with coping or being on the receiving end of change (cells III and IV).

Coping with change

Those in situations of having to respond to a particular change should assume neither that it is beneficial nor that it is useless; that much is clear from the previous analysis. The major initial stance should involve *critical assessment* of whether the change is desirable in relation to certain goals and whether it is 'implementable'. In brief, assess whether it is worth the effort, because it will be an effort if it is at all worthwhile. Several criteria would be applied. Does the change address an unmet need? Is it a priority in relation to other unmet needs? Are there adequate (not to say optimal) resources committed to support implementation (technical assistance, leadership support, etc.)? If the conditions are reasonably favourable, knowledge of the change process [. . .] could be used to advantage: for example, push for technical assistance, opportunities for interaction among teachers, and so on. If the conditions are not favourable or cannot be made to be favourable, the best coping strategy consists of knowing enough about the process of change so that we can understand why it doesn't work, and therefore not blame ourselves, and/or we can gain solace by realising that most other people are in the same situation of non-implementation. We can also realise that implementation, in any case, cannot be easily monitored; for most educational changes it is quite sufficient to *appear* to be implementing the change such as by using some of the materials. In sum, the problem is one of developing enough meaning *vis-à-vis* the change so that we are in a position to implement it effectively or reject it as the case may be.

Those in authority positions who are confronted with unwanted change (cell III in Figure 2) will have to develop different coping mechanisms from those in non-authority positions (cell IV). For the reader who thinks that resisting change represents irresponsible obstinacy, it is worth repeating that non-implementable programmes probably do more harm than good when they are attempted. The most responsible action may be to reject certain innovations which are bound to fail and to work earnestly at those which have a chance to succeed.[8] Besides, in some situations resistance may be the only way to maintain sanity and avoid complete cynicism. In the search for meaning in a particular imposed change situation, we may conclude that there is no meaning, or that the problem being addressed is only one (and not the most important or strategic) of many problems which should be confronted. The basic guideline is to work at fewer innovations, but do them better – the reason being that it is probably not desirable, certainly not humanly possible, to implement all the changes expected, given what we know about the meaning, time, and energy required for effective implementation.

We should feel especially sorry for those in authority positions (middle management in district offices, principals, intermediate government personnel in provincial and state regional offices) who are responsible for seeing to implementation but do not want or do not understand the change – either because the change has not been sufficiently developed (and is literally not understandable) or because they themselves have not been involved in deciding on the change or have not received adequate orientation in training. The psychiatrist Ronald Laing captures this situation in what he refers to as a 'knot':

> There is something I don't know
>   that I am supposed to know.
> I don't know what it is I don't know,
>   and yet am supposed to know,
> And I feel I look stupid
>   if I seem both not to know it
>   and not know *what* it is I don't know.
> Therefore, I pretend I know it.
>   This is nerve-wracking since I don't
>   know what I must pretend to know.
> Therefore, I pretend I know everything.
>   (R. D. Laing, 'Knots', 1970)

A ridiculous stance to be sure, as painful as it is unsuccessful.[9] Teachers know when a change is being introduced by or supported by someone who does not believe in it or understand it. Yet this is the position in which many intermediate managers find themselves, or allow themselves to be. Those in authority have a need for meaning too, if for no other reason than change will be unsuccessful if they cannot convey their meaning of the change to others.

Planning and implementing change

The implications for those interested in planning and implementing educational change (cells I and II in Figure 2) are very important, because we would all be better off if changes were introduced more effectively. It is useful to consider these implications according to three interrelated sets of issues: What *assumptions* about change should we note? What *knowledge and skills* will be necessary? What *guidelines for action* can be derived?[10]

Assumptions about change

The assumptions we make about change are powerful and frequently unconscious sources of actions. When we begin to understand what change is as people experience it, we begin also to see clearly that assumptions made by planners of change are extremely important determinants of whether the realities of implementation get confronted or ignored. The analysis of change carried out so far leads me to identify ten 'do' and 'don't' assumptions as basic to a successful approach to educational change.[11]

1 Do not assume that your version of what the change should be is the one that should or could be implemented. On the contrary, assume that one of the main purposes of the process of implementation is to *exchange your reality* of what should be through interaction with implementers and others concerned. Stated another way, assume that successful implementation consists of some transformation or continual development of initial ideas. (Particularly good discussions of the need for this assumption and the folly of ignoring it are contained in Bailey, 1975; Lighthall, 1973; Marris, 1975, ch. XVIII; Schon, 1971, ch. 5.)

2 Assume that any significant innovation, if it is to result in change, requires individual implementers to work out their own meaning. Significant change involves a certain amount of ambiguity, ambivalence, and uncertainty for the individual about the meaning of the change. Thus, effective implementation is a *process of clarification*.

3 Assume that conflict and disagreement are not only inevitable but fundamental to successful change. Since any group of people possess multiple realities, any collective change attempt will necessarily involve conflict.

4 Assume that people need pressure to change (even in directions which they desire), but it will only be effective under conditions which allow them to react, to form their own position, to interact with other implementers, to obtain technical assistance, etc. Unless people are going to be replaced with others who have different desired characteristics, resocialisation is at the heart of change.

5 Assume that effective change takes time. It is a process of 'development in use'. Unrealistic or undefined time-lines fail to recognise that implementation occurs developmentally. Expect significant change to take a minimum of two or three years.[12]

6 Do not assume that the reason for lack of implementation is outright rejection of the values embodied in the change, or hard-core resistance to all change. Assume that there are a number of possible reasons: value rejection, inadequate resources to support implementation, insufficient time elapsed.

7 Do not expect all or even most people or groups to change. The complexity of change is such that it is totally impossible to bring about widespread reform in any large social system. Progress occurs when we take steps (e.g. by following the assumptions listed here) which *increase* the number of people affected. Our reach should exceed our grasp, but not by such a margin that we fall flat on our face. Instead of being discouraged by all that remains to be done, be encouraged by what has been accomplished by way of improvement resulting from your actions.

8 Assume that you will need a *plan* which is based on the above assumptions and which addresses the factors known to affect implementation (see the section below on guidelines for action). Knowledge of the change process is essential. Careful planning can bring about significant change on a fairly wide scale over a period of two or three years.

9 Assume that no amount of knowledge will ever make it totally clear what action should be taken. Action decisions are a combination of valid knowledge, political considerations, on-the-spot decisions, and intuition. Better knowledge of the change process will improve the mix of resources on which we draw, but it will never and should never represent the sole basis for decisions.[13]

10 Assume that change is a frustrating, discouraging business. If all or some of the above assumptions cannot be made (a distinct possibility in some situations for some changes), do not expect significant change *as far as implementation is concerned*.[14]

Knowledge and skills

Assumptions, whether consciously or unconsciously held, comprise our philosophy of change. The realisation of change is furthered (or not) according to the knowledge and skills of those leading or managing change. It would be onerous and none too productive to attempt an inventory of all of the leadership and change agent skills which might be needed (see Havelock, 1973; Lippitt and Lippitt, 1978; Katz and Kahn, 1978, ch. 16). It is possible, however, to clarify the types of knowledge and skills required, and to classify them in three categories: (1) technical expertise related to *substantive content* area, (2) *interpersonal skills*, and (3) conceptual and technical skills pertaining to *planning and implementation*.

Technical knowledge and skills in the substantive area of the change require little elaboration. Those interested in promoting a given change should possess some technical understanding of what the change is and how to use it.[15] Otherwise, they would not be able to support its use effectively. (Indeed, lack of such knowledge raises the question whether they should be supporting it in the first place.)

Interpersonal or human relations skills have also been frequently acknowledged as essential. The abilities to communicate, listen, motivate, gain trust, and the like are all critical interpersonal skills necessary for effective leadership for change. So much has been written about these and other interpersonal skills that I need not repeat it here (see e.g. Lippitt and Lippitt, 1978).

On the other hand, and generally not adequately recognised, are the technical and conceptual knowledge and skills which relate to the ability to comprehend and organise the process of educational change and our own and others' places in it. This is unfortunate, for our cognitive ability to *conceptualise, understand, and plan the social processes* of educational change represents the most comprehensive and generative resource for dealing with change. In order to engage in successful change, we need to develop a way of thinking about change based on a thorough understanding of the processes analysed by Fullan, 1982.

It can also be seen that such knowledge, once obtained, is far more powerful as a resource than a memorised list of specific steps that we should follow. For this reason I consider Sarason's (1971) difficult-to-grasp treatment of educational change in terms of practical implications much more important than Zaltman, *et al.*'s (1977) seemingly more comprehensive formulation of the steps. Sarason talks about the importance of understanding the culture of the school, people's relationship to the change process, the murky areas of values and motivations, and the ubiquitous problems of communication. (See also Miles's 1980 discussion of eight dilemmas in planning.) Zaltman, *et al.* provide a more bloodless step-by-step set of recommendations. But change is never a wholly rational process. The fundamental goal for planners in my view is to achieve a feel for the change process and the people in it, which entails a blend of research knowledge and experiential knowledge. Lindblom and Cohen (1979) make a similar and more complete argument for the necessity of combining knowledge from 'professional inquiry' with what they call 'ordinary knowledge'. Both types of knowledge are necessary for solving problems.

In other words, change is not a fully predictable process. The answer is found not by seeking ready-made guidelines, but by struggling to understand and modify events and processes which are intrinsically complicated, difficult to pin down, and ever changing. Sarason explains that change agents do not confront their own conceptions of how to go about change, and thus do not learn to improve their approaches:

> I confess that I find it somewhat amusing to observe how much thought is given to developing vehicles for changing target groups and how little thought is given to vehicles that protect the agent of change from not changing in his understanding of and approach to that particular instance of change (Sarason, 1971, p. 217).

The conceptual factor, far from being an abstract exercise in theorising, represents a way of thinking about the process of change which in a practical way helps us plan and coordinate an approach to change. It helps us identify which factors need to be addressed. It helps us recognise that concentrating on one or two sets of factors while neglecting others is self-defeating. It provides ideas for formulating a 'plan' designed to address and review how these factors are operating in a given instance. I have frequently stated that good ideas, while necessary, are not sufficient for influencing others to change. To the extent that good ideas or visions of change are not combined with equally good conceptualisations of the process of change, the ideas will be wasted. Just as meaning about the substance of change is necessary, so is the development of a sense of meaning and competence about how best to approach it.

It should be evident that *all three* sets of skills are essential. Most of us could probably identify change projects in which leaders possessed only one or two areas of skills – the curriculum consultant who is a renowned expert in the subject area but a disaster interpersonally and a failure in conceptualising/planning on any scale which would allow work with larger numbers of people; the principal who is great with people but has few ideas when it comes to deciding on particular educational programmes; the superintendent who endorses a certain change but has little knowledge of the change process and thus cannot anticipate what might be needed to plan for and support implementation.

If we accept the premise that conceptual and technical planning knowledge and skills are essential to promoting effective educational change, two other issues immediately arise. First, how can we be sure that our conceptualisations are accurate and complete? Second, if we agree that better conceptualisations and skills are needed in planning for implementation, how can they be nurtured? That is, the need is not just to identify better conceptions and skills but to go about *changing* people's conceptions and skills. In answer to the first question, a great deal of knowledge has been developed during the 1970s. The conceptualisation of change in this Chapter is based on a large body of fairly consistent research evidence and descriptions of how change works. As such, it can contribute substantially to the conceptual knowledge we need to increase our effectiveness as participants in change.

The second question brings us back to the problem of regression. A 'theory of change' says that people *should* be able to conceptualise the change process in order to be more effective. A 'theory of changing' questions whether it is possible to alter (i.e. to increase) people's conceptual and organisational abilities merely by telling them what the concepts should be. Just as implementing the conceptual or philosophical basis for curriculum change is one of the most difficult dimensions of change to achieve, so is implementing new conceptions and beliefs among leaders and other participants concerning how to plan for and approach change. Some of the ways in which this might be attempted include (1) hiring or promoting new leaders who possess these conceptual abilities, and who will in turn develop them in others; (2) adding training in the processes of implementation to in-service workshops and other project training activities directed at programme change; (3) adding courses in the theory of practice of change to pre-service programmes for teachers, principals, and other administrators; (4) carrying out action oriented research as a collaboration between researchers interested in the process of change and practitioners interested in promoting and evaluating specific change projects; and (5) encouraging practitioners to reflect on their experiences by making available to them research knowledge on the change process. The most fundamental problem, of course, is that administrators and other planners of change frequently do not have adequate formal or on-the-job preparation to be change leaders.[16]

It should be clear that I am not advocating conceptual thinking for the sake of theoretical elegance. Conceptualisation must be integrated with the appropriate technical steps and human relations processes if it is to be useful; that is, it must be grounded in actual change events. Practical conceptual formulations can only be developed through experience *and* reflection. The ever-elusive nature of this process is described by Schon:

> The learning agent must be able to synthesise theory, to formulate new projective models out of his experience of the situation, while he is in the situation. He cannot operate in an 'after-the-fact' mode, taking as given or as *a priori* applicable, theory which is already formulated. And as often as not, his projective methods come apart. He must be willing for them to come apart, and to synthesise new theory in process as the old explodes or deacays (Schon, 1971, pp. 235–36).

Implicit in Schon's observations is that social change should never be treated solely as a rational, predictable phenomenon. Intuition, learning from experience, formulation and reformulation, getting something to work without necessarily knowing why it works – all have their place in planning and coping with change.

In summary, leaders of educational change to be effective must possess all three types of knowledge and skills, and use them in a way that allows learning from specific change attempts. Preoccupation with the content of proposed changes has resulted in neglect of the interpersonal and conceptual/organisational aspects of planning for change, which turn out to be the most potent barriers to progress. The most difficult factors also tend to be the most neglected, as Lindblom and Cohen remind us:

> Practitioners of PSI [Professional Social Inquiry] often incorrectly assume that policy makers want help from PSI on the substance of policy under their jurisdiction. A study of roughly a hundred different problems facing thirty policy makers disclosed that their PSI needs, in their own eyes, converged on problems in organization and interpersonal relations rather than on the substance of policy (Lindblom and Cohen, 1979, p. 55).

In short, knowledge and skills about how to plan for implementation are just as needed as ideas about the content of reform.

Guidelines for action: theories of changing and contingencies

In the final analysis, the bottom line for many people is what can we actually do to introduce change more effectively. Basically, this involves attempting to incorporate the assumptions and knowledge and skills about change into our ways of thinking and acting. The specifics present us with some problems, since it is difficult to alter the forces of change. Sixteen years ago, Bennis criticised theories of social change in the following words:

> They tend to identify and explain the dynamic interactions of a system without providing a clue pertaining to the identification of strategic leverages for alteration. They are theories suitable only for *observers* of social change, not theories for *participants* in, or practitioners of, social change. They are theories of *change* and not theories of *changing* (Bennis, 1966, p. 99).

Thus, the practitioner interested in planning and bringing about educational change requires a theory of changing. In the rest of this section, I take up the question of how to approach change in order to influence the direction of events more effectively. Essentially, the process involves being able to identify 'strategic leverages for alteration' (i.e. an orientation to changing) and being able to match strategies with situations (i.e. an orientation to contingencies).

Theories or ideas of changing

Given the number of variables which interact and potentially affect implementation, it would get us into a hopeless quagmire to attempt to spell out all the factors and contingencies which would need to be addressed. It is more fruitful and practical to provide an overview of the possible steps to be taken.

A theory of changing suggests that we determine to what extent factors conducive to implementation can be altered in favourable directions. [. . .] Fifteen factors affecting change in practice [can be] listed according to four major categories: (1) *characteristics of the change* (need, clarity, complexity, quality of materials); (2) *school system characteristics* (history of change, adoption process, administrative support, staff development approach, time-line and information, and school board/community support); (3) *school traits* (principal involvement, teacher/teacher relations, teacher characteristics); and (4) *extra-local characteristics* (role of government agencies, external assistance). These fifteen factors can be taken as a checklist for analysing existing change efforts or for planning new ones.[17] To illustrate, let us comment briefly on how factors from each of the four main categories can be used.

Whether or not a potential need is perceived by those who would have to implement a particular change should be tested early in the process. Several different outcomes could arise: (a) the need may be readily confirmed and an agreed-upon plan formulated; (b) the need may be generated through peer influence or other information (e.g. student achievement data); (c) the need may not be confirmed or it may be of low priority compared to other needs. Such a process may or may not operate as a decision making forum, but it is essential to know what situation is being faced. Situation (c) may lead the proposers of the change to abandon the idea in favour of another one, to redouble efforts, or to adopt a longer-term strategy. The point is that some explicit work should be done on ascertaining and/or creating the felt need for moving in a particular change direction.[18]

Whether the district- and school-level factors (categories 2 and 3) can be influenced will depend on several factors. There are three possibilities: (a) we are blessed with favourable existing conditions; (b) we alter the conditions by replacing existing personnel, especially leaders; or (c) we influence existing personnel development through some organisational or staff development programme. If condition (a) prevails, it is not a question of changing, since the favourable conditions already exist. Approach (b) represents the most powerful leverage for change, but depends on other conditions. It is a fact that the most successful examples of change occur when leaders are *replaced* with new leaders with different characteristics and a mandate for change. The Lakeville (Berman and McLaughlin, 1979) example referred to earlier involved major changes at the top (new board members, new superintendent, new central office personnel in key coordinatorship roles).

Condition (c) represents the usual situation. It is neither ethically nor practically possible to make wholesale replacements of school personnel. Professional development for existing staff is the only realistic approach when large numbers of principals and teachers are involved. If my analysis is correct, a number of school people (not all) are interested in change, but the conditions do not favour or otherwise facilitate or stimulate constructive change. The best combination seems to occur when there is a new person in the top leadership position (in the district or the school), who then provides the coordination, opportunity, and support for staff development and other activities likely to stimulate implementation of needed programmes. Professional development of teachers and administrators, in fact, represents one of the most effective strategies for implementation, if combined with other factors listed in this section.

Factors associated with the external environment – category 4 – are by definition extremely difficult to influence. For example, political pressures for reform in schools which come from the larger political arenas (states, provinces, the federal level, the media, etc.) will be almost impossible to influence. The best that we can do is take advantage of financial and other resources which these external agencies provide, and attempt to establish a supportive relationship with those agencies with which we have the most contact. Schon suggests other strategies for influencing and coping with those external sources he refers to as 'central' (as distinct from local):

> Propose what central wants to hear, but do what you want to do. Develop a rhetoric compatible with central policy.
>
> Play funding agencies off against one another.
>
> Seek minimum federal control over the use of money.
>
> Take advantage of the surplus of information about what is going on at the local level, and the high cost of finding out for central.
>
> Bring pressure to bear on the funding agency, exploiting its political insecurities.
>
> Attempt to gain central's commitment over time, so that it develops a heavy investment in the local venture and finds it difficult to back out (Schon, 1971, p. 154).

Manipulative, of course – but no more than what central planners do in figuring out what to do with local systems.

Thus, a theory of changing consists in formulating specific approaches to improving schooling, using our research and practice-based knowledge about what makes for success and failure. Effective approaches to change must include procedures for addressing and coping with issues related to characteristics of the change, the school district, the school, and the broader environment. I have not set out a complete list of procedural steps for two reasons: such a list is already implicit in the fifteen factors and need not be repeated; and specific applications of the ideas must be embedded in – and to an important extent generated by those in – *particular roles in particular situations*.[19] For example, a superintendent interested in stimulating improvements in elementary school science teaching will have to assess and draw on the expertise and commitment of central office staff to assist in developing the direction of the change; directly or indirectly establish orientation programmes to involve principals as programme facilitators; provide teachers access to resources and assistance and some say in the direction of the change; and so on. The fact that these activities do not constitute a linear sequence of steps – rather, the various factors must be attended to continuously – illustrates the futility of relying too heavily on a step-by-step checklist.

In summary, a theory of changing concentrates on those factors in a situation which are thought to be alterable. The extent to which certain factors cannot be altered is the extent to which we cannot go beyond explaining change and into the realm of bringing it about. We may also be discouraged to realise that identifying seemingly alterable factors is only one layer in the regress of change. For example, if our theory of changing leads us to develop an in-service training plan to change principals' leadership effectiveness, it is only the first layer, since the plan may not work. In other words, the plan itself has to be effectively implemented and have its desired outcome before any progress can be claimed.

It is important to dwell on these subtleties because what appears to be a theory of changing (a theory stating how to go about change) may turn out to be only a theory of what *should* change. A theory of changing should be judged only in terms of whether *it is successfully implemented* – whether it actually alters factors it sets out to change – not for what it claims to be. Otherwise, there is no real difference between those who claim that educational problems would be solved if only schools would adopt this or that *programme change*, and those who argue that problems would be solved if only schools would follow this or that *process of change*. Both are engaged in wishful thinking – the former on the substance of change and the latter on the form.

Theories or ideas of contingencies

Many of those who have been immersed in large-scale change efforts have concluded that it is next to impossible to alter situational characteristics at the district and school level when large numbers of schools and school systems are involved. Contingency theory is an extension of the theory of changing, but instead of focusing on changing conditions which might not be changeable (except perhaps through prodigious effort), it suggests that the most effective approach is to use different strategies in different situations. What we do is *contingent* on the characteristics of the change being attempted and the situations at hand. In answer to the question 'Where do you start?' Sarason states:

> I suggest that where one starts has to be a problem that is presented to and discussed with the target groups – not as a matter of empty courtesy or ritualistic adherence to some vague democratic ethos but because *it gives one a more realistic picture of what one is dealing with. An obvious consequence of this is that in different settings one may very well answer the question of where to start rather differently*, a consequence that those who need to follow a recipe will find unsatisfactory because there is no one place to start. Still another consequence is that one may decide *to start nowhere*, that is, the minimal conditions required for that particular change to take hold, regardless of where one starts, are not present. The reader should note that the decision not to proceed with a particular change, far from being an evasion, forces one to consider, *what other kinds of change have to take place before the minimal conditions can be said to exist* (Sarason, 1971, pp. 217–18; his italics).

At this level, a number of implications for planning change can be noted. First, it is clear that it is unrealistic to expect all situations to change. We may, depending on the circumstances, decide to work intensively with those schools or school districts which are interested in the particular change effort.[20] Many federal programmes in the United States are based on this approach. It is a testimony to the complexities of implementation that even programmes which involve apparently voluntary groups frequently fail. Put another way, even if we work with such groups, we will need most of our skills and knowledge about change in order to be effective. The first possibility, then, suggests that we might as well expend the energy where we will have at least some chance of success.

A second contingency possibility is to encourage different users to select different programmes according to their own goals and interests. Again, it will take much of our best knowledge of change to support effective implementation, even when implementers can choose in this fashion.

A third contingency would involve using quite different approaches depending on the readiness conditions in different settings. For example, the leadership and climate in one school may be so well developed that the provision of adequate resources (curriculum materials, consultants, etc.) will be sufficient; in another school the priority may be to replace the principal; in still another a programme of leadership and staff development may be the most effective starting point. Educational leaders, of course, make these types of contingency decisions all the time. The suggestion here is that knowledge about the process of change be used more systematically to inform the choices.

Berman (1978, 1980) has developed an initial promising framework along these lines. He suggests that there are at least five major situational parameters which vary and which must be taken into account in designing a change strategy. He states that there are two distinct implementation approaches which could be used depending on the five sets of conditions.[21] The following framework resulted (Berman, 1980, p. 214):

Situational parameters	Implementation Approach	
	Programmed	Adaptive
Scope of change	minor	major
Certainty of technology or theory	certain (within risk)	uncertain
Conflict over policy's goals and means	low	high
Structure of institutional setting	tightly coupled	loosely coupled
Stability of environment	stable	unstable

Berman argues that change situations vary in terms of whether the scope of change is major, whether the theoretical/technical soundness of the idea is established, whether there is serious conflict among potential implementers, whether the institutional setting is loosely or rightly organised and controllable, and whether or not the environment is relatively stable or turbulent. He claims that programmed approaches are more effective under some conditions, while adaptive ones are necessary under other conditions (see also Berman, 1981). For example, compare the problem of improving reading skills with that of integrating special education children in regular classrooms. The technology (the programmes) for improving reading is relatively well developed and specified, and the goal is almost universally endorsed. By comparison, the proven programmes to facilitate mainstreaming are not available, and consensus by no means exists. Contingency theory would suggest quite different approaches in the two cases. In the case of reading, the selection of a programme, specific staff development activities, and the like can be established relatively quickly. With mainstreaming a much slower, experimental, developmental strategy would be called for.

Contingency theories of implementation are only at an early stage of development. A word of caution is in order, because they do not have infinite value. The more we attempt to spell out all the details and contingencies pertaining to implementation, the more we become overloaded with complexity and fall into the trap of overrationality. The details of change *are* overwhelming. As before, the only manageable route is to develop a way of thinking about contingencies which can provide a framework and basis for generating ideas about where it might be best to spend our time and energy.

The scope of change

Are we better off in the long run if we attempt very small changes, or should we go big in the hope of reaching more people? The reader who by now has concluded that the theory of educational changing is a theory of unanswerable questions will not be too far off the mark.[22] It is a theory of probing and understanding the meaning of multiple dilemmas in attempting to decide what to do. The question of scope is no exception.

Sarason, as usual, identifies many of the underlying issues:

> A large percentage of proposals of change are intended to affect all or most of the schools within a system. The assumption seems to be that since the change is considered as an improvement over what exists, it should be spread as wide as possible as soon as possible. The introduction of a new curricula is, of course, a clear example of this. What is so strange here is that those who initiate this degree of change are quite aware of two things: that different schools in the system can be depended on differentially to respond to or implement the proposed change, and that they, the sources, ... do not have the time adequately to oversee this degree of change. What is strange is that awareness of these two factors seems to be unconnected with or to have no effect on thinking about the scope of the change. This is like a psychotherapist who, after listening to a patient present many serious personal problems affecting his life, decides that he will attack, simultaneously, all of these problems even though in another part of his head he is quite aware that the symptoms will not be equally vulnerable to change and that within the time he spends with the patient it will literally be impossible to deal with all of the symptoms (Sarason, 1971, pp. 213–14).

Several additional points put the problem of scope in perspective. First, in some situations it may be more timely or compatible with our priorities to concentrate on getting a major policy 'on the books', leaving questions of implementation until later. In other words, the first priority is adoption, not implementation. Major new legislation or policies directed at important social reforms often fit this mode – for example, new legislation on desegregation, special education, multicultural educational programmes, or decision making councils. There is no answer to the question of whether this is more effective than a more gradual approach to legislation, but it should be recognised that implementation is then an immediate problem.[23] Much social policy legislation is vague on implementation; some vagueness may be essential in order to get the policy accepted, but nonetheless it means that implementation can be easily evaded. In the face of major value or power resistance, it is probably strategically more effective in the short run to concentrate our energies on establishing new legislation, hoping that in the long run the pressure of the law and the emergence of new implementers in future years will generate some results. The only implementation guidelines are to realise that implementation will not be forthcoming in the short run, and to stress the need for specifying implementation criteria and resources. Many new policies in education are not clear about what implementation would look like, and do not contain reference to planning for the requirements of implementation. In short, those who decide to devote their energies to establishing new policies would be well advised to incorporate more deliberate implementation analysis into their thinking.

Secondly, it does seem to be the case that the reputation of innovation has suffered badly precisely because grandiose schemes were rampant in the 1960s and early 1970s – open education, large-scale curriculum projects, computer-assisted instruction, and the like. It is no criticism of the intentions of reformers to observe that faith and optimism in the power of big dreams, new technologies, and large-scale resources have little to do with the likelihood of successful implementation. The number of teachers, parents, and others who have turned against innovation because of negative experiences with previous change attempts is indeed a large price to pay for the wishful thinking of those who wanted to accomplish the big change. (See Smith and Keith's 1971 case study, and Sarason's 1971 discussion of the consequences of non-implemented proposals.)

Thirdly, most change theorists and practitioners agree that significant changes should be attempted, but they should be carried out in a more incremental, developmental way. Smith and Keith (1971) compare the 'alternative of grandeur', which was a colossal failure, to the 'alternative of gradualism', which might have been attempted at Kensington school. (See also Etzioni, 1966.) The issue is not to eschew large-scale change but to decide whether the problem is important enough, and the resources adequate, to warrant the attempt. In such an attempt, concreteness and incrementalism of implementation are important ingredients.[24] Large plans and vague ideas make a lethal combination.

Significant change can be accomplished by taking a developmental approach, building in more and more components of the change over time. Complex changes can be pursued incrementally by developing one or two steps at a time. Such a strategy is crucial when implementers are faced with major changes. The question of how widespread a change effort should be is a difficult one. Dissemination could be made more manageable if we concentrated early efforts on parts of the system (e.g., several schools, several districts) instead of the entire system. Given that universal reform cannot succeed (and may do more harm than good), Sarason wonders: 'Why not pick one's spots, learn from the experience, and then take up the tactics of extension? What if the schools that were not to receive service were part of an ongoing group to discuss and evaluate what was going on in the schools receiving service'? (1971, p. 214). Depending on the problem at hand, this approach may not be advisable (for example, in a question of legislative equity); but most field-based researchers now agree that it is essential to concentrate on more manageable portions of the problem and to build in ways of extending these critical efforts.

Even changes which are quite explicit and clear face the problem of scope of coverage when they are attempted with larger numbers than the support system (such as staff development and one-to-one assistance) can handle.

The problem of change

I am sometimes asked for specific recipes for how to implement particular programmes. I usually respond by listing the major things that must be done: opportunity (time) for training and interaction during implementation, good programme development or selection, allowance for redefinition of the change, a two- or three-year time perspective, supportive principals, and the like. The response to the list is frequently along the lines that it is impossible to do this or that because of lack of time, lack of resources, and so on. I then say, 'Well, don't expect much implementation to occur.' Needless to say, this answer is found to be unsatisfactory, but one cannot expect change to come easy or even to be possible in some situations. I say this not because I am a cynic but because it is wrong to let hopes blind us to the actual obstacles to change. If these obstacles are ignored, the experience with implementation can be harmful to the adults and the children directly involved – *more harmful than if nothing had been done.*

Understanding the central importance of 'meaning' for those who are implementing change gives us hints about the processes which may be required, and makes sense of the assumptions, knowledge and skills, and guidelines for action formulated above. It also reveals why the usual approaches to change fail. Many of those concerned with educational reform have been preoccupied with developing and advocating the goals of change, as if all that is needed are good intentions. Even good programmes are not enough, if it is simply expected that others will easily accept them or could be forced to.

It is easier – more tangible, clear, and satisfying in the short run – to concentrate on *developing* a new programme than to enter the conflict filled, ambiguous, anxious world of seeing what others think about the idea. But what is understandable is not necessarily right. Ideas about meaning, changing, and contingencies help to explain the perils of putting all our marbles into development. Curriculum development over the past fifteen years provides the best examples of developers and planners who lost their marbles. The subtleties of change are once again evidenced when we point out that these efforts failed regardless of whether they were engineered by university professors, federal or state/provincial departments of education, or local teacher committees. The main reason for failure is simple – the developers went through a process of acquiring *their* meaning of the new curriculum. And once it was presented to teachers, there was no provision for allowing them to work out the meaning for themselves of the changes before them. Innovations which have been succeeding have been doing so because they combine good ideas with good implementation support systems.

Planning and coping with change is not peaceful, because we can never let up for long. The implications for agents of change are well stated by Marris:

> They must listen as well as explain, continually accommodating their design to other purposes, other kinds of experience, modifying and renegotiating long after they would like to believe that their conception was finished. If they impatiently cut this process short, their reforms are likely to be abortive (Marris, 1975, p. 167).

Recognising the problem of educational change for what it is should help us bring about more effective implementation in some situations. While complex to use skilfully, the planning principles and guidelines contained and implied in this Chapter reflect more than anything else 'organised common sense'. Improvements in success rates seem achievable, if by success we mean attaining more and better implementation than in the past and reducing the number of wasted and ill-advised attempts. We should not underestimate the extent to which the latter would represent progress.

Success, however, depends on people. Understanding the orientations and working conditions of the main actors in schools and school systems is a prerequisite for planning and coping with educational change effectively.

Notes

1 This point is somewhat overstated in order to emphasise that zealous commitment to a change is not sufficient, and may get in the way if it results in impatience, failure to listen, etc. A certain amount of vision is, of course,

required to provide the clarity and energy for promoting specific changes. A more balanced summary of the basic point is that promoters of change need to be committed to the change *process* as well as to the change.

2 As George Bernard Shaw observed: 'Reformers have the idea that change can be achieved by brute sanity'.

3 The question of what is rational is too complicated to discuss in detail. My point is that focusing on the technical rationality of a change (goals, means, evidence) is not sufficient. We must also attend to the personal and social conditions of change. Indeed, it is eminently irrational to ignore these conditions. Moreover, these social conditions are frequently 'rationally' predictable if we take an implementation perspective.

4 See Lindblom and Cohen (1979); Schon (1971); Sarason (1978); Sieber (1979).

5 Further, there may be such an overload of problems that it is not possible to solve very many of them with the time, energy, and resources at our disposal.

6 It is also the case that the 'right combination' of variables has not been vigorously addressed – for example, the factors affecting implementation.

7 See, for example, Zaltman, *et al.* (1977); Rothman, *et al.* (1976); Havelock (1973).

8 There are those who will say that this advice gives a licence to anyone who wants to reject a change even though the change might be necessary to benefit, for example, a disadvantaged group. This may be the case in a particular instance. But let us remember two things. First, many inappropriate and/or insufficiently developed changes have been introduced in the last fifteen years which should have been rejected or delayed. Secondly, promoters of change also will receive guidelines (indeed, quite elaborate ones in the next section). Unless we assume that all change being promoted is good, it would be myopic to think that only the promoters need advice.

9 It can, of course, be successful in the sense of maintaining the status quo. Depending on one's capacity for self-deception, it can be more or less painful as well. It is also a very general phenomenon. Teachers pretend they know more than they do with students and with parents; university professors with students, colleagues, and the public; men with women; etc.

10 I will not address issues of how to get changes 'adopted'. The focus is on what it means to plan for effective 'use'.

11 For a somewhat similar set of assumptions applied to planning for school system curriculum implementation, see Fullan and Park (1981, pp. 24–6).

12 The time, of course, varies with the complexity of the change and the size of the system in question.

13 See especially Lindblom and Cohen (1979) and Lindblom (1959). Again the issue is that the complexity (e.g., the number of variables and contingencies) is so great that complete authoritative knowledge is a myth. We can increase the amount of good knowledge, but we will always have to rely on what Lindblom and Cohen call 'ordinary knowledge' which comes through experience, interaction, and so on. It is not so much that the latter type of knowledge inevitably gets in the way, but that it is vital to making effective decisions. (See also Corcoran, 1982.)

14 Recall that I am concerned with the question of whether new changes happen *in practice*. For certain types of reform which will be strongly resisted by some groups (e.g. desegregation and other issues which involve hard-core value conflict), the best long-term strategy may be to concentrate in the short run on getting new legislation adopted, and monitored. This will not represent implementation in the sense that implementers will pursue the intended outcomes of the policy, but it may be the best that can be done. These types of changes often take decades before real implementation becomes even partially

evident. The assumptions represent a guide for action when there is some possibility of change.

15 The degree of technical knowledge and skill required will vary by role. Curriculum consultants will need more detailed knowledge than the superintendent of schools.

16 Argyris and Schon (1977) analyse just how fundamental the problem is. Professionals' 'theories of use' are often discrepant from their 'espoused theories'; and the discrepancy is frequently not recognised.

17 See Fullan and Park (1981) for a number of action-oriented recommendations for planning and implementing change.

18 An alternative strategy is to attempt to create the need during implementation. This may be effective if the participants do not reject the idea at the outset because they have not been consulted in the initial decision. If the decision-makers are in tune with the felt needs of teachers, they may accurately decide on change programmes or directions which turn out to be well received.

19 For a short basic list of procedural steps compatible with the ideas in this section, see Howes and Quinn (1978), who suggest six steps in preparing for change under the category 'setting up adequate orientation', and a further six steps for 'setting up adequate support networks for implementation'.

20 Basically, the strategy is to work only with voluntary populations, since it will be extremely time-consuming to change involuntary ones, and since working effectively with the former probably will take all the time and energy at our disposal. (Recall that effective implementation is extremely difficult, even with districts or schools who volunteer.) It is important to emphasise that this is only one of several possible approaches. It will be acceptable politically, for example, if the change effort concerns a major problem of equity (e.g., desegregation). In the latter case, in a sense, people are still working at the adoption and early implementation stages. It is considered important enough that longer-term struggles are warranted.

21 The guidelines for action discussed in this Chapter do not adequately distinguish between programmed and adaptive approaches, because this would get us into fine detail. This brief illustration of contingency approaches by Berman partly addresses the distinction; but more would have to be done at the level of specific implications.

22 Harry Truman (and later Pierre Trudeau) said, 'We need more one-armed economists,' because he was frustrated at the advice he kept getting: 'on the other hand . . . on the other hand.' The same can be said about the scope of educational change efforts. No one knows for sure what is best.

23 Sarason and Doris (1979) in commenting on special education legislation warn us: 'To interpret a decision . . . as a "victory" is understandable but one should never underestimate how long it can take for the spirit of victory to become appropriately manifested in practice' (p. 358).

24 Van der Berg, et al. (1981) contains a very useful discussion of 'large scale strategies for supporting complex innovations in schools'. Suggestions include materials development, trainer of trainers, peer networking, demonstration sites, technical assistance systems, etc.

References

Argyris, C. and Schon, D. (1977), *Theory in practice: Increasing professional effectiveness*, San Francisco, Jossey-Bass.

Bailey, A. (1975), 'A re-examination of the events at Cambire school', unpublished paper, University of Sussex, England.

Bennis, W. (1966), *Changing organizations*, Toronto, McGraw-Hill.

Berman, P. (1978), 'The study of macro- and micro-implementation', *Public Policy*, 26 (2), 157–84.

Berman, P. (1980), 'Thinking about programmed and adaptive implementation: Matching strategies to situations', in H. Ingram and D. Mann (eds), *Why policies succeed or fail*, Beverly Hills, Calif., Sage.

Berman, P. (1981), 'Towards an implementation paradigm', in R. Lehming and M. Kane (eds), *Improving schools*, Beverly Hills, Calif., Sage.

Berman, P. and McLaughlin, M. (1979), *An exploratory study of school district adaptations*, Santa Monica, Calif., Rand Corporation.

Corcoran, T. (1982), Ordinary knowledge as a constraint on the use of research: The case of the comprehensive basic skills review. Paper presented at American Educational Research Association annual meeting.

D'Amico, J. (1980), *The effective schools movement: Studies, issues and approaches*, Philadelphia, Research for Better Schools.

Denham, C. and Lieberman, A. (1980), *Time to learn: A review of the beginning teacher evaluation study*, Washington, National Institute of Education.

Edmonds, R. (1979), 'Effective schools for the urban poor', *Educational Leadership*, 36, 15–27.

Etzioni, A. (1966), *Studies in social change*, New York, Holt, Rinehart and Winston.

Fullan, M. (1982), 'Causes/Processes of Implementation & Continuation', in M. Fullan (ed.), *The Meaning of Educational Change*, New York and London, Teachers' College Press, Columbia University.

Fullan, M. and Park, P. (1981), *Curriculum implementation: A resource booklet*, Toronto, Ontario Ministry of Education.

Havelock, R. (1973), *The change agent's guide to innovation in education*, Englewood Cliffs, N.J., Educational Technology Publications.

Howes, N. and Quinn, R. (1978), 'Implementing change: From research to a prescriptive framework', *Group and Organizational Studies*, 3 (1), 71–83.

Katz, D. and Kahn, R. (1978), *The social psychology of organizations*, 2nd edn, New York, Wiley.

Lezotte, L., *et al.* (1980), *School learning climate and student achievement*, East Lansing, Michigan State University, Center for Urban Affairs.

Lighthall, F. (1973), 'Multiple realities and organisational nonsolutions: an essay on anatomy of educational innovation', *School Review*, February, pp. 255–87.

Lindblom, C. (1959), 'The science of muddling through', *Public Administration Review*, 19, 155–69.

Lindblom, C. and Cohen, D. (1979), *Usable knowledge*, New Haven, Conn., Yale University Press.

Lippitt, G. and Lippitt, R. (1978), *The consulting process in action*, La Jolla, Calif., University Associates.

Lortie, D. (1975), *Schoolteacher: A sociological study*, Chicago, University of Chicago Press.

Marris, P. (1975), *Loss and change*, New York, Anchor Press/Doubleday.

Miles, M. (1980), 'School innovation from the ground up: Some dilemmas', *New York University Education Quarterly*, 11 (2), 2–9.

Rothman, J., Erlich, J. and Teresa, J. (1976), *Promoting innovation and change in organisations and communities*, New York, Wiley.

Sarason, S. (1971), *The culture of the school and the problem of change*, Boston, Allyn and Bacon.

Sarason, S. (1972), *The creation of settings and the future societies*, San Francisco, Jossey-Bass.

Sarason, S. (1978), 'The nature of problem-solving in social action', *American Psychologist*, April, pp. 370–80.
Sarason, S. and Doris, J. (1979), *Educational handicap, public policy, and social history*, New York, Free Press.
Schon, D. (1971), *Beyond the stable state*, New York, Norton.
Sieber, S. (1979), The solution as the problem. Paper delivered to Society for the Study of Social Problems annual meeting, 1978; revised 1979.
Smith, L. and Keith, P. (1971), *Anatomy of educational innovation: An organisational analysis of an elementary school*, New York, Wiley.
Van der Berg, R., *et al.* (1981), *Large scale strategies for supporting complex innovations in participating schools*, 's Hertogenbosch, Netherlands, Katholiek Pedagogisch Centrum.
Wise, A. (1977), 'Why educational policies often fail: the hyperrationalization hypothesis', *Curriculum Studies*, 9 (1), 43–57.
Wise, A. (1979), *Legislated learning*, Berkeley, University of California Press.
Zaltman, G., Florio, D. and Sikorski, L. (1977), *Dynamic educational change*, New York, Macmillan.

4.2

Curriculum Change: Management or Meaning?

Jean Rudduck

In this paper I want to argue that effective change is largely dependent on building a shared understanding of the intended change among members of a working group – and in particular the working group of a teacher and his or her pupils. Building such understanding is no easy task but without it attempts at change in other than trivial or uncontested areas of institutional life may end in failure or the kind of innocent self-deception which is captured in the phrase 'innovation without change'. Radical change in schools and classrooms (i.e. change that profoundly affects the basis of practice) involves change in the culture of the working group. One set of meanings has to be replaced by a new set of meanings, and until the new meanings can be reflected in a set of shared principles that will guide action within the working group, the change in question is likely to remain precarious.

A teacher talking about the difficulties and disappointments of his school's attempt at radical change in one area of the curriculum offers an explanation of the failure that is consistent with my thesis. He is in fact talking about pupils, but what he says could be true of colleagues too:

> Somewhere along the line we went wrong in not engaging them in some sort of discussion or at least information process where we told them why we were doing it and what was the rationale behind it all. There is still this feeling among some of them that if you haven't got a text book in front of you and a pen in your hand then you are 'not doing 'owt' (quoted by Ian Annis in work for an M.Ed. dissertation).

One problem is that there are few institutional conventions that support time spent in exploring the meanings that underpin practice. Staff meetings and departmental meetings are usually filled with 'business' and there is little time to deal sensitively and constructively with fundamental issues. When, in the context of research projects, we have interviewed groups of teachers from the same school or even from the same department we have noted how surprised they often are at finding out what their colleagues actually think about educational issues. And as far as pupils are concerned, the conventional authority relationships of the classroom lead us to overlook the pupils' right to understand what they are expected to do. For them, the curriculum is revealed day by day, like the tear-off sheets on a block calendar: rarely are they offered an explanation of the logic of particular courses of study or the logic of the curriculum as a whole (see Rudduck, 1984a). It is not surprising, then, that we fail also to make time to explain to them the point and purpose of new curriculum initiatives. For all those involved, curriculum change, if it is to be successful, must be construed as a 'communal venturing forth' (Aoki, 1984) on the basis of a common knowledge of what is at stake, a common sense of purpose and a common understanding of the principles that are to inform new practices. In short, the problem of change is a cultural problem, for the key is to achieve 'the idea in common' within the working group – 'and that is culture' (Barnett, 1953, p. 12).

The curriculum development movement, for interesting historical reasons, did not leave us, as part of its legacy, a view of the change process in which culture was an important concept. The possibility of such a perception was there, however, for in our early vocabulary of change the term 'diffusion' was used to refer to the process by which ideas are communicated beyond their originators. Diffusion is a term that educationists imported from social anthropology – where culture is a key concept. Linton (1961, p. 1372) describes diffusion as 'the transfer of culture elements from one society to another', and Kroeber (1964, p. 142) also suggests that diffusion is about the transmission of cultural content 'from one population to another'. In abandoning the term diffusion we lost access to a theoretical framework which might have enabled use to see more clearly the cultural implications of curriculum change. It was, I suggest, our increasing preoccupation with the 'management of change' that led us to neglect the 'meaning of change' and to define the change task in other than cultural terms.

One of the earliest curriculum development projects to swap terms as a matter of policy was a project that I worked on (the Humanities Curriculum Project, 1967–72). The term 'diffusion' had acquired (see Banks, 1969) overtones of an almost haphazard casualness, with good ideas being expected to make their own way through the system on the passport of personal recommendation, authority and trust. The time-scale for such an enterprise had to be easy. This is how new practices, new ways of thinking gain ground in the unplanned changes that Linton and Kroeber were reporting. But such casualness did not suit the ambitious and hyperactive members of a curriculum development team. Our lifespan was limited: we were a temporary system (Miles, 1964) and we had only a short time in which to justify publicly the intellectual and emotional energy that we had invested in the project. We wanted procedures for communication that were more strategic and structured. We confirmed that we meant business by hauling down the modest pennant of diffusion and marching under new colours – the bold banner of dissemination. We discarded more than we realised at the time.

The attitude of the major sponsor of curriculum development, the Schools Council, was also changing as they in their turn faced issues of accountability. There was a concern to gather evidence of the impact of new approaches, and 'take-up' came to be seen as an important measure of success. Where the Schools Council had once accepted leisurely progress of innovations, now, in the early 1970s, there was a new impatience and the term 'diffusion' did not suit the *zeitgeist*:

> The present contacts . . . are too often haphazard, fitful and limited . . . the day of the blushing violet has ended and . . . positive promotion should be the aim . . . Positive promotion, timely and relevant information, and widespread involvement should lead to successful adoption (Ralphs, chairman of the Schools Council, 1972).

The term 'dissemination' was part of the official new-speak:

> Projects should gear dissemination to certain defined ends . . . this insistence of planning and promotion will not be welcomed by some . . . this must mean an end to the chance encounters of the past (Schools Council, 1974, p. 28).

The first responsibility of projects was, according to the new policy, the efficient transmission of *information*. To be fair, the Council did express concern about the need to 'convey *understanding*' (1974, p. 28), but the burden of the message was the effective conveyance of information to target audiences within the system – a management task. Project teams, caught in the accountability imperative, became efficient. They quickened their efforts at communication by organising large-scale dissemination conferences which took teachers away, often for a number of days, from routine settings and routine pressures. Such conferences can be highly effective in supporting participants through an uneasy transition as they confront values embedded in past practice and explore alternative ways of seeing and acting. At their best they do what Herron (1971, p. 4) was calling for: they help teachers to 'perceive or understand the underlying philosophy, assumptions, design and purpose of the innovation'. But they dealt, usually, with only one or two delegates from any one school. When the teachers returned to their work places, they had little idea, it seems, how to set about communicating what they had been through to colleagues: there were often no structures for a searching reappraisal of values and practices. Colleagues might agree to go forward kindled by the excitement and optimism that bandwagons characteristically generate but without having 'worked out a reformulation of their position which made sense to them' (see Marris, 1975, in Fullan, 1982). They were to adapt Marris's phrase, like 'puppets dangling by a thread' from the conception of the innovation's originators. They moved their limbs but with no unifying understanding out of which they could achieve coherent performance. Given the disorienting effects of change anyway, it is not surprising if, in such circumstances, the initiative were not to survive.

The school based curriculum development movement has a better chance of building new meanings within the working group as a basis for new practice, but few institutions, even if they see the need, have been able to afford the extensive time commitment of exploring new ideas in depth so that the teachers involved all start with a relatively clear idea of the innovation (Gross, *et al.* 1971, p. 202; and see Sarason, 1971; Rudduck, 1983).

The inertia of past meanings

Failure to perceive the nature of the task, in curriculum change, as one of penetrating the tight weave of meanings that hold in place the existing culture of the working group and establishing new meanings, has led to some disillusionment with the idea of radical curriculum change. When such an absence of vision is complemented by a traditional neglect of the rights of pupils to understand the structure of the curriculum and the logic of different teaching styles, then the task of curriculum change at the classroom level is likely to be even more prone to failure.

Pupils are partners in the transactions of the classroom that we call teaching and learning. Too often they are cast as conscripts in the innovative campaigns launched by teachers, and their response to the unexplained and unjustified loss of stability that curriculum change represents is to lure their teacher back from the quicksands of innovation to the terra firma of the familiar past. A good example of this is the attempt at curriculum change reported by Denscombe (1980). The school set out to implement a policy of social and curricular integration, but high status subjects, which were more vulnerable to pressures from public examinations, tended to maintain their subject boundaries – and the innovation was coherently tried out only in the new humanities course. Here, 60 to 80 pupils worked in an open-plan area, with a team of 3 teachers following, in the main, individualised enquiries and using a centralised resource collection. Denscombe noted, over time, how the pupils pushed their teachers back into conventional patterns of classroom organisation within the open arena: the hall effectively became three classrooms without walls. In the old structure the pupils knew the rules of the game and it was to their advantage to return to familiar working conditions. Their challenges to the teachers' control were expertly adjusted to the new open setting. For instance, the teachers were not worried about noise in the new setting and so noise was no longer a weapon to be used against them. But the teachers *were* anxious about free movement in the hall since mobility made it difficult for them to check on whether work was being done, and their interrogation of pupils signalled a distrust of the autonomy that was a goal of the new course: it reinforced the old image of the teacher as disciplinarian rather than consultant. The pupils' strategy was, then, to wander about, and the teachers' counter strategy was to set up territories within the hall with sanctions for being 'out of bounds'. The innovation was losing its identity.

Denscombe is concerned primarily with the match between pupil strategies and the physical organisation of classrooms but his account is also evidence of the difficulty of establishing a new way of working in a setting where the innovation is not only shot through with reminders of the past which it is trying to break loose from but is also surrounded in other areas of the curriculum (humanities was only six periods a week) by conventions which embody the familiar norms of behaviour. The island of difference which the humanities course represented was not sufficiently clearly defined in the consciousness of the working group of teachers and pupils for it to survive alongside the strong protocols provided by classroom experience in more traditional areas of the curriculum. Denscombe explains the failure of the innovation to be realised in all but surface form in terms of 'the host of expectations and meanings based on current and previous experience' that the teachers and the pupils brought to the situation. There was no systematic attempt, it seems, to try to root the innovation in the minds of the participants – no attempt to build a common understanding out of shared experience and establish a stable alternative culture within the working group.

The paradox of communication

We often behave as though our authority as teachers is sufficient to enforce change in pupils but, as we have seen, change without understanding is an unsatisfactory basis for development within the working group. As Marris (1975) says: 'Those who have the power to manipulate change act as if they have only to explain'. But how does one communicate effectively something that is outside the shared experience of those who are to implement the change? Schwab (in Westbury and Wilkof, 1978, pp. 170–1), captures the essence of the problem:

If the enterprise is to be successful it is the new logic and not some radically mistaken version of it which must be tried. Yet this is the unlikeliest outcome of all. For, if the new logic be described in its own terms, its hearers must struggle hard for understanding by whatever means they have. These means, however, are the old modes of understanding, stemming from the old logic. Inevitably the new will be altered and distorted in this process of communication, converted into some semblance of the old . . . If the new logic is entirely converted into the terms of the old, a static and unrecognised misunderstanding is likely to result.

I have written elsewhere of such an experience (Rudduck, 1984b), and I will quote one passage from the account which sums up the nature of the difficulty. I was teaching at a local comprehensive school for a double period a week trying to introduce, to pupils who had no experience of discussion-based inquiry, a new way of working. I seemed unable to communicate, despite repeated efforts, what it was we were to do as a group (1984b, pp. 59–60):

Each week I began the session by explaining that I was acting as a chairman, not as a teacher; that discussion was an opportunity to learn from each other and not from me . . . The group listened, apparently attentively, for this bit was familiar: it was teacher talk. But they didn't ask questions about what I meant nor seemed to relate what I had said to what followed . . . My acting as a chairman and sitting at the table alongside the pupils marked a change from the conventional authority-based relationship of teacher and taught. But the pupils had no conception of any alternative convention for they could not realise the form of discussion for a long enough period of time to perceive what the structure of an alternative convention might be . . . We seemed to have arrived at stalemate in terms of progress with discussion. Maintaining my role was a severe strain. I could understand why teachers might give up.

We made an accidental breakthrough when we discovered that showing pupils video tapes of the innovation at work in other schools helped them to relate the abstract explanation to a concrete situation. We now had a shared sense of purpose and a common reference point for monitoring the progress of our performance. From this experience I drew four conclusions:

1 Pupils' understanding of the form of an innovation will be increased if they have access to concrete representation of the form in addition to oral explanations.
2 If an innovation requires a substantial shift in classroom roles and relationships, teachers and pupils will have to develop a mutual commitment to the work which will counter the pull of existing conventions.
3 The development of a mutual commitment to the innovation by teachers and pupils requires a shared understanding of the nature of the innovation and an agreement, tacit or open, about the management of control.
4 Alertness on the part of the teacher to aspects of the task of communicating the nature of the innovation to pupils will increase the likelihood of the innovation taking root in the classroom.

(Adapted from Rudduck, 1984b.)

Without a formal attempt to build a shared understanding and commitment, pupils may well choose to escape the innovation and press the teacher to reinstate the familiar. For the teacher, a return to the familiar ways may be a blessed relief from the stress of attempting to change established ways of behaviour.

Above all, the teacher as the mediator of change must struggle to understand the innovation in its own terms and must struggle to introduce it in its own terms to colleagues and to pupils in the working group. As the partners wrestle with the meaning of the curriculum innovation in their setting, so they build a new classroom culture that reflects new principles of judgement and action. This is dynamic change, rather than the dynamic conservatism that Denscombe's account exemplifies. Schwab describes it in these words – which can apply to a teacher and his or her pupils as well as to a team of teachers working together (Westbury and Wilkof, 1978, p. 173):

> As they (the participants in the innovation) translate their tentative understanding into action, a powerful stimulus to thought and reflection is created . . . The actions undertaken lead to unexpected consequences, effects on teachers and students, which cry for explanation. There is reflection on the disparities between ends envisaged and the consequences which actually ensue . . . The new actions change old habits of thought and observation . . . Energies are mobilised and new empathies aroused. There then arrives a new and further understanding of the ideas which led to it.

Summary

The strategies for curriculum change developed in the 1960s and 1970s have, by and large, not taken into account the complexity of the task of building new meanings within a working group – especially when that working group continues to operate within a context which is reminiscent of past habits and when it is obliged to accomplish change without the opportunity of withdrawing from its cycle of productivity. The inertia of past meanings is a formidable barrier to change. In education, you cannot create a vacuum in which to grow a new set of meanings and practices; you cannot stop teaching for a year in order to learn to work together in a different way. The show must go on. It is against such pressures that the task of change has to be undertaken.

References

Aoki, T. (1984), 'Towards a reconceptualisation of curriculum implementation', in Hopkins, D. and Wideen, M. (eds), *Alternative Perspectives on School Improvement*, Falmer Press, Lewes, pp. 107–18.

Banks, L. J. (1969), 'Curriculum development in Britain, 1963–68', *Journal of Curriculum Studies*, vol. 1, No. 3, November, pp. 247–59.
Barnett, H. G. (1953), *Innovation: the Basis of Cultural Change*, McGraw-Hill, New York.
Denscombe, M. (1980), 'Pupil strategies and the open classroom', in Woods, P. (ed.), *Pupil Strategies: Explorations in the Sociology of the School*, Croom Helm, London.
Fullan, M. (1982), *The Meaning of Educational Change*, Ontario Institute for Studies in Education Press, Ontario.
Gross, N., Giacquinta, J. B. and Bernstein, M. (1971), *Implementing Organisational Innovation*, Basic Books, Inc., New York.
Herron, M. (1971), 'On teacher perception and curricular innovation', *Curriculum Theory Network*, pp. 47–51.
Kroeber, A. L. (1964), 'Diffusionism', in Etzioni and Etzioni (eds), *Social Change*, Basic Books, New York, pp. 142–6.
Linton, R. (1961), 'Diffusion', in Parsons, T., *et al.* (eds), *Theories of Society, Vol. 11*, The Free Press of Glencoe, pp. 1371–80.
Marris, P. (1975), *Loss and Change*, Anchor Press/Doubleday, New York.
Miles, M. B. (1964), 'On temporary systems', in Miles, M. B. (ed.), *Innovation in Education*, Teachers' College Press, University of Columbia, pp. 437–90.
Ralphs, F. Lincoln (1972), 'Dissemination, the task of the working party', *Dialogue*, Schools' Council Newsletter, no. 12, p. 5.
Rudduck, J. (1983), 'In-service courses for pupils as a basis for implementing curriculum development', *British Journal of In-Service Education*, 10, 1, pp. 32–42.
Rudduck, J. (1984a), 'The hypothesis teacher and the problem of helping children gain power through understanding', in Simon, B. (ed.), *Margaret Gracise: a Teacher for our Time* (privately published; available from 11, Pendene Road, Leicester).
Rudduck, J. (1984b), 'Introducing innovation to pupils', in Hopkins, D. and Wideen, M. (eds), *Alternative Perspectives on School Improvement*, Falmer Press, Lewes, pp. 53–66.
Sarason, S. (1971), *The Culture of the School and the Problem of Change*, 2nd edn, 1982, Allyn and Bacon, New York.
Schools Council (1974), *Dissemination and In-Service Training*, Report of the Working Party on Dissemination, Pamphlet 14.
Westbury, I. and Wilkof, N. J. (eds) (1978), *J. J. Schwab: Science, Curriculum and Liberal Education – Selected Essays*, University of Chicago Press, Chicago.

4.3

Who's in Control? Pressure Group Politics and Curriculum Change

Bob Moon

The 1980s have seen a global resurgence of interest in the development of national curriculum policies. The movement has been characterised by a level of activity comparable to the curriculum development boom of the 1960s. Events, however, have been far more extensive in scope with the political and bureaucratic process fully involved in, if not leading, a variety of initiatives. Prime Ministerial involvement in Britain and Japan, for example, has given education in general, and curriculum in particular, a higher profile than any of the project workers two decades earlier could have hoped for.

Here, I want to look at the way educational systems promote and respond to the pressures for change. In particular I want to examine the classical division of systems into the categories centralised or decentralised, the focus of much political polemic. In England and Wales, opponents of the 1988 Education Reform Act took great pains to point out the number of increased powers given over to central ministerial authority. In France, curriculum has been excluded from the tentative moves towards decentralisation of the educational structure. Recent debates in the Netherlands and Iceland have focused on the issue of curriculum control. In Eastern Europe, in the decentralising reforms in Hungary, the central–decentral dichotomy has also provoked political interest.

The literature attaches great importance to the forms that systems take. A major comparative study of innovation at all levels in educational systems (OECD-CERI, 1973) stressed the significance of this distinction for understanding curriculum control and development. 'Over and over again we are faced with the issue of "centralisation" versus "decentralisation"' (vol. IV, p. 238), a view reinforced by observers such as Jackson (1974) who saw curriculum policy in a centralised system as determined on a national basis by a politico-administrative elite. Decisions are taken centrally by this group, transmitted to the schools and enforced by a national inspectorate. In contrast, in decentralised systems, central authorities take little active part in curriculum development. More recently Nicholas (1983) in a comparative study has suggested that a higher degree of centralisation makes it possible to generalise about the work of the system with some confidence and accuracy. Perhaps the most elaborate statement of system structure has come from Margaret Archer in her study *The Social Origins of Education Systems* (1979). An extensive range of evidence is amassed to characterise centrality and decentrality.

The pattern traditionally associated with England and Wales, in Archer's terms, is more elaborate than say, in France,

> instead of the simple convection current pattern of the centralised system (in which grievances were cumulated, passed upwards to the political centre, negotiated there through political interaction, before being transmitted downwards to educational institutions as policy directed changes) a more complicated pattern of cross currents characterises interaction and change in the decentralised system (Archer, 1979, p. 393).

Later in an important passage she argues:

> The supreme importance of political manipulation in the centralised system had two consequences for analysis. First, it was possible to describe educational interaction as a political story, with character, plot and outcome, which could be told chapter by chapter ... Second, it was possible to explain educational interaction in terms of the changing interrelationships between the political structure and the structure of educational interest groups. When dealing with decentralised systems the nature of both description and explanation differs considerably. On the one hand interaction cannot be described as a story (political or otherwise) because three different kinds of negotiations are going on simultaneously and are taking place at three different levels (those of the school, community and nation) instead of being restricted to the last of these ... This is no historic saga, but only a vast collection of short stories in which some of the same characters reappear and some of the same problems are tackled by different persons in different ways ... This serves to indicate the problems of describing interaction in decentralised systems, but it also helps to define the problem to be tackled when attempting to explain such interaction (pp. 396–7).

which leads her to conclude:

> the prospects for change are that future educational interaction will continue to be patterned in dissimilar fashions in the two systems and that the products of change will reproduce the main features of centralisation or decentralisation (p. 790).

There have been a number of criticisms of the Archer thesis. King (1979) and Warwick and Williams (1980) question the empirical basis for the overarching theory. Anderson (1986) is critical of the lack of clarity in the concept of system. He also feels that Archer's selection of evidence overestimates both the unification of the French system (her choice for an example of centralisation) and the extent of decentralisation in England and Wales.

Archer, however, has persevered with her central theory, publishing a shortened version of the book which included only exemplar material from France and England and Wales, archetypal representations of centralisation and decentralisation. She also, in a complex argument, has taken Bernstein and Bourdieu to task for overlooking the characteristics of the different systems within which each worked (Archer, 1983).

Recent legislative developments in England and Wales, however, paralleled by the findings of an increasing number of historical, case study, investigations have brought the value of the central–decentral dichotomy into question. I see the concept as increasingly problematic; an impediment to understanding of how policy develops and is implemented. Let me take two examples to illustrate this, one from France in the 1960s and more recently government legislation for the curriculum in England and Wales.

Reforming the primarily mathematics curriculum in France

I have set out the background to these events in a previous study (Moon, 1986). In the mid-1960s the reform of primary school mathematics was proposed by an influential group comprised primarily of University Mathematicians. Members of the group had already played an important role in advocating the place of 'New Maths' in the secondary school curriculum. In Primary schools the guidelines for Arithmatic (not Mathematics) dated back to the post war years and controversies surrounding the proposals ensued that the guidelines, although much debated, were not written until the early 1970s. A study of the formal system, however, would give little indication of the significant take up of New Maths in schools throughout France. The evidence from textbook sales is highly significant in revealing how extensive this transformation was. Television series, in-service education and subject association activities all proceeded regardless of central regulation. There were only limited connections between formal representatives of the system, such as the inspectorate, and those apparently holding more influence in the period, such as publishers and University mathematicians. From the mid-1970s onwards, however, the centre began to reassert control. The previously marginalised inspectorate, working within a more authoritative political structure, began to re-establish control. Publishers sensing the change of mood hedged their bets with new maths and traditional maths textbooks appearing simultaneously.

Centralising curriculum control in England and Wales

> The Secretary of State's policies for the range and pattern of the 5 to 16 curriculum will not lead to national syllabuses. Diversity at local education authority and school level is healthy, accords well with the English and Welsh tradition of school education, and makes for liveliness and innovation (*Better Schools: a summary*, p. 4, March 1985).

> The Government has announced its intention to legislate for a national foundation curriculum for pupils of compulsory school age in England and Wales ... Within the secular national curriculum, the government intends to establish essential foundation subjects – maths, English, science, foreign language, history, geography, technology in its various aspects, music, art and physical education ... the Government wishes to establish programmes of study for the subjects, describing the essential content which needs to be covered to enable pupils to reach or surpass the attainment targets (*The National Curriculum 5–16, a consultation document*, p. 35, July 1987).

How did the radical change of policy between 1985 and 1987 come about? In 1985 the publication of *Better Schools* marked the culmination of nearly a decade of government interest in educational, and particularly curriculum, affairs. The Ruskin College Speech of Prime Minister James Callaghan in 1976 had stimulated a succession of events and publications setting out critically to review the quality of education. Policy development, however, was characterised by the involvement of the full range of interest groups normally associated with educational debate. Local Authority organisations, Her Majesty's Inspectorate, Teacher and Headteacher views had all contributed, under both Labour and Conservative administrations, to the development of policy. The curriculum statements of *Better Schools* represented the evolving consensus about a non-statutory framework based around the HMI formulation of areas of curriculum experience.

A year later, however, the general election intervened. A group of ministerial, or Prime Ministerial, advisers took the opportunity to gain influence. Many were associated with right wing 'think tanks'. The Conservative Party Manifesto set out stridently worded proposals for testing and for curriculum legislation. This was quickly followed up in the post-election period by a rapid phase of consultation and extensive legislation. All the usual interest groups, including some with normally close links to the Conservatives, were excluded, or only nominally involved in the process. To some extent this included the central educational bureaucracy represented within the Department of Education and Science and in national bodies such as the Secondary Examination Council and the Schools Curriculum Development Committee. The destabilisation of these bureaucracies may have indeed contributed to the dominance of pressure groups politics in the 1985–7 period. The proposals of 1987,

despite extensive criticism (Haviland, 1988), passed on to the
statute books a year later. A decentralised structure of decision
making had, despite the prophecies of Margaret Archer, become
centralised almost overnight.

The challenge to French centrality in the 1960s and the usurping of
local control by central government in England in the 1980s
confound therefore the predictability of system theories. The evidence begins to give some substance to Patricia Broadfoot's assertion of the importance of looking beyond the rhetoric of control in
an education system to the reality that underpins it (Broadfoot,
1980, p. 119). Lawrence Stenhouse made a similar plea in his
Presidential Address to the Comparative Education Society in
Europe (Stenhouse, 1979)

> I am mounting a like criticism of the tradition in comparative education of
> studying and writing about the systems of other countries and asking that we
> develop in our field a better grounded representation of day-to-day educational
> reality resting on the careful study of particular cases (p. 10).

and Ian Westbury (1980) in looking at the problem of how systematic curriculum change can be conceptualised suggests that investigations based on a series of cases is perhaps the only way forward.

In the decade that followed cutbacks in funding have inhibited
research of the type proposed (although Broadfoot (1983) has
continued to explore the theories through some comparative study).
There is therefore an urgent need for enquiries that explore the
relationship between curriculum change and the operation of formal
procedures to promote, implement and evaluate such changes.
There is sufficient contradictory evidence to undermine Archer's
categorisations. What takes its place?

Investigations will need, in part, to be historical in character.
Tanner (1982) has suggested that the ahistorical character of
curriculum reform efforts has been identified as a substantive
problem in the curriculum field by curriculum specialist and educational historians alike. Recent work in subject histories has responded to this plea although the link to policy making processes
has often been weak and comparative material hardly exists.
Historical investigation could begin to answer the question as to
whether system categorisations ever had any validity. Margaret
Archer advanced the view that the central–decentral polarisation of
systems represented a second stage in the evolution of school
systems, a stage that marked the loosening of the catholic and
protestants churches respectively. Perhaps she underestimated the
extent to which systems had moved into a third phase where
national boundaries ceased to be significant. Rowlinson (1974)
suggests

the different national forms of European education, so much determined by historical, political and social developments within the separate countries, show a striking homogeneity when viewed from a non-European perspective.

Do the political and economic interdependencies between nation states allied to rapid technological change render the old categories meaningless? Are we in a third phase in the development of educational systems where global or at least continental forces are more significant than national systems in promoting change? The New Maths reforms, for example, represented a worldwide movement although subsequent resistance and retrenchment was more nationalistic in character. Will historical evidence show that the working of systems is nowhere near as differentiated as Archer and other observers suggest? My own view tends towards the latter. International trends may provide the justification for policy decisions. But there is nothing predictable about that, any more than it is predictable that systems will work in the way we expect them to.

In saying this I want to propose that the role of pressure groups and significant individuals is vastly underestimated in the study of the way educational or curriculum policies evolve. Here I make a distinction between pressure groups competing outside the formal policy process and interest groups working from within, although the former may eventually colonise the policy process as Downing Street educational advisers did during the latter part of the 1980s. The failure to examine the influence of individuals and pressure groups inhibits understanding of how influence is established and developed. As Ashford (1988) suggests in looking at the area of public planning, social science has great difficulty translating the mystique of influential persons into orderly conclusions. History therefore inherits all the questions that social science fails to ask. The danger is that the policy process becomes characterised by mystification, one of the key elements in pressure group politics. Greater theoretical awareness of how such groups interact with the different parts of the policy process is made more difficult as Regan and Wilson (1986) suggest because groups constantly seek new avenues of approach, new structures and new tactics to sway decision makers.

A preliminary analysis of successful pressure groups suggests two characteristic processes as essential to success. The first is orchestration and here I borrow the term from Michael Fullan's work on educational change (1982). The subtle forming of alliances and allegiances, the marginalising or incorporating of key groups and individuals, the exploitation of media and other means of securing influence are critical elements of the micro politics associated with orchestration. Reformers neglect such territory at their peril. Ducland Williams (1983) has gone so far as to suggest mapping as a technique for analysing the process. Mazey (1986) has stressed, again taking a historical perspective, the importance of looking at the way key groups and individuals move over, sometimes exten-sive, periods of time.

The second process concerns pace, speed of change. However long the gestation, when pressure groups gain a hold, when the pieces are in place, they move quickly. French University Mathe-maticians and Conservative party educational advisers both display-ed speed and agility in mobilising for reform. It could be argued that marginalised groups lack the strategic, political skills that seem so often to be associated with successful reform. Progressive educa-tors, for example, find both the process of orchestration and the requirement to move quickly uncongenial to the participatory, democratic value associated with their work at least from the 1960s onwards. Patriarcha and Buckman (1983) for example highlighted problems among curriculum developers identifying elaborate parti-cipatory arrangements as an important element in the failure of many of the projects. To regain influence therefore, progressive educators may need to reconceptualise ideas of authority and participation.

In summary therefore I have argued that the relationship between the formal processes for curriculum change and the way the system is worked is highly problematic. There is little evidence to suggest that the one determines the other except in so far as it is convenient for the dominant group to work within such structures. Analysis therefore of the way change occurs is essential if the policy process is to be demystified and if a wider public is to have access to influence and the form in which influence is exercised. The lack of evidence impoverishes curriculum policy debates.

References

Anderson, R. (1986), 'Sociology and history: M. S. Archer's social origins of educational systems', *European Journal of Sociology*, XXVII, pp. 149–61.

Archer, M. S. (1979 and 1984), *Social origins of educational systems*, London and California, Sage Publications.

Archer, M. S. (1983), 'Process without system', *European Journal of Sociology*, XXIV, pp. 196–221.

Ashford, D. E. (1988), 'In Search of French Planning: Ideas and History at Work', *West European Politics*, 11.3, pp. 150–61.

Broadfoot, P. (1980), 'Rhetoric and reality in the context of innovation: an English case study', *Compare*, 10, 2, pp. 117–26.

Broadfoot, P. (1983), 'Assessment constraints on curriculum practice: a compara-tive study', in Hamersley, M. and Hargreaves, A. (eds), *Curriculum Practice: Some Sociological Case Studies*, London and New York, Falmer Press.

Ducland Williams (1983), 'Change and authority in France', *West European Politics*, 6, 2, pp. 163–4.

Fullan, M. (1982), *The Meaning of Educational Change*, New York and London, Teachers College, Columbia University.

Haviland, J. (1988), *Take Care Mr. Baker*, London, Fourth Estate.

Jackson, R. (1974), 'The democratisation of curriculum control in four countries (England, West Germany, France and Italy)', *University of Newcastle Institute of Education Journal*, March–May, pp. 80–4.

King, E. J. (1979), 'Social origins of educational systems – a review', *Comparative Education*, 15, 3, pp. 350–2.

Mazey, S. (1986), 'Public Policy-Making in France: the Art of the Possible', *West European Politics*, 9, 3, pp. 412–28.

Moon, B. (1986), *The 'New Maths' Curriculum Controversy: an International Story*, Brighton, Falmer.

The National Curriculum 5–16, A Consultation Document (1987), London, DES.

Nicholas, E. J. (1983), *Issues in Education: a Comparative Analysis*, London, Harper Row.

OECD/CERI (1973), *Case Studies of Educational Innovation*, vol. IV, Paris.

Patriarcha, L. and Buckman, M. (1983), 'Conceptual development and curriculum change: or is it rhetoric and fantasy', *Journal of Curriculum Studies*, 15, 4, pp. 409–23.

Quicke, J. (1988), 'The "New Right" and Education', *British Journal of Educational Studies*, 26, 1.

Regan, M. C. and Wilson, F. L. (1986), 'Interest Group Politics in France and Ireland: Comparative Perspectives on Neo-Corporatism', *West European Politics*, 9, 3, pp. 393–411.

Rowlinson, W. (1974), 'German Education in a European Context', in Cook, T. G. (ed.), *The History of Education in Europe*, London, Methuen.

Stenhouse, L. (1979), 'Case study in comparative education: particularity and generalisation', *Comparative Education*, 15, 1.

Tanner, L. N. (1982), 'Curriculum history as usable knowledge', *Curriculum Inquiry*, 12, 4, pp. 179–85.

Warwick, D and Williams, J. (1980), 'History and the sociology of education', *British Journal of the Sociology of Education*, 3, pp. 333–46.

Westbury, I. (1980), Reflections on case studies in Steiner, M. G., Comparative Studies of Mathematics Curriculum – Change and Stability, 1960–1980. Proceedings of a Conference held in Osnabruck, PRG, 7–11 January. Institut für Didaktik der Mathematik der Universität, Bielefeld, Mataridien und Studien Band 19.

4.4

Towards an Understanding of the Values Issue in Curriculum Decision Making

Sue Johnston

Introduction

In the past, teachers were largely under the control of an externally imposed syllabus which rigidly prescribed all aspects of the curriculum. Today, in most countries, there is a trend towards school based curriculum decision making and, regardless of how complete the adoption of this philosophy has been, it is now more common for teachers to work within groups, discussing and planning curriculum policy. Much of the literature on curriculum decision making focuses on individual teachers and their instructional decision making role within the classroom (see, for example, Clandinin, 1986; Elbaz, 1983; Jackson, 1968; Leithwood, 1982). This interest is readily justifiable because of the importance of the individual teacher as the final arbiter of curriculum decisions in the isolation of the classroom. However, the propensity for studying curriculum decision making from this perspective has left a deficit in the area of curriculum decision making by groups and this remains little studied, with no theoretical framework. It is the aim of this paper to propose one possible framework to promote understanding in this neglected area. After establishing deliberation as a basis from which to study curriculum decision making, it will be argued that the values issue in group deliberation may be clarified by applying some notions borrowed from the field of teacher socialisation. Various factors which influence curriculum decision making will then be incorporated into the framework.

Rational models for curriculum development

Rational models for curriculum planning have abounded in the literature since Tyler's (1949) exposition of the objectives based model. Despite persistent criticism, rational curriculum models continue to draw a devoted following. As a basis for curriculum planning by groups, they are enticing because they offer a logical, neat prescription of the sequence to be followed. However, case studies present a very different view of how curriculum decision making occurs in practice (see, for example, Cohen and Harrison, 1982; Harrison, 1981; Reid and Walker, 1975; Shaw, 1972). These studies have exposed some serious shortcomings in the applicability of the rational models. Kelly (1982) reminds us that such models for curriculum development can take us only as far as recognising that various choices and selections have to be made and suggesting some of the factors which need to be considered when making the choices. In limiting ourselves to merely describing what needs to be decided upon, the rational models leave the most fundamental question unexamined – that is, how decisions about these choices and selections are made.

Orpwood (1985) attributes the failure of the rational curriculum models to their limited conception of the nature of curriculum. He argues that the rational models conceive a curriculum primarily as an 'artefact' which can be analysed into constituent elements with a view to its rational and systematic construction (p. 297). Such an approach might be useful for developing concrete curriculum materials, but is of limited value in planning curriculum policy where political impact plays a vital role.

In short, the rational curriculum models are limited in their ability to illuminate the process of group curriculum planning because:

1 they lack empirical data to support their application to practical contexts
2 their emphasis is on substantive elements of curriculum, rather than on the process of decision-making
3 they neglect the political nature of curriculum policy planning.

Deliberation

In searching for alternatives to the rational curriculum models, Schwab's (1969 and 1973) ideas provide some progress. His hard-hitting article of 1969, which criticises over-reliance on inappropriate and inadequate curriculum theories, did indeed bring about a form of renaissance of the field of curriculum (p. 1). Many writers have utilised his concept of deliberation as a means for understanding the process of curriculum decision making (Eisner, 1984; Orpwood, 1985; Pereira, 1984; Reid, 1979; Reid and Walker, 1975; Roby, 1985; Shaw, 1972). Deliberation, sometimes termed practical reasoning, is defined by Reid (1979) as:

an intricate and skilled intellectual and social process whereby, individually or collectively, we identify the questions to which we must respond, establish grounds for deciding answers, and then choose among the available solutions (Reid, p. 189).

Alone, this definition might appear to hold little that is inspiring or revealing for curriculum decision-makers. The deficiency lies, though, in the act of defining deliberation rather than in the nature of deliberation itself. Indeed, the mere act of defining and describing deliberation is laden with risk because the 'intricacy' of the process defies simple description. Attempts to do so readily lead to gross misrepresentation by way of over-simplification. There is a temptation to reduce the process of deliberation to a series of steps which, preferably, can be represented diagrammatically. Such accounts may be instrumental in understanding some aspects of the deliberative process, but they run the potentially 'lethal' risk of reducing the process to a procedural level – in direct contradiction of the very rudiments of the argument used to support the concept of deliberation. Roby (1985) warns us: 'The retrospective neatening of the process [deliberation] into discrete, linear stages, when mistaken for the process itself, can circumscribe its dynamics' (p. 21). This paper will not proceed by travelling the perilous journey of describing and systematically listing the elements of deliberation. Instead, the process will be accepted as a tentative basis for understanding curriculum decision making and a further issue emanating from this stance will be explored.

The element of discovery

A key aspect of deliberation which cannot be captured by listing the elements of the process is the role of 'discovery'. Schwab (1973) places great importance on the need for individual value stances to be exchanged, explored, contested and clarified by the planning group:

> it is the prime means by which each planner begins to discover himself [*sic*] – his values and their projections into educational intentions – begins to discover his colleagues, and begins to discover the loci at which each must begin to modify or contract himself to accommodate his colleagues' views and arrive at a collegiality which can function effectively in pursuing the task in hand (Schwab, p. 519).

Furthermore, Schwab believes that such a process, with its inherent balances and checks, will lead to the best decision being made, given that the group has sufficient time and that there is readiness on the part of the participants to be open-minded, honest and exhaustive in their deliberation. Schwab (1973) is the first to highlight the potential danger in these assumptions – that is, the tendency for individuals to reject values contrary to their own and to 'elevate automatically their own expertise to the role of ultimate arbiter of matters under consideration' (p. 519). Roby (1985) has elaborated on this and has delineated some of the habits likely to impede deliberation:

1 a tendency to rush to the solution
2 the imposition of a 'pet' solution
3 the use of 'universal' solutions
4 the pressures imposed by feeling as though there is a crisis
5 unwillingness to work within a group
6 'either/or' thinking – the lack of ability to develop compromise solutions
7 an expectation of a linear process
8 an intolerance of uncertainty associated with the process.

Although Roby (1985) suggests that at least some of these impediments can be minimised with more critical reflection incorporated into the process, the theoretical accounts which promote deliberation as a means of curriculum decision making can be readily accused of idealism. Schwab (1973) can suggest no device to overcome problems in resolving value conflicts other than 'a measure of humility and shame among the participants' (p. 250).

Value conflicts loom as a major barrier to any acceptance of deliberation as a process for explaining curriculum decision making. Little effort has been made to explore this problem and to search for a path around the obstacles that the values issue brings to curriculum decision making. There is a readiness to reject deliberation outright because of its deficiencies. Adopting a more optimistic attitude, this paper will pursue the glimmer of hope that the deliberative process offers curriculum decision making. An attempt will be made to seek some clarification of the values issue within the framework of deliberation.

Value conflicts in group deliberation

Values are the ideals and customs towards which group members have an affective regard, either positive or negative. Some writers attempt to define a singular school culture, stressing the homogeneity and cohesion within the teaching profession, delineating the shared identity, values, role definitions and goals of its members (Sarason, 1982). Indeed, such a perspective is useful for explicating some aspects of teaching and education. However, there is also considerable evidence to place the teaching profession into the Bucher and Strauss (1976) process framework which highlights the heterogeneous, fluid nature of any professional group. This conception suggests that the teaching profession is composed of many factions or segments which struggle for power and whose fates are interdependent and responsive to each other. Changes in the interrelationships and nature of these factions can be used to explain trends in curriculum innovation by the manner in which groups with different ideals become more powerful in the school or system policy making.

Whether or not one is willing to accept this highly political, 'social movement' approach to curriculum decision making, it still provides a useful legacy when translated to the level of group deliberation of curriculum policy. It serves to emphasise that, within any group of teachers, there is likely to be a wide range of value stances on any educational issue. The resolution of conflicts which might arise from these opposing, or at least varying, value stances is the key task when groups are working to plan curriculum policy.

The solution would be simple if values could be resolved arithmetically, like mechanical forces. Equal and opposite value stances would maintain the status quo and various other combinations would result in changed policy according to the relative direction and strength of the interacting value stances. Of course, such a mechanical representation of decision making is simplistic to the point of being ridiculous. It not only becomes unworkable when the complexity of group interactions is taken into account, but it also fails to acknowledge the social and political nature of curriculum decision making.

Emerging from the foregoing discussion is the need to search for a framework which takes into consideration the individual, as well as the interactions among individuals, within a specific group decision making setting. To this end, it is proposed that aspects of Lacey's (1977) framework for explaining the socialising of teachers may be profitably borrowed and adapted to the context of curriculum decision making.

Lacey argues that an individual's actions or strategies in a particular context are not only dependent on the background of the individual but are also importantly influenced by the intentions of the individual in that specific setting. Thus, individuals employ 'social strategies' which are determined by the constraints of the situation and the individual's purpose within that situation. Such strategies arc consequently context specific and, therefore, are not necessarily consistent or predictable. Lacey's emphasis on the 'intersection between biography and situation' is useful because it takes into account the socio-political nature of group decision making. Individuals are likely to consider the consequences of taking particular stances on issues in a group situation and influential in this consideration will be factors such as group composition and the individual's relative power or status in the group.

Lacey's categorisation of social strategies provides further insight into curriculum decision making. His framework suggests that an individual, when making a move within a group decision making setting, may choose either a strategy of *situational adjustment* or one of *strategic redefinition*. In the case of situational adjustment, an individual adjusts to or copes with the more powerful moves within the group. One way of achieving this is by *strategic compliance*, where the individual complies with the group decision but retains private reservations – that is, personal beliefs do not change but publicly the individual goes along with the group. The second means of situational adjustment is through *internalised adjustment*, where the individual complies because of agreement with the group and may internalise changed beliefs in order to do so.

Alternatively, the individual may publicly oppose the group's views and take an active role in attempting to change the situation – *strategic redefinition*. The risks associated with adopting such a strategy are obvious and the outcome is highly dependent on the perceived status and support for the individual within the group. The outcome is also likely to be dependent on the individual's social skills which determine how effectively the case is presented and argued as perceived by other members of the group.

The social strategies framework serves to emphasise the values that the individual brings to a group decison making setting, plus the interaction of that individual with the setting. Thus, an individual's intentions are modified according to factors such as interpersonal skills, the nature of the issue under discussion, the status of the individual in the group, composition of the group and socio political climate of the group and its wider context. The notion of social strategies readily explains the impotence of the young, inexperienced teacher to effect change at a school level. It portrays these teachers as most likely to opt for strategies of situational adjustment until their standing and security within the school are sufficiently established for them to question accepted procedures. Likewise, someone lacking self-confidence and the skills to sway group opinion is likely to take the low risk pathway of situational adjustment. The framework explains the adoption of strategically safe stances by those ambitious to climb the promotion ladder and who align themselves with policies and factions most likely to enhance that promotion opportunity.

Strategic redefinition can take many forms – from the powerful, effective moves made by an experienced, skilful and influential group member in swaying group decisions to the ineffectual, powerless calls by a low status group member taking a personal, but futile, stand on an issue. Successful strategic redefinition, regarded as a decision to adopt an innovative curriculum practice, is dependent on many factors and these may be related to personal qualities of the individual, to the school context or to the external context.

The social strategies framework, summarised in Figure 3, links much of the diverse literature on educational change, making the individual attempting strategic redefinition the focal point of all considerations.

Figure 3   *Social strategies framework*

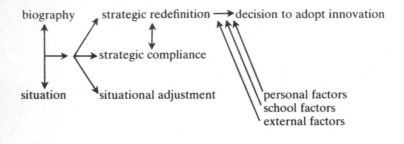

Aspects of *personal qualities* of successful innovators have not been well documented, with little to illuminate beyond Miles' (1964) somewhat outdated description of someone who is benevolent, strong, individualistic, creative and who has high verbal ability. A more recent study of teachers involved in decisions to diversify the curriculum in Australian schools suggests the importance of communication skills, commitment, professionalism, willingness to take risks, persistence and self-confidence.[1] Woods (1981) demonstrates the link between personal qualities and the decision making setting by defining a term called 'sociological awareness'. A prerequisite for successful strategic redefinition, sociological awareness relates to an individual's 'sensitivity to the environment and to significant others in it' (p. 290). This quality highlights the necessity to understand and operate within the particular social and political context of the workplace. Implied within sociological awareness is a good sense of timing and the ability to employ compliance procedures at crucial times.

The power of an individual is an important factor in determining the success of redefinition strategies. Power may be derived from official position or from expertise and experience. It not only increases the likelihood of others accepting and acting on proposals made, but it also gives the individual access to and control over resources which assist the change process.

A number of well-documented *school factors* play a vital role in facilitating strategic redefinition. Findings suggest the need for an open style of leadership which encourages participative decision making, a problem solving orientation rather than a bureaucratic orientation, support from administration and colleagues, provision of time and other resources and the availability of external support staff (Cohen and Harrison, 1982; Daft and Becker, 1978; Fullan, 1982).

Although *external factors* are unlikely to precipitate curriculum decisions, they may facilitate the strategic redefinition activities of a committed teacher or group of teachers. Fullan (1982) suggests that factors which influence decisions to adopt an innovation include community and parent acceptance for the desired change, funding support for resources and release time for teachers, provision of adequate information and policy changes at system level.

Conclusion

Importantly, the social strategies model places emphasis on individuals – their values and intentions – but, it also serves powerfully to relate these to the influences of group composition, the nature of the issue under discussion and the socio-political climate of both the group and its wider context. Additionally, the model highlights that group decisions may not reflect the wide range of views held privately by group members. The isolated nature of teaching often ensures that such private opinions remain unshared. The social strategies model transcends the simplistic notion of categorising teachers as either innovators or resisters. Innovative and effective curriculum decision making moves away from a belief that conservative, entrenched and obstructive teachers must be conquered.

The way forward is to accept deliberation as a basis for curriculum decision making. With such a commitment comes the realisation that effective curriculum planning is then achieved by assisting teachers to develop the knowledge and skills necessary for the deliberative process. As well as the need for sufficient time for group planning, an essential prerequisite is the provision of a safe, supportive and open climate for discussion. Only in such an environment can teachers, regardless of status and experience, be encouraged to expound and develop their beliefs collaboratively.

Note

1 The author is presently undertaking a study of teachers who have developed new subjects in the post-compulsory secondary school curriculum. Preliminary analysis of interview data suggests the importance of personal qualities in successful strategic redefinition.

References

Bucher, R. and Strauss, A. (1976), 'Professions in Process', in Hammersley, M. and Woods, P. (eds), *The Process of Schooling*, Routledge and Kegan Paul, London.

Clandinin, D. J. (1986), *Classroom Practice: Teacher Images in Action*, Falmer Press, Philadelphia.

Cohen, D. and Harrison, M. (1982), *Curriculum Action Project*, Macquarie University, Sydney.

Daft, R. and Becker, S. (1978), *The Innovative Organisation*, Elsevier, New York.

Eisner, E. (1984), 'No easy answers: Joseph Schwab's contributions to curriculum', *Curriculum Inquiry*, 14, 2, pp. 201–10.

Elbaz, F. (1983), *Teacher Thinking: A Study of Practical Knowledge*, Croom Helm, New York.

Fullan, M. (1982), *The Meaning of Educational Change*, Teachers College Press, New York.

Harrison, M. (1981), 'School-based curriculum decision-making: a personal viewpoint', *Curriculum Perspectives*, 21, pp. 47–52.

Jackson, P. (1968), *Life in Classrooms*, Holt, Rinehart Winston, New York.

Kelly, A. (1982), *Curriculum: Theory and Practice*, 2nd edn, Harper and Row, London.

Lacey, C. (1977), *The Socialization of Teachers*, Methuen, London.

Leithwood, K. A. (ed.) (1982), *Studies in Curriculum Decision-Making*, OISE, Toronto.

Miles, M. (1964), *Innovation in Education*, Teachers College Press, New York.

Orpwood, G. (1985), 'The reflective deliberator: a case study of curriculum policy making', *Journal of Curriculum Studies*, 17, 3, pp. 293–304.

Pereira, P. (1984), 'Deliberation and the arts of perception', *Journal of Curriculum Studies*, 16, 4, pp. 347–66.

Reid, W. (1979), 'Practical reasoning and curriculum theory: in search of a new paradigm', *Curriculum Inquiry*, 9, 3, pp. 187–207.

Reid, W. and Walker, D. (eds) (1975), *Case Studies in Curriculum Change*, Routledge and Kegan Paul, London.

Roby, T. (1985), 'Habits impeding deliberation', *Journal of Curriculum Studies*, 17, 1, pp. 17–35.

Sarason, S. (1982), *The Culture of the School and the Problem of Change*, Allyn and Bacon, Boston.

Schwab, J. (1969), 'The practical: a language for curriculum', *School Review*, 78, pp. 1–23.

Schwab, J. (1973), 'The practical 3: translation into curriculum', *School Review*, 81, 4, pp. 501–22.

Shaw, K. E. (1972), 'Curriculum decision making in a college of education', *Journal of Curriculum Studies*, 4, 1, pp. 51–9.

Tyler, R. (1949), *Basic Principles of Curriculum and Instruction*, University of Chicago, Chicago, Ill.

Woods, P. (1981), 'Strategies, commitment and identity; making and breaking the teacher role', in Barton, L. and Walker, S. (eds), *Schools, Teachers and Teaching*, Falmer Press, Lewes.

4.5

Towards a Kuhnian Approach to Curriculum Development

Derek Hodson

Inadequacy of the transmission model

According to Bennis, *et al.* (1976) top-down curriculum development comes in a variety of guises, the two most common being *power-coercive* and *rational-empirical*. Power-coercive strategies rely on the political/administrative system for their effectiveness. In other words, curriculum change is enforced by regulation or directive. By contrast, the rational-empirical approach assumes that teachers are reasonable and rational and is based on rhetoric, persuasion and intellectual appeal. While the second approach is more subtle, especially in its claim to present objective and unbiased information to potential users, it also assigns power and influence to the developer, rather than the teacher. In both approaches, teachers are regarded as 'receivers' of curriculum wisdom, who should readily change their ways in response to the new curriculum directives or rhetoric. Indeed, much concern is expressed when teachers don't respond quickly and 'appropriately'!

In my view, the frequent, and sometimes spectacular, failures of top-down curriculum development can be laid at the door of this basic assumption about the relationship between developer and teacher: that teachers simply receive and then act upon the curriculum wisdom transmitted by the developers. This approach ignores that teachers are people, too, who bring to the curriculum task their own ideas, experiences, perceptions and values. In fact, teachers possess a range of curriculum knowledge, skills and attitudes, ranging from theory based principles of procedure, through professionally acquired, experience based knowledge to taken-for-granted, 'common sense' knowledge and 'teacher folklore'. A style of curriculum development that adopts a prescriptive approach and ignores this wealth of background knowledge and theory is likely to be unsuccessful with many teachers, just as didactic teaching that ignores the knowledge, skills and attitudes of the learners is likely to be unsuccessful for many children. Understandably, teachers are suspicious of interference, impatient with rhetoric that ignores or undervalues their views and experience, and hostile to directives that appear to weaken their perceptions of their own professionalism. If we acknowledge the findings of the Children's Learning in Science Project (CLISP) in the UK and the Learning in Science Project (LISP) in New Zealand, that what a learner brings to a new learning task is crucial to the learning that ensues (Driver, 1983; Osborne and Freyberg, 1985), we should accept that what a teacher brings to the task of curriculum development is crucial to the success of that enterprise, too. It follows that it is appropriate to develop a programme of in-service curriculum development from teachers' existing curriculum knowledge.

Educational theory, and curriculum theory in particular, can be a number of things: a stock of principles that teachers *should* apply and use to guide their practice (a belief that seems to underpin much top-down curriculum development and INSET activity), descriptions and interpretations of teachers' actual practice (which often merely characterises the idiosyncracies of particular teachers), or a set of principles and theoretical structures developed alongside and concurrent with practice. The latter interpretation is advocated here. Theories and guidelines are formulated in response to experience of real classroom situations; tested in real situations; and refined, developed and applied in the appropriate classroom context. In this way, curriculum theory and practice are inextricably linked. Neither has absolute priority, but they develop together. The problem for the provider of INSET courses is how best to organise this complex, interactive development. Thomas Kuhn's work *The Structure of Scientific Revolutions* (Kuhn, 1970) may provide a suitable model.

Towards an alternative

Kuhn sees sciences progressing in a series of stages, as illustrated in Figure 4. In the 'pre-scientific' stage, little can be taken for granted, as practitioners struggle to delineate legitimate fields of study and establish theoretical structures and research methods. This period of uncertainty and dispute ends when the community of scientists agree on conceptual structures, theories, research methods, criteria of 'truth', standards of conduct, and so on. Practitioners then engage in what Kuhn calls 'normal science' – puzzle solving, in which the problem and its solution are defined in terms of the prevailing paradigm. Eventually, problems arise that resist solution. When such problems are long-standing, strike at the fundamental assumptions of the theoretical structure underpinning the paradigm, or are socially significant, a 'crisis' ensues, which deepens as further problems accrue and practitioners begin to lose faith in the paradigm. Speculation at a fundamental level eventually throws up a new theory or new procedure that resolves the problem. If the new position is seen to be capable of solving other problems, more practitioners agree with it, and a 'revolution' occurs, which establishes a new paradigm and initiates a new period of 'normal science'.

Figure 4   *Nature of scientific development (Kuhn, 1970)*

Pre-paradigmic phase	'Normal' science phase	Crisis phase	Revolution
(establishing the theoretical matrix)	(puzzle solving within established framework)	(problems resist solution by conventional methods or accepted theory)	(establishment of new theoretical matrix, followed by new period of 'normal' science)

Kuhnian ideas can be applied to understanding how children acquire new concepts in science. Just as the successful generation of scientific knowledge through scientific research starts from the existing theoretical matrix, so the learning of new scientific knowledge starts from children's existing understanding of scientific phenomena, and proceeds through periods of puzzle solving, elaboration, crisis and revolution. It follows that different teaching/learning strategies are appropriate at different stages of the Kuhnian cycle. For example, at the pre-paradigmic stage, children should be encouraged to explore and develop their understanding through discussion and writing. During the period of 'normal science', they should be encouraged to use their theories to explain phenomena, interpret experimental evidence and make predictions. Teachers might attempt to precipitate a crisis in understanding by introducing phenomena that resist explanation by the current paradigm, by providing counter examples or by introducing alternative theories. A revolution in understanding occurs when consensus shifts from the old to the new paradigm. Teaching strategies based on this interpretation of conceptual change have been discussed at length elsewhere (Hodson, 1986a, 1987).

Kuhnian theory may provide a suitable model for INSET courses on curriculum development. For example, part of curriculum development involves introducing teachers to new concepts, skills and attitudes on aims and objectives, content, learning methods and assessment and evaluation strategies. If children learn best by exploring, testing, sharing, communicating, challenging and developing ideas in an atmosphere of trust and confidence (Harlen 1985; Solomon, 1980), perhaps teachers best achieve a revolution in their curriculum understanding and expertise by similar methods. If so, any programme of curriculum development should start by considering current practice and the exploring teachers' perceptions of it. It follows that the conditions for satisfactory development are an atmosphere of mutual trust between all participants, such that no idea is ridiculed or rejected out-of-hand.

Crucial elements of a Kuhnian learning model are the principles of self-directed learning and self-evaluation and the avoidance by the teacher of any absolutes or dogma. If the translation of these principles to curriculum development activities is valid, curriculum developers should avoid presenting teachers with curriculum wisdom from 'on high'. Dispensing such curriculum wisdom seems, in many cases, to be doomed to failure, for the reasons outlined earlier. Moreover, it assumes that there is a universally applicable and unproblematic conventional theory, a view I find difficult to sustain. Transmission approaches to curriculum development can, of course, have many outcomes, including two unsatisfactory extremes: on the one hand, the kind of resistance and hostility described earlier and, on the other hand, the uncritical acceptance of 'official dogma'. As Carr and Kemmis (1986) pointed out, there is considerable danger in this latter position: 'taking theories too much for granted leaves us at the mercy of yesterday's good ideas'.

A more realistic and productive approach to curriculum development is to work with teachers to bring about a shift in understanding and expertise, based on a thorough, critical examination of current practice. This is not an argument for devolving all responsibility for curriculum development to the local level, for that approach may have its own problems of variable quality, incompleteness, superficiality and mediocrity. Even if these problems can be avoided, there is the inevitable risk that 'curriculum vision' is constrained and restricted by the immediate school perspective. Indeed, it may be necessary for an outsider to provide another perspective to re-focus the curriculum. This notion is similar to Paul Feyerabend's (1975) argument that in science it is frequently necessary to create a new, alternative theory before the inadequacies of the old one become apparent. So long as one remains within the constraints of a particular paradigm, all the available evidence seems to support it.

Thus, effective curriculum development would seem to require that groups of teachers 'on the inside', who know the children, the locality and the school environment well, are brought together to work on issues important in all schools, such as the compulsory-core curriculum, new models of learning, new assessment methods, multicultural education, in the company of an INSET provider acting as a 'change agent': a chairperson, a source of information who stimulates action. The principle underpinning this approach is that all curriculum knowledge should be regarded as problematic, and open to scrutiny, critical appraisal and revision. The first requirement, then, is that teachers' existing ideas are articulated and developed, analysed, criticised, compared and contrasted with others, and tested in the classroom. Because education is a practical activity, rather than an armchair amusement, curriculum development should be practical rather than the accumulation of abstract theory. The aim of transforming the consciousness of practitioners begins, logically, with reflection on existing practice, proceeds through critical consideration of alternatives, and culminates in deciding on future actions. In bringing about this transition, the role of the change agent may be crucial. That role may be filled by senior staff in the schools, LEA advisers, university or polytechnic staff, or any of the usual providers of INSET courses.

Role of the change agent

One could argue that teachers do not have the skills necessary to plan, design, implement and evaluate curricula. Indeed, my survey of departmental curriculum development strategies tends to support this view, for science teachers (Hodson, 1986b). However, I believe that, given an appropriate curriculum development climate, teachers *can* acquire and use such skills. The central concerns of curriculum development should be changing attitudes, skills, values and relationships, rather than the mere provision of curriculum information. I argue that teachers can aquire the skills, knowledge and attitudes necessary for effective curriculum development by refining and extending the skills they already possess and by articulating their intuitive practices, assisted by change agents, who improve problem-solving skills, foster the growth of awareness and work through value conflicts. This model of curriculum development is based on the belief that teachers are capable of creative actions if the working conditions are appropriate and specific expertise is provided when required. Figure 5 lists the kinds of activities that might comprise a programme for such interaction curriculum development.

Figure 5   *Activities for interactive curriculum development*

1 making curriculum ideas and theories explicit through writing and discussion with others. Free exchange of views;
2 exploring the implications of these ideas for curriculum practice;
3 matching and testing these theoretical ideas against one's own, and others', experience.

At this stage, the change agent might challenge the teachers to find classroom based evidence in support of their ideas.

4 using theories to explain curriculum phenomena;
5 applying theoretical ideas to new curriculum situations;
6 criticising the ideas of others. Subjecting one's own ideas to criticism;
7 modifying and refining ideas;
8 reaching consensus about the most appropriate ideas and strategies;
9 making predictions; testing theories and predictions in the search for support, refutation and refinement.

At this point, the change agent might begin to shift understanding, to bring about further skill development or modify certain attitudes.

10 introduction of activities to challenge and contradict existing views;
11 encouraging the generation of alternative frameworks and explanations by 'brainstorming' activities and the consideration of other literature based ideas;
12 introduction of the change agent's intended explanatory framework/theoretical notion/set of attitudes, or whatever, as one of the alternatives;
13 exploration and testing of all alternatives, repeating steps (1)–(7);
14 comparison, judgement and selection of the most acceptable alternative to the learning group (including the change agent), i.e. reaching consensus;
15 use of that alternative in a real school situation;
16 self-evaluation of the new curriculum modification in action;
17 sharing evaluation data;
18 generating ideas for further modification, i.e. go to step (11).

Conclusion

Time and again, research into the factors underpinning academic success has identified 'quality of the school' as a key variable. This is usually defined in terms of the professional competence of the staff. I contend that successful involvement of teachers in curriculum development activities enhances professional competence and, therefore, raises academic standards. The problem for the providers of in-service curriculum development courses is how best to engage teachers in these activities and assist them to make better sense of the world of the classroom.

Many teachers are indifferent (or even hostile) to research evidence, dismissive of theoretical arguments and resistant to directives as reasons for engaging in curriculum development, preferring instead to respond to personal hunch and teacher 'folk-lore' (Hodson, 1986b). Consequently both the rational-empirical and power-coercive models of top-down curriculum development seem doomed to failure. The model proposed here provides a workable alternative through its emphasis on practical classroom matters and its orientation towards enhanced job satisfaction and cooperative professional development. In this approach, teachers identify and discuss their own curriculum problems and concerns, use specialists to input the specific expertise they require, as they require it, in their attempts to solve these problems, and evaluate the changes for themselves within their own institutions (both projects involved teachers in extensive 'in-house' evaluation). This approach brings curriculum development into the classroom, where it is seen to address real concerns of real teachers, something that cannot be claimed for all in-service courses. In other words, teachers are seen as *active constructors* and *reconstructors* of their own curriculum knowledge, rather than as the passive recipients of transmitted curriculum wisdom. In this way, the impetus for change, the direction of change and the evaluation of change are seen to reside in the school and not in the DES or the LEA.

References

Bennis, W. G., Benne, K., Chin, R. and Corey, K. (1976), *The Planning of Change*, Holt, Rinehart and Winston, New York.

Carr, W. and Kemmis, S. (1986), *Becoming Critical. Education, Knowledge and Action Research*, Falmer Press, London.

Driver, R. (1983), *The Pupil as Scientist?*, Open University Press, Milton Keynes.

Feyerabend, P. K. (1975), *Against Method*, New Left Books, London.

Harlen, W. (1985), *Teaching and Learning Primary Science*, Harper and Row, in association with the Open University, London.

Hodson, D. (1985), 'Philosophy of science, science and science education', *Studies in Science Education*, 12, pp. 25–57.

Hodson, D. (1986a), 'Rethinking the role and status of observation in science education', *Journal of Curriculum Studies*, 18, pp. 381–96.

Hodson, D. (1986b), 'The role of assessment in the "curriculum cycle": a survey of science department practice', *Research in Science and Technological Education*, 4, pp. 7–17.

Hodson, D. (1987), 'Toward a philosophically more valid science curriculum', *Science Education*, in press.

Kuhn, T. S. (1970), *The Structure of Scientific Revolution*, University of Chicago Press, Chicago, Ill.

Osborne, R. and Freyberg, P. (1985), *Learning in Science*, Heinemann, Auckland.

Solomon, J. (1980), *Teaching Children in the Laboratory*, Croom Helm, London.

4.6

Backward Mapping: Implementation Research and Policy Decisions

Richard F. Elmore

Students of implementation repeatedly argue that implementation problems should be considered when policies are made. Better policies would result, we are told, if policymakers would think about whether their decisions could be implemented before they settle on a course of action. The argument is often made in an accusatory way, as if policymakers were somehow deficient for not routinely and systematically thinking about implementation problems. Yet when one looks to the implementation literature for guidance, there is not much to be found.

Implementation research is long on description and short on prescription. Most implementation research is case studies. This fact, by itself, is neither good nor bad. But it does present special problems when it comes to translating research into useful guidance for policymakers. Cases, if they are well written, focus on a particular sequence of events and a specific set of causes and consequences. When drawing conclusions from their data, case writers are characteristically and honestly cautious. They are typically careful not to generalise more than a step or two beyond their data, and they do that very apologetically. Thus, when we look to the most influential implementation studies for guidance about how to anticipate implementation problems, we find advice that is desultory and strategically vague.[1]

Vague advice is better than none at all. But one wonders whether this is the best that implementation researchers have to offer. Wringing more out of the literature, however, requires a brand of risk taking that academics and policy analysts typically find uncomfortable. It requires offering *a logically ordered sequence of questions* that policymakers can ask, prior to making a policy decision, that will provide prescriptions for action. The problem with this approach, as opposed to, for example, cataloguing the fragmentary advice that falls out of case studies, is that one can err in a variety of ways: in interpreting the literature, in determining the logic that ties the questions together, or in choosing the questions. It is this fear of erring, I suspect, that has resulted in a failure of nerve among implementation researchers. The important issue is not whether the framework of analysis is 'right' or 'wrong', but whether it is sufficiently clear to be controvertible. It is less important to agree on a single framework for analysing implementation problems than it is to be clear about the consequences of adopting one framework over another.

The essential argument of this Chapter is that there are at least two clearly distinguishable approaches to implementation analysis: *forward mapping* and *backward mapping*.[2] Forward mapping is the strategy that comes most readily to mind when one thinks about how a policymaker might try to affect the implementation process. It begins at the top of the process, with as clear a statement as possible of the policymaker's intent, and proceeds through a sequence of increasingly more specific steps to define what is expected of implementers at each level. At the bottom of the process, one states, again with as much precision as possible, what a satisfactory outcome would be, measured in terms of the original statement of intent. Forward mapping of a federal policy might begin with a statement of congressional intent. It would then outline federal agency regulations and administrative actions consistent with that intent. It would elaborate a division of responsibilities between central and regional offices of the federal government (or among federal, state, and local administrations) such that each implementing unit had a clearly defined mission. It would then state an outcome, usually in terms of an observable effect on a target population, consistent with the initial purpose of the policymakers.

Numerous variations of this approach are possible. One need not map only administrative actions and organisational arrangements. If political feasibility is a problem, one can describe the major political actors and the agreements necessary among them at each level. If the implementation of the policy depends on the adoption of some form of technology (for example, emission controls, medical equipment, or plant construction), one can describe the state of technology necessary at each stage. The analysis may also be elaborated by describing a number of alternative streams of action under varying assumptions about organisational, political, and technological factors.

The details of forward mapping are less important for our purposes than the underlying logic. It begins with an objective, it elaborates an increasingly specific set of steps for achieving that objective, and it states an outcome against which success or failure can be measured. It is consistent with the standard framework of policy analysis and with conventional techniques of management science and decision analysis (programme evaluation and review technique (PERT) and critical path method (CPM)). In so far as implementation analysis is treated at all in textbooks on policy analysis, it is treated as forward mapping.[3]

What the textbooks do not discuss, however, are the weaknesses of forward mapping and its severe limitations as an analytic technique. The most serious problem with forward mapping is its implicit and unquestioned assumption that *policymakers control the organisational, political, and technological processes that affect implementation*. The notion that policymakers exercise – or ought to exercise – some kind of direct and determinant control over policy implementation might be called the 'noble lie' of conventional public administration and policy analysis. Administrators legitimate their discretionary decisions by saying that their authority is delegated and controlled by elected and appointed policymakers. Policy analysts justify their existence by arguing that informed, rational choices by policymakers are necessary to guide and control administrators. Neither administrators nor policy analysts are very comfortable with the possibility that most of what happens in the implementation process cannot be explained by the intentions and directions of policymakers.

By assuming that more explicit directives, greater attention to administrative responsibilities, and clearer statements of intended outcomes will improve implementation, forward mapping reinforces the myth that implementation is controlled from the top. This myth is increasingly difficult to maintain in the face of accumulating evidence on the nature of the implementation process. Moreover, forward mapping, as an analytic strategy, treats only a narrow range of possible explanations for implementation failures.[4] The most persuasive explanation for the persistence of forward mapping in the face of its obvious limitations is the lack of a suitable alternative. It is one thing to appreciate intuitively that policymakers may not exercise decisive control over the implementation process; it is quite another to formulate an analytic strategy consistent with that intuition.

Backward mapping shares with forward mapping the notion that policymakers have a strong interest in affecting the implementation process and the outcomes of policy decisions. But backward mapping explicitly questions the assumption that policymakers ought to, or do, exercise the determinant influence over what happens in the implementation process. It also questions the assumption that explicit policy directives, clear statements of administrative responsibilities, and well-defined outcomes will necessarily increase the likelihood that policies will be successfully implemented.

The logic of backward mapping is, in all important respects, the opposite of forward mapping. It begins not at the top of the implementation process but at the last possible stage, the point at which administrative actions intersect private choices. It begins not with a statement of intent, but with a statement of the specific behaviour at the lowest level of the implementation process that generates the need for a policy. Only after that behaviour is described does the analysis presume to state an objective; the objective is first stated as a set of organisational operations and then as a set of effects, or outcomes, that will result from these operations. Having established a relatively precise target at the lowest level of the system, the analysis backs up through the structure of implementing agencies, asking at each level two questions: What is the ability of this unit to affect the behaviour that is the target of the policy? And what resources does this unit require in order to have that effect? In the final stage of analysis the analyst or policymaker describes a policy that directs resources at the organisational units likely to have the greatest effect.

Although backward mapping takes the policymaker's perspective on the implementation process, it does not assume that policy is the only – or even the major – influence on the behaviour of people engaged in the process. Furthermore, it does not rely on compliance with the policymaker's intent as the standard of success or failure. It offers instead a standard of success that is in all respects *conditional*; that is, one's definition of success is predicated on an estimate of the limited ability of actors at one level of the implementation process to influence the behaviour of actors at other levels and on the limited ability of public organisations as a whole to influence private behaviour.

Forward mapping assumes that organisational units in the implementation process are linked in essentially hierarchical relationships. This assumption has two corollaries: the closer one is to the source of the policy, the greater is one's authority and influence; and the ability of complex systems to respond to problems depends on the establishment of clear lines of authority and control. Backward mapping assumes essentially the opposite: the closer one is to the source of the problem, the greater is one's ability to influence it; and the problem-solving ability of complex systems depends not on hierarchical control but on maximising discretion at the point where the problem is most immediate.

Backward mapping and implementation research

Applying forward and backward mapping to the same problem gives much different results. The analytic solution offered by forward mapping stresses factors that tend to centralise control and that are easily manipulated by policymakers: funding formulas; formal organisational structures; authority relationships among administrative units; regulations; and administrative controls (budget, planning, and evaluation requirements). The analytic solution offered by backward mapping stresses the dispersal of control and concentrates on factors that can only be indirectly influenced by policymakers: knowledge and problem solving ability of lower-level administrators; incentive structures that operate on the subjects of policy; bargaining relationships among political actors at various levels of the implementation process; and the strategic use of funds to affect discretionary choices. The crucial difference of perspective stems from whether one chooses to rely primarily on formal devices of command and control that centralise authority or on informal devices of delegation and discretion that disperse authority.

The stakes involved in choosing an analytic approach are clearer when they are put in the context of current thinking about implementation. As the literature on implementation has accumulated, certain issues have emerged that demonstrate the consequences, both intellectual and practical, of seeing implementation either as a hierarchical ordered process or as a dispersed and decentralised process.

Organisational processes and outputs

The emergence of implementation as a subject for policy analysis coincides closely with the discovery by policy analysts that decisions are not self-executing. Analysis of policy choices matters very little if the mechanism for implementing those choices is poorly understood. In answering the question, 'What percentage of the work of achieving a desired governmental action is done when the preferred analytic alternative has been identified?' Allison estimated that, in the normal case, it was about 10 per cent, leaving the remaining 90 per cent in the realm of implementation.[5] Hence, in Nelson's terms, 'the core of analysis of alternatives becomes the prediction of how alternative organisational structures will behave over . . . time.'[6] But the task of prediction is vastly complicated by the absence of a coherent body of organisational theory, making it necessary to posit several alternative models of organisation.[7]

Those policy analysts who are economists, impatient with the complexities of bureaucracy and the lack of precision in organisational theory, have tried to reduce implementation analysis to a simple choice between market and non-market mechanisms. Schultze states the basic argument when he says that the 'collective-coercion component of intervention should be treated as a scarce resource' in the formulation of policies, and that policymakers should learn to 'maximise the use of techniques that modify the structure of private incentives.'[8] Wolf furthers the argument, stating that the whole enterprise of implementation analysis can be reduced to a diagnosis of the pathologies of non-market structures, or as he calls it, 'a theory of nonmarket failures.'[9] The simplicity of the argument is comforting, but its utility is suspect. It seeks to solve one type of organisational problem, the responsiveness of large-scale bureaucracies, by substituting another type of organisational problem, the invention and execution of quasi markets. There is little evidence to suggest that the latter problem is any more tractable than the former. One would hardly expect, though, that a detailed framework for analysis of organisational alternatives would emerge from an intellectual tradition that regards organisational structure of any kind as a second-best solution to the problem of collective action.[10]

Defining implementation analysis as a choice between market and non-market structures diverts attention from, and trivialises, an important problem: *how to use the structure and process of organisations to elaborate, specify, and define policies*. Most policy analysts, economists or not, are trained to regard complex organisations as *barriers* to the implementation of public policy, not as instruments to be capitalised upon and modified in the pursuit of policy objectives. In fact, organisations can be remarkably effective devices for working out difficult public problems, but their use requires an understanding of the reciprocal nature of authority relations. Formal authority travels from top to bottom in organisations, but the informal authority that derives from expertise, skill, and proximity to the essential tasks that an organisation performs travels in the opposite direction. Delegated discretion is a way of capitalising on this reciprocal relationship; responsibilities that require special expertise and proximity to a problem are pushed down in the organisation, leaving more generalised responsibilities at the top. For purposes of implementation, this means that formal authority, in the form of policy statements, is heavily dependent upon specialised problem solving capabilities further down the chain of authority. Except in cases where a policy requires strict performance of a highly structured routine (for example, airline safety inspections), strong hierarchical controls work against this principle of reciprocity. To use organisations effectively as instruments of policy, analysts and policymakers have to understand where in the complex network of organisational relationships certain tasks should be performed, what resources are necessary for their performance, and whether the performance of the task has some tangible effect on the problem that the policy is designed to solve. Analysts and policymakers do *not* need to know how to perform the task, or even whether the task is performed uniformly; in fact, diversity in the performance of the task is an important source of knowledge about how to do it better.

The notion of reciprocity lends some concreteness to the strategic calculations involved in implementation analysis. Instead of stating the central analytic problem as a choice between competing abstractions – market and non-market alternatives – it focuses on the *process* by which organised problem solving occurs and the *output* that results from problem solving. Understanding reciprocal dependencies in organisations also simplifies the conduct of analysis considerably. One is not concerned with mapping all the formal authority relationships that could possibly bear on a policy problem but with isolating the one or two critical points in a complex organisation that have the closest proximity to the problem and describing what needs to happen at those points to solve the problem.

Shrewd organisational analysis does not preclude the selection of market-like structures to implement policy. In fact, it clarifies the choice considerably. There is nothing to prevent the analyst or policymaker from concluding that, for purposes of a specific problem, the best strategy is to move problem solving responsibilities outside formal organisations and rely on individual choices. But the decision to pursue that strategy is based on a prior understanding of the setting and the actors, rather than a presumption that market-like structures are more effective.

The complexity of joint action

Pressman and Wildavsky were the first to observe the inverse relationship between the number of transactions required to implement a decision and the likelihood that an effect, any effect, would result. Even when the probability of a favourable result is high at each step, the cumulative product of a large number of transactions is an extraordinarily low probability of success.[11] This analysis is complemented by Bardach's extended discussion of the devices that administrators use to delay, divert, and dissipate the effect of policies and by attempts of other scholars to specify the effect of bureaucratic structure on implementation.[12] These notions have now become part of the standard repertoire of explanations for why policies fail. But they have had surprisingly little pay-off in increasing our understanding of how to prevent failure. If we accept that the complexity of joint action is a serious problem, for both policy analysts and policymakers, what can we do about it?

Very little can be done about the problem if analysts and policymakers persist in viewing implementation as a hierarchically ordered set of authority relationships. That is, to the extent that the implementation process is dominated by regulation, formal organisational structure, and management control, one would expect problems of complexity to increase. The tighter the structure of hierarchical relationships, the greater the number of checks and decision points required to assure compliance, the more opportunities for diversion and delay, the greater the reliance of subordinates on superiors for guidance, and the lower the reliance on individual judgement and problem solving ability. One of the great ironies of increased attention to implementation is that the harder we try, using conventional tools of hierarchical control, the less likely we are to achieve.[13]

Forward mapping, as an analytic strategy, reinforces the pathologies of hierarchy. With a sharp pencil, a good eye for detail, and a pocket calculator, one can demonstrate without much trouble that any policy will fail, simply by counting the number of discrete clearances and decisions, assigning a probability to each, and multiplying them seriatim. The flaw in this kind of analysis lies not in its internal logic, but in its failure to perceive an alternative to hierarchy. Demonstrating so simply that hierarchies increase the probability of failure should suggest the need for an alternative model of the process. A promising lead comes from Bardach's discussion of 'fixing', by which he means the skilful and selective intervention of policymakers at various points in the implementation process.[14] The key element of fixing is its deliberate disregard for hierarchy; a good fixer is one who is willing to intervene wherever a breakdown occurs, with scant regard for the line of authority relationships that precedes it. The difficulty with Bardach's account of fixing is that it does not provide very clear guidance about formulating a strategy of intervention: How does one decide among a number of possible points of intervention? What does one do when a point of intervention is identified? And how does one determine whether fixing has succeeded or failed? In other words, fixing, by itself, is a kind of behaviour, not an analytic strategy. Having decided to fix something, one is still left with deciding how to do it, and that requires a logic of some sort.

Street-level discretion

Distrust of discretion is deeply ingrained in conventional theories of administration and government. Kaufman confidently asserts, without argument:

> If leaders exert but little influence on the actions of subordinates, then one of the axioms of democratic government, ceases to apply . . . democracy in the modern state presupposes that changing a handful of officials in high places will ultimately change the actions of thousands of employees throughout the system.[15]

Substituting 'changing policy' for 'changing a handful of officials in high places', yields the essential statement of implementation as a process of hierarchical control. Kaufman argues that the 'major contribution' of his own work 'lies in the enhancement of leaders' capacities to neutralise tendencies toward non-compliance'.[16] Discretion, though inevitable in any complex administrative system, is to be carefully bounded, contained, and controlled by an assortment of devices (selection, monitoring, routinisation) that strengthen the top of the system against the bottom. Even theorists of public administration who argue that policymaking and administration cannot be separated harbour a strong distrust of discretion:

> Much of the actual discretion used in administration is used at the very bottom of the hierarchy, where public servants touch the public. The assessor who walks into the home and sees the furniture and the condition of the house, the policeman who listens to the motorist's story, the health inspector who visits the dairy, the income tax auditor who sees the return and interviews the taxpayer – all these people are compelled to exercise more discretion, and more important discretion, from the point of view of the citizen than many other functionaries further up in the organisation. While this is the actual situation in badly organised and poorly directed administrative units, it cannot be completely eliminated even in the best.[17]

This theme has been picked up and extended in the implementation literature by Weatherly and Lipsky in their analysis of the role of street-level bureaucrats. The heavy overload of demands and expectations resulting from new policies, they argue, means that street-level bureaucrats are essentially free to develop their own 'coping devices' for simplifying, and often distorting, the aims of policymakers. The solution to this problem, they suggest, lies mainly in devising more sophisticated ways of bounding and controlling discretion.[18]

The dominant view that discretion is, at best, a necessary evil and, at worst, a threat to democratic government pushes implementation analysis toward hierarchically structured models of the process and toward increased reliance on hierarchical controls to solve implementation problems. Uniformity of implementation, or low variability in the response of street-level bureaucrats to policy directives, has a positive value, whether or not it is positively related to outcomes. Compliance with orders and procedures displaces competence, or becomes the equivalent of competence, in interactions between lower-level public servants and clients. Nowhere in this view is serious thought given to *how to capitalise on discretion as a device for improving the reliability and effectiveness of policies at the street level*. Standardised solutions, developed at great distance from the problem, are notoriously unreliable; policies that fix street-level behaviour in the interest of uniformity and consistency are difficult to adapt to situations that policymakers failed to anticipate. Adaptation under these circumstances consists either of subversive, extralegal behaviour or a complex procedure of hierarchical clearance. There is little or no room for the exercise of special skills or judgement, not to mention deliberate invention and experimentation.

When implementation consists essentially of controlling discretion, the effect is to reduce reliance on knowledge and skill at the delivery level and increase reliance on abstract, standardised solutions. Hence, a certain proportion of the learning that is required to adapt a broad policy to a specific set of circumstances is lost; adaptive behaviours by street-level bureaucrats are never well understood by policymakers because they are viewed as illicit. Variability and discretion at the delivery level can just as easily be viewed as an asset – a broadbased body of data on unanticipated, adaptive responses to highly specialised problems. To capitalise on this knowledge, however, one's views of implementation has to put a higher value on discretion than compliance.

Coalitions and the bargaining arena

One of the earliest and most robust findings of implementation research was that the local effect of federal policy depends, in some critical sense, on the formation of local coalitions of individuals affected by the policy. Derthick documented the helplessness of federal administrators, trying to use surplus federal land as an incentive for the development of 'new towns', when local support for the projects failed to gel into a strong coalition.[19] Pressman concluded an analysis of federal programmes in Oakland with the observation that their impact depended upon the existence of 'effective bargaining arenas', in which the competing demands of local groups could be worked out.[20] Banfield concluded his analysis of the Model Cities programme with the observation:

> As perceived from Washington, a city government was an entity capable, if sufficiently prodded and when provided with a grant, of making decisions in a rational manner. . . . City officials knew, however, that only in a rather limited sense did such a thing as a city government exist; for them the reality was bits and pieces of power and authority, the focuses of which were constantly changing. Bringing the bits and pieces together long enough to carry out an undertaking was a delicate and precarious operation requiring skills and statuses that few persons possessed.[21]

Unless the initiators of a policy can galvanise the energy, attention, and skills of those affected by it, thereby bringing these resources into a loosely structured bargaining arena, the effects of a policy are unlikely to be anything but weak and diffuse. Once bargaining is recognised as a key element of implementation, certain other conditions follow. Bargaining, for example, requires real stakes. Local actors have no incentive for participation in a bargaining arrangement unless the possible pay-off is tangible and valuable. The terms of the deal cannot be fixed in advance by law and regulation; sufficient flexibility must exist in the outlines of a policy to allow the local bargaining process to work. Carefully specified, hierarchically controlled policies limit incentives to form strong local bargaining coalitions.

Another consequence of local bargaining is that policy implementation has no clear, decisive end point. The outcome of one bargaining episode is the starting point of the next. Success in bargaining is completely relative in one important respect: each participant judges success in terms of his own objectives, not in terms of an overall set of objectives that applies to all participants. The only measure of success that all participants can agree on is maintenance of the bargaining arena, since it provides them access to the goods that are dispensed there. To acknowledge that bargaining is essential to the process of implementation is to accept the consequence that policy outcomes will never be discrete, determinate end points that can be measured and objectified. An analytic framework that requires the comparison of a clearly specified outcome with a clearly specified intent – a comparison implicit in forward mapping – is inconsistent with a conception of implementation that includes bargaining.[22]

To summarise, the implementation literature provides strong support for an analytic framework that takes account of reciprocity in the relationship between superiors and subordinates in organisations; the connection between hierarchical control and increased complexity; discretion as an adaptive device; and bargaining as a precondition for local affairs.

Recall the logic of backward mapping outlined earlier: begin with a concrete statement of the behaviour that creates the occasion for a policy intervention, describe a set of organisational operations that can be expected to affect that behaviour, describe the expected effect of those operations, and then describe for each level of the implementation process what effect one would expect that level to have on the target behaviour and what resources are required for that effect to occur. The advantage of beginning with a concrete behaviour and focusing on the delivery-level mechanism for affecting that behaviour is that it focuses attention on reciprocity and discretion. It puts the policymakers' problem in the following form: 'If we propose to affect that behaviour, where is the closest point of contact we have with it?' It emphasises, in other words, that it is not the policy or the policymaker that solves the problem, but someone with immediate proximity. Problem solving requires skill and discretion; policy can direct individuals' attention toward a problem and provide them an occasion for the application of skill and judgement, but policy cannot itself solve problems. Hence, the connections between the problem and the closest point of contact is the most critical stage of analysis. After that, analysis consists of describing the most direct means of reaching the point of contact, focusing resources on those organisational units and coalitions that have the greatest likelihood of affecting delivery-level performance. Strategically, the more direct the path for reaching the point of contact – that is, the greater the reliance on delegated discretion, and the less the reliance on hierarchical controls – the greater the likelihood of affecting the target behaviour. Rather than reasoning from top to bottom, through successive layers, trying to discover how each layer can control the next, one begins at the point of the problem and tries to find the most parsimonious way of reaching it.

Notes

1 Pressman and Wildavsky conclude that the 'length and unpredicability' of implementation processes should lead policymakers to consider 'more direct means' (Jeffrey Pressman and Aaron Wildavsky (1973), *Implementation*, Berkeley, University of California Press, pp. 143–4). Bardach advises policymakers to base policies on explicit theories, to prefer market-like mechanisms to bureaucratic ones, to forecast problems by using scenarios, and to 'fix' implementation problems with political intervention (Eugene Bardach (1977), *The Implementation Game*, Cambridge, Mass., MIT Press, pp. 250–83). Berman and McLaughlin suggest policymakers should pay more attention 'to all stages of the local change process', provide 'adaptive implementation assistance', and improve 'the capacity of school districts to manage change' (Paul Berman and Milbery McLaughlin (1978), *Federal Programs Supporting Educational Change*, Santa Monica, Calif., Rand Corporation, vol. VIII, pp. 35–43). Weatherly and Lipsky conclude that policymakers should attend more closely to the behaviour of street-level bureaucrats, rewarding behaviours that are consistent with policy and penalising those that are not (Richard Weatherly and Michael Lipsky (1977), 'Street-level bureaucrats and institutional innovation: implementing special education reform', *Harvard Educational Review*, 47, May, 196).

2 I am indebted to Mark Moore of the Kennedy School of Government, Harvard University, for introducing me to the notion of 'backward mapping', though he should not be held accountable for my version of it.

3 See, for example, Harry Hatry *et al.* (1976), *Program Analysis for State and Local Government*, Washington, D.C., Urban Institute, p. 97; Edward Quade (1975), *Analysis for Public Decisions*, New York, Elsevier, p. 253; Grover Starling (1979), *The Politics and Economics of Public Policy*, Homewood, Ill., Dorsey, p. 430.

4 For a detailed discussion of alternative explanations of implementation failures and their consequences for modelling the implementation process, see Richard F. Elmore (1978), 'Organisational models of social program implementation', *Public Policy*, 26, Spring, pp. 185–228.

5 Graham Allison (1971), *Essence of Decision: Explaining the Cuban Missile Crisis*, Boston, Mass., Little Brown, p. 267.

6 Richard Nelson (1977), *The Moon and the Ghetto*, New York, W. W. Norton, p. 40.

7 See for example, ibid., p. 41; Elmore, 'Organisational models', pp. 187–9.

8 Charles Schultze (1977), *The Public Use of Private Interest*, Washington, DC, Brookings Institution, pp. 6–7.
9 Charles Wolf (1979), 'A Theory of Non-Market Failures', *Public Interest*, Spring, pp. 114–33.
10 For examples of this argument, see Kenneth Arrow (1974), *The Limits of Organisation*, New York, W. W. Norton; and Oliver Williamson (1975), *Markets and Hierarchies*, New York, Free Press.
11 Pressman and Wildavsky, *Implementation*, pp. 87–124.
12 Bardach, *The Implementation Game*, p. 65; see also, Allison, *Essence of Decision*, pp. 67–100; and Elmore, 'Organisational models', pp. 199–208.
13 Richard F. Elmore (1979), 'Complexity and Control: What Legislators and Administrators Can Do About Implementation', Policy Paper no. 11, Institute of Governmental Research, University of Washington, Seattle, Washington, April.
14 Bardach, *The Implementation Game*, pp. 274–83.
15 Herbert Kaufman (1973), *Administrative Feedback*, Washington, DC, Brookings Institution, p. 4.
16 Ibid., p. 5.
17 Luther Gulick, quoted by Herbert Kaufman (1977), 'Reflections on Administrative Reorganisation', in Joseph Pechman (ed.), *The 1978 Budget: Setting National Priorities*, Washington, DC, Brookings Institution, p. 400.
18 Weatherly and Lipsky, 'Street-Level Bureaucrats', pp. 172 and 196.
19 Martha Derthick, *New Towns in Town*, Washington, DC, Urban Institute.
20 Jeffrey Pressman (1975), *Federal Programs and City Politics*, Berkeley, Calif., University of California Press, pp. 143–4.
21 Edward Banfield (1976), 'Making a New Federal Program: Model Cities, 1964–68', in Walter Williams and Richard Elmore (eds), *Social Program Implementation*, New York, Academic Press, p. 210.
22 Elmore, 'Organisational Models', pp. 217–26; Helen Ingram (1977), 'Policy implementation through bargaining: the case of federal grants-in-aid', *Public Policy*, 25, Fall, pp. 499–526.

4.7

School Based and Centrally Directed Curriculum Development – the Uneasy Middle Ground

Mary Simpson

Introduction

One of the recommendations of the Munn Report (SED, 1977) which were accepted by the Government (SED, 1980) was that room should be found within a predominantly subject based curriculum for a small number of multidisciplinary courses to deal with such general areas of concern as guidance, health and social education. The procedures by which such courses could be planned and implemented were not made clear, but it was recognised 'that a good deal of experimentation and imagination will be needed to discover the most effective ways of providing the opportunity and means for pupils to explore these vital issues', and that 'when such courses have been developed and adopted by an increasing number of schools, account will have to be taken of them in arrangements for assessment' (SED, 1977).

In 1980, the development of one such multidisciplinary course, to be called 'Health Studies', was initiated as part of phase two of the Munn and Dunning Development Programme. At first sight, the procedures used by the Scottish Education Department (SED) to effect this curriculum innovation appear exemplary.

The allocation of resources to the development was generous. In 1980 an HMI team was appointed, comprising a District Inspector and specialists in Biology, Physical Education and Home Economics. Discussions within this HMI team resulted in a first draft of Proposals for a Health Studies course. In 1981, two Field Development Officers, one full-time and one part-time, were appointed. Their remit was to assist the HMI team in the development of the course at Foundation level and to work with the twelve pilot schools (later increased to eighteen) recruited to the development exercise.

Later, two members of staff of Jordanhill College of Education were recruited to give curriculum development support to the two FDOs. These four comprised the Writing Team, the remit of which was to produce exemplar material for the pilot schools. In September 1982, a Joint Working Party, comprising mainly teacher members, was established and charged with the responsibility of producing a report for the JWP Steering Committee. If accepted, this report would be used by the Scottish Examination Board (SEB) as the basis for 'Conditions and Arrangements' for the nationally certificated course due to commence in 1985, and to be first examined in 1987. Considerable effort was put into the organisation of two pilot national examinations in 1983 and 1984. An input to the development from the research community was assured by the funding of two projects, one concerned with the implementation of the assessment of the course (Simpson and Arnold, 1985), the other with aspects of collaboration within multidisciplinary courses (Munn and Morrison, 1985).

The time allocation for the development of the course – five years to the projected national start to the certificated course, seven years to the first national examination – appeared to be generous.

Finally, care was taken to involve teachers in the development programme. In 1981, after discussions with teachers, a Central Team, comprising one of the members of the original HMI team and the two FDOs, produced a second draft of the proposals. Early in 1982, two conferences for all the teachers involved in the pilot schools were held, as a result of which draft Guidelines were produced. In the same year, and again in 1983, national conferences for the leaders of the multidisciplinary teaching teams considered assessment and moderation procedures.

Despite the care with which the Health Studies development had been mounted, it gradually became clear that serious difficulties were being encountered. There were rumblings of discontent in the pilot schools; in May 1984 the report from the JWP was rejected by the Steering Committee; a new working group was convened with one teacher member and a majority of SEB staff who prepared a considerably revised set of draft Guidelines; the course was relegated to a later stage of the Development Programme; and the researchers involved in the project on assessment advised the SED that due to these circumstances their remit could not be fulfilled.

The Health Studies development comprised two major strands – a curriculum development based largely in the schools and supported by external guidance; and a curriculum development which was an integral part of the national development of the Standard Grade, subject to the requirements of external certification and with its mechanisms for development within the central administrative structure of Scottish education. The compatibility of these strands and their successful interweaving would determine the viability of the Health Studies course.

The school based development

The draft proposals produced by the early HMI team were for a course which fitted 'the scientific mode of activity and learning outlined in the Munn Report' and which had a compulsory core (30 per cent) of biological information which linked the course to Foundation level Science. The draft Proposals formed the basis of discussion between the members of the Central Team and the teachers in the pilot schools. Scrutiny of the draft Guidelines and exemplar material which resulted from these consultations shows that major changes had occurred in the underlying philosophy of the course. The four core areas of study envisaged in the proposals – Human Biology, Nutrition, Defence and Protection, and Family and Community, were replaced by three Fields of Study, 'The Individual', 'The Individual and the Family' and 'The Individual and the Community', signalling the change from a scientifically oriented knowledge based course to one which was pupil centred and concerned with the perceptions, actions and feelings of the individual pupil in his or her daily life. Only one third of the course content was prescribed, allowing schools, in the remainder, the 'utmost freedom to respond in their Health Studies courses to local needs and circumstances and to adapt them to the available resources'.

The style of the new approach, applied to both the prescribed core and the options, is illustrated by the example given in the Guidelines of a plan for designing a learning unit on the handicapped. The titles of the sub-units included 'My name is Joey Deacon', 'What's it Like to be in a Wheelchair?', 'What's it Like to be the Parent of a Mentally Handicapped Child?' and the activities proposed included simulation events and role-playing. The assessment scheme suggested for the course was complex, ambitious and innovative. At least 70 per cent of the final assessment was to be internally applied and based on a continuous scheme designed to test not the acquisition and retention of knowledge, but the pupils' performance, at three grade levels, of 'tasks' which were themselves learning experiences.

These draft Guidelines were generally well received by the teachers, who saw a course developing along these lines as filling a gap in educational provision, as a response to the needs of adolescent pupils, particularly those of lower academic attainment, and as a means of describing fairly the attainments of those pupils whom they regarded as being disadvantaged by the normal end-of-course external examination procedures. But innovations must be judged not by their initial reception but according to their successful implementation.

It was clear from our discussions with teachers (Simpson and Arnold, 1986) that there was a wide range in the extent to which teachers were trying to implement the Guidelines: some teachers were enthusiastic innovators while others took the more cynical view that since the Guidelines had merely a draft status, and might later be modified, it was unnecessary to take action until 'they' had made up their minds. These disparities in response may have been a reflection of the way in which teachers had been recruited to the pilot enterprise; some had been fairly keen volunteers; others had been assigned to the development, with little or no consultation, by enthusiastic or compliant headteachers.

There was also a considerable diversity in the way in which the Guidelines were implemented. It was intended that developments within the school should be by multidisciplinary teaching teams, supported by communications from the FDOs, conferences, the SED and SEB. The extent to which the classroom teachers received much of this support was dependent on the frequency and regularity of the team meetings. It appears that in some schools local management, having agreed to take part in the development, did not, by appropriate timetabling, ensure that the team members could meet. Team leaders not uncommonly had so many other responsibilities that they were precluded from exercising their proper role in the dissemination and the coordination of responses to incoming information. The great diversity in the effectiveness of the teams resulted in wide differences in the teachers' awareness of key features of the development, which ranged from excellent to grossly unsatisfactory.

Teachers had not only to receive these communications, they also had to interpret them. Some of the differences in assessment practices in schools appeared to be the result of different percep-tions of terms such as 'continuous assessment', 'criterion-referenced assessment' and 'diagnostic assessment', which have no history of practice or commonly accepted meanings. The first term, for example, was used by the SEB, the Central Team, and some teachers, to denote three quite different practices. It was perhaps insufficiently recognised that there is a major difference between the conceptual frameworks of those who are developing educational policy and those who have to implement it in the classroom. This difference was at the root of the difficulties experienced by teachers in understanding some of the communications they received and was exemplified by the comment 'the Field Development Officer came and explained, but we didn't understand'.

Finally, the course was intended to offer experiential learning, to address itself to questions to which there are no definitive answers and to have as a major objective the exploration by pupils of their individual, personal lifestyles. It required that teachers should function outside their specialities and as resources rather than authorities. The difficulties which are encountered by teachers in attempting to adopt such a role are almost always underestimated.

The influence of these features of the development was felt in several ways. Because they had few resources (of text-books, worksheets, past experience and training) on which they could draw, teachers needed a great deal of time to assemble their classroom materials, and to think, plan and reflect. That time was not made available.

Many teachers were uncertain and needed reassurance about teaching outside their own subject discipline. Some were sure that parts of the course might be better taught by others from outside the three involved specialities.

The national certification of the course had been almost universally welcomed as giving the course status in the eyes of the pupils (and the teachers) although there were fears that it might distort the selection of course content. Furthermore, teachers recognised that they were being asked to assess things which they had not explicitly taught, for example, skills of social interaction. Indeed, many thought it likely that pupils would have been able to pass the final examination without undergoing the course.

The centrally directed curriculum development

The assessment scheme which was conceived by the Central Team and further developed in conferences and in the pilot schools was undoubtedly appropriate to the content of the Health Studies course and to its underlying philosophy. Its purpose was expressed as follows: 'The basic function of assessment in our course is to provide pupils with information on their progress and achievements with the intention of showing where, when, how and why they can, or should, improve their performance'. It accordingly won a real, though cautious, acceptance in the pilot schools. Teachers recognised that it presented many difficulties, but looked to some central authority to resolve these and subsequently provide an amended, standardised version which could be adopted nationally.

However, the assessment had not only to be appropriate to the content and aims of the course and to the learning needs of the pupils, it also had to be accommodated to the national certification procedures for Standard Grade. This task fell to a Joint Working Party, comprising seven teacher members, one of whom was appointed as an 'independent', the others being nominated by the

Consultative Committee on the Curriculum (CCC) and the SEB. One HMI from the original HMI Team attended as Assessor and professional support was given to the JWP by an Examination Officer (SEB) and a member of staff of the Scottish Curriculum Development Service (SCDS). The full-time FDO attended most meetings.

The remit for the JWP was to detail for the Health Studies course those factors (e.g. grade-related criteria, assessable elements, Foundations/General differentiation mechanisms) which would allow conformity to the general guidelines set out by the SEB for Standard Grade. The basic function of *this* system of assessment was to describe pupils' performances in terms of a small number of assessable elements, to be defined in terms of numbered grade levels, and to be summarised, ultimately, in terms of a single grade level.

The JWP had available to it two sources of authoritative advice: the FDOs who formed the sole formal and regular channel of communication between the pilot schools and the JWP, and an Examination Officer from the Scottish Examination Board who presented and interpreted a series of papers, advisory and informative, from the SEB on the requirements of the Standard Grade.

The FDOs advised that the problems identified within the piloted task based system of assessment were more imagined than real, and the Central Team was defensive against the possibility of changes to the system which they reported to be working well. The Examination Officer, while concerned that the integrity of the course which had been developed in schools should be respected, had nevertheless to advise that the requirements of the Standard Grade system *must*, by some means, be met.

In the early stages of its work, the JWP (and the Central Team) believed that the Munn Committee's recommendation on the innovative multidisciplinary courses, that 'account will have to be taken of them in arrangements for assessment', would find practical expression in a considerable negotiability of the SEB's requirements for certification. The experience of the JWP was otherwise. As time passed, the requirements appeared to become progressively more demanding.

It became apparent to the JWP that there was a fundamental incompatibility between the philosophy and content of the course and the requirements being framed up for external certification. An innovative form of external examination, devised largely by the FDOs, had been trialled at the end of the first year of the pilot study, and the outcome was reported by the FDOs as affording a high degree of correlation between the grades achieved by pupils in the examination and those derived from internal task based assessment. The examination comprised a small number of questions, each using a scene-setting approach, and requiring pupils to use the information presented and to suggest appropriate action in everyday life situations. It provided evidence of what pupils could do in specific life situations and was wholly compatible with the course's holistic and experiential approach to learning. In contrast, the SEB required that the attainment of single elements, comprising identifiable skills and knowledge, should be assessed at five levels of performance specified by grade-related criteria. One teacher described the incompatibility of the course content and the SEB's approach to assessment by likening the course experiences to 'a good novel'. The benefit to be gained from reading it is to be found in its generation of insight, understanding and compassion, and should not be assessed by measurement of the reader's ability to 'spit out at the end' the names of characters and details of the plot.

The task of the JWP was to effect a reconciliation. One possible accommodation, that the external examination should be of factual material only and that appraisal of more holistic attainments should be conducted internally, was ruled out by the SEB's requirement that for aggregation purposes internal and external assessments should report on the same elements, and was also resisted by the FDO and members of the JWP, who feared that this might lead to an undesirable emphasis on the teaching and retention of facts at the expense of the more difficult task of promoting experiential learning.

In a long series of working papers, the JWP attempted to formulate some means of resolving the tension between the school based development and the SEB requirements. The procedures set out in the final report of the JWP to the Steering Committee represented a considerable compromising of the holistic approach underlying the course, but when compared with the assessment procedures detailed in the reports of other JWPs, appeared to be in a form which would be acceptable to the SEB.

The report produced by the JWP in May 1984 was sent for approval to the JWP Steering Committee. It was not found to be acceptable as the basis for a national course. Although the reasons for failure were reputedly associated with assessment, no formal statement of the Steering Group's decision was sent to the JWP, which convened its last meeting amid considerable uncertainty.

The SEB hastily convened a new working group comprising representatives from the SEB (five), SCDS (one), and the SED (one), together with one teacher (the former chairman of the disbanded JWP). As a result of its deliberations, second and third drafts of the report were speedily produced, in which the course content was revised and reorganised in such a way as to further the process of reversion to the knowledge based, depersonalised course which had been reluctantly begun by the JWP.

Following consultations with teachers, health educators (e.g. the Scottish Health Education Group) and other interested parties, who expressed reservations about the usefulness of a knowledge based health course, the SED decided that a compromise, combining features of a pupil centred 'Health Education' course and a knowledge based 'Health Studies' course might provide a solution to the dilemma. The original JWP was accordingly reconvened early in 1985, although with a considerably reduced teacher attendance, and following advice from a representative of the SED, it set to work to produce Guidelines for such a course.

The terrain of curriculum development

Despite the element of democracy introduced into educational decision making by the establishment of the CCC, the predominant method of curriculum development in Scotland has, in the past, been strongly centralist. In its most extreme form, a relatively small number of people decided what aspects of education should be considered to be problems, formulated solutions and disseminated relatively untested instructions and advice to classroom teachers. More recently, it has been recognised that classroom teachers are not the passive recipients of advice on innovation, but have an active role in its adoption. In its most extreme form, this has found expression in the view that *only* those developments which are school based can succeed.

However, there never can be any national curriculum development which is so wholly centralist as to ignore the views and needs of the classroom teachers, nor one which is entirely based within schools. The introduction of national curriculum developments involves the negotiation of a middle ground between two domains – the central administrative structure of Scottish education and the schools on the periphery. The nature of the terrain, safe or uneasy, is determined by the underlying structures of these domains – the organisation, attitudes and methods of operation of the SED, the SEB and the schools. The two models which are appropriate to the analysis of central and peripheral organisations are those of 'power' and 'participatory problem solving' (Havelock and Huberman, 1977).

The national curriculum development – the power model

Organisations for effecting curriculum change under this model have the following characteristics: there is an involvement and direction by political leadership; there is a clear administrative hierarchy for decision making and implementation; use is made of directives, laws, rules and procedural guidelines; use is made of negative sanctions for failues to conform to project procedures or to meet specified objectives; use is made of agents or intermediates to communicate central decisions or to provide technical help.

Many features of the national Health Studies development conformed to this model. There was a clear hierarchy which comprised the Government, the SED and SEB, the Joint Working Party Steering Committee, the Joint Working Party and the Central Team, and the teachers. Formal remits were given to the JWPs. Directives and advisory papers were issued by the SEB concerning 'elements', 'profiling', 'rating', 'grade related criteria' and on other features of summative reporting. The Central Team issued Proposals and Guidelines, exemplars, and guides on procedures for moderation and grading.

There was considerable pressure on the JWP to deliver its draft report on time and according to specifications. The major negative sanctions were the threat of rejection of the report by the Steering Committee, and the possible relegation of the subject from phase two to phase three of the national development programme.

The agents of communication and technical help to the school teams were the Field Development Officers and representatives of the SED, the SEB and the SCDS. The independent researchers from the two research projects associated with Health Studies had no remit to participate in the development process.

The curriculum development in the schools – the participatory problem solving model

The general characteristics of developments which conform to this model are that they are locally controlled, responsive to local needs and draw on local resources. They reflect an underlying belief that local development groups can solve their own problems with a minimum of outside assistance and a maximum amount of mutual support. The group generates a high cohesiveness but allows latitude for individual initiative and choice. In the Health Studies development these characteristics were exemplified by the following.

Teachers from the participating schools were involved in discussions on the content and philosophy of the course particularly in its early stages when the knowledge based, scientifically oriented course originally proposed began to be displaced by the pupil centred, experiential learning, process based course. It was initially expected that teachers would be primarily responsible for the assessment – 'at least 70 per cent' was to be internally applied. For the common core material, 'fields of study' were identified rather than 'compulsory topics'. The content to be covered was not explicitly specified and the exemplars confirmed the low status to be given to the coverage of specific factual material. Local resources and local needs were the key factors which were to determine what was covered in courses, two-thirds of which was to be entirely optional.

The uneasy middle ground

Considerable resources had been allocated to the Health Studies development. Staff of the SED and the SEB had devoted time, conferences of teachers had been funded, a JWP supported, Field Development Officers had been employed, all in order to establish a course which would form part of the national plan for curriculum and assessment reform. The result was a course which was radically different from that which was originally intended and for which the suggested methods of assessment would be difficult to accommodate within the requirements of Standard Grade.

From the viewpoint of the schools the Health Studies development may be regarded as a success which failed. It encountered some difficulties in schools but it fulfilled the hopes of many teachers for a course which met the needs of a section of the school population which had previously been neglected (Gow and McPherson, 1980). Its only serious, but by no means insoluble problems were those associated with assessment and certification. The most recent draft of the revised course (SEB, 1986) will undoubtedly be regarded by those teachers who were most committed to the development as being a conventional and inadequate response to the perceived needs of their pupils.

The Health Studies course floundered in the middle ground because, prior to the development proceeding, agreement had been assumed rather than reached on the ways in which this difficult terrain should be negotiated. The underlying causes of the floundering should not be thought peculiar to Health Studies, or to multidisciplinary courses, but as being particular expressions of general deficiencies in the procedures used to effect curriculum development in Scotland.

First, no consensus of aims had been established. The SED's concern was perhaps for a course which would allow the lower-achieving members of the pupil community to gain some nationally recognised certification, the SEB's that the integrity of the national certification process should not be compromised and that an award for one subject should be recognised by society as having the same value as a similar award for another subject. The teachers' concern was for a course which would be relevant to the life needs of their pupils and which would be motivating to the lower achievers. They had little regard for certification except in so far as it gave the course status and they valued internal assessment as a means of serving learning needs rather than of sorting pupils. These differences were not explored in the teachers' conferences. Instead, teachers were urged to develop an innovative course without regard to assessment, even although it must have been recognised that any national system of assessment and certification would impose constraints. If the middle ground is to be successfully negotiated, the different parties must be aware of the limits of their freedom. It is not surprising that the experience of abandoning promising lines of curriculum development in order to conform to some later, centrally imposed assessment procedure should have alienated so many innovative and committed teachers (Simpson and Arnold, 1986; Eleftheriou, 1985).

Second, there was no clear understanding of what the role of the Field Development Officers should be. They had a remit to assist the development in the pilot schools. In the event, they took an extremely active part in initiating and encouraging highly innovative procedures. In doing so they supported and encouraged the defection from the original course aims. But they retained the authority vested in them as agents of the central institution, and, as the sole means of communication between the JWP and the pilot schools, exercised a 'gate-keeping' function on the exchange of information. It is not surprising that teachers in some pilot schools began to feel that they were merely trialling the course of the FDOs and the central institution, and that they showed reluctance to respond until firm decisions had been taken. However, the FDOs failed to act as agents in ensuring that the course in schools did not get too far out of step with the emerging requirements for Standard Grade assessment. What was critically absent from the Health Studies development, and indeed from all other Munn and Dunning developments with the notable exception of Social and Vocational Skills, was a guide to the middle ground – a 'change agent', an independent consultant committed to the need for some form of development, but whose task it is to negotiate that particular form which meets the needs of the schools and central institutions (Hoyle, 1970). The requirement that the change agent is genuinely independent, free to criticise and able to initiate the kind of debate which leads to a reconsideration of organisational solutions (Weir and Currie, 1985) makes it impossible for FDOs and HMIs to function in this role.

Third, the power to take decisions rested solely with the central institution. No transfer of power was effected, even to deal with issues of direct and immediate importance in the classroom. Thus, the realistic request that schools should have the power to decide that certain teachers with expertise in social education, but whose specialities lay outside Biology, Physical Education and Home Economics, might contribute to the course was rejected. Similarly, schools felt themselves powerless to effect any negotiation of the levels of budgetary and manpower support.

In conclusion, it has been argued that, left to themselves, schools would innovate slowly, if at all, and that curriculum innovation initiated centrally and imposed on schools is likely to fail in important respects (McIntyre, 1985). If effective curriculum development can only take place in the middle ground, then action must be taken to make it less uneasy than recent experience has demonstrated it to be.

Acknowledgments

The author is grateful to the Scottish Education Department for funding the research project on assessment in Health Studies. The views expressed here should not be taken as representing those of the Department.

References

Eleftheriou, M. (1985), 'School-based developments in foundation English', in Brown, S. and Munn, P. (eds), *The Changing Face of Education 14 to 16: Curriculum and Assessment*, Windsor, NFER-Nelson.

Gow, L. and McPherson, A. (1980), *Tell them from me: Scottish school leavers write about school and life afterwards*, Aberdeen, Aberdeen University Press.

Havelock, R. G. and Huberman, A. M. (1977), *Solving Educational Problems: the Planning and Reality of Innovation in Developing Countries*, Paris, UNESCO.

Hoyle, E. (1970), 'Planned Organisational Change in Education', *Research in Education*, 3, pp. 1–22.

McIntyre, D. (1985), 'A school-based development programme', in Brown, S. and Munn, P. (eds), *The Changing Face of Education 14 to 16: Curriculum and Assessment*, Windsor, NFER-Nelson.

Munn, P. and Morrison, A. T. (1985), *Approaches to Collaboration in Scottish Schools, in Multi-Disciplinary Courses, 14–16*, Stirling Educational Monographs, University of Stirling.

Scottish Examination Board (SEB) (1986), Joint Working Party on Health Studies at Foundation and General Levels.

Scottish Education Department (SED) (1977), *The Structure of the Curriculum in the Third and Fourth Years of the Scottish Secondary School (The Munn Report)*, Edinburgh, HMSO.

Scottish Education Department (SED) (1980), *The Munn and Dunning Reports, The Government's Development Programme*.

Simpson, M. and Arnold, B. (1985), *The Development and Implementation of Assessment in Health Studies: A Study of a Curriculum Development at Standard Grade*, Aberdeen, Aberdeen College of Education.

Simpson, M. and Arnold, B. (1986), *The Development and Implementation of Assessment in a Standard Grade Multidisciplinary Course: The Teachers' Views*, Aberdeen, Aberdeen College of Education.

Weir, D. and Currie, R. (1985), 'Social and vocational skills: an alternative approach', in Brown, S. and Munn, P. (eds), *The Changing Face of Education 14 to 16: Curriculum and Assessment*, Windsor, NFER-Nelson.

Appendices

Appendix 1
Extracts from James Callaghan's Speech at Ruskin College, Oxford, 18 October 1976

I was very glad to accept your invitation to lay the foundation stone for a further extension of Ruskin College. Ruskin fills a gap as a 'second chance' adult residential college. It has a special place in the affections of the Labour movement as an institution of learning because its students are mature men and women who, for a variety of reasons, missed the opportunity to develop their full potential at an earlier age. That aspect of the matter is a particular interest of my own.

Ruskin has justified its existence over and over again. Your students form a proud gallery and I am glad to see here this afternoon some of your former students who now occupy important positions. They include leading academics, Heads of State of Commonwealth countries, leaders of the trade union movement and industrial life and Members of Parliament. Indeed, 11 of the present Labour Members of Parliament graduated from Ruskin and five of them are either in the Government or have served there, including one present member of the Cabinet, Eric Varley, the Secretary for Industry.

Among the adult colleges, Ruskin has a long and honourable history of close association with the trade union movement. I am very glad to see that trade unions are so strongly represented here today because you are involved in providing special courses for trade union officials and I hope that this partnership will continue to flourish and prosper.

The work of a trade union official becomes even more onerous, because he has to master continuing new legislation on health and safety at work, employment protection and industrial change. This lays obligations on trade unionists which can only be met by a greatly expanded programme of education and understanding. Higher standards than ever before are required in the trade union field and as I shall indicate a little later, higher standards than in the past are also required in the general educational field. It is not enough to say that standards in this field have or have not declined. With the increasing complexity of modern life we cannot be satisfied with maintaining existing standards, let alone observe any decline. We must aim for something better.

I should like to pay tribute to Billy Hughes for his work at Ruskin and also for his wider contribution to education as Chairman of the Adult Literacy Resource Agency. This has been a strikingly successful campaign for which credit must go to a number of organisations, including the BBC. It is a commentary on the need that 55,000 students were receiving tuition this year with a steady flow of new students still coming forward. Perhaps most remarkable has been that 40,000 voluntary teachers have come forward to work, often on an individual, personal basis, with a single student. When I hear, as I do in so many different fields, of these generous responses to human need, I remain a confirmed optimist about our country. This is a most striking example of how the goodwill, energy and dedication of large numbers of private persons can be harnessed to the service of their fellows when the need and the opportunity are made plain.

There have been one or two ripples of interest in the educational world in anticipation of this visit. I hope the publicity will do Ruskin some good and I don't think it will do the world of education any harm. I must thank all those who have inundated me with advice: some helpful and others telling me less politely to keep off the grass, to watch my language, and that they will be examining my speech with the care usually given by Hong Kong watchers to the China scene. It is almost as though some people would wish that the subject matter and purpose of education should not have public attention focused on it; nor that profane hands should be allowed to touch it.

I cannot believe that this is a considered reaction. The Labour movement has always cherished education: free education, comprehensive education, adult education. Education for life. There is nothing wrong with non-educationalists, even a Prime Minister, talking about it again. Everyone is allowed to put his oar in on how to overcome our economic problems, how to put the balance of payments right, how to secure more exports and so on and so on. Very important, too. But, I venture to say, not as important in the long run as preparing future generations for life. R. H. Tawney, from whom I derived a great deal of my thinking years ago, wrote that the endowment of our children is the most precious of the natural resources of the community. So I do not hesitate to discuss how those endowments should be nurtured.

Labour's Programme '76 has recently made its own important contribution and contains a number of important statements that I certainly agree with. Let me answer the question 'what do we want from the education of our children and young people?' with Tawney's words once more. He said: 'What a wise parent would wish for their children so the State must wish for all its children.'

I take it that no one claims exclusive rights in this field. Public interest is strong and legitimate and will be satisfied. We spend £6 billion a year on education, so there will be discussion. But let it be rational. If everything is reduced to such phrases as 'educational freedom versus State control', we shall get nowhere. I repeat that parents, teachers, learned and professional bodies, representatives of higher education and both sides of industry, together with the Government, all have an important part to play in formulating and expressing the purpose of education and the standards that we need.

During my travels around the country in recent months, I have had many discussions that show concern about these matters.

First let me say, so that there should be no misunderstanding, that I have been very impressed in the schools I have visited by the enthusiasm and dedication of the teaching profession, by the variety of courses that are offered in our comprehensive schools, especially in arts and crafts as well as in other subjects; and by the alertness and keenness of many of the pupils. Clearly, life at school is far more full and creative than it was many years ago. I would also like to thank the children who have been kind enough to write to me after I visited their schools: and well-written letters they were. I recognise that teachers occupy a special place in these discussions because of their real sense of professionalism and vocation about their work. But I am concerned on my journeys to find complaints from industry that new recruits from the schools sometimes do not have the basic tools to do the job that is required.

I have been concerned to find that many of our best trained students who have completed the higher levels of education at university or polytechnic have no desire to join industry. Their preferences are to stay in academic life or to find their way into the Civil Service. There seems to be a need for a more technological bias in science teaching that will lead towards practical applications in industry rather than towards academic studies. Or, to take other examples, why is it that such a high proportion of girls abandon science before leaving school? Then there is concern about the standards of numeracy of school-leavers. Is there not a case for a professional review of the mathematics needed by industry at different levels? To what extent are these deficiencies the result of insufficient coordination between schools and industry? Indeed how much of the criticism about basic skills and attitudes is due to industry's own shortcomings rather than to the educational system? Why is it that 30,000 vacancies for students in science and engineering in our universities were not taken up last year while the humanities courses were full?

On another aspect there is the unease felt by parents and others about the new informal methods of teaching which seem to produce excellent results when they are in well-qualified hands but are much more dubious when they are not. They seem to be best accepted where strong parent-teacher links exist. There is little wrong with the range and diversity of our courses. But is there sufficient thoroughness and depth in those required in after life to make a living?

These are proper subjects for discussion and debate. And it should be a rational debate based on the facts. My remarks are not a clarion call to Black Paper prejudices. We all know those who claim to defend standards but who in reality are simply seeking to defend old privilege and inequalities.

It is not my intention to become enmeshed in such problems as whether there should be a basic curriculum with universal standards – although I am inclined to think that there should be – nor about other issues on which there is a divided professional opinion such as the position and role of the Inspectorate. Shirley Williams, the new Secretary of State, is well qualified to take care of these issues and speak for the Government. What I am saying is that where there is legitimate public concern it will be to the advantage of all involved in the education field if these concerns are aired and shortcomings righted or fears put at rest.

To the critics I would say that we must carry the teaching profession with us. They have the expertise and the professional approach. To the teachers I would say that you must satisfy the parents and industry that what you are doing meets their requirements and the needs of our children. For if the public is not convinced then the profession will be laying up trouble for itself in the future.

The goals of our education, from nursery school through to adult education, are clear enough. They are to equip children to the best of their ability for a lively, constructive place in society and also to fit them to do a job of work. Not one or the other, but both. For many years the accent was simply on fitting a so-called inferior group of children with just enough learning to earn their living in the factory. Labour has attacked that attitude consistently, during 60 or 70 years and throughout my childhood. There is now widespread recognition of the need to cater for a child's personality, to let it flower in the fullest possible way.

The balance was wrong in the past. We have a responsibility now to see that we do not get it wrong in the other direction. There is no virtue in producing socially well-adjusted members of society who are unemployed because they do not have the skills. Nor at the other extreme must they be technically efficient robots. Both of the basic purposes of education require the same essential tools. These are basic literacy, basic numeracy, the understanding of how to live and work together, respect for others, respect for the individual.

This means acquiring certain basic knowledge, and skills and reasoning ability. It means developing lively inquiring minds and an appetite for further knowledge that will last a lifetime. It means mitigating as far as possible the disadvantages that may be suffered through poor home conditions or physical or mental handicap. Are we aiming in the right direction in these matters?

I do not join those who paint a lurid picture of educational decline because I do not believe it is generally true, although there are examples which give cause for concern. I am raising a further question. It is this. In today's world higher standards are demanded than were required yesterday and there are simply fewer jobs for those without skill. Therefore we demand more from our schools than did our grandparents.

There has been a massive injection of resources into education, mainly to meet increased numbers and partly to raise standards. But in present circumstances there can be little expectation of further increased resources being made available, at any rate for the time being. I fear that those whose only answer to these problems is to call for more money will be disappointed. But that surely cannot be the end of the matter. There is a challenge to us all in these days and a challenge in education is to examine its priorities and to secure as high efficiency as possible by the skilful use of existing resources.

Let me repeat some of the fields that need study because they cause concern. There are the methods and aims of informal instruction; the strong case for the so-called 'core curriculum' of basic knowledge; next, what is the proper way of monitoring the use of resources in order to maintain a proper national standard of performance; then there is the role of the Inspectorate in relation to national standards; and there is the need to improve relations between industry and education.

Another problem is the examination system – a contentious issue. The Schools Council have reached conclusions about its future after a great deal of thought, but it would not be right to introduce such an important change until there has been further public discussion. Maybe they haven't got it right yet. The new Secretary of State, Shirley Williams, intends to look at the examination system again, especially in relation to less-academic students staying at school beyond the age of 16. A number of these issues were taken up by Fred Mulley and will now be followed up by Shirley Williams.

We are expecting the Taylor Committee Report shortly on the government and management of schools in England and Wales that could bring together local authority, parents and pupils, teachers and industry more closely. The Secretary of State is now following up how to attract talented young people into engineering and science subjects; whether there are more efficient ways of using the resources we have for the benefit of young people between the ages of 16 and 19 and whether retraining can help make a bridge between teacher training and unemployment, especially to help in the subjects where there is a shortage.

I have outlined concerns and asked questions about them today. The debate that I was seeking has got off to a flying start even before I was able to say anything. Now I ask all those who are concerned to respond positively and not defensively. It will be an advantage to the teaching profession to have a wide public understanding and support for what they are doing. And there is room for greater understanding among those not directly concerned of the nature of the job that is being done already.

The traditional concern of the whole Labour movement is for the education of our children and young people on whom the future of the country must depend. At Ruskin it is appropriate that I should be proud to reaffirm that concern. It would be a betrayal of that concern if I did not draw problems to your attention and put to you specifically some of the challenges which we have to face and some of the responses that will be needed from our educational system. I am as confident that we shall do so as I am sure that the new building which will rise here will house and protect the ideals and vision of the founders of Ruskin College so that your future will be as distinguished as your past and your present.

Appendix 2
Extracts from Margaret Thatcher's Speech to the Conservative Party Conference, 1987

Our most important task in this Parliament is to raise the quality of education. It's in the national interest. And it's in the individual interest of every parent and above all, of every child. We want education to be part of the answer to Britain's problems, not part of the cause.

To compete successfully in tomorrow's world – against Japan, Germany and the United States – we need well-educated, well-trained, creative young people. If education is backward today, national performance will be backward tomorrow.

But it's the plight of individual boys and girls which worries me most. Too often, our children don't get the education they need – the education they deserve. And in the inner cities – where youngsters must have a decent education if they are to have a better future – that opportunity is all too often snatched from them by hard-left education authorities and extremist teachers.

Children who need to be able to count and multiply are learning antiracist mathematics – whatever that may be.

Children who need to be able to express themselves in clear English are being taught political slogans.

Children who need to be taught to respect traditional moral values are being taught that they have an inalienable right to be gay.

Children who need encouragement – and so many children do – are being taught that our society offers them no future.

All those children are being cheated of a sound start in life – yes cheated.

Of course – in the country as a whole – there are plenty of excellent teachers and successful schools. Every good school, and every good teacher, is a reminder of what too many young people are denied.

I believe that government must take the primary responsibility for setting standards for the education of our children. And that's why we are establishing a national curriculum for basic subjects.

It is vital that all children master essential skills: reading, writing, spelling, grammar, arithmetic; and that they understand basic science and technology. For good teachers this will provide a foundation on which they can build with their own creative skill and professionalism.

But the key to raising standards is to enlist the support of teachers.

The Labour left – hard, soft and in-between – hate the idea that people should be able to choose. In particular, they hate the idea that parents should be able to choose their children's education.

The Conservative Party believes in parental choice. We are now about to take two dramatic steps forward in extending choice in education.

First, we will allow popular schools to take in as many children as space will permit. This will stop local authorities from putting artificially low limits on entry to good schools.

And second, we will give parents and governors the right to take their children's school out of the hands of the local authority and into the hands of their own governing body. This will create a new kind of school funded by the State, alongside the present State schools and the independent private schools.

These new schools will be independent state schools. They will bring a better education to many children because the school will be in the hands of those who care most for it and for its future.

There's no reason at all why local authorities should have a monopoly of free education. What principle suggests this right? What recent experience or practice suggests it is even sensible?

In these ways, we are furthering our Conservative tradition of extending opportunity more widely.

This policy will be of the greatest advantage, not to those schools where the parents are already satisfied with their children's education, but to those schools where the parents are dissatisfied and believe that their children could do a lot better. Nowhere is this policy more needed than in what have become known as 'inner cities'.

Appendix 3
Curriculum Chronologies

England and Wales – *John Raynor*

1861 Report of the Commissioners appointed to enquire into the State of Popular Education in England (*The Newcastle Commission*). In reviewing a number of unsatisfactory features in English Elementary Education (provision of places, grants, quality) the Commission concluded that standards of teaching were poor and that while senior classes were being offered a sound education in the 3Rs the Commissioners were anxious to see the standard basic subjects taught to a 'larger body of inferior schools and inferior scholars'.

1862 The Revised Code (*Robert Lowe*). Following the Newcastle Report, the Code attempted to: grade the syllabus according to the age of the pupil; annually examine children in the 3Rs; organise teaching in stages or standards, and pay teachers by results. The Code was modified in 1867 following the charge that it made teaching too mechanical. Schools were then awarded for introducing some additional subjects, with Religious Instruction being regarded as a non-examined subject.

1864 Report of Her Majesty's Commissioners appointed to enquire into the Revenues and Management of certain Colleges and Schools, and the studies pursued and instruction given therein (*The Clarendon Commission*). The report into the older Public Schools reaffirmed that classical language and literature should be the principal subjects of the curriculum but proposed that every boy should be taught mathematics, a modern language, either drawing or music, some knowledge of ancient and modern history and geography, with limited specialisation in later years of school life.

1868 Schools Enquiry Commission (*The Taunton Report*). Established to review those schools which lay between the Elementary Schools (reported by Newcastle Commission) and the great Public Schools (Clarendon Commission), the Report proposed a three-grade system of schools to reflect the three grades of society, each with its own curriculum. First grade schools were to prepare children for Universities and their curriculum should be that of classics, elements of political economy, modern languages, maths and natural science. The Second grade schools were to prepare pupils for professions, business and the army and should have a curriculum of Latin, Maths, Science and a Modern Language. The Third grade schools were for those who would be artisans who should enjoy a curriculum of basic subjects plus inorganic chemistry, practical geometry and drawing. An independent Examination Council was proposed.

1870 The Elementary Education Act (*The Forster Act*). The beginning of the dual system. Religious liberty and a 'conscience clause' afforded to all parents of children in public elementary schools. No religious catechism to be taught in Board Schools.

1871 The Elementary Code. Following the Forster Act, the Code increased the number of subjects that could be taught – natural science, political economy, and languages. These 'specific' subjects were restricted to Standards 4, 5 and 6. Drill also appeared for the first time and infant teaching recognised by provision of special grants for classrooms.

1872–5 Report of the Royal Commission on Scientific Instruction and the Advancement of Science (*The Devonshire Report*). The 6th Report on teaching in public and endowed schools recommended no less than six hours a week on Science teaching and that science in the elementary schools should be strengthened by being taught by certificated science teachers.

1875 The Elementary Code. Curriculum now divided into 'obligatory' subjects – 3Rs, 'specific' subjects (following the 1871 Code), and a category entitled 'class' subjects – grammar, history, needlework, which were taught to a class as a whole.

1882 The Elementary Code (*A. J. Mundella*). The Code introduced a new Standard 7 – for those staying on at school – with elementary science being taught from Standards 1–7. Practical training in cookery for girls recognised. Inspectors graded schools (fair, good or excellent) as a means of paying grants, with a merit grant for outstanding work.

1882 Report on the Royal Commission on Technical Instruction (*The Samuelson Report*). Established to enquire into the 'instruction of the industrial classes . . . in technical and other subjects and the influence of such instruction on manufacturing and other industries'. Considerable use of comparative material from other countries was built into the terms of reference. Second Report urged not only the teaching of elementary science but also drawing and writing as 'specifics' across all standards with further specific grants for the introduction of working with tools in wood and iron.

Natural science, drawing and maths to replace Latin and Greek in selected schools. Local Authorities should be empowered to establish secondary and technical schools and colleges.

1888   Report of the Royal Commission on the Elementary Education Acts (*The Cross Commission*).   The Commission considered it essential to include within the elementary school curriculum the 3Rs, needlework for girls, drawing for boys, singing, English, English history, geography (especially of the British Empire) plus elementary science in the higher standards. Because of the time taken up by needlework, it was proposed to modify the requirements of the Code in mathematics for girls.

1895   Report of the Royal Commission on Secondary Education (*The Bryce Report*).   While principally concerned with organisational issues and while eschewing a model curriculum for schools it proposed that a well balanced education would consist of literary, scientific and technical studies.

1900   The Elementary Code.   'Obligatory', 'class' and 'specific' subjects abandoned and replaced by a list of subjects all elementary schools were expected to teach: English, arithmetic, geography, history, singing, physical exercise, drawing for boys, needlework for girls. French, science and algebra could be introduced where practicable. Infant classes to teach elements of 3Rs. Payment by results ended. No examination requirements for elementary school curriculum.

1904   The Day School Code.   Following the 1902 Education Act, the Elementary Code still operated but was further formalised into what we would now call a compulsory core, namely English, arithmetic, drawing for boys, needlework for girls, object lessons in history, geography and common things, singing by rote and physical training. Additional subject could be added (from a list of 22) if Inspectors thought it to be desirable.

1904   Regulations for Secondary Schools.   Thought to be the work of Sir Robert Morant, the Code attempted to steer the new county secondary schools away from a scientific and technical curriculum with the insistence that they model their curriculum on that of the Grammar Schools. Specialisation was only to be permitted after a broad general education and must be planned to lead up to a defined 'standard of acquirement in the various branches of instruction'. The course to include English Language and Literature, one language other than English, Geography, History, Mathematics, Science and Drawing with provision for Manual work, Physical Exercise and Housewifery. 'Not less than four and a half hours per week for English, Geography and History; three and a half or six hours for language where one or two are taken; seven and a half hours for Science and Mathematics of which at least three were obligatory for Science.'

1917   Board of Education. Examination of Secondary Schools. Introduction of the School Certificate. For pupils of 16, a five-subject grouped examination was introduced across the areas of English subjects, maths and science and foreign languages. Secondary School Examinations specialised in one of three groups: classics, modern studies and maths/science. Secondary Schools Examination Council established.

1922   Board of Education. Curriculum for Secondary Schools in England.   Report consolidating the findings and conclusions of a number of subject enquiries into natural science, classics, modern languages and English. Curriculum was seen as congested, over-crowded and impossible to meet the requirements for a general education.

1926   Report of the Consultative Committee on the Education of the Adolescent (*The Hadow Report*).   The report recommended that there should be a separation between primary and secondary education at age 11, that allocation to either Grammar or Modern school should be by examination at 11 and that the modern school curriculum should be similar to that of the Grammar school but shorter and more practical.

1931   Report of the Consultative Committee on the Primary School.   Supported the Hadow recommendation that the age of transfer to Secondary school should be at 11. Until then the curriculum of the Primary School was to be thought of 'in terms of activity and experience rather than knowledge to be acquired and facts to be stored'. Physical Education, dance, drama, maths and science and aesthetic subjects all regarded as desirable parts of the curriculum though not to be thought of as separate subjects or distinct lessons.

1938   Report of the Consultative Committee on Secondary Education with reference to Grammar Schools and Technical High Schools (*The Spens Report*).   Proposed three types of secondary school – Grammar, Modern and Technical with 'parity of esteem' between them. Modern schools would have a less academic curriculum for the more practical child, while Technical schools should concentrate on science and technical subjects. Children aged 11–13 to have a similar curriculum to facilitate transfer.

1943   Curriculum and Examinations in Secondary Schools: Report of the Secondary Schools Examination Council (*The Norwood Report*).   The report provided a further reinforcement for tripartism with different curricula for different types of pupils. The report also proposed to replace the grouped subject examination of the School Certificate by a single subject examination which led the way to O and A level examinations. Committee also proposed that the examination should be run by schools on curricula devised by teachers.

1944 Education Act. The great Education Act which changed the whole administrative structure of education and in which the word curriculum is never used. Religious Education became the only subject that was required.

1956 Ministry of Education. White Paper on Technical Education. Aimed at stimulating scientific and technical education, the paper concluded that they were indispensable elements in a 'liberal education'.

1959 Ministry of Education: 15–18 (*The Crowther Report*). Recommended that the school leaving age be raised to 16 with part-time education in County Colleges to age 18. Considered the issue of early specialisation especially in the 6th form, and in its plea for a balanced curriculum suggested two-thirds of the timetable be spent on specialist subjects, with one-third being spent on common studies (arts and science, pupils studying together) plus a 'complementary' element to 'save the science specialist from illiteracy and the arts specialist from innumeracy'.

1960 Secondary School Examinations other than GCE (*The Beloe Report*). In response to the growing demand by parents and employers for external examinations (and the growing use by schools with subsequent proliferation of different exams) the Committee recommended a new examination – the CSE – for the 40 per cent of the pupils who lay below the 20 per cent who took GCE O level. Report appeared to accept a tripartite examination system with three types of curriculum.

1963 Central Advisory Council: Half Our Future (*The Newsom Report*). Established to consider the education of young people 13–16 of less than average ability, the report sought to find a way of marrying the old elementary tradition of the 3Rs with progressive education. The Committee rejected any idea of a 'universal fixed curriculum' because of the age range and differing capacity of young people. The curriculum it was felt should be more related to the world of work and adult life.

1964 Working Party on School Curricula and Examinations (*The Lockwood Report*). Recommended the establishment of the Schools Council for Curriculum and Examinations.

1967   Central Advisory Council for Education. Children and their Primary Schools (*The Plowden Report*).   The Committee urged a structure of First schools (5–8) and Middle Schools (8–12). It proposed the idea of 'positive discrimination' (on which basis the subsequent EPA projects were based) and endorsed the progressive and flexible primary curriculum. For the younger children the more broadly based divisions of learning were deemed appropriate, while the more rigidly defined subjects were to be deferred until the children were older. The teacher to take a more stimulating, guiding and consultative role than a narrowly didactic one.

1968   Inquiry into the Flow of Candidates in Science and Technology into Higher Education (*The Dainton Report*).   The swing against science in schools led the Committee to urge that there should be a broad span of studies in 6th forms and irreversible decisions against early specialisation should be resisted. All pupils to study maths until they left school, and science teaching should be infused with breadth and humanity and should consider up-to-date issues.

1972   DES. Education: a Framework for Expansion.   While reviewing all sectors of education from pre-school to University, no mention is made of the curriculum at any level except for the view that the pre-school child was capable of 'developing further in the use of language, thought and practical skills than was previously supposed'.

1974   HMSO. A Language for Life (*The Bullock Report*).   The report based its recommendations on the principle that reading, writing, talking and listening were a unity and not discrete skills. No one method was held to guarantee the key to reading. All teachers were seen as involved in the development of language skills of their pupils. The need was for a language policy for the whole school which was to be embodied in the organisational structure of the school.

1975   Schools Council. Working Paper 53, The Whole Curriculum.   An attempt, in part, to answer criticisms that Schools Council projects were solely subject or issue bound and therefore failed to reflect the significance of whole school curriculum planning.

1976   Ruskin College Speech (Prime Minister, Rt. Hon. James Callaghan, Speech printed in Appendix 1).   A critical polemic about existing standards and the relevance of the school curriculum. Initiated a series of nationwide meetings discussing all aspects of schooling.

1977   DES. Education in Schools: a Consultative Document (Cmnd 6869).   Against the background of the Ruskin Speech, and the subsequent regional 'great debates', but set against the wider background of recent history, the Green Paper followed the main topic areas of the debate – curriculum, teachers, assessment and school and working life. On curriculum, after reviewing the criticisms (overcrowding of timetable, variation between schools, insufficiently matched to modern industrial life, etc.) the paper calls for an agreed 'framework for the curriculum' and for a 'core or protected part'.

1978   DES. Primary Education in England.   A survey by HMI of 547 schools. Report covers teachers, teaching methods, attainment of children and the curriculum. Report indicates the need for some specialisation of teaching and giving teachers some specific curriculum responsibilities. Despite schools' attention to basic skills, standards in maths were disappointing; rising trend in reading standards noted but children were not encouraged to extend their range. Lack of science noted and better planning called for in history and geography. A better planned curriculum called for.

1978   Special Educational Needs: Report of the Committee of Enquiry into the Education of Handicapped Children and Young People (*The Warnock Report*).   The first full-scale review of special educational provision in Great Britain this century. The report widened the scope of special education to cover the 1 in 5 children said to have learning difficulties at any one time. It called for a systematic approach to the assessment of special educational needs, and for the official 'recording' of children with particularly marked needs. Though commonly believed to have promoted the integration of children with special needs into ordinary schools, the report made no firm recommendations on this, and saw a substantial and continuing role for special schools. Pre-school and post-school provision, and in-service training, were accorded top priority in the recommendations. The curriculum was not central to the report's concerns, and the curriculum recommendations have received only scant attention since its publication.

1979   DES. Aspects of Secondary Education in England.   A report by HMI. General pattern of a broad curriculum for the first three years followed by options identified. Only 11 per cent of schools agreed that they followed a common curriculum, the majority of schools claiming there was a differentiated curriculum according to sex and ability of pupils. Option schemes were seen to be unbalanced and 'choice' was deemed illusory – the result overall was an ill-balanced education. Calls were made for more specialist teaching in English, Maths, Modern Languages and Religious Education. Comprehensive reform and raising of school leaving age had not led to a re-shaping of the curriculum. Suggestion that it was 'time to think again for a more explicit rationale for the curriculum as a whole'.

1979   DES. Local authorities' arrangement for the school curriculum following the issuing of Circular 14/77 (a questionnaire sent to all LEAs).   The Department published the results, which showed 'substantial variations' in policies towards the Curriculum. Observations were made on the teaching of maths, English, modern languages and science. The report affirms that it is the duty of the Secretary of State to ensure that the 'work of the schools matches national needs'. LEAs have a duty to 'formulate curriculum policies and objectives which meet national needs and command local assent'. This points, the commentary says, towards a 'nationally agreed framework for the curriculum'.

1980   DES. A Framework for the School Curriculum.   Addressed to LEAs in the light of Circular 14/77 the document offers an essentially centralist and bureaucratic, rather than professional set of proposals. The Core appears to be English, Maths and Science with other subjects having a lesser status. Little discussion of aims, but each school should set out clearly its own curriculum aims and objectives.

1980   HMI. A View of the Curriculum.   By contrast to the DES view in the 'Framework . . .' document, HMI set out a curriculum in terms of 'areas of experience'. For primary schools, language and literacy, maths, science, aesthetic and social aspects. For secondary, aesthetic and creative, ethical, linguistic, mathematical, scientific, social and political and spiritual. Document refers to equality of opportunity, forms of knowledge, needs of the individual child, racial and cultural diversity, etc.

1981   Education Act.   Following the Warnock Report (see above) this Act abolished statutory categories of handicap and replaced them with a new definition of special educational need as a learning difficulty which calls for special provision to be made. A 'statement of special educational need' is to be made for all children for whom the LEA has to determine the provision to be made. The Act set out complex assessment procedures, including new rights for parents, leading up to the making of a statement. Children with special educational needs were to be educated in ordinary schools where this was consistent with the efficient education of the child concerned and other children in the school, and with the efficient use of resources.

1981   DES. The School Curriculum.   Perhaps the first document directly offering guidance on the school curriculum 5–16. Document holds back from specificity, this being the responsibility of the schools and LEAs. Curriculum not static but must be periodically reviewed. While guidance is in terms of conventional subjects it acknowledges that many aspects must be taught 'across the curriculum' or seen in terms of skills or areas of experience. Curriculum must 'reflect fundamental values of our society'. It should have breadth to include health education, preparation for parenthood and family life. All pupils from 11–16 should have a curriculum of a 'broadly common character' designed to ensure a balanced education 'in order to prevent subsequent choices being needlessly restricted'; primary curriculum should contain more breadth than a narrow 'back to basics'. Britain as a multicultural society and knowledge about our place in Europe is stressed. For Secondary, as well as the customary core, report pleads for special importance of CDT, of preparation for adult and working life, and for exams to 'serve the educational process'.

1982 DES. A Report of the Committee of Enquiry into the Teaching of Mathematics in Schools in England and Wales. Mathematics Counts (*The Cockroft Report*). The mathematics outcome of the Ruskin College 'Great Debate'. Well received nationally for brevity and for the identification of a central core of mathematical knowledge.

1983 DES. Curriculum 11–16. Towards a statement of entitlement (*HMI Red Book 33*). HMI's expression of the way a more unified curriculum band on 'areas of experience' would be introduced into secondary schooling.

1985 DES. Report of the Committee of Enquiry into the Education of Children of Ethnic Minority Groups. Education for All (*The Swann Report*). In a long account covering most aspects of education in a multicultural society, the committee concludes that the issue is not simply that of educating ethnic minority children but rather all children who must be enabled to understand the nature of Britain as a multicultural society, with schools leading the attack on racism and stereotyping. LEAs urged to declare a commitment to 'education for all'; to adopt a pluralist curriculum, with HMI giving clear guidelines on the practical application of adopting a pluralist approach. The SCDC asked to review curriculum materials, and the Exam Boards to reflect cultural diversity in syllabuses. LEAs to expect schools to produce clear antiracist policy and to monitor implementation and practice.

1985 HMI. The Curriculum 5–16 (*Curriculum Matters* Series). A further development arising from the Curriculum 11–16 exercise. HMI conclude that the curriculum of all schools should be so designed to include learning and experience in the following areas: aesthetic and creative, human and social, linguistic and literary, mathematical, moral, physical, scientific, spiritual and technological. Schools should ensure that 'each of the areas of learning and experience ... makes its unique contribution ... to ensure the development of knowledge, concepts, skills and attitudes'.

1985   DES. Better Schools. Cmnd 9469.   Concerned to improve the quality of education, the report covers all aspects of education from that of the under-fives, discipline, ethnic minority children, role of parents, resources, etc. The important changes in the primary and secondary curriculum over the previous 30 years are reviewed, but the report concludes that the standards achieved are neither as good as they can or need be. Expectations by teachers of pupils are not high and teaching is often inferior and lacking in challenge. The lack of agreed curriculum policies in schools is noted and didactic teaching and unimaginatively set homework commented on. The need for broad agreement on objectives at Secretary of State, LEA and school level is called for. The report, however, draws the line at prescription, though chapter 2 does list the purposes, contribution of subject areas, organisation of content and attainment levels.

1986   Education (No. 2) Act.   Local education authorities required to keep up to date written statements of policy in relation to the secular curriculum. School governors required to publish statements of school curriculum aims indicating any points of divergence with LEA policies.

1987   DES. The National Curriculum. Test Group on Assessment and Testing (*TGAT*).   Established to advise on examinations and testing for the National Curriculum, the Report makes 44 recommendations among which are the following:

1 National assessment at ages 7, 11, 14 and 16.
2 Ten levels of attainment identified within each profile component.
3 Record of achievement to be used as a means of recording progress and achievement within the national curriculum.
4 Basis of assessment system to be formative but so designed to identify where diagnostic assessment is required.
5 Tests, practical tasks, observations with moderated teacher rating as component elements of the national assessment system.
6 Results to be confidential, though those for a class or a school as a whole should be available to parents.

1987   DES. The National Curriculum 5–16: a consultation document.   The document issued at the end of July set out the Government's proposals for a prescribed curriculum based on ten subjects and testing and assessment throughout the compulsory years of schooling.

1988 Education Act.   Among many other things, the Act establishes a National Curriculum with responsibilities for its implementation resting on the Secretary of State, the LEAs, and the
Governing Bodies of maintained schools. The aim is to meet 'the
spiritual, moral and cultural, mental and physical demands of pupils
and society'. The Curriculum to consist of a 'core' of English, Maths
and Science (plus Welsh in Welsh speaking schools) plus further
'foundation' subjects. The act legislates for attainment targets for
each subject, and a definition of programmes of studies within each
subject area. Departures from the National Curriculum have to be
agreed by the Secretary of State.

Northern Ireland – *Jenny Meegan*

1831 'A bill for the establishment and maintenance of parochial
schools and the advancement of the education of the people of
Ireland'.   Introduction of a new state system of 'national schools' in
Ireland. Formal control was entrusted to the 'commissioners of
national education' who controlled school finances and curriculum.
Textbooks published by the commissioners were used widely in
Britain and the Commonwealth as well as in the national schools.
They emphasised loyalty to the British crown and had virtually no
reference to Ireland or Irish history and writers. Any other books
used in schools had to be approved by the commissioners. Teaching
of Irish was discouraged and almost non-existent. (By contrast, the
Christian Brothers Schools, which received no state funding until
early twentieth century, published textbooks emphasising Irish
culture and history.)
    The national schools were founded as non-denominational in
1831 but by 1851 were, in practice, denominational.

1870 Royal Commission of Inquiry into Primary Education in
Ireland. (*Powis Commission*).   The Commission reported low
standards of education in all schools and recommended the English
system of payment of teachers by results. All children in Irish
national schools were to follow an obligatory programme in reading,
writing, arithmetic, spelling, grammar and geography. Boys were to
study agricultural theory and girls needlework. This was implemented in 1872. The commission also recommended that the
national school commissioners should no longer publish textbooks
but retain the right to veto books. Denominational schooling was to
be encouraged.

1875 '42nd report of the commissioners of national education in
Ireland'.   Twenty-one extra subjects were listed for which the
commissioners would pay grants for teachers' salaries, e.g. geomet-

ry, algebra, trigonometry, navigation, magnetism and electricity, physical geography, geology, botany, Latin, Greek, French, sewing machine, cookery, poultry management. Irish could receive a grant if taught to advanced pupils outside school hours.

1892 'A bill to improve national education in Ireland'. This introduced compulsory school attendance of at least 75 days/year and abolished fees for national schools.

1898 'Commission on Manual and Practical Instruction in Primary Schools under the Board of National Education Ireland' (*Belmore Commission*). This resulted in a major revision of the national school curriculum and a new curriculum known as the 'Revised Programme' came into effect in all national schools in September 1900. Payment by results was abolished and replaced by regular inspections. In addition to reading, writing and arithmetic other subjects, i.e. educational handwork, drawing, elementary science and singing, were compulsory. Agricultural (practical farming) was rejected as part of the elementary school curriculum and replaced by elementary science. Cooking and needlework were seen as useful for girls but not compulsory. Irish could be taught as an optional subject in schools hours as long as it did not interfere with other instruction.

1923 Education Act (Northern Ireland), 'The Londonderry Act'. This was the first Education Act after the partition of Ireland in 1921. It created county borough education authorities and committees and made provision for the transfer of existing schools to these authorities. It implemented the findings of the Lynn Committee (1923). It defined elementary education (up to 14 years) as literary and moral, based on reading, writing and arithmetic. There was no other mention of curriculum except the controversial one that religious instruction was forbidden within the hours of compulsory school attendance. (The authorities were made responsible for catechetical instruction of children according to parents' denomination, outside school hours.)

1930 Education Act. This gave the Education Minister power to nominate up to a quarter of the membership of Education Committees (it being understood the nominees would be clergymen). The education authority was *required* by law to provide Bible instruction in any school during school hours if the parents of ten or more children demanded it.

1932 Programme for Primary Education.

1944 White Paper 'Education Reconstruction in Northern Ireland'. This considered the implications of the Hadow Report for Northern Ireland. Recommended that the public elementary system should be replaced by a new system with a break at 11+ and secondary education for all. The aim of the primary schools should be teaching essential skills (3Rs) plus 'to train the hand, to encourage grace and freedom of movement and give full scope for self reliance and originality'. Two types of secondary school were proposed: senior (up to 18 years) and intermediate (to 15 years). The latter was to have emphasis on practical subjects and physical training. Junior technical schools should continue as separate for pupils of 13+. Religious education was compulsory and each day was to begin with an act of collective worship. This was put forward in the Education Bill (Northern Ireland) of 1944 and made law by the 1947 Education Act (Northern Ireland). Educational Amendment Act (1953) postponed raising the school leaving age from 14 to 15 until 1957.

1955 Report of the Committee on Secondary School Examinations. Ministry of Education. Government of Northern Ireland (*The Macbeath Committee*). This recommended that no external exams be specially provided for secondary schools but they should be at liberty to enter suitable pupils for any appropriate external examination.

1956 New Programme for Primary Schools. Based on the report of a committee of teachers and inspectors and differs radically from 1932. The Primary 1–3 curriculum is to be based on physical education including play out of doors, art, handwork, nature studies, drama, music, and basic skills of reading, number, writing. Primary 4–7 should include basic skills, PE, geography, nature study, music, handwork, art, needlework (girls). Irish is optional Primary 4–9. In non-reorganised schools students remaining until 14 studied domestic economy (girls) and science, horticulture, woodwork (boys) plus other subjects.

1960 Ministry of Education. Exams for Secondary Intermediate, (including Technical Intermediate Schools (*The Johnston Report*). This recommended that secondary schools should be allowed to do Junior Certificate exams (formerly only allowed for grammar schools) and that Junior Certificate be changed into a subject exam. Senior Certificate was considered unsuitable for Intermediate Schools.

1960 Report of the Advisory Council for Education in Northern Ireland on Selection of Pupils for Secondary School (Third Report). This established selection on the basis of a qualifying exam with tests in English, arithmetic and verbal reasoning.

1964 Educational Development in Northern Ireland. Government White Paper. Deals mainly with selection and intermediate school organisation. It recommends elimination of Junior Technical Schools. It stresses the need for every child to develop in accordance with their aptitude and to develop the full range of courses in some secondary schools. There is tentative questioning of selection but against the background of entrenched grammar school privilege. Encouragement given to alternative school organisation resulted in the Craigavon two-tier system in 1965.

1964 The 5th Report of the Advisory Council for Education. 'Selection Procedure'. Recommended replacing the qualifying exam by teachers' estimates of suitability for grammar school in rank order plus two verbal reasoning tests. Implemented 1966.

1967 Ministry of Education. The Curriculum of the Secondary (Intermediate) School. Report of the Working Party set up following the White Paper on Educational Development in Northern Ireland 1964. This recognised that pupils in secondary schools could achieve success in external exams but felt pupils would not benefit from academic O level courses. Recommended a reduction in the number of exams attempted by Secondary Schools but not in the number of pupils entered.

1968 Educational Amendment Act (Northern Ireland). Created a new category of 'maintained' schools. These were voluntary schools on whose management committee the education authority was represented and for whose building and equipment they took financial responsibility (mainly Catholic intermediate schools).

1968 Primary Education in Northern Ireland. Report of the Advisory Council for Education.

1970 Education (Examinations) Act (Northern Ireland). This set up a Northern Ireland GCE and CSE Examinations Board. The first CSE exams were held in 1973 (although some schools had taken the NW England Board CSEs since 1968).

1972 Education and Libraries Order. Creation of five Education and Library Boards which from 1 October 1973 became responsible to the Department of Education, Northern Ireland (DENI) for local administration of education and library services. This followed the introduction of direct rule from Westminster.

1973 Reorganisation of Secondary Education in Northern Ireland (*Burgess Report*). Recommended the abolition of selection at 11+.

1976 The Reorganisation of Secondary Education in Northern Ireland (*Cowan Report*). Consultative document setting out the findings of a feasibility study into the practicalities of reorganising post primary education.

1977   Speech by the Minister of State, Lord Melchett, declaring his intention to 'eliminate selection at 11+ through a restructuring of the school system'.   Following this a new 'Alternative Transfer System' was introduced 1977–80 based on transfer reports by principals and no external testing.

1980   Announcement by Lord Elton, Parliamentary Under Secretary with responsibility for education in Northern Ireland, of a return to formal 11+ testing consisting of two verbal reasoning tests which contained questions on English and mathematics.

1984   Secondary Schools: A New Development for 11–16 year olds, DENI.   This document established a province-wide programme of curriculum review and development under the auspices of Northern Ireland Council for Educational Development (NICED). This scheme known as the 11–16 Review is the main curriculum initiative for secondary and grammar schools and is currently (1989) operating in more than 100 schools.

1984   Primary guidelines.   These arose from a meeting of the Standing Conference on Primary Education and a document produced by NICED, *Primary Guidelines: an Introduction*. They have been followed by publication of a series of subject guidelines for all schools in Northern Ireland. This is the main curriculum initiative for primary education and is currently (1989) being followed by all primary schools.

1986   Education and Libraries (NI) Order.   This is based on the Warnock report but does not adopt all its recommendations. It encourages the education of children in ordinary schools wherever possible though some children will still attend special schools.

1986–8   Four reports on the transfer procedure. Published by Northern Ireland Council for Educational Research, 'Transfer and the Primary School', Sutherland and Gallagher (1986), reported a growing effect of the Transfer Procedure on each year of the upper primary curriculum. (Maths and English were identified as over-emphasised.) Nearly two-thirds of those interviewed thought it would impede implementation of the NICED Primary Guidelines.

'Transfer Pupils at Sixteen' (Gallagher, 1988) raised serious questions about the fairness of treating boys and girls separately for transfer grades and that boys did not 'catch up' with girls by 16. As a result of this some parents of girls who were not awarded grammar school places took a case against DENI under Equal Opportunities legislation and this resulted in an additional 400 girls being awarded grammar school places in 1988.

1988   'Education Reform in Northern Ireland: The Way Forward',

DENI. (White Paper to be followed by draft Order in Council in late 1989.) Recommends:

1 A common curriculum. Religious education will be compulsory. The Paper recognises the contribution of Primary Guidelines and 11–16 Programme to the development of curriculum organisation but considers it necessary to now legislate for a basic curriculum. Prescribed areas of study are English, Maths, Science and Technology, the Environment and Society, Creative and Expressive Studies and Language Studies (secondary schools only). Irish can only be studied as a second foreign language in addition to French or Spanish or German. New statutory curriculum body – NI. Curriculum Council to be set up.
2 Quotas for grammar schools to be abolished and schools to be constrained only by accommodation. Transfer procedure to be abolished and admission to grammar school is left to the schools' discretion and parental choice.
3 No grant maintained schools as in England but a new category of grant maintained integrated schools created.

Scotland – *Jim Rand*

1867 Report of Royal Commission to investigate the state of education in Scotland (*The Argyll Commission*). Throughout the nineteenth century the general pattern of school provision in Scotland had become increasingly complex. There was no coherent system of schools; there was no central control or organisation; there was wide variation in standards of the different types of school and about one-fifth of Scottish children still attended no school at all. Report of the Argyll Commission led to the passing of the Education (Scotland) Act, 1872. The Argyll Commission produced three separate reports it 'corresponded to the Newcastle, Clarendon and Taunton Commissions rolled into one'.

1872 The Education (Scotland) Act. The Act established a framework for national system of public education and made schooling compulsory between the ages of 5 and 13. Public schools were opened to children of all denominations and were subject to inspection but not with regard to religious instruction. Local management of schools was vested in 984 schools boards, one for every parish or burgh in Scotland. Essential controlling and coordinating body, the Scottish Education Department, was established.

1873 First Scottish Education Department Codes. System of 'payment by results' extended to Scotland (abolished 1886; minimum standards in basic skills laid down in annual code, based on the performance of classes rather than individual pupils.

Until 1939 separate Codes for Elementary and Secondary Education, printed annually with alterations, giving specific instructions on grants, fees, curricula and size of classes – reading, writing, arithmetic from ages 5–12; and with them physical exercise (military drill for seniors), drawing, poetry, 'singing by note', and needlework for girls, nature knowledge and 'object lessons'.

1888 Leaving Certificate Examination instituted, adopted by almost all 'higher class' schools both public and private, gave clear goal and raised and equated standards.

1903 The Qualifying Examination replaced the Merit Certificate as a determinant of which children were to proceed to post elementary education.

1908 Education (Scotland) Act.   Broadened the interpretation of the scope of education including medical examination and supervision of pupils.

Two distinct forms of post-primary education came into existence: *intermediate* providing a three-year course of instruction in languages, mathematics and science and *secondary* which offered a five-year course of instruction leading to the Leaving Certificate.

1918 Education (Scotland) Act.   Extended unit of educational administration, education authorities, and facilitated development of secondary and technical education.

1922 Circular 44.   The Qualifying and Intermediate examinations, which were no longer needed for purposes of grant, were abolished, they had come to dominate both the curriculum and teaching. Introduction of Day School Certificate (Lower), Day School Certificate (Higher), and Senior Leaving Certificate.

1945 Education (Scotland) Act, (Consolidation Act, 1946).   Like the 1944 Act in England and Wales, the 1945 Act created the general context for postwar education. Emphasis on an education suited to age, ability and aptitude.

After the Education (Scotland) Act 1945 and the raising of the school leaving age to 15 in 1947, secondary courses of five or six years duration became generally known as 'senior' secondary courses and those of three years duration 'junior' secondary courses.

1946 Primary Education: A Report of the Advisory Council on Education in Scotland.   The report was progressive and persuasively written. It advocated a 'wider' philosophy for primary education and called for a shifting of emphasis from merely intellectual training to the development of the whole personality with new emphasis on physical and emotional training and from a passive reception and memorising of facts to the encouragement of every child to develop actively. Report discarded 'with little regret the narrow and obsolete view that reading, writing and arithmetic are the three fundamentals of education . . .'. It is suggested that the report was ahead of its time. There was little support in the profession for its ideas.

1947   Secondary Education: A Report of the Advisory Council on Education in Scotland. A further imaginative and progressive report; claiming that the function of secondary schools was to provide a rich environment, it recommended a larger place for practical and aesthetic activity, and constant cooperation between departments. Held English division of grammar, technical and modern schools to be unsound. However, the philosophy of the report could not be translated into action and in reality there continued to be two courses: certificate/non-certificate, the curriculum division of academic/non-academic.

1950   SED. Report on the Primary School in Scotland.   Report written by HMI, while apparently supportive of the Advisory Council Report it was more cautious when assessing priority of basic subjects but stressed the importance of schools being child centred rather than curriculum centred.

1955   SED. Memorandum on Junior Secondary Education.   Offered generalised advice and encouraged experimentation in three-year secondary courses, many authorities established their own leaving certificate.

1956   The Schools (Scotland) Code Regulation 21 (1) set out that 'in each year of attendance in the primary department pupils shall be given instruction in reading, writing and arithmetic; in the use and understanding of spoken and written English; in music; in art and handwork; in nature study; and in physical education. They shall also, from such stage as is appropriate having regard to their age, ability and aptitude be given instruction in geography, history, written composition and, in the case of girls, needlework.'

1959   Report of Working Party on Senior Secondary Curriculum. This 'shattered the complacency of secondary schools'. Recommended new examination structure – Ordinary grade in secondary 4 (16 years), Higher Grade in secondary 5 (17 years), and new subjects were proposed (modern studies). Most of the recommendations were implemented and the new Scottish Certificate of Education was introduced in 1961.

1963   SED. From School to Further Education (*Brunton Report*). This report endorsed the conventional wisdom that the most able 35 per cent of population should follow certificate courses; for the remainder recommended the 'use of the vocational impulse as a core around which the curriculum should be organised'.

1965 Circular 600.   Circular 600 was the Scottish equivalent of Circular 10/65 introducing comprehensive reorganisation in Scotland.

1965 The Consultative Committee on the Curriculum (CCC) established.   The CCC set up by the Secretary of State for Scotland with a three-fold remit.

1 To maintain general oversight of the whole school curriculum – primary and secondary.
2 To draw the Secretary of State's attention to any aspect of the curriculum which seemed to call for consideration by specialist bodies.
3 To give the Secretary of State its comments on the recommendations made by any working party set up by the Secretary of State on its advice.

Unlike the Schools Council in England where the curriculum advisory body involved a 'partnership' of central government, local government and teaching professions, members of the CCC and its committees were nominees of the Secretary of State.

1965 SED. Primary Education in Scotland (*The Primary Memorandum*).   The Primary Memorandum was written by a panel including teachers, college lecturers and HMI. Prior to the publication of the Plowden Report (England and Wales), the 65 Memorandum was significant for its emphasis on child centred education. It placed great stress on the integration of subjects (language, arts, environmental studies); flexibility of timetable; and the child's needs and interests as the key leading to meaningful learning.

1967 CCC. Organisation of Courses Leading to the Scottish Certificate in Education (*Ruthven Report*).   This was established to consider 'lack of balance' and the view that in most schools 'too little time was being given to subjects which were not examined'. Essential aspects were described as 'English (spoken and written); mathematics; social subjects; scientific; practical and aesthetic; social moral and religious; physical education'. No more than three-quarters of the school week should be spent on examination courses.

1968 SED. Guidance in Scottish Secondary Schools (Orange Book).   Introduced structure for curricular, vocational and personal guidance in secondary schools.

1971 Primary Education: Organisation for Development: A Progress Report.   Document prepared by officials from the Scottish

Education Department attempted to assess the effectiveness of the implementation of the ideals set out in the Primary Memorandum (1965). Stressed key role of head teacher in formulation of overall school and curriculum policy, and the importance of in-service training for head teachers.

1977   Scottish Education Department/Consultative Committee on the Curriculum. The structure of the curriculum in the 3rd and 4th years of the Scottish Secondary Schools (*Munn Report*).

1977   Scottish Education Department: *Assessment for All*. Report of committee to review assessment in the 3rd and 4th years of secondary education in Scotland (*Dunning Report*).

1977   Scottish Education Department: *Truancy and Indiscipline in the Schools in Scotland* (*Pack Report*).

The *Munn Report* provides an analysis of supposed 'claims' on the curriculum, aims secondary schools might be expected to meet and goes on to argue that all pupils should follow a curriculum model of core-plus options, based on eight 'modes' of activity. (Literary and linguistic studies, mathematical studies, social studies, scientific and technological studies, physical, religious and moral education.)

The *Dunning Report* wished to do away with the certificate/non-certificate divide, recommended assessment and certification for all, a move to criterion reference assessment and over-lapping internal and external assessment elements for certification.

The *Pack Report*, which was over-shadowed by the reports of the other two committees, took a more experiential view of Scottish education. In many senses it raised the most fundamental questions about curriculum and assessment.

1978   The Education of Pupils with Learning Difficulties in Primary and Secondary Schools in Scotland: a progress report by Her Majesty's Inspectorate.   This report presaged the transformation of the education of children with learning difficulties in ordinary schools from remedial education to a system of learning support. It argued that the main cause of learning difficulties was the curriculum, and that up to half of all pupils could be said to experience learning difficulties. The education of children with learning difficulties should become the responsibility of the whole school, it should be delivered across the curriculum, and the practice of withdrawing children for basic skills work should be minimised. The report had a major impact on Scottish and English practice in this field.

1980   Learning and Teaching in Primary 4 and 7. A report by HM Inspectors of Schools.   Report based on sample of 6 per cent of primary schools. Areas of the curriculum surveyed: language arts, environment studies, mathematics, music, art and craft, physical education. Report concluded that schools had remained 'remarkably unaffected by change over the years'. Knowledge was still regarded as a body of content to be imparted and there was a 'two category' approach to the curriculum, i.e. the basic skills (language and number) in the morning and other studies (less important) in the afternoon.

1981   Scottish Education Department: A Framework for Decision. The new Conservative government's plan for implementation of the Munn and Dunning proposals. The development exercise resulted in Standard Grade courses being introduced in the classroom on a phased basis beginning in 1988.

1981   Education (Scotland) Act.   The so-called 'Parents' Charter' giving parents rights, with certain qualifications, to choose schools. Parents were also given rights of access to information regarding aims, curriculum, methods and organisation.

1983   Primary Education in the Eighties: A COPE Position Paper (Consultative Committee on the Curriculum). The document takes a broad view of the development of primary education in Scotland since 1965. It comments 'pronouncements from HM Inspectorate and the Consultative Committee on the Curriculum since then have been expressed in terms of pursuit of and usually failure to achieve the goals set out at that time'.

1983   SED. 16–18s in Scotland – An Action Plan. The Action Plan introduced a new framework for non-advanced further education. The development of modular courses certificated by SCOT-VEC was to have a particular impact on curriculum in secondary schools, this development was aided by the introduction of TVEI in Scotland in 1984 (one year later than in England).

1986   CCC. Education 10–14 in Scotland: A Report of the Programme Directing Committee.   In 1981 the CCC set up a major development programme focused on the 10–14 age group in Scottish schools. The report is the official account of that programme. The recommendations were judged, at a time of declining resources, as too extensive to be supported.

1987   CCC. Guidelines for Secondary Headteachers.   The document attempts to draw together current curriculum advice and provide a framework for the secondary school. It develops the Munn modes and introduces the notion of 'permeating elements' – process skills and personal and social development, which should be the responsibility of all teachers.

1988   Curriculum and Assessment in Scotland: Policy for the 1990s.   Following the publication of a consultation paper in the Autumn of 1987 a programme of national curricula guidelines is to be introduced and testing in language, mathematics and science.

introduced and testing in language, mathematics and science.

1988   The Consultative Committee on the Curriculum is dissolved and a new advisory body, limited by public guarantee, the Scottish Consultative Committee on the Curriculum is established.

1989   Introduction of Schools Boards giving parents and local community greater involvement in running of schools.

List of Contributors

Dena Attar, freelance writer.

Richard Elmore, Assistant Professor of Public Affairs, University of Washington, Seattle.

Michael Fullan, Professor of Education, Ontario Institute for Studies in Education.

Caroline Gipps, Lecturer, University of London, Institute of Education.

Mike Golby, Reader in Education, Exeter University.

Derek Hodson, Lecturer, Department of Education, University of Auckland, New Zealand.

Sue Johnston, Department of Curriculum and Teaching Studies, Brisbane College of Advanced Education, Carseldine, Australia.

Sheila Lawlor, Deputy Director, Centre for Policy Studies.

Catherine Manthorpe, Centre for Studies in Science and Mathematics Education, University of Leeds.

Jenny Meegan, Assistant Staff Tutor, The Open University, Northern Ireland.

Bob Moon, Professor of Education, The Open University.

Peter Mortimore, Professor of Educational Research, University of Lancaster.

John Quicke, Lecturer, University of Sheffield.

Jim Rand, Jordanhill College of Education, Glasgow.

John Raynor, Formerly Professor of Education, The Open University.

Jean Rudduck, Professor of Education, University of Sheffield.

Mary Simpson, Research Officer, Aberdeen College of Education.

Martin Skilbeck, Vice Chancellor, Deakin University, Australia.

John Tomlinson, Professor of Education, Warwick University.

Harry Torrance, Lecturer, University of Southampton.

Barry Troyna, Lecturer, University of Warwick.

Index

Source Acknowledgments

The publishers would like to thank the following for permission to reproduce material in this volume:

The Academy of Political Science for 'Backward mapping: implementation research and policy decisions' by Richard F. Elmore from *Political Science Quarterly* 94(4) Winter 1979–80; Mr L. Barton of Bristol Polytechnic for 'The origins and development of mental testing in England and Wales' by H. Torrance from *Journal of Sociology of Education* 2(1) 1981; Basil Blackwell Ltd for 'The "New Right" and education' 26(1) 1988, by John Quicke and 'The debate over standards and the uses of testing' 26(1) 1988, by Caroline Gipps, both from *The British Journal of Education Studies*; Carfax Publishing for 'Beyond multiculturalism: towards the enactment of antiracist education in policy, provision and pedagogy' by Barry Troyna from the *Oxford Review of Education* 13(3) 1987, 'Curriculum change: management or meaning?' by Jean Rudduck 1986, 'Towards an understanding of the values issue in curriculum decision making' by Sue Johnston Vol. 8 1988 and 'Towards a Kuhnian approach to curriculum development' by Derek Hodson Vol. 8 1988, all from *School Organisation*; The Centre of Policy Studies for 'Correct Core' by Sheila Lawlor, (1988) and 'Grounding comes first' by Oliver Letwin (1988); Fourth Estate Ltd for 'Curriculum and the market: are they compatible?' by J. Tomlinson in *Take Care, Mr Baker* edited by J. Haviland (1988); The Institute for Economic Affairs for 'Curriculum and the Market'; Longman Group Ltd and Lord Callaghan of Cardiff for the extracts from a speech given by Prime Minister James Callaghan published in *Education* 1976; Catherine Manthorpe for her article 'Reflections on the scientific education of girls' in *School Science Review* March 1987; The Organisation for Economic Co-operation and Development for 'A changing social and educational context' by M. Skilbeck from *School Development and New Approaches for Learning: Trends and Issues in Curriculum Reform* report (1988); The Open University for 'Curriculum traditions' by Mike Golby, 'A national or nationalist curriculum?' by J. Raynor, 'Now you see it, now you don't . . .' by Dena Attar, 'Who's in control? pressure group politics . . .' by Bob Moon and 'Curriculum chronologies' by John Raynor, Jenny Meegan and Jim Rand; Open Books Publishing for 'School matters' by Peter Mortimore from *School Matters: The Junior Years* by Mortimore, Sammers, Stoll, Lewis and Ecob (1988); The Scottish Academic Press for 'School based and centrally directed curriculum development – the uneasy middle ground' by Mary Simpson from *Scottish Educational Review* 18 1986; Teachers College Press and the Ontario Institute for Studies in Education for 'Planning, doing, and coping with change' from *The Meaning of Educational Change* by M. Fullan (1982); *The Times Educational Supplement* for extracts from their treatment of Margaret Thatcher's speech to the Conservative Party Conference, October 1987.

Every effort has been made to trace and acknowledge ownership of copyright. The publishers will be glad to make suitable arrangements with any copyright holders whom it has not been possible to contact.